THE ROSSETTI FAMILY
1824-1854

VASTO IN 1836   The Rossetti House

From a painting by GABRIELE SMARGIASSI

THE
ROSSETTI FAMILY
1824–1854

BY

R. D. WALLER, M.A.

*Lecturer in English Literature in
the University of Manchester*

MANCHESTER UNIVERSITY PRESS

1932

Republished 1972
Scholarly Press, Inc., 22929 Industrial Drive East
St. Clair Shores, Michigan 48080

Library of Congress Cataloging in Publication Data

Waller, Ross Douglas.
  The Rossetti family, 1824-1854.

  Original ed. issued as no. 21 of Publications of the
University of Manchester, English series, and as no. 217
of Publications of the University of Manchester.
  Bibliography: p.
  1. Rossetti family. 2. Rossetti, Gabriele Pasquale
Giuseppe, 1783-1854. I. Series: Victoria University
of Manchester. Publications. English series, no. 21.
II. Series: Victoria University of Manchester.
Publications, no. 217.
PR5236.R9W3 1972   851'.7 [B]   73-145352
ISBN 0-403-01261-9

Published by the University of Manchester at The University Press
(H. M. McKechnie, M.A., Secretary), 23 Lime Grove, Oxford Road, Manchester

TO

H. B. CHARLTON

TO WHOSE UNWEARIED PROMPTINGS

THIS BOOK OWES ITS EXISTENCE

Che poteva io ridir, se non " Io vegno " ?

PREFACE

WHILE every book on the Rossettis has a preliminary account of Gabriele Rossetti, his exile and his Dante theories, no one in England seems so far to have given any special attention to the naïve and interesting figure who presented this country with such an extraordinary family. A good deal of material, however, is available for anyone who wishes to make his acquaintance, and much of it is embodied in this book. The Biblioteca del Risorgimento in Rome has a vast collection of letters to and from Gabriele Rossetti. He was a relentless correspondent, in times of agitation sometimes sending two or even three letters to the same friend on the same day. Although the student must endure an almost insufferable tedium whenever Rossetti, in the handwriting of a gnat, gives rein to his unending speculations on Dante, the Papacy and mediaeval Freemasonry, he is frequently rewarded by the discovery of intimately human documents, expressing the hopes and fears, the vanities and self-deceptions, the ambitions and disappointments, the affections and hostility of an open and ingenuous character in all the phases of its career, from the ardour of young manhood to the melancholy decline of old age. In their original form these letters could hardly fail to affect any reader of ordinary human sympathies. If, translated and summarised in the form in which I here present them, they do not so affect the reader, I may say with Arrian, τυχὸν μὲν ἐγὼ αἴτιος, τυχὸν δὲ καὶ ἀνάγκη οὕτως ἔχειν.

Closing with the death of Gabriele Rossetti in 1854, when Dante Gabriel was twenty-five and Christina twenty-three, I have attempted to sketch his career, his personality and his literary occupations ; also to give a fairly intimate account of the fortunes of his family and to relate the early work of the Rossetti children to the circumstances and influences of their home.

All letters in Italian have of necessity been translated, out of consideration for the general reader. It should be understood, however, that Gabriele Rossetti always wrote in Italian, except on rare, occasions, which are duly noted when they occur. A number of passages from his often very prosaic verse have been done into English verse by my wife, whose initials would have been appended but for the fact that in the interests of fidelity I have sometimes tampered with her handiwork to its disadvantage in all other respects. The originals in every case may be found in the Appendix. My wife has also helped so much, at all stages of the book's preparation, that in some parts it is virtually a collaboration.

I have to express my grateful thanks to Gabriele Rossetti's four grandchildren, Mr. G. A. Rossetti, Signora Rossetti Agresti, Signora Rossetti Angeli, and Miss M. E. M. Rossetti, all of whom have shown me the most obliging kindness. I am also much indebted to Mr. John Purves of Edinburgh University, who has taken a helpful and generous interest in my work, and to Professor Rébora of this University, who has given me useful information on various points, literary and linguistic, and has allowed me to use three autograph letters in the Notes. For all their sakes, I wish the book more deserving than I can hope it is.

Finally I have to state that the translations of Gabriele Rossetti's letters to Frere are in several places quoted from Gabrielle Festing's *John Hookham Frere and his Friends*, by permission of Messrs. Nisbet & Co., Ltd.

THE UNIVERSITY,
   MANCHESTER,
      March, 1932.

CONTENTS

Illustrations

LIST OF ILLUSTRATIONS

(Illustrations follow this list)

Birthplace of Gabriele Rossetti

AUNT CHARLOTTE
From a portrait by D. G. ROSSETTI, 1853

MRS. ROSSETTI
From a drawing by D. G. ROSSETTI, 1854

38 CHARLOTTE STREET

CHARLES LYELL

From a portrait by JOHN PHILLIPS

JOHN HOOKHAM FRERE
After a portrait by JOHN HOPPNER

CHRISTINA
DANTE GABRIEL

WILLIAM
MARIA

From miniatures by F. PISTRUCCI, c. 1838

GAETANO POLIDORI

From a drawing by D. G. ROSSETTI, 1848

ANTONIO ROSSETTI, THE BARBER OF VASTO
From a portrait by FILIPPO PALIZZI, 1848

GABRIELE ROSSETTI IN 1853
From a drawing by D. G. ROSSETTI

MRS. ROSSETTI WITH HER DAUGHTERS, MARIA FRANCESCA AND
CHRISTINA

From a daguerreotype, c. 1855

GABRIELE ROSSETTI IN 1848
From a portrait by D. G. ROSSETTI

DANTE GABRIEL ROSSETTI
From the portrait of himself in The National Portrait Gallery, 1847

WILLIAM MICHAEL ROSSETTI
From a drawing by D. G. ROSSETTI, 1847

CHRISTINA ROSSETTI
From a portrait by D. G. ROSSETTI, 1848

CHAPTER ONE

FROM VASTO TO MALTA

About half a day's journey to the south of Ancona, on its precipitous perch above the Adriatic, lies the little town of Vasto, overlooking sunlit slopes of vine and olive.   The town itself, though boasting an antiquity carried by enthusiasts as far back as the Diomed of Homer, offers but little attraction to the modern eye, the unabashed squalor of its narrow streets contrasting strangely with the blue and green of nature's perfect setting.   Hens peck and scratch their way in and out of the dilapidated houses ; herds of tousled goats invade the town at morning and evening, give up their milk from door to door and shuffle off again to generate a new supply outside the walls ; while a process of decay which seems to have begun in the dim ages of the past goes on unchecked, and for the most part disregarded.

So the old Vasto crumbles, while here and there a Bank—a block of flats—a school of commerce—a villa in process of erection, bespeak the efforts of a later generation, obviously imbued with the spirit of Italy's new age.   Vasto in 1931 cares more for the future than the past.   However, she has had distinguished offspring, whose memory she still proudly preserves in the somewhat damp security of her public museum.   After one of them, indeed, she has named a street, a theatre, and a public square.   In the latter, with his back to a tall white column, stands a frock-coated figure, book in hand, and looking out over the fast-disappearing township of his youth. It is Vasto's most famous poet, Gabriele Rossetti.

In the days of Rossetti's youth Vasto was less decayed, and of its attractions he has left a poetical record.

Thou ancient citadel of Roman days
Where first my eyes beheld the morning's rays ;
Thou who adornest the Frentanian shore,
Glad hills around thee, Adria's blue before ;
Thou who to show the merit of thy line,
Palladian olive on thy brow dost twine.

Wonderful shores whose mirror and whose murmur
Only a mental image now can be,
Where is reflected still the vivid azure
Of the bright sky and emulating sea ;
Beautiful fields where dewy day presents
Emeralds and pearls to be her ornaments.

Crownèd with clouds, thou lofty Apennine,
Upon whose flanks the woolly herds are fed ;
Ye sunny hills that as a child were mine,
And shady valleys where my songs have sped ;
Farewell for ever, never to my view
Can ye return, for evermore adieu.[1]

The passage was written toward 1846, when the poet had passed
his sixtieth year.   Age always recollects the scenes of childhood with
tenderness ; but the poet's farewell to his birthplace was final long
before it need have been, for once Rossetti left Vasto he never
returned—apparently not even during the eighteen years which as
a young man he spent in Naples.

He was born on 28 February 1783, receiving, as he puts it himself,
" with no waft of fortune a humble cradle from a worthy pair ".[2]
In one of his prefaces, written while he was a professor at King's
College, London, he shows some pride in his plebeian origin.
" Now I, born of the people, wish once more to throw in my lot
with theirs."   This is not merely rhetorical ; Rossetti never forgot
his humble origin nor acquired any social affectations.   His verse
made its most direct appeal to simple minds, and his vanity is often
ingenuously attractive, being so obviously the pride of a man who
has risen from obscurity to fame and esteem and who never loses
his delighted surprise at having done so.   His father was a black-
smith and locksmith who died about 1800 ; he is reported to have
been a man of character, harsh but upright and respected.   His
mother, Francesca Pietrocola, the daughter of a shoemaker, who
survived her husband by twenty-two years, could neither write nor
read.   Gabriele had a strong affection for her, and when addressing
a honeymoon poem to his wife, he can pay her no higher compliment

[1] In the translations from G. R.'s verse which appear in this book,
fidelity to the sense has been the first consideration.   The critical
reader is advised to consult the Appendix, where the original passage
is given in each case.

[2] For quotation from G. R.'s *Autobiography*, William Michael
Rossetti's translation is used, except where otherwise stated.

than to declare that Love has given him again the mother he had
lost :

> No, diverse thou canst not be ;
> I discern her still in thee
> Who presentest to mine eyes
> All the former sanctities.

There were six other children. Of the sisters very little is to be
heard, but Gabriele's three brothers, all considerably older than he,
attained a degree of distinction which qualified them for an occasional reference in his letters. Andrea, the eldest, became *decano*
of a cathedral ; Antonio, who will enter these pages again, described
himself as a *barbitonsor, frisore*, and what is more, an *inculto natural
cantor plebeo* ; he was in fact a barber at Vasto, and a fluent though
very minor poet. His verses exist still in manuscript in the Museum
of his native town ; some of them are merely doggerel, but others
leave the reader wondering whether with his brother's opportunities
he might not have been the better poet of the two. Neither the
barbitonsor nor the *inculto cantor*, however, seems to have met with
much reward from the world, and poor Antonio died in great poverty
at the age of eighty-two, after years of privation. Domenico, last of
the three brothers, was the most distinguished. He was a lawyer
and a poet by no means *inculto*, whose printed work may still be read
in Italian libraries, if not with pleasure, at least with some respect.

We see then that humble as Gabriele Rossetti's origin may have
been, he grew up in a home from which the influences of literature
and learning were by no means absent. He himself indeed claims
on two occasions that the family could boast of illustrious men of
letters in past generations, and from a remark in one of his letters
to Charles Lyell it would appear that the Rossettis had fallen somewhat in the social scale in the course of two preceding generations.
He talks of an estate or property called *Val Terrae*, of a Cardinal,
of a librarian at St. Mark's, Venice, and of a family device and seal.
However this may be, his brothers were certainly men of parts, and
they encouraged his early pursuit of the muse.

> I was escorted by this goodly three
> Into Apollo's and Minerva's fane.
>
> [W. M. R.]

The house in which he was born was a fit place of origin for a
family of poets ; to-day it is a mean and pathetic ruin. The
towering front which it used to present to the sea fell away in 1922,
the outer rooms lie open to wind and rain and sun, grass and

weeds grow all about them, and neighbours hang their washing from wall to wall. After its collapse the municipality suddenly recalled the fame of its poet son, and built a sustaining wall to prevent further ruin; but the wall runs across the house front cutting off half its height, and all that was grand and impressive in the old building has disappeared for ever. In the days of Niccolo and Francesca Rossetti its five floors rose sheer from the rock on which the town is built, to a height of eighty or ninety feet. Gabriele was born in one of the top rooms overlooking the sea.

Of his childhood Rossetti has left little record. He loved the hills no doubt and delighted in the sea; once he narrowly escaped drowning; but nature makes so rare, formal, and figurative an appearance in his poetry that it is difficult to suppose that he was ever at any time a very faithful or patient lover of her beauty. However, some of the chief interests of his later life already make a tentative appearance during the twenty years of his life at Vasto. His study of Dante and of mediaeval literature began there under a certain Benedetto Betti. Poetry came to him early as to his children, poetry of an easy and spontaneous kind described by himself as avoiding the abstruse, though his mind at all times was so free from intellectual complication that the abstruse could never have been a very pertinacious enemy. At the same time he discovered a considerable aptness for painting and drawing. It was not a pronounced gift and was not long pursued. Some of his pen-sketches have been reproduced; they are neatly executed, but while they are sufficient to attest that in Dante Gabriel the gift was hereditary, they lack invention, and to an even greater degree the touch of unmistakable genius. For these pen-sketches he used to obtain sepia himself from the belly of the *calamarello* or cuttlefish. There were other uses for this serviceable creature—it was a favourite Neapolitan dish for which the poet longed in Bloomsbury, as an Englishman in Vasto might long for beef and carrots.

Even the political enthusiasms which were later to change the whole current of his life were touched to their first faint stirrings in those early days. In 1799, when Gabriele was sixteen, the podestà of a neighbouring town was strangled in a riot. He was told that it was part of a revolution in favour of the throne and the Catholic religion, threatened by Jacobins. "'This'," he is said to have thought, "'is not the way to defend monarchy and the altar'; thenceforward the name of liberty began to whisper in his mind." For the time being, however, his mind had other pressing occupations and he needed quiet for study. As Vasto was becoming a nest of factions, it must have been with great joy that the poet received a summons to Naples from the Marchese di Vasto, Majordomo to the King of Naples, who had séen his drawings and heard some of his poems. He left Vasto in 1804, at the age of twenty-one, and came to Naples as Secretary to the Marquis and with the intention of becoming an artist. His patron sent him to the university, but after only thirteen months of study there, " a political whirlwind " upset everything. The French came and " the Marquis vanished with the perjured king." This was the end of all disciplined instruction for Rossetti. The mass of ill-organised learning which he brought in later years to the study of Dante bears the mark of this early dislocation.

His patron gone and the Napoleonic era begun in Naples, the poet gave up all idea of painting and took up his lyre resolvedly.

> A poet I was born
> And such I will be in my future course.
> [W. M. R.]

He wrote plays, or rather librettos, of a Metastasian kind for the theatre of San Carlo, enough he says to fill a volume, artificial but melodious celebrations of Giulio Sabino, Hannibal, Hercules and others. These were all successful, he declares, and certainly they earned Rossetti the post of official poet to the theatre, a burdensome office from which the irritable race of composers, managers and prima donnas soon drove him in despair. In the meantime he had become well known as a lyric poet, even it is said as a source of lyric poems, for many nobles begged sonnets and odes from him and then passed them off as their own. Anyone who has looked through (let us not venture to say read) his unpublished autographs, will not much regret the loss of these purloined poems. If ever poet was in a position to lend to the needy it was Rossetti. Some of his early verses were published in a volume of 1807, and the best of them reprinted in the better known *Versi* of 1847. The poet was then twenty-four and the theme of love is frequent, although in sterner times he declared that his " soul from childhood onwards leaned towards more noble themes ". Indeed one might suppose from these conventional rhymes that love was not a deep concern of the poet in his Neapolitan days ; and as those who read these lines will probably have been drawn to them by an interest in his children rather than in Rossetti himself, it may be worth while to offer here

B

an example of Gabriele's love poetry, so empty and artificial when compared with that of Dante Gabriel or Christina.

Springtime Entreaty

With tremulous flowerets
The hillside is pretty,
O leave, lovely Nice,
The troublesome city.

And come, for affection
Is pure in the fields,
Where love will reward
What the true lover yields.

The stream purling down
From this slope in the sun,
Seems to murmur in passing
" Oh, when will she come ?

For her at my banks
The sweet blossoms I lave ;
To mirror her beauty
I offer my wave."

Come ! a wreath of fresh roses
Love weaves by his art,
He wishes to crown thee
The queen of my heart.

The soft dewy breezes,
Sweet daughters of spring,
To cheeks so vermilion
Caresses would bring.

On the hillside, encircled
With crocus and thyme,
An altar I've raised,
And would hallow it thine.

Revive the soft airs,
And thy blessing extend ;
The place and the altar
Their goddess attend.

Nice, Lidia, Clori, Eleonora, Nina, Cloe, all have their tributes, or are entreated to take pity in neat, sometimes graceful, always melodious stanzas. Sometimes the tone rises to a more sensuous warmth as in *Ad Amor Pittore*, a poem which Rossetti saw fit to chasten in the Lausanne collection of 1847. But the real Rossetti is not to be found here ; he remains to be awakened to his most vigorous work by the pressure of political circumstance.

We left him escaping from his connection with the Teatro San Carlo. In later days he thought that in himself a great dramatist had somehow lost the way. " Oh ! if they had only left me in peace," he says, " I would have presented Italy with plays better perhaps than those of Metastasio." The possibility will scarcely be endorsed by readers of the operatic librettos composed in his early London days ; several of them may be read in the British Museum, and there is an unfinished libretto on the subject of Mary Queen of Scots preserved in Rome.

He betook himself to the Minister for Home Affairs, who gave him a subordinate place in the King's Museum at a salary of 15 ducats a month,[1] later rising to 28 ducats a month. Rossetti was custodian of the ancient statuary and was proud of the post in spite of the miserable pay. That he did not accept the latter without protest may be seen from the following, a good example of Rossetti's epistolary style in times of agitation :

" ECCELLENZA,

I am inspired to address you by nothing else than the natural instinct to defend oneself against oppression ; a right that pertains even to the most timid hare . . . and shall a man be less regarded than a hare ? Signore, until this moment patience and silence have been my only answer to violence and tyranny : now the cup is full ! and my patience has become fury. Or rather I shall do better to say that humility has turned into courage. Cavaliere Arditi is my oppressor. Signor Eccellentissimo, it is impossible to understand him fully if you have not first been so unfortunate as to have been his subordinate, (and may Heaven deprive you of life before you come to such misery). He (the mark of a base mind !) ever places his head beneath the feet of those above him, in order afterwards with greater tyranny to put his own feet upon the head of those beneath him. But I will tear the bandage from the eyes of justice, or rather of virtue, and expose his iniquities and oppressions. Signore it is now five years since I first entered the Royal Museum (Oh day fatal to my peace !) . . . as curator of the statuary. And what has been the rich reward that was then assigned to me ? . . . fifteen ducats that have now been reduced to thirteen."

[1] Stated by W. M. R. (*Aut.* p. 18) to be equivalent to £31 2*s*. 6*d*. a year (1901).

In the meantime, however, Rossetti was able to " commune with the living bronze and marble animate ", and to browse in the " immense choice library ",

> And thus a double discipline exalts
> My soul in beauty's pathways and in truth's.
> [W. M. R.]

He met kings and emperors, artists and writers ; and had time to write a good deal in prose and verse. Thus from Vasto to the University of Naples, from the Teatro San Carlo to the Museo Borbonico, the young poet's life followed a comparatively uneventful course.

In more peaceful circumstances he would no doubt have passed on into the tranquil old age of a writer both popular and respected, well known as the prolific author of graceful verses, as an adept in the art of extemporisation, as a member of numerous literary academies in Naples, Palermo, Viterbo, and Rome. Perhaps he would have married and brought up a family of young Italians as versatile as himself, and nobody in England would have known anything about him. *Dîs aliter visum.* He lived like John Evelyn in " an age of great events and revolutions." Another and more violent whirlwind carried him off his feet, blew him to Malta, and afterwards, its fury abating, dropped him gently in London, where for the rest of his life he settled into the uneventful peace which was the instinctive desire of his essentially peaceful nature. Perhaps the events of the Italian risorgimento had no stranger consequence than this. Into the life of a talented and voluble curator of the Neapolitan Museum Il Re Nasone came, and Carbonarism, and political frenzy ; and from it not only all Rossetti's best poetry and all his volumes on Dante and the antipapal spirit, but also Dante Gabriel and Christina, *The Blessed Damozel*, *Beata Beatrix*, and *Goblin Market* ; and a good deal of the spirit of the whole Pre-Raphaelite movement.

It is now necessary to follow briefly the course of the political disturbances which took Rossetti to Malta. In 1759 Ferdinand, third son of the King of Spain, became King of Naples at the age of eight. He married Maria Carolina, sister of Marie Antoinette, in 1768. Ferdinand was well-meaning but incompetent, his wife callous and domineering ; and their joint career was chequered and nefarious. Hostility to France which followed upon the Revolution caused their first misfortune. Obliged to take refuge in Sicily in

1798, they were soon restored, and began to rule with great vigour and barbarity. Forced to abdicate by Napoleon in 1806, the King and Queen again retired to Sicily, and with them this time went Rossetti's Marquis of Vasto and whatever academic ambitions the poet may have cherished. Joseph Buonaparte was installed in Naples.

It is worth noticing that a good deal more than half of Rossetti's life in Naples was spent under the Napoleonic régime, to which he had no difficulty in accommodating himself. His political complexion was indeed extremely simple. Long afterwards in a letter to Frere he remarks whimsically, " To tell the truth I understand these matters not at all. Truly it is a strange thing that I who don't at all understand what politics are, should for politics be persecuted and exiled." The vast bulk of his political writings is the product partly of simple moral instincts ; partly of vanity—at first the vanity of an easily excited and versatile poet, asked by his compatriots for songs and immensely flattered by their applause—and partly, later on, of acquired habit. He hated cruelty and corruption, he hated tyranny and loved freedom. He shared in the general abhorrence of Ferdinand and his wife, and in the general delight with which Naples saw them go to Sicily in 1806. " Thank heaven the tomb has swallowed them ere now," he says in his *Autobiography*. He sympathised ardently with the French revolutionaries so far as they stood for liberty and fraternity ; but inveighed against Napoleon and his despotism. He had " dug out his grave," he said, " when he called himself Emperor." But Rossetti was no real revolutionary. He might write long tirades against kings and priests, he might declare over and over again, " I am a republican because I am a Christian," he might exalt tyrannicide as if he were an Orsini— in his heart of hearts he was really a lover of law and order if they could be secured without palpable injustice ; and. what suited him best of all was a constitutional monarchy.

So with some misgiving lest Joseph might " stifle liberty " as Napoleon had in France, he " gave homage to the new-built throne " in verse. Under Murat, who soon followed Joseph, the poet rose to his highest eminence, occupying for a short time a minor office in the Provisional Government in Rome. Meanwhile democratic feeling was growing strong around him. It is well known that Murat's régime was a great incubator of liberal sentiment. He protected the Carbonari either openly or secretly throughout his reign, and Ferdinand found the kingdom swarming with them on his return in

1815, when their number in the kingdom of Naples alone is said to have been 200,000. There is no doubt that in this atmosphere Rossetti's vague political feelings grew more compelling. In a letter written to Charles Lyell in 1830, he says he had been a Freemason from 1809—the year after Murat's arrival. He became a Carbonaro at least as early as 1812, for a document of that date exists summoning him to one of their meetings. In the second half of 1820, when the organisation was no longer illegal, he was secretary of its Neapolitan section.

In 1815 Ferdinand, now bereaved of his wife, returned to Naples, and for a time all went well. He patronised the arts, he did what he could for the people in plague and famine ; the offending Adam seemed to have been quite driven out of him. Rossetti addressed verses to him, and celebrated with joy his recovery from an illness. But before long the King began to make himself a party ; and when in 1818 Rossetti failed in his candidature for the Chair of Eloquence at the University he held the King responsible :

> Who got the chair ?   A certain Bianchi did
> Who had salient merits as a loyalist.
>
> [W. M. R.]

Actually Rossetti had not acquitted himself at the test as well as he supposed ; but though Ferdinand may not have stooped to defraud the poet of a University chair, he certainly was soon engaged in much worse activities. Determined to exterminate the Carbonari, he recruited from the dregs of the people, through his Minister of Police, a new society called the Calderai del Contrappeso [Braziers of the Counterpoise], " a loathly scum " Rossetti calls them. The attempt failed and feeling rose higher and higher. At such times no man of good heart and courage needs any understanding of politics or indeed any interest in them to know which side he is on ; and the poet was now heart and soul with the insurgents.

We come to the events celebrated in Shelley's *Ode to Naples.* The Carbonari grew rapidly more ardent and more numerous ; a mutiny broke out at Monteforte ; the king's troops, sent to deal with it, sympathised with the mutineers ; Ferdinand, now powerless to resist, granted the Constitution.

> July's ninth day is flaming in the heaven,
> And to the people's will the king accedes,
> With rage in bosom and with joy in face.
>
> [W. M. R.]

It lasted for nine months. Parliament re-opened in August; the fleet and the army were rejuvenated; " the strenuous presses creak and everywhere the country's intellect displays its fruits." And the poet breaks into patriotic song.

That day of delirious joy, 9 July 1820, is the opening of Rossetti's career as a political poet. He has a lively account of the occasion in his *Veggente in Solitudine*. Naples that morning, he says, lay by the sea like a great giant, awake but feigning sleep. A great cry breaks out; the king has yielded to the people; and the giant leaps to his feet and goes singing through the streets. Everybody is shouting *Viva Ferdinando!* and then suddenly the poet is surrounded by an excited throng, hurrying to him like wind-driven waves. At their cry of " Art thou silent, poet of thy country ? " the poetic flame springs to life within him and he sings :

> At the holy inspiration
> Of a hid angelic breath,
> Blazes forth the love of country,
> Hid till now in sleep of death ;
>
> Shines resplendent on the weapons
> Of our youth assembling fast,
> Dream I yet ? I dream no longer,
> Liberty is come at last.

and so on through seventy-two exultant lines, not likely to be at all pleasing to the king, and yet assuring him that now a ray of reason has dissipated the mists of his mind he need fear nothing from the heroes who will surround him. The song raised a tempest of applause, like a great wind in a forest; the poet in confusion " bent his modest head ; " all wept with joy, and he wept with them. Three days of revelry followed, the glad hours passed in singing and dancing, all the streets were garlanded with flowers. On the night of the third day the king took his oath of observance. At the following dawn, the poet, turning to the east, " in his breast received the god ", the glorious Apollo of political as of other song ; the people gathered round him, and their common joy found vent in Rossetti's most famous poem, *Sei pur bella* :

> Lovely art thou, stars within thy hair,
> Shine as with the living sapphire's ray ;
> Sweet indeed the fragrance of thy breath,
> Rosy-vestured harbinger of Day.

With the smile of realized desire
  Thou declarest from the neighbouring height
  That in all Italia's garden bright
  Bondage is for ever done away.

He the branch of Henry and of Charles,
  Who resembles each so happily,
  Has to-day his family enlarged,
  Not desiring slaves, but children free.

To the treaties we have made and signed
  Willingly he now has set his hand ;
  And the sacred compacts we have sworn
  Laid upon the altar of our land.

Lances shook, a forest in the breeze,
  At the warlike trumpet's gath'ring call ;
  In the shadow of the sacred flag
  No dissentient voice was heard at all.

Dauno, Irpin, Lucan, and Sannita,
  Brothers all, shook brothers by the hand ;
  Not extinct in them the ancient virtue,
  Sleeping, it awaited the command.

But what sound of festive trumpets this ?
  Who a hundred cohorts thus can bring ?
  Lo the strong returning with the strong,
  Whom the country honours with the king.

Pomp and triumph ! armèd phalanxes
  Fill the streets like rivers deep in flood ;
  Yet amid so many thousand swords
  Not a blade is stained with human blood.

Happy scene ! what praises and what tears !
  Hyacinths and violets flung above ;
  Conquerors and conquered all as one
  Met together with the kiss of love.

Passing from the palace to the hut,
  Festal joy in each doth nothing feign ;
  Rather it increases as it goes
  From the cottage to the throne again.

Mother of heroic champions,
  What art seeking with thine eyes of fear ?
  Doubt not ; at the sacred banner's call
  All thy sons are safely gathered here.

They do not return from hostile lands
  Instruments of any tyrant's power,
  But from thy redemption's happy field,
  Where the branch of peace did lately flower.

Happy she among so many maids,
  Happy nymph who sees her lover now
  Mid the valiant company return
  With such noble moisture on his brow.

Now the secret of her modest heart
  Rosy cheeks may openly declare ;
  And the blest reward so long denied
  Beauty now for Valour doth prepare.

In the shade of laurels harvested,
  Comrades let us rest in peace assured ;
  But to guard our native country yet,
  Keep we still our hand upon our sword.

He in peace must still prepare for war
  Who in wisdom folly would upset ;
  And though peace may smile upon our brow
  War doth stir within our bosom yet.

Jealous foreigners why look ye thus ?
  Sally from your warrens if ye dare !
  For the ancient lion's noble brood
  Slumbers now no longer unaware.

You may still adore your heavy chains—
  Who would envy you such treasure meet ?
  But beware you do not now provoke
  Those who scorn to feel them round their feet.

Should you come, your consorts sorrowful,
  Heaping curses on the standard dread,
  May prepare them vesture funeral ;
  Hope for them will certainly be sped.

You will satisfy the maw of kites,
  Mercenary phalanxes of slaves ;
  He who combats for his fathers' rights
  Mercy cannot feel nor mercy craves.

As a flashing thunderbolt of Jove
  Is the sword in any freeman's hand ;
  But within the bondman's trembling grasp
  Vacillates the steel like willow-wand.

Death itself for us be glorious,
  Our last murmur a triumphant cry !
  All the thousands of the Persian host
  Did before three hundred Spartans fly.

These remained, their hands upon their swords,
  O'er the bodies of the bleeding slain ;
  And those hands, albeit frozen then,
  Seemed about to strike and strike again.

Such disdain is instinct in the son
  Who was cradled in his father's shield ;
  He to whom his mother murmured still,
  " So thou mayest die, but never yield."

O thou goddess of the rights of men,
  Who the broken yoke doth smiling greet,
  Now at length the blessed day is here
  When a king doth worship at thy feet.

O'er the smoke of Tiber's bloody wave
  Thou to pass in shuddering haste wert fain ;
  But serenely as the laughing dawn
  O'er Sebeto thou dost sit and reign.

Once a phantom with thy sacred name
  Came to us with promises most free ;
  We believing it to be thyself
  Still adored the phantom form of thee.

She at length, amid the stolen hymns
  Gleaming with a luminous deceit,
  Vanished like the fragments of a dream,
  Leaving us with chains about our feet.

But at last thou camest, thou thyself
  Nothing veiling or obscuring thee ;
  And a ray of light from Heaven above
  Shining on thy blessed face I see.

In thy crown perennial lilies blow ;
  And as an example to thine own,
  Thou a palace for thy temple chose
  Where as altar thou dost use the throne.

The original poem well illustrates the strength and the weakness of Rossetti as a poet. Read in quietness in a foreign land it may well seem exaggerated and rhetorical ; at the same time there is in it a naïve simplicity which at this distance of time is even slightly amusing. The rhythm has little variety, and save for the very fine opening line the language lacks magic. But it is wrong to dissociate the poem from its occasion. Poetry is here fulfilling the function which Shelley lays down for it in the *Defence of Poetry*, and the result illustrates the dangers which threaten verse written under such stresses as Shelley has in view. In its abandon, its spontaneity, its simplicity of emotion and style, in its very exaggeration, it was the voice of the Neapolitan people ; the poet was their instrument, their mouthpiece. Carried away by the general excitement, like the bards of ancient times he unlocked his word-hoard and distributed largesse to the people. Truly he could not help himself. However much in later years Rossetti liked to think of himself as the suffering and principled exile patriot, he was neither a Settembrini calmly enduring years of imprisonment for a patriotic ideal ; nor a Mazzini who would have risked a hundred lives for the cause he held sacred. He was simply an enthusiastic and eloquent poet who found himself able to give expression to his countrymen's feelings and did so with inordinate pride. His vanity, as Frere suggested to him, had of course a good deal to do with it ; but it would be unfair to emphasise this unduly. He rushed blindfold into consequences, and his indignation and astonishment when they fell upon him would be diverting in circumstances less serious. But at all events his conduct had been entirely honourable. Settembrini, at his own trial, said, " In this world there are only two parties, that of honest men and that of scoundrels. I have always obliged myself to belong to the former, and I have never paid much attention to names because I have seen much evil done by men called Royalist or Liberal, Absolutist or Republican or Constitutionalist. I love freedom, which for me sig-nifies the exercise of one's own rights without giving offence to anyone—which signifies severe justice, order, respect for the laws and obedience to them and to the authorities. This freedom I warmly love, this it is which is desired by honest men, and if to love it be a crime, I confess myself guilty and accept the penalty." Rossetti could never have spoken with such dignity and restraint ; but his demands were no less virtuous, his political aims no less vague.

The next year was, in its excitement and activity, the climax of Rossetti's life. Nowhere in the kingdom was a more enthusiastic Carbonaro than he. Not only did he compose patriot songs which were on everybody's lips, and were even quoted in Parliament ; he became a member of the General Assembly of the Carboneria ; he wrote more than sixty manifestos which circulated among all its members ; and he published a brochure of some length called *Alla Difesa o cittadini*. [*On guard, Citizens*.] It is even possible that like Tyrtaeus or Archilocus of old he accompanied the patriot troops into battle. For Ferdinand did not appreciate the " band of heroes " who the poet said were to surround him, and soon forgot his oath. He secured an army of 50,000 from the Emperor of Austria, and on 7 March 1821 the Constitutionalists under General Pepe were defeated, though not discreditably, at Rieti. There now began an era of persecution. Parliament was at once dismissed.

Condemnation followed condemnation. According to Rossetti the Church joined with the oppressor and " published her anathema with unanimous howls."

On the 31 March the poet abandoned the Museum and took refuge with a family in the Concordia quarter of Naples. He had evidently decided that the country was too hot to hold him, for on 18 March he managed to secure a passport for either Spain or Malta. For reasons unknown the document, which must have been difficult to obtain, was never used. Possibly Rossetti hoped things might grow quieter, and flight seemed a painful and drastic step. He remained concealed wondering what to do next. While he was waiting Ferdinand helped him to decide by decreeing his exile. This was on 10 April. Fortunately the means of escape were at hand. Lady Dora Moore, wife of Sir Graham Moore, an admiral of the British Fleet and brother of the famous Sir John Moore, had for some time been an admirer of Rossetti's verses. When in the course of time she came to Naples on her husband's flagship, the *Rochfort*, she expressed a wish to see the poet. This being intimated to Rossetti by an English officer who saw him in the Museum, he called on Lady Moore and was graciously received. It was shortly before the fall of the constitutional government, and the new acquaintance could hardly have been more opportune. The *Rochfort* remained in the harbour, while Lady Moore grew more and more anxious about the poet's fate. According to him, she implored her husband to

> Save from the axe that guiltless man ; if love
> Of country be a crime, you are guilty too !
>
> [w. m. r.]

Three times Sir Graham offered refuge on his ship while the poet hesitated. At last in the dead of night a friend mysteriously warned Rossetti of approaching danger. A note was sent next morning to Lady Moore, and towards evening two English subalterns came to the house with a suit of British uniform. The poet meanwhile had packed up a few belongings, leaving a portrait and some manuscripts in the hands of a friend ; and now left the house in the full glory of a British lieutenant. They went by carriage to the shore, passing a police official who exclaimed, " By God ! the man in the middle looks to me like Rossetti ! " He did not, however, venture to inter-fere, and they reached the ship in safety. Rossetti's first action was to kiss the planks of " that wooden Albion ", a very Italian and poetic gesture which seems to have amused the crew. He then went to the Admiral's cabin to thank his two deliverers, Thetis and Neptune, as he liked to call them. They were certainly for him a joint *Deus ex machina* and theirs was the first and most sensational of the many services rendered to him by English or Scottish sympathisers. He was amazingly fortunate in his friends.

Now at the point of leaving Naples for good, Rossetti's feelings against Ferdinand rose to their bitterest and most violent. He breathed curses against him and against all his subjects. He saw in vision a hundred daggers seeking the traitor king's heart; but declared he was too vile even for assassination. Never let history tell that the iniquitous Ferdinand died the death of Caesar. But these ebullitions of rage mingled with gentler feelings as Naples and Italy died away into the night distance.

> " Farewell land of misery ! "—
> But the land he could not see.
> He in deepest sorrow bowed,
> Bent his head and sobbed aloud
> Ah, the love of country blest,
> Ah, the strife within his breast !
> Wretched man ! his heart must yearn,
> Knowing he will ne'er return.

It should be added that everything so far related about the poet's feelings during these unhappy months is based on poems written at the time, or on his own account in the *Autobiography* and *Il Veggente*. The last two were written many years later, and since Rossetti's retrospects were always full of high lights, we should take what he says in them with a certain amount of caution.

Rossetti's arrival at the rocky shore of Malta is described by himself as being attended by circumstances so admirably in keeping with the arrival of an exiled patriot that it would be ungracious to follow one of his Italian critics in doubting their truth. If they are not true, they deserve to be. No sooner had he set foot on land than he heard a loud cry of " Hail, Tyrtaeus of Italy," and saw a boat full of lovely women close in to the shore. When they had come within hearing they raised their gentle voices in the poet's already famous song *Sei pur bella*. The crowd on land were loud in applause and all the shore echoed with their cries.

Here then is our poet, cast like St. Paul upon the shores of Malta, but by another kind of tempest ; and it was his public celebration of St. Paul in an extemporised poem which brought him to the notice of various eminent persons, among them John Hookham Frere. His fame as an improvisor as well as a poet had gone before him, and he was induced to give a demonstration of his powers before a large assembly. This was on 12 August 1821, and the poem he then improvised may be read at the end of his son's translation of the *Autobiography*. He improvised on five other themes as well as the one originally chosen, with so much success that several eminent persons called on him next day. Frere had been present at the recital and was much astonished at the poet's skill. Before long Rossetti had established a respectful friendship with that very admirable Englishman which was of lasting benefit to the poet. Frere's recommendation was the passport to everybody that mattered in Malta and later in England; he continued to send wise and friendly letters almost up to the date of his death; and frequently he sent timely gifts of money. We may well believe the poet's declaration that he felt himself grow better by so great a pattern; certainly the lifelong admiration and respect he felt for his patron does credit to both men. Frere had by this time settled into the cultured and indolent seclusion which he was never to abandon. His wife's health had taken him to Malta; after her death his own conservatism kept him there. He lived on with his sister in the beautiful villa he had built for himself on the Pietà creek until 1846, translating Aristophanes and Theognis, giving help to the poor, taking the interest of a very able dilettante in antiquities and all matters of intellectual concern, and enjoying the conversation of any sensible visitor who came to the island.

Rossetti was naturally interesting to him. The poet at this time was thirty-eight years of age, of slightly less than average height, inclined to fullness of contour, dark-haired and dark-eyed. His manner was disarming and simple, straightforward and cheerful. He was fundamentally friendly and good-natured, having an emotional excitability which would lend warmth to his voluble and sonorous speech. Frere liked him, and so fortunately did his wife and sister. Some may think this friendship between the Anti-Jacobin and the revolutionary poet strange and unlikely, but it is hardly necessary to emphasise again the very moderate nature of Rossetti's political views. Frere saw at once with amusement the incongruity between the poet's hot-headed eloquence and the honest harmlessness of his nature. In an undated letter to Rossetti he says that he has heard about his obnoxious verses; he attributes them to a time of great popular excitement, and knows how little they signify.

He thinks no worse of Rossetti for them. As for the assassins Sand and Louvel, to whom he had made ominous reference in one of his poems, it was a pity he had not chosen the great classical scoundrels like Brutus instead of these little modern good-for-nothings. *Lovello*, Frere suggests, merely came in as a rhyme for *coltello*; and Sand murdered a poet, like Rossetti, a good fellow too. It is painful to think that " a new Sand may be sent by the Carbonari to plunge a coltello into an excellent Rossetti who wouldn't wish knives to be used for anything other than pigeon pies." [1]

This letter was in French, which was probably the language of their conversation, for as yet Rossetti knew no English. Sometimes they appear to have resorted to Latin, for there is in Rome a document in that language addressed by Rossetti to Frere during the Malta period. It apparently followed some conversation about the origins of the Italian literary language, and begins thus:

H. Frerio. V.C.
G. Rossettius
S. D.

Cum in meo, clarissime vir, quod heri de italico sermone adserui tacito animo volverem ne quid dixerim metuens, quod confermare auctorita non possem, monimenta diligentius perscrutenda existimavi : et certius ex illis iam mea assurgit sententia. In sicula Frederici II aula nostram praesertim florissime linguam quam plurimi comprobant. . . .

The sequel to such intellectual exchanges is the long correspondence about Dante and the Freemasons, which will demand our attention in another chapter.

Meanwhile it was necessary to make some money, and not only for his own needs, for Rossetti had already domestic responsibilities of an irregular kind. Some seven years before this, in a distracted letter to his friend Ferretti, he had reported the loss of his new-born son, his " perfect image in miniature," who lived only some six hours. " Donna Peppina ", its mother, followed the poet to Malta. In a letter to some person unnamed and written at an uncertain date in 1823, Rossetti says she " is in the most deplorable state of health ; for seven months she has been getting worse and worse ; it is the only thing which troubles me ; for the rest I am ready to face my destiny with courage." What became of Peppina eventually is not known. There is no further reference to her,

---

[1] Sand assassinated the poet Kotzebue. Louvel assassinated the Duc de Berri, heir to the French throne.

except perhaps in a remorseful passage of the *Autobiography* where the poet expresses regret for the irregularities of his earlier life. He was evidently too attached to her to desert her altogether, and it seems probable that before he entered upon his eminently respectable married life in Bloomsbury, the illness referred to had resulted in her death. Possibly too it may have been due to Peppina that the poet did not come earlier to England. It is evident that he contemplated such a step long before he finally took it; a letter to Ferretti dated 24 March 1822, hints that the right hand of Fate which has thrown him on that rocky isle may soon lead him to make *un salto vitale ad uno scoglio più grande* [a jump for his life on to a greater rock]—by which he explains that he means England.

Frere must have given him a good deal of practical assistance, and for the rest the poet kept himself alive by teaching and giving improvisations. He soon had a numerous and distinguished clientèle, among whom he turned his " lengthened studies to account "; he knew many of the Italian classics by heart, and diligently spreading a taste for them among his pupils, he became, or at least thought he became, " the foremost of professors in the isle." At the same time he was prosecuting his own studies, " sifting out of fallacies the truth ", as he puts it in the *Autobiography*. It would be interesting to know if he meant by this that his Dantesque studies had already begun. On the whole it is not likely. The prophetic vision of Dante which came to him on the journey to England seems to suggest that his exhausting labours in that field were still to begin. William Michael Rossetti, moreover, definitely states that it was not until the poet arrived in England that he gave the *Commedia* that close scrutiny which resulted in the *Comento* and its sequels. However, if the commentator was not yet at work, the poet was still busy. It was in Malta that he conceived and wrote the greater part of his *Psaltery*, of all his sustained works the best planned and the most level in execution. It was published in 1833 with the title *Iddio e l'Uomo, Salterio*, [*God and Man, a Psaltery*], and as its name suggests it is full of deistic and humanitarian sentiment which has an obvious connection with the central ideas of his Dante interpretation. A beautifully written copy in three volumes was made in Malta by a friend of Rossetti's and given to Frere, to whom the work was eventually dedicated.

Rossetti stayed in the island for some three years, during which his position was never secure. Naples was far too close at hand. Castlereagh, it appears, had ordered the expulsion of the fugitives, in the execution of which decree the Neapolitan Consul, Gerardi, was only too ready to co-operate. Rossetti, who had to see friend after friend expelled, one of them driven to madness and afterwards suicide, curses the Consul in good round terms. He himself was no doubt protected by his powerful English friends, but was nevertheless thrown into some apprehension by Gerardi's machinations. We find him writing an indignant letter to the Consul in October 1822.

" SIGNOR CONSOLE,

I have been informed by trustworthy persons that you have been going about spreading the report that I am an *unfrocked priest.* . . . I believe you would admit that there is little difference between a man who having had the glory of exercising the august ministry of our holy religion, chooses to relinquish it, and one who having had the good fortune to be born in her bosom, should choose to abjure her. . . . If then I should fail to rebut your charges. . . . I should voluntarily assume the wretched character of an *apostate.* . . .

My offended honour requires satisfaction. . . . Pray therefore give me a reply by to-morrow : and take warning that if you fail to do so, you will lose all right to complain of the steps which the law allows me to take to protect my honour."

Later in life Rossetti was to have a good deal to do with the class of unfrocked priests for whom he here shows so much disgust ; but the letter throws an interesting light on his attitude to the Catholic Church at this time, even allowing for the probability that he was more angry at Gerardi's malignity than horrified at the suggestion of apostasy. A challenge of this kind could do him little good. Gerardi appears to have had recourse to the Maltese police, for on 3 January 1823, Rossetti writes to their Inspector General to excuse himself for not having yet left the island, " after the government's orders officially communicated to me ", and promises to put them into execution as soon as possible. The letter of 1823 about Peppina, already quoted, declares that he is going to leave for England within two months ; his actual departure was in January 1824.

Rossetti's voyage to England was made again under the care

of Thetis and Neptune. Indeed only the staunch friendship of
the Admiral prevented its being drastically interrupted, for the
vigilant Gerardi had sent news of his departure, and when the
ship anchored off Naples, the king demanded Rossetti's surrender.
Why, asks the poet, should the king whom he had so often praised
have been so incensed against him? He had been excepted from
the general amnesty of 1822; the king, so a friend had told him,
had threatened him with death under the bastinado. The only
explanation that Rossetti could think of was that Gaspar Mollo,
Duke of Lusciano, a jealous rival poet, had poisoned the king's
mind against him. Had he forgotten the *Odi Cittadine*, his sixty
odd Carbonaro manifestos, his many provocations of which the
following is an example :

> Sire, wherefore do you wait? But now in Spain
> A shattered sceptre hurtled to the ground,
> Terrible portent for who waits to reign.
> Vengeance already for herself hath found
> A murderous hand that wills to work him bane.
> Sire, wherefore waitest thou? pride most insane
> Must grant a people's will, who all around
> Require thy death; Temple and Forum sound
> But this; the weak and vile resist in vain.

When Count Giovanni Arrivabene was arrested at Mantua in May
1821, a copy of *Sei pur bella* found on his person was regarded
alone as sufficient incrimination, and he was imprisoned for
seven months. Camillo Ugoni once got into trouble for merely
listening to it. Pietro Giannone was imprisoned by the Austrians
on suspicion of having written it. Ferdinand knew only too well
who had written it, and knowing all the other things Rossetti had
written as well, he did not need the Duke of Lusciano's jealousy to
spur him on. When Frere tried in 1822 to get the authorities at
Naples to overlook Gabriele's offences, writing for that purpose
to Mr. Hamilton the British representative there, the reply was
inauspicious. " Even his best friends and admirers are loudest in
condemning him for the pains he took during the Revolution to
preach up the Carbonaro doctrines; and only yesterday or the
day before, one of his dicta was quoted to me, as descriptive of his
usual language—' I giorni dei Santi [*sic*] e dei Lovelli [*sic*] non son
finiti ancora ' [The days of Sands and Louvels are not yet over] [1].

[1] See page 19.

. . . I fear he must submit to his lot." In his more excited moments Rossetti was a supporter of tyrannicide—" Does he who kills a tyrant slay a man ? No ! He destroys a dragon." Words for him are often sufficient for the occasion, and have little relation to permanent principles ; they seem to have intoxicated him to the point of unconsciousness so that he was astonished to hear them remembered against him afterwards.

Whatever the causes may have been, it would certainly have gone ill with him at Naples if Moore had not firmly refused to give him up. The ship remained two weeks in harbour, while a hundred spies set by the vigilant police kept watch to see if any-body visited the ship. These were miserable circumstances in which to leave one's native country. Even the weather was un-kind—the poet's last sight of Italy was on a bad day—" Nor could I say, ' Oh sun of Italy, adieu ! ' "

The journey was a long one, taking in all about six weeks ; ten days to Naples, two to Leghorn, eight to Gibraltar ; from there he wrote a letter to the Freres. He was in good spirits. " To the wonder of all the oldest sailors, I have been eating like a wolf, digesting like an ostrich, and sleeping like a dormouse." The Admiral has been endlessly kind and Rossetti has almost finished his work [the *Psaltery*]. But alas, he spoke too soon. From a letter written to Lady Moore after his arrival in England, we hear that on the second day after leaving Gibraltar he could hardly move a foot, for gout had claimed him. " The lack of exercise on board ship, the quantities of food I had eaten, my laborious studies . . . and the extraordinary exertion of climbing Calpe's beetling rock, together caused this malignant germ to develop within me."

As he thus approaches England, " a poet with the gout " as he calls himself, we may inquire how much he knew, if anything, of the English language. He had not of course spent three years in Malta without acquiring some knowledge of English. Among the Rossetti manuscripts in Rome are some sheets of notes made in studying it. Why he preserved them for so many years is matter of wonder, but the preserving instinct was very strong in him, and he may have felt a sentimental attachment to his first steps in the language which his children were afterwards to master to such effect. The notes appear from the writing to belong to the Malta period, their elementary nature suggests it too. " I have been, said Thomas, to your country house. Lubin the farmer's house. John out good miller's wife. The man who was here last night's house (*meglio*) [1] the house belonging to the man who was here last night. He sells cheese. Does he sell cheese? A hundred ducks and a thousand geeses. I have more than sixty livers. Mr. Such a one has been here to-day. I am. It is I. He is as old as I. He writes better than she. He loves me better than her (*questa distinzione è difficilissima e a dir vero non la intendo*)." [2]

The progress he had made in the written language may be estimated from the letter he wrote to the Freres when the ship was approaching English shores. We give it with Rossetti's own alterations, which are not always for the better.

My Lady

In approaching to your ~~happy~~ glorious country I feel even here ~~already~~

good
its influences; and ~~then,~~ of it there is a proof in my letter which is written in your language.

I have been at Naples; but I have seen it from very far ~~it~~. I am unable to express you my thauts tumultuous and my pointing sensations at that sight. After three days we left that ~~country as~~ bia beatiful and ~~handsome as~~ wretched country

and from the poop of our ship, I was repeating ~~too~~ in miself ~~that~~ ~~I sung so.~~ these verses:

> Must I then leave thee, Paradise! thus leave
> Thee native soil, these happy walkes and shades
> Fit haunt of gods! Where I had hope to spend
> Quiet though sad the respite of my days?

And then addressing my speech to ~~whom that~~ barbarous my oppressor I added:

> What sorrow and abjection, an despair
> My frailty can sustain ty ~~tidings~~ cruelty brings
> Departure from this happy place, my sweet

[1] Better.

[2] "This distinction is extremely difficult and to tell the truth I don't understand it." These little sentences have been selected; they do not occur continuously.

My Lady

In approaching to your ~~happy~~ glorious country I feel ~~already~~ ~~even here~~ its good influences; and ~~then~~ there is a proof of it in my letter which is written in your language.

I have been at Naples; but I have seen it from very far ~~it~~. I am unable to express to you my ~~thoughts~~ triumphant and my pointing sensations at that sight. After three days we left that ~~country as~~ big ~~handsome as wretched~~ beautiful and country and from the poop of our Ship I ~~sung it~~ was repeating ~~glory in myself~~ these verses:

Must I thus leave thee, Paradise! thus leave
Thee native soil, these happy walks and shades
Fitt haunt of gods! Where I had hope to spend
Quiet though sad the respite of my days?

And then ~~at~~ addressing my speech to ~~whom that~~
my barbarous oppressor I added:

What sorrow and abjection, an despair
My frailty can sustain ty ~~endures~~ crudelty brings
Departure from this happy place, my sweet
Recess, and only consolation left
Familiar to my eyes: all places else
Inhospitable appear and desolate
Nor knowing me and nor known... O ruthless things

~~Well~~ Hott What do you say of my ~~sorrowfull~~ sorrowfull song?
Is it not very good? I am already so learned in
your poetry as your great Milton.
I hope that your health may be improved every day after
my departure; and that my wishes may had been
~~exhaused~~ granted.
I beg your pardon of my daring in writing a bad letter
in ~~bad~~ most more bad lenguage. I am ~~beginning~~ a

LETTER FROM GABRIELE ROSSETTI TO LADY ERROLL,

beginner and your tongue is very difficult; for it
absolutely necessary that I may learn it
I have also directed another letter also to Miss Frare, and
another to your respectable husband. and I beg of
you, will permit to me to do same time thing
with regards you; respect for giving me
the pleasure to repeat me

Your most obedient humble servant
Gabriel Rossetti

WIFE OF JOHN HOOKHAM FRERE, (? APRIL) 1824

Recess, and only consolation left
Familiar to my eyes ; all places else
Inhospitable appear and desolate
Nor knowing me and nor known . . . o ruthless King.
~~Watt~~ What do you say of my ~~sorrofull~~ sorrowfull sang ?

Is it not very good ? I am already ~~so~~ as learned in
your poetry as your great Milton.
I hope that your health may be improuved every day after
my departure ; and that my wishes may had been
~~exhaused~~ granted.
I beg your pardon of my daring in writing a bad letter
in ~~best~~ more bad language. I am ~~beginning~~ a
beginner and your tongue is very difficult ; but it
is absolutely necessary that I may learn it.
I have directed ~~another~~ also letter ~~also~~ a to Miss Frere, and
another to your respectable husband ; and I beg of
you, ~~will~~ to permit to me to do ~~same tin~~ sometime the same thing ~~to~~
with ~~wards~~ you ; ~~and most respect~~ to for giving me
the pleasure to repeate me
Your most ~~obeissan~~ humbel ser.

GABRIEL ROSSETTI

What was the nature of his " tumultuous thauts " when the
white walls of England came in sight ? The hope of meeting old
friends, fellow exiles ? The excitement of seeing at last a great
country long admired ? Renewed grief and regret for the country
he had left, perhaps for ever ? It is at least not likely that any
apprehension was mixed among them. Rossetti never lacked self-
confidence and was armed besides with powerful recommendations.
He had already experienced enough generosity in Englishmen to
encourage the hope of finding stores of it in their native land.
Probably he did not then expect his exile to be as irremediable
as that of Milton's hero, whose words he had so aptly quoted ;
and he must have had some hope that sorrow would endure but
for a night and joy return to him in the morning. In any case he
was faced with the unknown and the unguessable. Had he been
able to foresee the long years in Bloomsbury, the much-loved half
Italian wife, the toiling and moiling with articles and prepositions

in young ladies' seminaries, the children whose fame was eventually to eclipse his own, his sensations would have been poignant indeed. He came bringing nothing but letters of introduction with him ; but was ever a foreigner's arrival on these shores more full of significance for English literature ?

CHAPTER TWO

THE POET IN LONDON

THE poet received a welcome before he set foot on shore. Henry Munroe, in a letter to him on board the *Rochfort* at Chatham, suggested lodgings near Berkeley Square, and told him that Lord Holland and the poet Campbell had been informed of his arrival by the Moores ; while Lady Moore herself shortly after sent a kind note of regret that she was unable to be in London at his arrival. " I am afraid you will be very sad in that great city with few friends, but have courage and I am sure that with time and patience you will do very well." Unfortunately, the retributive gout which had so promptly punished him for overeating on board ship, still held him in its clutches. Arriving in London on 7 April, and finding his first lodgings at 37 Gerard Street, Soho, he there took to his bed, not to arise from it for some ten days or more. This interval of retirement he seems to have spent in putting the finishing touches to his *Psaltery*. " I rely on it ", he writes to Lady Moore, " to make me known here, and if in Italy my verses were thought to be something, I hope that in England they will not be without worth for those who love our poetry " ; and he asks her if she knows some English poet whom he may consult about the tastes of her countrymen.

At length he was able to go out and look about him. Of course, one of the first things he noticed was the opaque atmosphere, " the radiant torch of day turned into a ball of glass glowing red hot from the furnace, even that soon to be hidden behind black clouds of thickening fog." Apart from this notorious disadvantage, the place is a paradise on earth. " London, or rather England, is an object of the greatest wonder to me. What seemliness and order, what wealth, what . . . but what is there not ! The very bells play tunes." Still he disapproves—in 1824—of the advertisements, " all the walls are full of them, London is written all over like a book."

His first personal intercourse was with his " co-mates and fellows in exile ". There were many of them, though not all known to Rossetti either now or later. In 1823 a committee had been formed to help Italian exiles ; and between 1 December 1823 and 1 July 1824, some £2020 were collected and paid out by the committee to needy Italians, some of them already friends of the poet. At the end of that period some of the exiles were receiving help at the rate of two shillings a day. It does not appear that Rossetti had ever to depend on this excellent organisation—he had more English friends than most of his countrymen, and Frere, who was so generous later on, would hardly have allowed him to arrive penniless in England—but his fellow-exiles certainly did not fail in friendly attentions. Within a fortnight of his arrival he had been visited by Pepe, Menechini, Poerio, Paladini, Pistrucci and others. Still others had been visited by him. In his *Autobiography* he says that at this time the continent sent to Albion its best and its worst ; he was to have long experience of both kinds, but from the first he seems to have feared there were only too many of the worst. " Italians, Spaniards, Portuguese, floods of them, and they would all be in the greatest distress if they were not generously helped ; but there are very few educated men among them as I hear to my great regret." And yet as the month of May went on and the problem of finding work became more urgent, he found himself lamenting that the supply of Italians capable of teaching their own language was so much in excess of the demand. Everybody tells him of the scantiness of readers or would-be readers of Italian and " the great plethora of professing instructors. . . . Italian they say is known by few, and the political circumstances of the continent have cast upon this solitary refuge a swarm of unfortunates who have undertaken teaching. Arduous truths for me." However, he will do what in him lies. " I too will enter the ball and we shall see who has the best legs." Good conduct, love of work, few needs, many acquaintanceships, abundant assiduity, talent not deficient, must surely produce some result. In a postscript he says his pocket has just been picked of a lettercase in which was a valuable letter of introduction.

A few days later one of the many acquaintances sent an account of his impressions to Frere. This was Edward Davenport, who had been recommending Rossetti to everybody and who later staunchly supported his edition of Dante. " The man appears to me to be good and clever, and possessed of uncommon powers of writing, though not without the national fault of redundancy, of which I have been endeavouring to cure him. I fear, however, that a certain Parson-Adams-like simplicity (of which the pick-pockets have already twice availed themselves) will prevent his keeping his money, should he make any. . . ." Meanwhile Frere's recommendations had secured him interviews with various distinguished men. He had met his patron's two brothers ; Lord Holland received him cordially, Mr. Gurney with warmth. Dr. Young, Mr. Heber, and W. S. Rose were all on his list. The Moores had introduced him to Campbell, who evidently received him politely since Rossetti describes him as " the most courteous of the tuneful family ", and who appears to have helped him to find work. On 4 May he had three pupils, but having lost them all before the middle of July he was still finding it necessary to present his inexhaustible letters of introduction. No wonder that he says London soon ceased to be a forest to him.

We have seen that Rossetti had some hope of the *Psaltery* as a means of getting himself known. Some of his new friends told him that he ought to publish it " so that the author may accredit the instructor." Murray had read it in April and had advised him to publish it in three instalments. But this was not to be. Per-haps his readings from it did not meet with as much applause as he had hoped. Certainly Davenport, who suggested a list of celebrities to whom the poems should be shown, could hardly expect them to be much impressed, since he himself had already expressed to Frere his doubt whether Rossetti would make any money by a work executed in a metre so ill-chosen. It was still on hand for reading purposes in January of the next year, when the poet spent a day with Coleridge and read him part of it ; but it was not published until 1833, when according to his own account he salved a conscience made uneasy by close studies of the heresies of Dante by turning back to his own sacred poem.

The amazing powers of improvisation which had attracted the attention of Frere in Malta might, one supposes, have served Rossetti in some stead in this situation ; but he was resolved to use them as little as possible. He believed that improvisation was a practice harmful alike to the nerves and the poetic style of the improviser. He held it responsible for the early death of his brother Domenico, and believed that his own overfluent and neglectful composition to some extent resulted from it. He thanks his exile for putting an end ·to this activity, although he would occasionally indulge acquaintances in their wish to hear him. Thus one of Dante Gabriel's earliest letters, in 1835, informs Aunt Margaret that the Turkish Ambassador had asked papa to improvise at a party.

Otherwise we may be sure that Rossetti left no stone unturned in his effort to establish himself. There is some reason to believe that from the very beginning he had hoped to gain some profit by renewing his connection with the theatre. As soon as he was able to leave his bed he had visited Signor Benelli of the Teatro Italiano, who returned his visit; and called upon Rossini, who apparently undertook to do something for him, though the promise was apparently unfulfilled. He came to know various luminaries of the contemporary operatic stage. Lablache the tenor used occasionally to give the Rossettis tickets for performances; Pasta the soprano he knew well—she had heard of him in Paris in 1824, and sought him out when she came to London in the same year. For a few years he did a little in the libretto line—the dreary results of it may be seen in the British Museum, in cantatas based on Byron, and books of words by other writers of which he had revised the translation.

It was perhaps his operatic connections which first brought Rossetti into touch with Cipriani Potter, Principal of the Royal Academy of Music, who was godfather to William Michael and whose family was the only one with which the young Rossettis were familiar. Potter once gave Rossetti £40 for a libretto, possibly *Medoro e Corrado*; on another occasion the poet received £30 from some young ladies through Maestro Negri for a similar composition. Had much of this kind of work been available his fortune would have been assured, for the remuneration seems extravagant and our fluent poet could hardly have found it difficult to reel off *ad infinitum* verses of which the following are a fair example:

> Ladies dear, your charming beauty
> In dispute could never be;
> But you seem more fair than ever
> When for long we've been at sea.

> All the charms your sex deviseth
> I know not from whence they be;
> But I know I always feel them
> Disembarking from the sea.

The part of Gonsalvo who experiences these tender feelings w sung by Lablache, who no doubt looked as much like a Corsair as the song sounds like one.[1]

We have a lively and amusing glimpse of Rossetti in his first year in England in an account he sent Lady Moore of a visit to Cambridge in company with Pasta. (It was before 13 July, on which date Lady Moore replied.) The poet had gone there chiefly to see Frere's brother, the Master of Downing, a " very good-natured man, who has inspired even his household cats with his own natural goodness of heart." He met two other brothers as well, Bartholomew and Temple and all Temple's family, who were kindness itself not only to him but also to his travelling companion, Signora Pasta, and two other gentlemen who came with her. " She sang four airs in Cambridge, two in church in the morning, and two more in the evening in a great hall. The audience was immense, and the applause, or rather the enthusiasm, quite indescribable. There was such a crowd that we were obliged to enter the hall through a window. . . . I perceive that the English are music mad, and the sums they will disburse to delight their ears are truly alarming. Signora Pasta, for these four airs sung in less than an hour, received about £200. Mrs. Frere, who seems to live on music, and all her numerous band of musical friends, have conferred a thousand marks of distinction on the celebrated Italian singer, who returned with me to London altogether astonished and delighted with the courtesy of English gentlewomen." There was some reflected glory for her countryman in this, but some cause for envy too had he been of an envious disposition. As for him, the music-loving Mrs. Frere had presented him to " all the most distinguished persons of her religion ", and for this service he was grateful. It was not as useful as £200, but it subserved his leading principle of action at the moment— " acquaintances in England are like the good seed." He was nothing if not optimistic ; in the next sentence he says he is losing all his scholars.

At what point Rosseti found enough pupils to secure a living does not appear from the material at our disposal, but since there is no suggestion of distress in the letters of 1825 it is probable

---

[1] Among other acquaintances in the world of music was Paganini, whom the poet knew well. At one time (27 May 1831) the famous virtuoso will hardly let Rossetti out of his sight, and is anxious to have his company on a tour of the provinces. " If he pays me," says Rossetti, " I will go, but he is a terrible miser."

that the good seed broadcast so indefatigably in 1824 had borne fruit by the end of the year. Early in July he had thought of going to Liverpool for six or seven months, " until the nobility return to London ", but the project for some reason fell through. Meanwhile the sojourn of the nobility in their country houses was not without advantage for Rossetti. Some of them offered him what must have been a pleasant respite from treading the hard London ways. The Moores invited him to Cobham in June. In July he thinks of going to spend two months in the country at the invitations of Rose and Davenport. A certain Thomas Witby invites him to Lymington for Christmas.

II

The year 1824 sees Rossetti transplanted indeed in the alien soil, but not yet striking root ; going from one rich man's table to another ; meditating upon Dante in unwelcome leisure ; making friends among the Italian colony, and being spied upon by its few treacherous members. In the course of 1825 he was to become firmly established in London, the commentary on Dante was to take form and be published, life-long friendship was to be made with Gaetano Polidori, life-long love and devotion to be found in Polidori's daughter. In the following spring he set up house in Charlotte Street and the history of the English Rossettis begins.

Gaetano Polidori, one-time secretary to Alfieri the dramatist, had been in England for about thirty-five years, and spoke the language perfectly except for some slight trace of foreign accent. He came of a Tuscan family among whom the poetic gift seems to have been as widely distributed as among the Rossettis. His father, who was a doctor, wrote among other things a long poem on the bones of the human body, a composition which Gaetano thought readable and recommended to his daughter. His profession descended to the ill-fated Dr. John Polidori, Byron's travelling companion, and would have descended still further to his great-grandson William Michael Rossetti but for Gabriele's chronic impecuniosity. Agostino Polidori was a man of the most admirable integrity, so modest that he would never have his portrait made, and such a lover of decency that hearing the improper songs sung in the streets, he is said to have composed sacred ones and had them sung by those around him. The austere Polidori tradition is evident enough in Gaetano who would not allow his daughters to learn dancing, and composed moral fables in Italian to supply the lack of reading material edifying to young ladies; it appears in full grandeur in the formidable array of Polidori aunts, and in the well-tempered asperity of Mrs. Rossetti's family control; and has to be remembered in any consideration of Christina Rossetti's rigid outlook.

There is a good deal of nonsense written about what is and what is not Italian or English in the Rossetti children, and we shall have occasion to return to the subject later. Meanwhile, we may notice in Gaetano the Tuscan the existence of many admirable qualities of the kind proclaimed as British, his strong common sense and level-headedness, his independence, his hatred of pretence and dishonesty, his steadiness of judgment, his love of the open air and gardening, his sturdy dependability. He remains in the background of Rossetti's life up to its last year, a tower of strength and health and activity.[1]

In 1793 Gaetano Polidori had married Anna Maria Pierce, an English governess—it was a profession as natural to the women of the family as medicine to the men. She was a chronic invalid for at least the last twenty years of her life, never leaving her bedroom; and so could hardly have been an active influence in the development of her grandchildren. Nevertheless, anyone who wishes to make the hazardous attempt to connect Christina's temperament with her family inheritance, would do well to consider closely this entirely English and not very cheerful invalid, whose eyes were Christina's eyes, whose father had been remarkable for "faultless precision and imposing decorum", and who had

---

[1] In Polidori's *Poesie Varie*, London, n.d. [? 1806], pp. 72–4, occurs the following passage:

To Myself. Anacreontic

Of the present could I justly
Now bewail me? No, no, no!
Health is mine, and I robustly
Eat and sleep and stand and go.
I've a wife who very often
Sad and troubled seems to be,
But the sunshine is most pleasant
When its light we seldom see.
Five fine children, gay and bonny,
All around me frisk and play;
Never one of them I'd barter
For the Empire of Cathay.

brought up all her daughters to be, like herself, earnest members of the Church of England.

The Polidoris had a cottage at Holmer Green in Buckinghamshire, but Gaetano supported himself until 1835 by teaching, and so kept two rooms in London, in Wells Street, Oxford Street. By the time Rossetti met him he had written and published a good deal, and had a family of four sons and four daughters. Gaetano being a professing (though not by any means ardent) Roman Catholic, it was arranged that his sons should be brought up in that faith, while the daughters should follow that of their mother. Of these four sons one died in infancy, another was Byron's Polidori, whose death was so grievous to Gaetano that his name had never to be mentioned in his father's hearing,[1] a third was Philip Robert who could never settle into doing any work at all, and the fourth was Henry Francis who was an unsuccessful lawyer. The daughters were a more satisfactory group, being all women of ability in their own ways. Margaret, the eldest, was in early days a governess, afterwards living with her family, and subsequently in the household of William Michael. She occasionally took charge of the Rossetti children when their mother was ill or away at Holmer Green. Charlotte, the second daughter, figures more prominently as time goes on ; she is the Aunt Incarnate. Governess and later companion to the Marchioness of Bath, she was a touchstone of propriety and decorum ; her dress approximated more closely to prevailing fashion than that of the other Rossetti women, who were always several years behind the times ; she also had more money than the other relations, although William remarks that she never seemed to have any when required. Her relations with her sister Frances were very affectionate—they were called substance and shadow ; to the children she was an object of some awe. Eliza Harriet, the youngest, had the least pretension to intellectual accomplishment and preferred house-keeping. When Gabriele presented her with a copy of his *Arpa Evangelica*, she sent the following reply :

My Dear Sir,

Many thanks for the copy of your book that you have been so kind as to give me. I have heard Margaret read some of the Hymns and like what I have understood but my head not being poetical I cannot appreciate its beauties. Pray give my love to

---

[1] John was Mrs. Rossetti's favourite brother, and on that account alone Dante Gabriel thought his memory deserved some respect.

your wife and daughters and trusting you are all well as I am I remain attached

Sister-in-law

ELIZA H. POLIDORI.

After her mother's death in 1853 she went out to the Crimea with Florence Nightingale and earned a Turkish medal. Her long life of eighty-three years came to an end in 1893, a year before Christina Rossetti's—it was she who found comfort in the consoling thought that no day lasts longer than twenty-four hours, which was a good thing since she had to endure so many.

III

At what date Rossetti first made the acquaintance of Polidori is not certain. The older man lay rather out of the beaten track of exiles and letters of introduction. By July 1825, in any case, Rossetti is corresponding with him in terms of the greatest politeness and respect, in just such terms in fact as one would expect from a man writing to another whose daughter has begun to attract him. " If you do not think it too bold in me to ask you to present my respects to your family, please do so." Rossetti was writing particularly about Dante, sending the first sheets of the *Comento* and asking for remarks and suggestions ; Polidori replies with equal politeness and offers comments with enthusiasm—his tone is that of a man who is aware of a possible son-in-law and entirely approves of him. Not that he could agree with all Rossetti's hazardous speculations, particularly not with his interpretation of *pape Satan aleppe*.[1] Gaetano was a genuine admirer of Dante and his poem. Christina, who loved her grandfather dearly, perhaps even more than she loved her father, remarks with her quiet discrimination that, of the two, Gaetano knew more about Dante *as a poet*. But at no time does he appear to have offered any strong opposition to Rossetti's theories, and for the present he is very ready to help and to admire. Gabriele was delighted. He will mention Gaetano in a note (which he did very handsomely) ; he takes to the *Voi* ; he blesses the day they met ; he will always have the satisfaction of repeating to himself, whatever the envious critics may say, *Sufficit mihi unus Plato pro cuncto populo*. " You are the only man, or at least the first in this country, who understands Dante humanly. A hundred learned unfeathered bipeds are for me not worth a single

[1] See p. 86 and note.

hair of one of those animals which can be called rational : I like men, not parrots, and I who believe myself to belong to the former species have been drawn to you with delight on the ancient principle of *omne simile*." Gaetano for his part declared that Rossetti had not only rent asunder but had altogether torn down the dusty curtain which had concealed the meaning of Dante to that day. " I cannot thank you for the honour you have done me in mentioning my name with so much courtesy and with a generosity which is never found except in those who are gifted with the highest genius ; I lack words adequate to express the feelings of my heart, which will always be full of esteem, friendship, and gratitude towards you."

Amid this shower of compliments Rossetti marched towards his marriage, Dante paving the way. Polidori's daughter Frances, then twenty-five years old, had engrossed his attention from the beginning.

> Upon the day when I returned his call
> And saw him 'mid his well-bred family,
> I twice and thrice fixed my admiring eyes
> Upon the second daughter's comeliness.
> A single moment regulates a life :
> My heart became the lodestone, she the pole.
>
> [W. M. R.]

On 7 December 1825, he enclosed a formal proposal in a letter to Polidori, asking him to throw it into the fire if he disapproved ; he was accepted the next day. It must have been a time of great excitement. The *Comento* was being printed and published during this month, there was the usual daily grinding at articles and prepositions, and there was much to plan for the future. The tone of his feelings as a lover may be seen from the following scrap of a love-letter, the only one that remains, and that only a preliminary draft, for his wife had little of his instinct for preserving such relics of the past. " I have stopped a moment to re-read this letter : I have found it contradictory like the mind it came from ; I promised not to talk of my distraction and then I went on to describe the tempests that disturb my heart ; I was tempted to tear it up ; but instead I have made up my mind to send it to you, if only to show you my sincerity ; you will begin to get some idea from it of the sort of man who is to be your fellow-pilgrim here on earth : he has need of your companionship and of your counsel ; but yet he is not one of the *bad Italians*. You will see that this letter does not need a reply, so do not let it cause you to lose moments that you could better employ in other ways."

A complete decorum and steadiness is noticeable from the outset. His love was sincere and deep and lasting ; but it was also quiet and in a sense business-like ; it did not carry him away as his political enthusiasms had done five years ago ; it came to him in the even tenor of his present way, and he took it in his stride. The verses he sent to " Fanny " on New Year's Day 1926 are full of roses, lilies, stars and swans, pretty and graceful, not in the least passionate. Writing to his friends Rossetti accounts for his marriage in matter-of-fact terms that are very surprising in a poet so excitable. Thus he tells Lyell that he has taken a step that will make it necessary for him to remain permanently in England. " That is to say I am going to marry Signor Polidori's daughter. It was necessary for me to engage in a more regular system of life in order to give proper attention to my studies, and that helped me to come to such a decision." [1]

Altogether his own naïve account in the *Autobiography* probably presents in the right light this act which was the foundation of his happiness and his peace. Having settled in England, he says, and seeing the future less ambiguously,

> Like Dante's, ' *Vita Nuova* ' was my word :
> He wrote, but I resolved to practise it.
> ' Let warm affections in my novel lot
> Arise ', I said, ' to populate my breast.'
>
> [w. m. r.]

He needed a wife, and had found one better and more capable than he could ever have hoped. It was not a matter of high romance, but what it may have lacked in ecstasy, it made up for in durability and common sense.

Gabriele Rossetti and Frances Polidori were married according to the Roman Catholic rite by a certain Dr. Baldacconi on 8 April 1826, and then again in the English Church on 10 April—a date which Christina Rossetti still piously observed as late as 1893. Then or soon after they went to the Polidori cottage at Holmer Green. On the eve of their departure Gabriele composed a sort of honeymoon piece which is printed among his poems.

[1] In the *Veggente in Solitudine* the poet declares that he had refrained from being married in his native land,

> Che altri servi a tirannia
> Disdegnai di generar

[for new bondsmen to tyranny I disdained to beget].

> Little garden, humble roof,
> Fanny mine, will greet us there,
> Happiest of all retreats
> Liberty and country cheer.
>
> Happy, happy little field
> Thee to-morrow shall I see ;
> Cincinnatus born again
> With his hand hath tended thee.

Cincinnatus is of course Polidori, whose character, occupations, and outlook have certainly a pronounced air of classical antiquity. The poet goes on to say that in Fanny his mother is given back to him again, and he again addresses the cottage :

> Hail, sweet Inn, where we shall offer
> Each to each our loving days ;
> Thou a temple art of Hymen,
> Where an altar Love doth raise.
>
> Hail, oh wood ! to whom are given
> Shades and breezes April loves ;
> Now within thy leafy bosom
> Take two newly mated doves.

IV

It will be well to pause at this point and to form as clear an idea as possible of the admirable woman whom the poet had so fortunately met and married, and who was to determine the tone of the Rossettis' family life. Whoever is to understand the work of the Rossetti children must begin by understanding the character of their mother. There is no such wealth of material for this purpose as there is in the case of her husband ; few of her letters have been preserved, none at all of this early period. Her part in any case was a quietly pervasive one ; she was far too unassuming ever to do anything sensational or to put herself forward in any unusual way. However, from the writings of her son William, and from occasional passages in the works and letters of other members of the family, a tolerably clear outline emerges. At the time of her marriage she was almost twenty-six. Brought up in the severe but kindly atmosphere of the Polidori home, the natural firmness of her nature and the refinement of her mind had had the most favourable opportunities of development. For young ladies of education but no means, there was then only one respectable method of earning a living. She took to it at the age of sixteen and was governess in three families before meeting Rossetti. In the third a colonel related to the family fell in love with her, but before there was time for him to decide whether or not he could marry the governess, Rossetti arrived on the scene and carried her off.

Her appearance in middle age, as portrayed by her son, was one of grave and regular beauty ; in youth she must have been very beautiful indeed. She was of about the average woman's height, had abundant full-tinted brown hair, grey eyes, fresh complexion, very regular features, and an expression of composure and self-control. Her voice was clear, and excellent for reading. Her mind was well-instructed and acute without having any kind of creative power, or intellectual originality. She accepted her world as she found it, observing its absurdities with a shrewdly critical eye, but never questioning her own position in it. She could both speak and write in French and Italian, although English was her natural language, and she had read widely in the three literatures. Her manners were extremely simple and dignified. Any kind of pretence was hateful to her—it could hardly be otherwise in a daughter of Polidori—and she had no liking at all for ' evening parties ' or the other observances of society. Morning calls she hardly ever paid or received.

She rose regularly at seven to a busy day, though she had little instinctive interest in cooking or dressmaking or similar domestic occupations for their own sake, any more than her two daughters had afterwards ; however, she was ready to deal with them when necessary with the unostentatious ability which characterises all her activities, and this too may be remarked with equal truth of her daughters. As Rossetti says in his poetical way, " at the touch of her industrious hands order ever flourishes around me." She was, of course, a close observer of all the reasonable proprieties and naturally not untouched by the conventions of her day, but she was by no means bound to them. She was deeply and unpretentiously religious, in the first half of her life evangelical, later leaning toward the Puseyism which her husband took to attacking so violently in other people—what he thought of it in his own home does not appear. Her beliefs were simple and literal, though not without occasional assertions of individual judgment—she was once moved to say with decision, " I will never believe that Socrates is condemned to eternal punishment."

It is not likely that the world would ever be allowed to know what such a woman thought about her husband's weaknesses and foibles, his childish vanities, his theories about the Manichees and the Freemasons, his violent literary quarrels. That she loved him for his finer qualities is very certain; that she was sometimes amused, and sometimes even irritated, by his failings may with hardly less certainty be surmised. She promptly burnt all the copies of his *Amor Platonico* after his death; she objected to his bringing home lollipops for the children, calling them *porcherie* [trash]—and in an often-quoted conversation of 1873 she is reported to have said, " I always had a passion for intellect, and my wish was that my husband should be distinguished for intellect, and my children too. I have had my wish; and I now wish that there were a little less intellect in the family, so as to allow for a little more common sense."

But it is impossible either to praise her worth adequately, or to estimate the effect of her influence upon the family. " To her more than myself ", says Rossetti, " is due our children's educating discipline." He calls upon them to thank him for having chosen such a mother to give life to them. " Your inculcations on many points ", said Dante Gabriel in 1876, " are still the standard of criticism with me." William Michael, at her death in 1886, made the following entry in his diary: " My dearest mother, the pattern to me of everything that is simple, sweet, kind, and noble, died on 8 April at 25 minutes past noon." Christina, who was her daily companion for the greater part of her life, loved better than any other her

> Blessed Dear and Heart's Delight,
> Companion, Friend, and Mother Mine.

When Christina Rossetti was on her deathbed she had some conversation with William about their mother. He said that her life might be considered on the whole a happy one, " as lives go "— much affection bestowed by her, and not a little received. " Christina did not reply very definitely, but I inferred that she is less prepared than myself to regard our mother's life as happy." There are, of course, two very different sets of values involved here, and one imagines that Mrs. Rossetti herself would have agreed with her prosaic and realistically minded son rather than with her poetic and other-worldly daughter. There was indeed much that Christina might have had in mind which might often have clouded her mother's rather limited family horizon. As William Michael himself points out, her deep religious instincts undoubtedly suffered a good deal from the indifference of her father, the curious heterodoxy of her husband, the agnosticism of her sons. And apart from the losses that afflict any long life, she appears to have felt deeply the discords that eventually separated Christina and herself from William Michael and his family, while her pride in the fame of Dante Gabriel must have been chastened by who knows what anxiety over his life and actions. " I send you ", he wrote on one occasion, " my sonnets, which are such a lively band of bogies that they may join hands with the skeletons of Christina's various closets and entertain you by a ballet." That must have seemed to her very tragical mirth—the sonnets included the series called *Willowwood*. However, she was in the best sense of the word an ordinary woman, though one of the finest ; and by the ordinary student of the family, William Michael's judgment, which is that of an ordinary man, may very well be allowed to stand. She loved much and wisely, she was well beloved. She had anxieties, but many compensations. Her life was a happy one " as lives go ". At the moment, however, she is twenty-six, and her griefs as well as most of her joys are all before her. We have to see her bringing her four children into the world, looking after them in health and sickness (very often the latter), keeping Gabriele's home in order, supporting the family by her own labours when his health declines. Or rather we shall be aware that she is doing all these things, but what she thought about them and how she did them we shall hardly know at all, while we hear enough about her husband's views on Dante and the Papacy to fill many volumes, as large and tedious as those he published. It will be amusing to remember her quiet and efficient figure in the background when we consider those endless lucubrations.

CHAPTER THREE

EARLY MARRIED LIFE

I

THE contrast between Rossetti's life in Italy and his married life in Bloomsbury could not be better symbolised than in the contrast between the house where he was born and that in which he and Frances Polidori began their life together. Neither of them still exists—the first is a ruin as we have seen, the other has been demolished and has given place to a set of flats called Rossetti House—but both may be seen in photographs. It is the contrast between the romantic and the ordinary, between poetry and prose. No. 38 Charlotte Street is described by William Michael as having been " fairly neat but decidedly small ". The street itself began to " go down " soon after the Rossettis set up house there, and the petty warfare between the respectable and the undesirable which always sets in under such circumstances had already begun within the children's memories. A sordid environment for a family of poets ; in itself it helps to account for *Goblin Market* and *The Blessed Damozel*, and it is certainly a sufficient explanation of the entire lack of intimacy with nature noticeable in all the Rossetti work (even in Christina's). Their visits to Holmer Green were no doubt delightful and long remembered, but they were at most only holidays in the country.

The house was humble, for the Rossettis had little money to dispose of. Later on, while he was professor at King's College, Rossetti was able to make some £300 in a good year, not receiving this amount directly, but securing more private pupils through his status at the College.[1] At this time, however, he must have made a good deal less. Now and then Frere would send £50 or so, and he had a happy way of sending it at the moment when it was most needed. Mrs. Rossetti had what are called expectations : at the death of

[1] The usual fee for lessons was 10s. 6d. per hour.

42

her mother she was entitled to a fortune of £2000 ; but her mother did not die until 1853. However, although they were comparatively poor, they never experienced absolute poverty. No debts were ever allowed to accumulate ; " no butcher nor baker nor candlestick-maker ever had a claim upon us for sixpence unpaid." This was Mrs. Rossetti's doing ; but their living was insecure, and remained so until William Michael's salary and one or two legacies had put things on a more settled footing. That was not until 1853.

Rossetti now settled down anew to his lessons and his theories, and gradually gave up the habit of dining out, in which he had been obliged to indulge up to the time of his marriage. And soon his wife had more to think about than the preparation of his conservatively foreign dishes. Early in 1827 Gabriele composed the following lines, which were subsequently pricked by Frances into a baby pincushion :

> Offspring of love, grow thou to happiness,
> Like a sweet floweret in the wind's caress ;
> Thy father's and thy mother's inmost hearts
> Compunction feel and deepest tenderness.

This was for Maria Francesca, who came into the world on 17 February. She was the firstborn and the first to die, the least known, but it might be contended the best-balanced character among the children. Of Maria's earliest experiences in the world she was later to renounce, and of her parents' feeling about the event, there remains nothing to be known apart from Gabriele's pincushion verses. He probably wished for a son with the proper Italian predilection for that sex ; and in a year's time the desire was gratified.

Meanwhile he had entertained the hope of becoming professor of Italian at the newly founded University College.[1] The matter first comes to light in a letter of Lady Moore's on 30 April 1827. If Rossetti will let them know the form it should take, the Admiral will be glad to write him a testimonial ; what is more, when the time for electing the professor arrives, he will speak to Brougham about it. We find later that Moore also recommended him to Campbell, who was the presiding genius of the new institution. But both avenues were unfortunate—Brougham's ear had been gained in another quarter, and Campbell, who had read the *Comento*, thought much more highly of Foscolo. And Rossetti could have

---

[1] So too had his father-in-law, as it appears from the College records, though no hint of this rivalry appears in the family letters.

no access to men more influential in the matter than these. He was supported by Cary the translator of Dante, Davenport, and W. S. Rose whom he knew fairly well and to whom he had given some help in his translations from the Italian. He tried every way at his disposal although, as he said himself, if the post had been open to competitive examination he would have asked for no man's recommendation.

Unfortunately, it was not ; and Rose in writing to say he had spoken to various people, expressed a fear that Rossetti had moved too late—he had heard of the good hopes of a competitor from Liverpool. Now steps before the curtain the villain of the piece, *il mago maggior di tutti i maghi*,[1] Antonio Panizzi, the Liverpool competitor himself, who was elected to the chair, and was considered by Rossetti throughout his life as an inveterate and diabolically cunning enemy. Panizzi had come to England a year before Rossetti, having fled in danger of his life from Modena ; he subsequently received from Reggio a bill for the expenses of his accusation, sentence and execution, a matter of 225 fr. 25. His first experiences in London seem to have been more distressing than Rossetti's, but he had many valuable friends ; among them, Santarosa who advised him to note all the most important points in English habits, which he did with much success, and Ugo Foscolo who urged him to go to Liverpool. He went there—it was *reculer pour mieux sauter*. The climate depressed him, he had to trudge long distances on foot to give lessons, he lacked comfort and even proper food. But Roscoe, the famous biographer of Lorenzo de' Medici, befriended him, and it was Roscoe's recommendation to Brougham more than anything else which secured for him the chair at University College, and laid the foundation of his future prosperity. He was naturalised in 1832, became Principal Librarian of the British Museum in 1856, and subsequently received an entirely deserved knighthood. Mazzini, with whom for a time he was intimate, disapproved of his absorption into English life. " By force of making himself English in opinions, in manners, in everything, he has become Librarian in the British Museum, has a splendid salary. . . . But would I consent to serve this noviciate ? No, indeed ; it is better to be poor." But Panizzi was neither so great nor so fanatical as Mazzini ; he had found his proper métier, and followed it with outstanding skill

[1] " The greatest sorcerer of all the sorcerers." The phrase occurs in the *Autobiography*.

and devotion. Nor had he forgotten his own country. His influence on liberal opinion and sympathy in England was considerable ; Gladstone, Lord John Russell, Salisbury and others were intimate friends. He hated the Austrians as long as he lived ; and he energetically organised a rescue expedition to extract Settembrini and Carlo Poerio from their island prison.[1] He visited Naples itself, interviewed Ferdinand, reported on the state of the Neapolitan prisons.

Rossetti, however, feared and hated this excellent man more than any other single person. Even in America, he said, he would not be safe from such a " demon sorcerer " ; only in heaven would he be secure, for——

Hatred, howe'er persistent, comes not there.

An eloquent anthology of abuse could be compiled from his letters on this subject. What was the cause of it all ? There can be little doubt that most of the magician's enmity was as imaginary as the conspiracy that Dante Gabriel supposed to be working against him, after the attack of Robert Buchanan. But Panizzi, as we shall see, certainly attacked the Dante theories with very open contempt ; he was elected to a chair that Rossetti coveted, and that without any previous reputation for learning ; fortune subsequently smiled on him as she refused to do upon the poet, and his growing importance made his critical hostility seem more dangerous. Rossetti attributed his supposed malignity to *stolta invidia* [stupid envy], but the occasion for such feeling was all on the other side. Certainly there is no ground for believing that Panizzi did anything worse than to call Rossetti's Dante interpretation nonsense.

By February of 1828 Rossetti knew that his application had been unsuccessful. " The Council of the University of London which seemed very well disposed to elect me as professor of Italian literature ", he writes to Lyell, " through the influence of Mr. Brougham has preferred to me a nobody who has not even given the world an alphabet, a certain Panizzi whose name for the first time sounds in the ears of men." Lyell tries to give him friendly consolation. " It grieves me to see that a gloom has been cast on your prospects by the election of Signor Panizzi at the London University. It has been known for some time that he had the zealous support of Messrs. Brougham and Roscoe. What consolation can I afford you ? It will not be a satisfactory one to say

[1] Unfortunately the ship which was chartered to make this desperate attempt 'was lost on the way'.

that since the breaking up of our liberal administration the University has less chance of becoming a prosperous concern. . . .

> *Quand on n'a pas ce que l'on aime*
> *Il faut aimer ce que l'on a.*

Now you have lost the Professorship, but you have your Dante, so love it, give your whole soul to perfecting it, as to a darling child, and put it forth on to the world as soon as you can to make its fortune. It will not disappoint you, but will repay you richly at last, and keep away the gout, which will soon be in the fingers again if you sigh at the good luck of Panizzi who must be laughing in his sleeve at John Bull's choice of *him*. . . . I wish I could offer you any better antitode [*sic*] than my French proverb against despondency, which it would be well to fight against with the insouciance of a Frenchman." Perhaps Rossetti went about expressing his opinions about Panizzi's nonentity with so much freedom that they came to that gentleman's ears. It is very likely, and in that case the acerbity of Panizzi's review of the *Comento*, which appeared in the *Foreign Quarterly*, in October,[1] would be better explained. At all events he was disappointed and his pride hurt, while his feelings may have been exacerbated by the fact that the book did not yet look like making its fortune.

II

The need for establishing his worldly security was at the same time becoming urgent. Another child was expected, and eventually arrived on 12 May 1828. Writing to Lyell about Dante on the 28th, Rossetti says, " To make memorable to myself the sad epoch in which I illustrate him in my exile, I am going to renew his name in my family. A few days ago my wife gave birth to a little Rossetti. I shall call him Dante ; and if I could flatter myself that a certain gentleman whom I greatly respect would consent to be godfather by proxy to my little protestant, I should call him at the holy font Dante Charles Rossetti. I shall not have him christened until I hear from that gentleman whom I so much honour. If he consents, the new Dante will have two Philodantes, one as his father by nature and the other as his father in God." Lyell undertook to discharge the office in person, and on 8 June the child was christened Gabriel Charles Dante. At the festivities which followed Rossetti made the following

---

[1] See pp. 95–6

Impromptu Toast.
On the day when Charles Lyell, Esq., held at the baptismal font my
son Gabriel Charles Dante.

'Mid our company convivial
Forth I pour auspicious wine ;
For my little son Dantino
Briefest wish shall now be mine.

Briefest wish, but countless blessings
To his lot will surely fall,
If his Godfather he only
May resemble—that is all.

III

By the end of July Mrs. Rossetti had gone off to Holmer Green
with her baby, and we get the first glimpses of the Rossetti
family relations. There is nothing particularly striking about them,
much that is quietly interesting. Maria was already there. " I
am glad to hear ", writes Gabriele, " that all are well, although
our dear Tuppitiello has still got a bit of a cold. Poor little thing !
I envy you the pleasure of having our two little images with you.
. . . So Maria Francesca didn't recognise you at first ? I can
imagine your disappointment. But now she makes up for it by
being with you, by calling you Mamma, by caressing her little
brother, and by showing you how well she can walk. . . .
This house is like a desert. I try as well as I can to forget your
absence in my books, but with little success. Yet once or twice,
absent-mindedly, I have thought that you and my son were still
here, have gone up twice into the bedroom to see you both . . .
and have been disillusioned ; and, miserable and oh so cold, I
have returned to my books again, but for some time without understanding a word of them." Meanwhile he has been buying a
" nest for our turtle dove ", a cot with a good woollen mattress and
soft feather pillow and castored feet. It will cost £3 altogether,
no small sum for Rossetti in those days. " Don't forget ", he ends,
" to write whenever you can and to tell me about our dear Cupid
and our dearest Psyche."
The next day he writes again with important news.

" MY DEAREST FRANCESCA,
I have just come back from Camberwell, and not being able
to see you I want to talk to you. (I went out at 8 because Miss

Goldsmid had asked me to come two or three hours earlier. There were no carriages so early and I was obliged to walk). Mr. Goldsmid had not left home, and on seeing me, showed me infinite kindness ; and told me (supposing I didn't know about it) that a new university is being established, which according to him, will be much more splendid than the other. . . . He asked if I had any intention of applying for the professorship of Italian literature there, and hearing that I had, replied ' You will get it, without any doubt ' ; and then added emphatically, ' I will bet a thousand pounds that you will get it. I shall go about talking to everybody who has anything to do with it, and I am sure of succeeding with them. They have done you one wrong but they shall not do you another. I know how that affair came to pass, I know who contrived it ; but it is not right for me to talk about it ! ' Then I told him that I had heard . . . that Panizzi has no intention of serving in the chair conferred upon him, or at least that he doesn't care whether he does or not. He replied, ' If that were true, I should be very pleased about it : you would have the Professorship : but I don't believe what Panizzi says : it is just a conceited gesture.'

He asked me to come on Sunday at eight, and I have accepted. I must certainly keep on good terms with this very courteous gentleman, who shows me so much friendliness. So, my Francesca, I shan't be able to come next Sunday ; but I hope that you will come back to your husband on Monday with our two beloved pledges. . . .

Coming back from Camberwell and going down Oxford Street, I stopped at a shop where there was a great crowd ; I went in with them and found that the entire stock was being sold cheap, perhaps because the owner had gone bankrupt. It came into my mind that I might buy something for you and Tuppitella ; so I got you half a dozen cotton stockings very white and fine (for four shillings), another half-dozen for you at fourteen pence a pair : two pairs of half-hose for me, a silk handkerchief also for me, a pair of black gloves for you—but these last two purchases were neither cheap nor good. I have put everything aside for your return. And I hope that on the whole you won't be displeased with what I have bought."

This gentleman, whose friendship it was so important to retain, was Sir Isaac Goldsmid, a wealthy Jewish stockbroker, and well known in London. Rossetti taught in his family, and he remained a very useful friend for many years ; it was he who eventually placed William Michael in the Civil Service.

IV

Leaving for the time being any consideration of the poet's literary occupations and of his circle of friends, we shall limit our view until we see him surrounded with his complete family. There were frequent anxieties, and inordinate suffering from childish complaints. Maria was seriously ill in February 1829, and again in December. Mrs. Rossetti was again at Holmer Green during the summer, no doubt resting in preparation for the third child then expected. " Coming home to-day at four and not finding a letter from you, I was very troubled and didn't know what to make of it, when at half-past five Henry arrived ; having seen and read your letter I felt entirely reassured. I delight in what you tell me, and I envy you the pleasure of seeing that dear little Gabriel running about among the plants and stopping at the currant bushes. If I were there, I would chase him, and I can just imagine him running away shouting with glee and staggering with his little hand to his ear. I hope that his present liveliness will strengthen and loosen his legs, so that when he comes back he will be able to walk about our rooms unaided like a little sparrow or at least a little fledgling bird. So he is afraid of the lowing of the cows ! What a strange thing ! But soon it will become welcome music to those big ears of his which you are so kind as to laugh at.

I hope that Maria still feels the joy that shone in her eyes on the day she left here. You are in good company, and I here

<blockquote>
Alone and thoughtful, pace the empty rooms
With mournful steps and slow." [1]
</blockquote>

As he oftens appears to have done, Rossetti made arrangements on this occasion to go down himself to Holmer Green for the week-end.

William Michael was born on 25 September 1829, and from an account of the family sent to Frere in December he seems to have been the strongest of the three from the beginning. " My daughter has overcome a long illness which at one time made us lament for her death, and has recovered as a flower is revived by the dew. My little Dante walks, talks and plays ; and my baby William who

---

[1] Solo e pensoso le deserte stanze
   Vo mesurando a passi tardi e lenti.
      —An adaptation of Petrarch, *Canzoniere*, xxxv.

is only three months old, is as lively and gay as a little Hercules. They make life dear to me and help me to forget my exile ; they increase my desire to work hard, and I have nothing at all to complain of except that the work there is to do hardly corresponds to my desires."

There are frequent references to Dante Gabriel in the letters of the next year, indicative of his father's delight in him. He is " as lively as a sparrow and as fresh as a flower ", he is " big and fat and playful and loving ", he is " an impertinent darling ". By the end of September he has become " a little giant and very beautiful, the prettiest of the family ", and in November it is his turn to be a " little Hercules ". But still the endless anxiety to make ends meet goes on, and this year things are worse than usual. The expenses of printing the *Comento* hung heavy on Rossetti's shoulders—whatever other cause to dislike his researches his wife may have had, this is likely to have been one of the most vexing— £100 remained to pay in March 1830. " If God thought me worthy of his providence, I should escape this year from a burden which so weighs on my mind that death itself could be little worse. What particularly alarms me is the very marked decline in my affairs this year. The season is already well advanced, and my lessons are fewer by a good third than last year ; whether the cause be these hard times which make gentlemen disinclined to incur the usual expenses ; or the fact that many families in which I used to teach have gone on to the Continent ; or that some of my pupils have been married ; or that others have been ill ; or that not a few others have stayed in the country ; or that several others have learnt as much as they wanted to learn ; one thing is certain and that is that I find myself with many vacant hours which in past years were occupied ; wretched and black hours which depress my spirits, and colour my prospects quite other than rose." It appears to have been a bad year for other teachers besides Rossetti, for Gaetano was hard pressed too, and was obliged to consider the sale of his library.

In December the quartet was completed by the arrival of Christina on the 5th. The event was announced to Miss Polidori (this probably means Charlotte) in the following letter :

" DEAREST SISTER-IN-LAW.,

You have now another niece, born at the due time, last Sunday night, at ten minutes past three. Her mother suffered little, and now lies nursing the dear pledge who, to judge by her appetite, could not be doing better. She is considered to be the very picture of Maria, but more beautiful. She is fairer, and looks, with that round face of hers, like a little moon risen at the full. All the rest of the family is well, and I thus fulfilling my duty in writing to you, sincerely sign myself

Your affectionate brother
GABRIELE ROSSETTI."

The subject of this letter subsequently pencilled on it the following comment :

"*How could my dear Father give such a report?*
Dearest Mamma had a fearful time with me. CGR."

V

On 4 May 1831 Frances is again at Holmer Green with all the four children. She had left her husband in considerable anxiety ; his lessons in April had been only eight in number, whereas two years before he had had as many as forty-five. He now writes to give her reassuring news. The lessons have gone up to seventeen ; Mr. Potter is going to give him £40 for a drama ; he hopes to have £80 for her when she returns. (The Rossettis had no bank account—they used to keep their little accumulations in a box at home.) What is more, the King's College chair is now well up on the horizon ; many persons have been interesting themselves in Rossetti's behalf. " The Principe di Cimitile, who recommended me to some member of the Council of the College, learned from him that the election of the Professors depends chiefly on the Bishop of London ; and I quickly procured two letters of introduction to the Bishop. Mr. Barclay who is his intimate friend, gave me one, and the other came from Sir Gore Ouseley, who has also handed me two others for the patrons of the College. I trust that Providence will second my efforts. Be in good spirits then, Frances mine, because that God who gives nourishment to the worms in the earth will not abandon us, with our four little children, innocent and in need."

On 8 May lessons have gone up to twenty-two. Rossetti has been to see the Bishop and found that he spoke Italian fairly well. The Bishop was non-committal, doubted whether there would be any professors of modern languages, had had strong recommendations of Panizzi, and was surprised to hear that he was already at University College—he had chosen an unfortunate prevarication. Rossetti bravely offered him the manuscript of his new work, the *Spirito Antipapale*, no doubt thinking it might not only attest his scholarship, but remove some of the odium attaching to his native creed in that very Anglican institution. On 21 May the Bishop has not yet read the manuscript, and Rossetti fails to obtain an interview with him after a long wait in the episcopal anterooms. Eventually his lordship succeeded in reading at least the first two chapters, and his goodwill evidently survived the ordeal, for on 7 June Rossetti received notice of his appointment, acknowledging it on the 9th. with assurances of his pleasure, gratitude, and zealous intentions. He was and remained vastly proud of his appointment. In a stanza of his *Autobiography* which William Michael omitted in the translation, he says :

> Not in vainglory do I here declare
> But thinking that posterity should know it,
> That first appointed to the Italian Chair
> In our King's College was the exile poet.
> " What truly diverse sovereigns," then I said,
> " One honours me, the other wished me dead."

The King of course had nothing at all to do with it, the Bishop a good deal. All the professors had to be Anglican, except the Orientalists and the teachers of modern languages, and that even they might find it useful to be Anglican too is clearly shown by the notes made by some member of the Council when Valerio Pistrucci was elected to succeed Gabriele in 1847. Having examined the claims of Gallenga and Beolchi, the writer of the notes goes on to consider Pistrucci's qualifications with favour, and concludes, " When it appears further that he is a Protestant married to an Englishwoman, that their children are baptized in our church, and that he himself is a member of it, I prefer him to Mariotti, alias Gallenga, a liberal refugee, who thinks it a point of honour to be, as well as duty to remain a Roman Catholic, and to Beolchi, who will never introduce a subject of religion."

It is to be remembered to Rossetti's honour, as his son points out, that though it would have been much to his advantage in the early years in London to have formally joined the Anglican communion, he considered it unworthy of an Italian and never took any steps in that direction ; although at the same time the confusion of his principles in religious matters allowed him to make the most ferocious attacks on the Papacy, and even on one occasion to declare that if Catholicism were the only religion on the earth he would, if he could, blot it out without hesitation. Professor Hearnshaw has called his appointment at King's an anomaly; having in mind his religion and even more his political views—an additional objection to Gallenga later was that he was " a bona fide liberal "; but then Rossetti was a Catholic who hated the Pope and a liberal who profoundly admired the English constitution, and no doubt he fulfilled his academic duties without much disturbance of the religious and political principles of his pupils.

As we have already said, Rossetti made little profit directly out of his new post. The major chairs carried a guarantee of £200 a year, plus a share of the fees. The other professors had a share of the fees alone, in most cases three-quarters, and were really only visiting masters. Naturally under such conditions Rossetti threw himself with enthusiasm into the task of attracting pupils. His inaugural address, delivered on 1 November and afterwards published, was a discourse on the text *Omne tulit punctum qui miscuit utile dulci*. The study of Italian is useful because of its close connection with Latin, because of the indebtedness to its literature of many English poets; delightful for many reasons and particularly because Italian song cannot be appreciated without a knowledge of the language. With so much then of utility and pleasure to make it attractive, he does not doubt that many will wish to follow in the steps of the great English poets. " O you their descendants, come and study this beautiful language if you wish to open for yourselves an easy approach to Latin, French and Spanish; if you wish to commune with all the authors who have made it rich and precious; if by its means you wish to command the enchanting harmonies which are wedded to it; if by its means you wish to prepare yourselves for a profitable visit to the land where it is spoken; and to open a hundred paths into oriental regions where it is understood."

The response to this appeal was discouraging. By 16 November only two of the descendants of the great English poets had presented themselves. In May 1832 there were four. In October 1836 there were three. In October 1840 for the first time there was no class at all. William Michael says there were fewer students from about 1840 when German began to supersede Italian in public favour, but apparently they could not have been much fewer than they were. The most Rossetti ever made out of the institution

was about £10 a year, but he might have had the consolation of
knowing that the sorcerer at University College did no better
than he. Moreover he does not appear to have taken advantage
of whatever opportunities of intercourse with other members of
the staff the post may have offered ; for he had a dislike for social
functions with which it is easy to sympathise. He writes to his
wife in May 1832, " I spent Saturday evening at that tedious
professors' dinner, for which I had to pay eight shillings. This
shall be the last time. I don't want to spend money on being
bored." But the post was a matter of much pride to him ; his
status must have brought him private students, and he liked to call
himself *Professore nel Collegio del Re* on the title pages of his
books.

VI

We return to his family and more private concerns, which we
left in the middle of May 1831 to follow his hot pursuit of the
chair. His wife was in the country with the four children, while
her husband interviewed bishops and stayed talking about Dante
from nine at night to one in the morning with Lyell who was then
in London. It all caused him to neglect his correspondence with
her, a fault not to be passed over without a protest. " Dearest
Francesca," he writes, " I see from your letter which begins and
ends *ex abrupto*, without my name and without ceremony, without
telling me of our children, without a word about your mother, I
see clearly enough that you are offended and angry with me, like a
sheep running amok. . . . God save us ! To punish you for
this anger I have done so little to deserve, I won't tell you the
reason why I have not written before. There is no greater punishment for a woman than to leave her curiosity unsatisfied." It
appears later in the letter that his long discussions with Lyell are
the chief cause, and a little nemesis has already attended those
midnight sittings, for " the other evening on my way there I tripped
over a stone, fell on my face, and broke my nose. . . . When
you come back you will find it in an amazing condition."

When we next meet with a batch of those letters to Francesca
which are almost our sole source of information about the children
at this time, the babies have gone and little boys and girls have
appeared in their place. In the spring of 1832 " our skittish
little Christina with those rosy cheeks and sparkling eyes, so like
her grandmother's, [is] walking all alone about the garden, like a

little butterfly among the flowers." She is a year and five months old but not yet weaned ; Rossetti is anxious about it, thinks the long-continued breast-feeding does her more harm than good. Maria and Gabriel are rapidly developing their childish minds and childish appetites. Mrs. Rossetti collects and sends on their little sayings ; Gabriele sends them picture books, and a box of figs. They have their childish indispositions, sometimes from overeating. " What you say about William grieves me ; poor child ! I am sure that if it had happened here, you wouldn't have failed to blame me for it, so as to have the satisfaction of reproving me for every mouthful I give them of what you call trash." Sometimes their health gives their father grave cause for alarm. " Every word that you wrote pierced like a dagger into my heart. My sweetest Gabriele, then, is so ill ! My baby Christina suffers with her teeth and has wounded her forehead ! Oh my poor children ! . . . And William, you tell me nothing about him. You said in your last letter that he had a return of those fevers from which he suffered here : and now, how is that going on ?—how is he ? . . . Tell me all about them ; hide nothing from me, absolutely nothing. . . . Who knows but what the figs I sent may have done them harm ! But this constant change of weather has more likely been the cause, first hot, then cold, now hot again. This belief is strengthened by your telling me that Maria and Christina have sore throats. . . . I should be the most frantic and most inconsolable man in the world if I were to lose a son, that dearest little Gabriel, the very core of my heart, and lose him thus, far from my sight. My eyes are already full of tears whilst writing these words, and unless I dry them I cannot continue writing, as I do not see the paper. But take heart, my wife, it may turn out to be nothing serious ". Here there is still something of Parson Adams left. Gabriele may often thus be seen working himself up by the sheer force of writing and imagination. When his wife writes to tell him all is well, the letter comes to him " like dew to a dying flower." So full of sad thoughts had he become, that at first sight he had taken the red seal on her letter for a black one and feared to open it. When he did he shed tears of happiness. " God be a thousand times thanked for removing my anguish and giving me back my dear Gabriel whom I seemed to love immensely more than any of my other children. . . . Tell my darling Gabriel that he shall certainly have the very nicest wood lamb and also a pretty little picture book. And assure

William that if he is a good boy there will be a book for him too. I suppose those sheep and shepherds that you bought the day you left will have already gone their way to the slaughter house. Children will be children. Maria has been given by her grandfather two beautiful and expensive books, bought specially for her. . . . She will be able to read bits of them to her little brothers and in instructing others will instruct herself." He himself has been unable to sleep for anxiety, and besides has been suffering agonies from gout. He asks for news about each one of the children; "tell me particularly if Christina's tumor which had to be lanced has left any mark. Tell me if she still manages to walk alone, if she has grown as rosy as I have sometimes seen her, and if she has those bright, bright eyes which so remind me of her grandmother's. May she resemble her in her severe virtue, but with better health and fortune."

The infantile expressions which Mrs. Rossetti was reporting to her husband were English, but while they were in the country Gabriele was making an attempt to restore them all to Italian citizenship. He had sent a petition to the King of Naples and was full of hope that he might soon be invited to return. His friend Leopoldo Curci bestirred himself in the matter, and actually had an audience with the King about it. But all was in vain. This was not the last time that such hopes were entertained by Rossetti, and one would like to know what his wife thought about them; whether she quietly waited for the disillusionment she thought certain; whether she was prepared to go with her husband and family wherever fate led them; whether to her as well as to him it might have been gratifying if he could have received public honour and perhaps lucrative office in his own country. It is not possible even to guess, except vaguely from a letter in which Rossetti sounds a little apologetic on the subject. "Yesterday evening I met Beolchi, who told me that the King of Sardinia is recalling some of the exiles, so that it will be easy for him to return to his country. . . . If I could find means of living honestly by my own application, I shouldn't concern myself about leaving England. If I have desired and still desire to return to Naples, it is solely with regard to making a living. Meanwhile you see that it is getting more probable that the King of Naples will recall me, and it seems as though the Kings have agreed among themselves to give up for a time the barbarities they have practised hitherto. Whether by some improvement in my resources here, or whether by my being recalled by the King to some office, we may hope that our affairs will soon take a better turn."

At some point in those early years the Rossettis could have disposed of a small part of their responsibilities. Mr. Tallent, the local doctor at Holmer Green would have liked to adopt William Michael, who might then have become a medical man as he always wanted to be, after the decline of his earliest aspiration to be a sailor—but at the cost of missing how much ! This proposal is not likely to have exercised his parents' minds for very long.

At the end of 1832, then, Rossetti was Professor at King's, had published the *Comento* on Dante's *Inferno*, and the *Spirito Antipapale*, was still cheerfully struggling with the daily round of private pupils and " keepers of establishments ", as the proprietresses of young ladies' schools called themselves, his affairs fluctuating, and his desires occasionally turning back to the scenes of his young manhood. The children were passing from Bloomsbury to Holmer Green, from illness to illness, growing nevertheless, talking and beginning to read. Maria was five, Dante Gabriel four, William three, Christina two. The distinctive marks of their characters were beginning to become apparent, and at this point we will leave them to consider their father's researches and the environment of family friends and visitors. For relying as we have done for information on the letters of Rossetti to his wife, we have seen the children almost entirely at Holmer Green ; whereas for the greater part of the time they were in London going for walks in Regent's Park, playing together in 38 Charlotte Street, and being moulded by the circumstances of their home.

CHAPTER FOUR

FELLOW EXILES

I

THE character and interests of Gabriele, the unassuming and home-loving nature of his wife, their Italian origin and the general quietness and sobriety of their life, made the inhabitants of 38 Charlotte Street very much a household apart. The children grew up in a seclusion from ordinary English life which only drew the boys more reassuringly back into itself when they began to go to school. That their early environment was almost entirely Italian is a fact that has been repeated by every writer on the Rossettis since Hall Caine's *Recollections*; and there is no wonder that all of them, except Dante Gabriel, felt themselves to be to some degree foreigners to the end of their days. And if Dante Gabriel often talked and felt very much like an Englishman and expressed very English prejudices, it must be remembered that the Polidori relations had always brought something of English habits of thought into the family life, that Dante Gabriel launched out into the world earlier than the others, that he was always the most recalcitrant of the children to family influences, and finally that when all is said there remained much more of the Italian in him than of the Englishman.

Some English friends they had of course even in the early days. The aunts already referred to, like Mrs. Rossetti herself, seem to have been more English than Italian; and the awe-inspiring great-aunt Harriet Pearce who occasionally descended upon them had no Italian blood at all. Apart from these, the only English family with which the Rossettis had any close relations was that of Cipriani Potter, whose children were much of an age with theirs. Lyell and Keightley, of whom we shall hear more in the next chapter, were close friends, but not frequent visitors. There was somewhat distant and occasional friendly intercourse with two of the families in which Rossetti taught, those of Sir Isaac Goldsmid and Swynfen Jervis. But all this amounted to very little.

However, if the Rossettis went forth little into the world around them, the world came to them in Charlotte Street in sensational and colourful forms. Gabriele's fellow-countrymen, many of them political exiles and most of them picturesque, were accustomed to visit him daily hardly ever less than three in an evening. William Michael has given an excellent summary account of them in the *Memoir* of his brother ; and it is not intended here to attempt any full enumeration of them or detailed description of their careers. We shall content ourselves with seeing the main figures, as much as possible through their own eyes or those of their host.

There were hundreds of Italians in London in Rossetti's time, educated and illiterate, distinguished and commonplace, noble-minded and base. The cultured were for the most part engaged in teaching young ladies Italian ; the others were organ-grinders, plaster-cast sellers, models, waiters, or merely mendicants—the ice-cream seller had not yet made his appearance. All classes suffered alike from physical indigence, the more sensitive also endured a great deal of mental distress. The story of Foscolo's sufferings and miserable death is well known ; Panizzi would have had to endure penury a good deal longer than he did had his char-acter not been better equipped than Foscolo's for dealing with the world around him. Mazzini himself was forced to make a living by selling oil and sausages before he began to command the atten-tion of Englishmen. For though the exiles occasionally figured as heroes at the time of their arrival, and though here and there sympathetic philanthropists continued to support them, the general opinion was that they were all rather foolish to have brought such disasters upon themselves, and as conspirators and revolutionists they were regarded with suspicion. Queen Victoria herself, " brightest of stars, angelic Victoria ", as Rossetti once called her, thought that the Austrians had as good a right to Lombardy as we had to the colonies ; Prince Albert was strongly Austrophile, and so consequently were both court and government.

As for the mute and inglorious among the exiles, their condition was truly pitiable. Strangers in a strange land, they often had not even the slightest acquaintance with the English language, and, many of them no more than boys, they were hired like slaves for a few pence a day, following their wretched street trades for the profit of others. Mazzini was much stirred by the sight of them, and in 1844 started an association for the protection of destitute boys, from which grew later a union of Italian working men. Three years earlier he had established the school for Italian working men of which Pistrucci was secretary. It had 109 scholars within a fortnight. " These poor devils work," says Mazzini, " or go about with their organs all day, and when they are tired, if they have a penny to spare, wander into a public house and drink till they fall asleep." He insists on their being taught more than reading and writing —for instance geography and the history of Italy. On the first anniversary of the school, 10 November 1842, Professor Rossetti made a speech to a crowded hall. The scene was touching. Prizes were received by little boys of ten or twelve as well as by old men just learning to read, who were highly excited at having won them. " Most of them were dressed in their best, but others, organ-grinders, etc., came in the same clothes as they wear when they go about the streets. . . . The grand moment was when supper was brought in. Just imagine the delight of perhaps a hundred and fifty of these lads at seeing before them *maccheroni asciutti* garnished with butter and Parmesan cheese."

Rossetti's intimate friends were of course educated men, but he did not by any means hold himself aloof from the others. Indeed the plebeian origin which left very obvious traces on his general bearing and outlook, made it easy for him to associate with the most humble on friendly terms. He would sometimes stop organ men or others in the street to ask them what part of the country they came from ; many came to seek him at his house and received a genial welcome there, particularly if they gave a masonic knock at the door or made a masonic sign on entering. The Neapolitans called him Don Gabriele, the title having continued in Naples from the Spanish occupation. Some of them came merely to beg for help, which he gave as far as his small means allowed ; so, in May 1831 he tells his wife that he has bought her a pair of carpet slippers from a poor Italian who said he hadn't a penny to buy food. Sometimes they wrote to him for assistance, as in the case of a certain Prati who sent an unstamped letter from Switzerland in 1848 to say that he was trying to get money to return to England. " What do you think about it ? " Rossetti asks his wife. " All the bloodsuckers round me ! I have sent the enclosed letter to his wife, but I don't know whether I shall reply to him. What shall I say ? " Rossetti used to divide his less desirable visitors into two classes, the *cercatori* and the *seccatori*, the begging and the boring, and there were very many of both.

Many others however came " for to admire ", and their talk was sweet music in his ears ; these, one imagines, were never *seccatori* ; they poured balm into the grievous wounds inflicted by unkind reviewers and over-candid friends ; they helped Rossetti to feel a great hero and made his patriotism soar to the most exalted heights. On 30 August 1836 he writes to his wife, " Among others three young Italians have been to visit me, as if I were a holy relic ; a Roman, a Tuscan, and a Neapolitan. If you had only seen what reverence and what worship they paid me ! " And only a week later came the Marchesa Marchegiana, paying three calls in two days. " She talked for ten. She expressed great concern for your illness and exclaimed several times, ' Oh, if I had seen her, I would have made her know what a husband she possesses ! ' To hear her, I am the idol of Italy. She told me that . . . were I to return . . . youthful admirers would come about me in shoals, and would unharness the horses from my carriage to drag me in triumph. Matter for laughter. Sangiovanni, who was present at all this (which I can but suppose exaggerated) had to wipe his eyes from time to time—the loving friend. In short, dear Frances, without your having observed it nor yet myself, you have as husband the greatest man of Italy, indeed the idol of Italy ! Who would ever have fancied it ? " Let us beware of supposing this to be all a matter of flattery and vanity. Carducci who had a high opinion of Rossetti's verse, relates that his poems, either printed or in manuscript, used to run like a flame through towns and villages from one end of Italy to the other, the more ardently sought for as they were the more ferociously suppressed by the enemies of liberty. His songs were still being sung in 1848 ; and Mazzini himself was glad to enlist the aid of his pen. There is no wonder then that young men and ladies of high repute should come to worship at his shrine.

II

Most of these visitors had had exciting adventures, some of them were odd to the point of absurdity, others desperate to the point of suicide. There was a certain Galli for instance who came one evening and in a long and mysterious speech attempted to prove himself to be Christ.[1] There was Galanti whom Rossetti first

---

[1] " The day you left ", Rossetti writes to his wife, " . . . came that poor madman Fiorenzo Galli, who thinks himself to be Jesus Christ, and who made that delusion the subject of a speech so mysterious, earnest, and intimately persuasive as to leave the most vivid impression on our minds." (25 August 1839.)

describes as " this bird of ill-omen, Giacinto Galanti, who does nothing but foretell disasters, and who seems to me to be a mere wind-bag, singing his own name all the time like that tedious bird the cuckoo."

Galanti's end was sudden and dramatic, and we may leave Rossetti himself to describe it as he did over and over again to various correspondents. " One evening he called to read me a writing of his entitled *The Three Years*, 1848 (it was just in June that year), 1849, and 1850. The first of these three years he defined as a Year of Roses and Thorns (and you will take note that the thorns had not yet begun) ; the second, Year all Thorns ; and the third, Year of Death. And such, haplessly, they all turned out. . . . On hearing that writing I was staggered, and yet, not being able then to give credence to it, I smiled incredulously, and shaking my head, I called Galanti a bird of ill omen and a visionary. He rose incensed, and exclaimed : ' You will see whether I speak the truth, and you will confess it ; but not to me, for I will not await the direful time that is coming upon us.' Saying this, he departed, returned to his house, not far from mine, and cut his throat. This terrible event produced the deepest impression on me ; and soon afterwards began our disasters. The days of Novara, Verona, and Mantua, ensued. . . ." Like many other deep impressions, this one had ended by submitting to the mind's unconscious artistry. Galanti did cut his throat, but not in horror of the future he had foreseen. He may have read Rossetti his forecast in 1848, but he did not finally despair until after Novara itself, when Rossetti wrote to Ricciardi, 2 April 1849, " Perhaps you do not know that poor Galanti on hearing the news cut his throat and is now buried. If it were not for love of my family I should already have done the same." The children were all about twenty at this time—such an event must have made the woes of Italy come very near to them.

Another strange figure was a certain Anichini, a friend of Janer, who himself was an intimate friend of the Rossettis. " Janer came yesterday ", writes Gabriele to his wife, 9 February 1836, " and gave me a letter to read from his dear Anichini which wasn't fit to be sent to the hangman. That example of urbanity and friend-liness began thus, ' Janer, take good care never again to cross the threshold of my house, if you don't want to be treated as you deserve ' . . . and went on in this tone, or rather worse in every line. And what is the reason for so many insults ? Because Janer hasn't been to see him for some weeks, wishing to avoid being rudely insulted by those well-bred children of our very cultured Anichini, who not only call him Ass and Beast and other sweet names, but tear his clothes off, play football with his hat, put out the light so that he cannot read, give him great whacks on the back, or even go for his nose with a red-hot poker, to see if they can make a scar or poke an eye out. Now after all that I've told you, will you be able to credit what I have to add ? This evening Anichini came here looking for Janer, and delivered a panegyric on him such as a Catholic priest would hardly dare to make over a saint of the Roman Church. Fine intellect, great heart, learned, virtuous, generous, and goodness knows what." There is a sequel to this a month later, which shows that Anichini reaped the due reward of neglecting family discipline. He is in a terrible state. He wife has sold everything in the house, and run away again, taking their daughter with her. He rushed to France after them but fell out of the diligence and broke his arm. Now he is almost delirious with fear that his wife may sell his daughter as a prostitute, as she threatened to do when money ran out. Her deplorable conduct has been revealed by bundles of letters he has found in a trunk from four different lovers. Janer hearing all this forgot his anger and went to see Anichini, who by that time had received an insulting letter from his daughter saying that he brought it all on himself, including the broken arm, and that he was the worst husband in the world and unworthy of such a good wife.

William Michael and others have made it easy to visualise the family hearth of 38 Charlotte Street on any evening of the years 1847–49. We can imagine the strange visitors arriving one by one in the little parlour, their elaborate deference to Mrs. Rossetti and her daughters, their excited expansiveness to Rossetti himself. He, who had been tired at the end of his day's teaching, is revived and reanimated by their arrival. They are given little to eat or drink ; a cup of tea or coffee and a slice of bread and butter suffices for their small needs, for they have come not to eat but to talk. They hold forth endlessly about Pio Nono and the Austrians, they listen to Gabriele's declamation of his poems with sonorous applause ; they exchange anecdotes and jests and reminiscences of their adventures and their home country.

Holman Hunt has a vivid description of his first visit to Charlotte Street. " The father arose to receive me from a group of foreigners around the fire, all escaped revolutionaries from the Continent, and addressed me in English in a few words of welcome as Mr. Madox Brown, a slip on which his eldest daughter rated him pleasantly. He was so engrossed in a warm conversation that some minutes afterwards he again made the same mistake. The conversation was in Italian, but occasionally merged into French, with the obvious purpose of taking into the heat of the conference refugees unfamiliar with the former language. The tragic passions of the group around the fire did not in the slightest degree involve either the mother, the daughters or the sons. . . . The hearth guests took it in turn to discourse and no one had delivered many phrases ere the excitement of speaking made him rise from his chair, advance to the centre of the group, and there gesticulate as I had never seen people do except upon the stage. . . . Each orator evidently found difficulty in expressing his full anger, but when passion had done its measure in word and gesture, so that I as a stranger felt pained at not being able to join in practical sympathy, the declaimer went back to his chair, and while another was taking up the words of mourning and appeal to the too tardy heavens, the predecessor kept up the refrain of sighs and groans. When it was impossible for me to ignore the distress of the alien company, Gabriel and William shrugged their shoulders, the latter with a languid sigh of commiseration, saying it was generally so. As the dinner was being put on the table, some of the strangers persisted despite invitation in going ; some still stayed round the fire declaring solemnly that they had dined. . . . We had an excellent dinner. Our circle conversed in English ; the father talked with his friends from the hearth, and at the end of each course he got up and joined them, until he was once more called to the head of the table by the appearance of a new dish. At the conclusion of the meal the brothers and I saw the remainder of the company established at dominoes and chess before the arrival of the other members for the P.R.B. meeting upstairs."

Rossetti was very good-tempered as a general rule and was on good terms with most of the members of this extraordinary circle. Indeed, the only one of the Italians who visited his house with whom he appears to have seriously quarrelled was Luigi Angeloni, a well-known exile and closely associated with Santarosa, the Cianis, and the Committee of Help that had been set up in 1823. There is a group of letters about him in 1836 which give an excellent illustration of Rossetti's generosity, no less than of his fury when his literary vanity was wounded.

In May we see Rossetti amicably procuring an opera ticket for Angeloni from Lablache. In June he is searching on his behalf for a passage in Cicero. In August a cloud is seen " no bigger than a man's hand " when Janer informs Rossetti that Angeloni has written resentfully of him in the last pages of a book which is just going to press. Rossetti cannot guess what offence he may have given to deserve this. He will not ask that the hostile passage be deleted ; it will indeed make no difference to the esteem and veneration in which he holds Angeloni's knowledge, character, and years. " To anybody who tells me what you have written I shall reply that . . . you have not ceased to be in my eyes . . . the model of true gentlemen and true patriots, a great Italian in whom time and fortune can make no change." What is more, on the day the book is published, Rossetti will publish also the *canzonetta* he has written for Angeloni so that everybody may know what he thinks of him. " You may succeed in abusing me but you will never be able to alter my good opinion or my affection towards you ; and you will never succeed in making me other than

> Your true and unchangeable friend,
>
> GABRIELE ROSSETTI."

The *canzonetta* itself praises Angeloni's songs about English ladies, in its last verses declaring they are Venus Pallas and Juno all in one, and Angeloni a new Paris awarding the apple to the whole sex.

Carducci presents this letter as an example of Rossetti's nobility of mind ; it is certainly sufficient to show his nobility of impulse. But all this forgiveness and loving-kindness was quite unable to stand the shock of discovering what Angeloni had actually written. Rossetti's next letter on the subject, addressed to his wife, reads as follows : " Pistrucci has been to the printer's to find out what that curious old man has vomited forth about me, and tells me that it all comes down to making me look ridiculous—about the way I blow my nose, the way I sit in my easy chair ; he says I am conceited and think I know everything, swollen with vanity and going up in the air like a balloon ; he calls me a fool and simpleton for believing in that heap of nonsense (as he considers it) called the Bible ; and says that he was sorry for me when he saw my horror at what he had written about it, and sorrier still when he heard that I wanted to dissuade him from printing such things.

Pistrucci assured me that he had read all his gibes attentively and that they all boil down to that. And indeed what could he find to say against Gabriele Rossetti ? I dare assert, Francesca mine, that you have a husband not unworthy of you, one about whom nothing truly dishonourable could be written by anybody, unless he were willing to descend to calumny. My innocent and stainless life gives no opening to the malevolent, and this man's opinion of me is merely ludicrous. The impotent efforts of a malevolent mind. Oh, I forgot to add that he decides I am a sonorous but empty poet, and says that I have taken in the shallow world with my verses while those who love substantial things think nothing of me at all. . . . Well, be it so. A great poet he is himself in any case. I confess that that arrogant old man's white hair and blindness and poverty served for merit with me ; for as far as knowledge is concerned, I have always regarded him as a . . . I will content myself with saying a miserable pedant. Thank heaven he has taken himself away of his own accord ; I think it a very good riddance."

Later on we find Rossetti writing to Angeloni himself again, but in more strident tones. " Since you wish to offer to the ardent Italian Youth whom you exhort to agree in the great cause of their country, the edifying spectacle of two Italian exiles, and both suffering for the same most holy cause, tugging at each other's hair like oyster wives and tearing each other's eyes out like mad crows. . . . I shall be reduced to the necessity of taking up the gauntlet and saying ' Let him have war who does not wish for peace '. . . . Let me tell you at once that I have no fear of you ; I wanted to be your friend, but I am not frightened at finding you my enemy. . . ." He goes on to point out that Angeloni has ill-treated him in the very book that Gabriele had helped him to publish—he had collected seventeen pounds and two of them came from his own pocket. He finds it hard to think of Angeloni as an enemy. " There is always before my eyes the spectacle of an exile, a wanderer expelled from Italy, hounded out of France, grievously burdened with years, almost friendless and deprived of the sweet gift of sight." But he no longer professes any admiration for his talents, " No, Angeloni, you are not so great in the world's eyes as you like to imagine, nor am I so mean an object as you would like to make people think." But still he will not write against him in spite of all. This letter bears no signature and no address ; it may never have been sent. It is unkind and one hopes it was not.

But it seems unlikely that the quarrel was ever made up. Rossetti tells Lyell with some glee in January 1838 that Sarti has written a poetical satire against Angeloni and " other Italian impostors who dishonour their country." Poor Angeloni eventually died in a workhouse in February 1842.

III

The inner circle of constant and intimate visitors was small in number. There was always of course Polidori, the most friendly of fathers-in-law, there was the cultured Tuscan Janer, able and often malicious, who has already been mentioned. More attractive is the faithful Sangiovanni who shed tears of joy when the Marchesa Marchegiani sang Rossetti's praises. References to him are plentiful in the Rossetti correspondence. He was an uneducated man, and was supposed to have knifed somebody in his early days; before coming to England he led a band which set out to suppress brigands in the Kingdom of Naples, and in appearance he seems to have looked something of a brigand himself.

He supported himself in London by modelling in clay. The children remembered him well; according to William he had more to do with their early family life than any of the others, and Dante Gabriel, reading Benvenuto Cellini's *Autobiography* in 1853, was irresistibly reminded of him at every page, " it is absolutely like hearing Sangiovanni speak." The family seems to have regarded him with affectionate pity—he is usually referred to as " poor Sangiovanni ". When Rossetti first knew him he was, so far as anybody then knew, unmarried. Going over to America in 1853 at the invitation of Achille Murat, he there met a young woman whom he brought back as his wife, and whom he proceeded to keep, according to the southern Italian fashion, closely immured in their dingy dwelling-place. This no doubt gave her wings, and when she suddenly found that he had a wife still living in Italy, she promptly vanished to Utah. Sangiovanni was much upset, and soon afterwards went to live in Brighton whence he wrote at times to Rossetti; and in 1849 was able to report having heard high praises of his painter son there. He died at Brighton in 1853, some said blaspheming God, though this Pistrucci as an eye-witness strenuously denied. " I knew that Sangiovanni ", writes Gabriele to a friend in Rome, " he was a good man but unbelieving to an amazing degree." Pistrucci sends Rossetti a more formal epitaph :

Qui solo dopo aver fatto la guerra,
Qui l'italiano Sangiovanni giace.
Contro la tirannia trovò la pace.
[Here alone, his warfare over,
Lies the Italian Sangiovanni.
In spite of tyranny he found peace.]

Pistrucci himself was hardly less familiar to the family than Sangiovanni, and more of his letters have been preserved. He was a man of considerable ability and an active figure among exile circles, a close friend of Mazzini whom he served as lieutenant in that great patriot's schemes for the benefit of the Italians in London as faithfully as his son Scipio served him in continental conspiracies. He was also well known as an improviser, and had a certain gift for portrait painting, to which we owe several likenesses of the children at early ages. No doubt his poverty is also responsible for this, as Rossetti had various portraits done to help his friend out of difficulties. About the same age as Rossetti and of a deeply religious nature, Pistrucci was interested with an even greater ardour than his in Italian politics and religion ; his hatred for the Church of Rome was positively ferocious. Partly perhaps because he was less fortunate in his circumstances than Rossetti, his temperament was more sombre ; all his letters bear witness to that gloom which according to Mrs. Carlyle earned him the nickname of " Heraclitus the weeping philosopher ". When visiting Rossetti at Charlotte Street, he was no doubt one of the more eloquent and heartrending of the fireside conversationalists.

Another friend was Count Carlo Pepoli, who eventually returned to Italy and became a senator of the united country. He lived in England for many years, and was one of Panizzi's successors in the Italian chair at University College. In 1839 he married an Englishwoman—a highly unsatisfactory match according to Rossetti whom Pepoli asked to be a witness at his wedding. " At the moment when he takes his bride home he will enter into possession of six thousand pounds, apart from what he will get later on, that is twelve thousand more. I fear that he is sacrificing himself, for she appears to be old, and when I said I hoped to see him soon surrounded with Pepoletti, he replied with a melancholy smile that that was impossible." A few days later Rossetti describes the ceremony. " On Monday morning at about eight, Count Pepoli came for me in a carriage to take me to be best man and witness at his wedding. I should like to say his happy and auspicious wedding, but that I dare not say after having seen his wife. She has certainly passed forty and I should think by a good deal. She came to the nuptial altar from a bed of no slight sickness, and at the moment of pronouncing the solemn *yes* she trembled like an aspen. She is as lean and pale as a corpse ; I very much hope that after a space of holy matrimony she will make a complete recovery ; and perhaps when she has put on a little flesh she will not look quite so old. . . . When you come back I will give you more details about the marriage service ; I will tell you about the gigantic brother who accompanied the bride to the altar, and of the little sisters who were her bridesmaids. My fellow witness was Dr. Belluomini : but a doctor called to Hymen's altar doesn't seem to me to be a good omen."

IV

All the men described up to this point were permanently or temporarily cut off from any active part in the service of their country, although their interest in it suffered no diminution. But there were others who came and went between Italy and England, such as like Count Ricciardi, an ardent republican and active agent in continental organisations. Becoming known to Rossetti in 1833, he assisted in smuggling our poet's publications into the Continent ; he was moreover the recipient of a lengthy correspondence valuable for the study of Rossetti's political feelings ; and eventually wrote an obituary notice of his friend. Ricciardi was introduced to Rossetti by the latter's old acquaintance General Pepe, who was in England when Rossetti arrived, and who occasionally revisited this country in the intervals of his indefatigable exertions on behalf of the Italian cause. " Pepe is coming ", exclaims the poet in September 1849, " venerable old man, admirable patriot ! I shall embrace him with a cry of joy." It was Pepe who in 1833 had wished him health, wealth, and no more children. And it was Pepe who in April 1848, when things were going hopefully, had told a meeting of the Neapolitan ministers at the time that gratitude and national honour demanded the bestowal on Rossetti of some post of dignity. " All agreed that the execution of my request was a matter of justice, so leave London and come back to your country where you will be received with rejoicing by all." But the hopes of 1848 were short-lived ; and after all his heroic exertions had proved to be in vain, Pepe took to writing his *Memoirs*, of which he sent a copy to Rossetti in June 1850. He died in 1855.

With Mazzini, the greatest of Italians then living in England,
Rossetti was never intimate. Indeed he disagreed with Mazzini's
aims and entertained some jealousy of his influence among the
London Italians. The great Genoese for his part was ready to
use any man's talent in the cause which never left his mind, and
he knew the value of Gabriele's gift of popular song. He sometimes put his network of correspondents at Rossetti's service to
help in the dissemination of the poet's writings in Italy, and as
late as 1851 he was sending messages to him through Pistrucci
asking for even stronger things. He was anxious to secure
Rossetti's co-operation in the Italian school, that " nest of young
conspirators " as Carlyle called it, and implored him to join Young
Italy and to cease recommending constitutional monarchy. And
in 1867, long after the poet's death, he spoke with great regard
for him to Swinburne. His attitude to Rossetti seems quite consistent ; he recognised his gifts and valued his help ; on the other
hand he was no doubt well aware of his weaknesses, and his flat
disagreement on the subject of Dante was once at least expressed
in public. Rossetti, for his part, knew the greatness of Mazzini
and saw the importance of his work for Italy, so that he could on
one occasion urge Ricciardi to make up his differences with Mazzini
for the sake of the cause to which they were both devoted. But
on many occasions he says very hard things of the great conspirator.
It was partly a matter of political disagreement. Rossetti did not
like Mazzini's untiring activity in the raising of insurrections ; he
refused to join Young Italy ; he disapproved of the republican
ideal and thought Mazzini's activities in 1848 and 1849 were partly
to blame for the country's disasters. " It is the fate of Italy ", he
says, writing of Mazzini in 1851, " that those of her sons who love
her most should do her most harm." This is the point of view
expressed in the *Autobiography*,[1] where, speaking of the good and
the bad Italians who came to live in England, he says:

> To you, Mazzini, first I turn my gaze
> Who for your land would give a hundred lives ;
> For her you faced swift death in perilous ways ;
> In you the former ardour still survives.
> But to what end ? Your country in distress
> Not more would have you undertake but less.

---

[1] Not, however, in W. M. R.'s translation, where the passage given
above is not represented, while a long interpolation explains how it
came about that Mazzini was not mentioned. I have been unable to
explain the discrepancy.

Sometimes, however, in his excited way, probably only half believing what he says, he has graver complaints than this to make. " Almost all those who cry ' Italian Independence ', beginning with Mazzini, are no other than abominable self-seekers who throw themselves into the troubled waters and disturb them the more so as to fish the better." He and his like " cry that they do not want a king because they hope to be one themselves." Rossetti was particularly embittered about all this in the winter of 1850–51, because various members of his fireside salon had attached themselves to Mazzini and no longer came to see him. " Saliceti has never been to see me, and I know that he is often with Mazzini, who is still here although he had set a rumour about that he had gone to America, perhaps to avoid the sight of so many wretched refugees who complain on all sides, or to avoid having to receive some of those who, having followed him in his mad enterprises, lost everything, and are now countryless and many of them without shelter and food. He has made a convenient habit of refusing to see them, and of not replying to their letters. That is what is being said, and very often." And it is not only Saliceti, he never sees Petrucelli, De Vincentiis, or Lazotti now ; Mazzini has conjured them away. " But he who has lost country, sight, and health, and well-nigh life itself—what do other losses matter to him ? "

V

It is as unprofitable to spend much time in examining Rossetti's political views as it is in considering his religious beliefs. In both cases we are concerned with a few elementary moral notions, a great deal of easily expressed emotion, and an almost complete absence of rational and consistent theory. He could raise any of his feelings to the nth degree by giving free play to thought and fancy, as is so often to be seen in his letters. An impression of insincerity often results, but it would be quite unfair to dwell on this ; one may be amused at an excessive display of feeling without questioning the genuineness of the original impulse. Besides, what he demanded for Italy was at bottom simple and sensible : a constitutional monarchy, the unification of the country under an Italian king, the abolition of the secular power of Rome, and fraternity with the other nations of the world. Within twenty years of his death, events were to justify him, as William Michael pointed out in a sonnet more remarkable for filial piety than poetic skill :

Is this thing known to thee ?
Known or unknown, the fruitless enterprise
Beaconed thy life, and last the fruit appears.

His patriotism certainly admits no doubt. He loved Italy and particularly the Kingdom of Naples. But he had been exiled almost accidentally, and that his defiance was not in its nature unbending and intransigent like that of a Mazzini or a Settembrini is evident enough from the fact that he would willingly have returned to Naples under the Bourbon if Ferdinand had invited him. His was not a character that could wait and watch and plan to serve its country's freedom, although nothing pleased him better than to think of himself as one of the great heroes of the cause, suffering with glorious fortitude the penalties of his heroism. And yet there is no need to disbelieve him when he says, " I am passing my days in disquiet and my nights in anguish, thinking of Italy." The Psalm called *Love of Country* in the *Psaltery* gives a clear illustration of the truth and its exaggeration.

O holy love
Of native land oppressed,
Delight and torment
Of the noble breast ;
Our spirits feed on thee,
Yet art thou still,
To me the source and root
Of every ill.

Thou art my fault,
At least in other's eyes,
Whence I must lose
The very land I prize.
But vainly wrathful storms
On me are spent ;
Of fault so fair
I know not to repent.

Turning my gaze
To bid a last adieu,
Sweet native nest
My heart was riven in two.
And now when memory brings
Hid things to mind,
The old unchanging grief
At heart I find.

Of course his ills were not so great as all this. " Lives there the man with sadder fate than mine ? " he asks in the *Veggente*. There were and there are many. But still he never felt at home in England. " You ", he says, addressing his children, " are in your own country but I am in exile." The sun and warmth and loveliness of southern Italy remained in his mind distilling a nostalgia which only grew the stronger as the recollection of them became more remote. It was a simple and very natural state of mind.

The democratic instinct was strong in him. He ardently believed in the right of the individual to think and say what he liked. And yet, as in the conduct of his every-day life in London, he was cautious. If kings could be persuaded to grant constitutions and allow honest men to do what they chose, then there was no sense in doing away with kings altogether. England seemed to him an almost perfect example of the *via media*. He could say, " I am a republican, because I am a Christian and God made us free and equal ", but it was only a sentiment the logical consequences of which he did not approve. He sometimes speaks with horror of the French Revolution ; and only on exceptional occasions supports the republican enthusiasms of his Italian friends. When Frere suspected him of having dealings with Young Italy he was very disturbed, declared that he desired liberty not licence, the republic was a dream of maniacs. Now and again, however, on the occasion of some overt act of tyranny when the rights of the people have clearly been violated, he felt constrained to regard the republic as the only solution ; if it is impossible for princes to reconcile their interests with those of the people, then " good-bye for ever to despots and even to constitutional kings "—except, he adds significantly, in England.

> Here duties and rights
> Each do balance the other ;
> The use of man's reason
> Is here not a crime.
>
> Thou wielding thy empire
> From Nile to Abila,
> Thou ultimate refuge
> For virtue's distress ;
> Thy sheltering coast
> With its numberless havens,
> The just man rejected
> Doth welcome and bless.

It has been suggested by more than one writer that Rossetti's regard for constitutional government may have been derived from his long residence in England ; but there had been constitutions within Rossetti's experience before he came to England, and the constitutional ideal seems in any case well adapted to his compromising temperament. Still, he admired the English political system and the freedom of the people, he was deeply indebted to English gentlemen of high standing, his wife's sisters had more than a little of English Toryism. All this would tend to moderate his political views. At the same time he was not prepared to admit that England was the paradise he had first called it. In one of the poems of the *Inedite* he assigns praise and blame in a judicious survey. There are too many social injustices and inequalities ; England is a mother to some, a stepmother to others. She should check the growing power and arrogance of her proud clerics. These use their possessions badly—let them return their estates to the nation whose property they rightly are.

> So schools and hospitals you then might raise,
> And feed your people, not their evil ways.

Moreover, she makes her children pay for their education while France, Germany, and even Spain, have a hundred universities open to all. What mother charges her baby for milk ! Let the clerical harpy be dislodged from Oxford and Cambridge ;

> Thus to your sons good fruit would surely fall,
> Cambridge and Oxford being free to all.

Indeed the clergy and aristocracy have always been a check on England's progress—if their disastrous league could only be dissolved what a splendid land this might be !

Gabriele did not always find himself in agreement with the more English of his relatives in his tentative views on English matters. Though his wife shared his liberal sentiments, her sister, Eliza, did not, nor one imagines did Charlotte. He took some interest in the fate of the Reform Bill in 1832 and feared there would be great disturbances should it not be carried. On its safe passage through Parliament triumphant messages are sent to Holmer Green. " Tell that Tory Eliza that her champions are making themselves immortal, but all their resistance will be as successful as Christina's when you are giving her medicine ", and later he wishes " the aristocratic Eliza better judgment." He is noticeably playful—it was impossible to get so excited about such things as he did about the doings of Metternich and King Ferdinand.

A motto that was frequently on his lips was *age quod age*, and no one can say that he did not live up to it. Reading through the complete *epistolario* it is impossible not to be struck with the contrast between the calm domesticity of his daily life as it appears in the letters to his wife, and the feverish excitement that besets him when he writes about Italy to his Italian friends.

> A double life the poet lived,
> And with a double burthen grieved,

as Francis Thompson says. Appointments had to be kept, and house removals had to be attended to ; there were clothes to buy, children to feed, money to husband. But all the while that riotous imagination could not keep still, and continued, in ineffective denunciations and high-minded declamation among his daily guests, to exercise itself upon abuses which had become fixed and centred for him in his own irrevocable exile ; and something of the same political excitement was carried on with equally uncritical ardour into the study of Dante. If the children were little interested in politics and all opposed to their father's views on Dante, it was not only because they had heard quite enough of these things in early youth ; is it not likely that what they heard seemed very much in the air, out of keeping with the rest of their father's life as they saw it daily, in a word unreal ? Unreal, and even at times comical (though smiles were surreptitious and not at all unfilial) ; but still not by any means unimpressive or easily forgotten. Dante Gabriel's *Last Confession* was indebted for its central figure to one of his father's visitors ; William Michael's republicanism had its roots in conversations he had heard in his own home. Above all the atmosphere of emotional excitement, the constant declamation of poetry, the romantic unordinariness of it all, made life in Charlotte Street a fertile soil for the growth of young poets. The training they received from their mother might possibly have curbed their imaginations, as it undoubtedly did violence to their instincts ; that is problematical. Their father's contribution to their environment may have been in some respects ineffective, but in others it must have been stimulating to a high degree. At all events it is strange to think that while the company in Charlotte Street was probably among the most interesting and the most bizarre in London, the family that lived there must surely have been among the most efficiently regulated and disciplined. Company and discipline alike helped to make the children a group apart in the literary disposition of the century.

CHAPTER FIVE

THE SHADOW OF DANTE

*Circa sensum mysticum dupliciter errare contingit ;
aut quaerendo ipsum ubi non est, aut accipiendo aliter
quam accipi debeat.*

DANTE, *De Monarchia*, III, 20.

*Egli ha da combattere con Dante medesimo, il
quale non concederà mai ch'altri sappia più di lui
quel ch'egli ha voluto dire.*

ROSSETTI, *Comento*, II, p. v.

I

IN one of the most visionary parts of his *Veggente in Solitudine*
Rossetti relates that when he was being carried away from the shores
of Italy for the last time in 1824, he saw the great Apennine range
stretched out in the darkness, like a giant lying prone with Italy for
a bed ; and it seemed that Italy amid all the relics of her past greatness was asleep. " Sleep then ", he thought, " and rest in peace,
but may there come a day when the trumpet blast shall waken thee."
" She will awake ! " said a great voice at his side, and turning he
saw a titanic winged warrior, helmeted and sword in hand. " Take
courage, and when you see me again, she will have ceased to sleep."
So saying, he disappeared. The poet, wondering, dreamed on
through the night, until near dawn he saw an even greater marvel.
A cloud gathering out of the night sky slowly descended towards the
ship, and as it came, strange lights encircled it. At last a form could
be seen, a grave and well-known figure, he " who visited in mental
pilgrimage the world in three divided." Looking gravely upon the
poet, he spoke :

Thou sufferest—hear and hope. A stern decree
Now bids thy feet traverse the vale of pain.
Myself have proved how salt another's bread,
Myself have known how hard a path it is
Going and coming by another's stair.

76

All this in scorn I threw behind my back,
And if thy bosom burns with equal fire
For a like cause thou wilt the same endure.
Were we not driven both from hearth and home,
Both very vilely ?—Who more wronged than we ?
I by the citizens so dear to me,
Thou by the fury of a perjured King.
Show then in equal suffering equal pride,
Which in the great must be its own reward.
Go then, and take as I did on the way
Sorrow and not remorse for company ;
A noble sorrow rich in noble thought,
Whence man becometh wise in many ways.
And to reward thee for thy fortitude,
The secret ordering of my holy hymns
Profound and difficult I will reveal.
Once purged away the darkness of the world,
Thou wilt be able in my covert words
To hear the voice of Truth ineffable,
Truth hidden from the most, revealed to few.

So saying, he veiled himself again in his cloud and disappeared from sight. But the poet betaking himself again on the boat to the mystic song, saw to his amazement a new heaven and a new earth opening before his eyes. So the shadow of Dante had fallen across his life, as it fell indeed over that of all his family.

The passage in the *Veggente* was written long after 1824 and is certainly not to be taken *au pied de la lettre*. We do not know at what point Dante finally took possession of the poet's imagination, but it appears to have been after leaving Malta, and was probably soon after his arrival in England. A letter from Susan Frere in September 1824 asks, " Do tell me what are these new views about Dante's poem ? " They had apparently not been heard of before he left the island. On the other hand the radical ideas of his *Psaltery*, which was very largely composed in Malta, bear a close resemblance to what Rossetti thought were the radical ideas underlying the *Divine Comedy*. The sequence of events was no doubt something like this. In 1809 he says, at the age of twenty-six, he became a Freemason, but only reached the third degree. Ten years afterwards he was deeply involved in Carbonarism, which was free-masonry with a difference. Carbonarism had been excommunicated *en bloc* by the Pope. It stood for ideals which the philosophy of the eighteenth century had been long preparing, humanitarian and secular ; its aim was political, its methods were secret and symbolical. When Rossetti in exile began, through the exigencies of his new and enforced profession, to turn a closer eye upon the *Divine Comedy*, he no doubt noticed for the first time that Dante's position was in some respects very like his own. Next the possibility presented itself to his mind that Dante was equally a member of a secret society with political aims as ardent as those of the Carbonari. That theory started an avalanche which, rolling down the years of the poet's life in London, grew and grew until it was like to have buried its author and all his household under its weight. It drew absurdities to itself as easily as a magnet gathers iron filings ; but that it was absurd in all its details is more than any but the very uncautious will now say. Rossetti covered so enormous a field in his unsystematic way, that few men can ever have had knowledge enough to disprove the whole of his case, and those few have never undertaken a task so thankless.

Opposite one passage in Frere's copy of the *Amor Platonico* stands the comment " Enquire into this ". It represents the constant experience of the student of Rossetti's system. At point after point arises the query, " Can this be true ? If so, then . . ." But enquiry leads to enquiry, till the enquirer is lost in the wilderness of the unknowable and the spirit fails, feeling life too short for the verification of so many strange hypotheses. " The work of ten men ", says Rossetti, " would not suffice to explain these things " ; and certainly it would require at least ten more to explain them away.

II

Before entering into any detailed consideration of the Dante theories, it will make for clarity if we pause for a moment to examine Rossetti's own religious beliefs. Certain facts about them are clear. He was of course brought up in the beliefs of the Roman Church and never definitely renounced them. He was sufficiently faithful to that communion to be married according to its rite, although he afterwards cheerfully gave up his children to Mrs. Rossetti's evangelical training. At the same time, he was for the greater part of his life, like most of the Risorgimento exiles, strenuously antipapal and anticlerical. The lordly and well-fed bishops of the Church of England were disliked by him hardly less than those of Rome. He regarded the Roman hierarchy as the cause of the irreligion of his country, as well as an obstacle in the way of liberty—the two went together in his mind, since he thought it a property of the truly Christian mind to have regard to the liberty and physical well-being of one's fellows. That is why he could say that a liberal government such as he desired for Italy was the object of evangelical law. For the same reason he attacked the Puseyites—they were blind devotees of the Pope and would steal England's political liberty. The invasion of England by the new Catholic hierarchy in 1850 infuriated him ; it was a new gunpowder plot with Wiseman as Guy Fawkes. And his pamphlet, *Roma verso la metà del secolo decimonono* [*Rome towards the middle of the nineteenth century*], extracted from the *Amor Platonico*, was published as a warning to Englishmen of what might be expected to happen to England if they let the Pope and his minions gain a footing What is more, the spread of Roman Catholicism in England was one of the alleged causes for his having completed the *Amor Platonico* itself.[1] In spite of all this, until the last phase, in which he became involved with the Italian evangelicals in London, he often called himself a faithful son of the Catholic Church ; even at the end of the pamphlet mentioned above, he identifies himself with the good Catholics whose dearest wish it must be to see the Pope simplify and purify his holy church ; while shortly before his death he received the sacraments from a Catholic priest.

So far this is ascertainable fact. What is more difficult to define is the kind of belief which was left after Rossetti asserted the right to private judgment and turned his back upon the Catholic hierarchy. It was in all probability very simple, the offspring of long-established habit of thought and natural goodness of heart. In the main it seems to have consisted of a firm belief in the Christian ethic with practically no consciousness of any implicit doctrinal background. Great as was his love of symbols, it is impossible to read his *Psaltery*, his hymns, his *Amor Platonico* without realising that his mind was definitely not of a mystical order. Discounting inconsistent episodes, as when he offended the editor of the *Eco di Savanarola* by suggesting that the souls of the saints might intercede with Christ for the salvation of Mapei after his death, and occasional remarks which have led one Italian critic to say that he was Protestant when he thought he was Catholic and Catholic when he thought he was Protestant, one may confidently assert that he never held any persistent belief in the traditional Christian conception of a supernatural world, at least from 1824 onwards when his mind begins to be known to us. He believed in God as the source of goodness and truth, as a majesty and power felt without and within.

[1] Between 1837 and 1851 the number of Roman Catholics in England increased from 400,000 to 800,000.

> By two books Thou art presented
> Clearly to the spirit's sight ;
> Nature's self a volume opens
> Written over with Thy might ;
> Thought itself to him who thinketh
> Is a book of inward light.

Christ for him is the saviour, the teacher, the great exemplar of love to man ; and in this sense certainly the very son of God. The Gospels were to him a school of virtue, giving counsel in peril, and comfort in distress :

> Souls by Thee are edified
> Into purest love fraternal ;
> Human reason sanctified,
> Holy book, I find in thee ;
> And in thee the word eternal
> Speaking to my faith I see.

But in ritual and sacraments he appears to have had no interest at all. In general he seems to have been a deist with strong evangelical leanings. Settembrini said of him that " arrived in England he too made a god of the Bible." If " Bible " is replaced by " New Testament " there is a good deal of truth in the remark. For the Old Testament he seems to have had no great liking ; perhaps from the ancient heresies he studied so closely he came to feel in it the power of the Demiurge which the Marcionites thought presided therein. The only occasion on which he interfered in the religious education of his children was when his wife was telling them the story of Abraham's sacrifice of Isaac—" If I had been Abraham I should have said, ' Thou art not God, thou art the Devil.' " The texts he chose to give as the basis of his belief are all instructions to love one's neighbour from the New Testament, such as 1 John iv. 20, " If a man say, I love God, and hateth his brother, he is a liar ; for he that loveth not his brother whom he hath seen, how can he love God whom he hath not seen ? " Or iii. 17, " Whoso hath this world's good, and seeth his brother have need, and shutteth up his bowels of compassion from him, how dwelleth the love of God in him ? "

It is here perhaps that the mind of Rossetti diverges most clearly from the mind of the Roman Church, in so far as she asserts that everything rests on the First Cause, that knowledge precedes love, and that thereafter knowledge and love increase each other. For her the world of men is a secondary consideration. Men are only to be loved in God and for God ; God alone is to be loved for himself. That is the first and greatest commandment. Rossetti, however, drew all his deductions from the second. Instinctively loving his brother, he was content to discover in that way the love of God ; and his attitude consequently was much rather ethical than religious. Still, to this simple form of Christian belief he clung with tenacity. Once when Mazzini was declaring that the creed was outworn, Rossetti opened the window and said, " Look at that sun ! It is older than Adam, and yet it is still beautiful."

At what point he developed or began to develop his naturalistic, freethinking, and ethical point of view is matter for debate. It is sometimes said that his protestantism, like his constitutionalism, was the product of his life in England. It is certainly not true. No doubt he was confirmed in both matters by his English environment, and no doubt he would not have written the hymns of the *Arpa Evangelica* but for the example of the English hymnaries, though even then it must be remembered that he had always held that poetry ought to be sung, and he who thought his political poems might be made into marching songs may well have thought that his religious poetry might take the form of hymns. In the sphere of religion we have the incontestable evidence of the *Psaltery*, the main lines of which were laid down in Malta, and which is so definitely non-Catholic that it was put on the *Index*. And yet even at that time Rossetti was protesting his loyalty to the Church,[1] as he did almost throughout his life, and the *Psaltery* itself was innocently presented to the Pope in the vain hope that he might be pleased with it.

There seems consequently some reason for supposing that Rossetti's anticlericalism, humanitarianism, and exalted rationalism may have been connected with his membership of the Freemasons from 1809 onwards. The suggestion is made with some diffidence since it is impossible to know with certainty what the central masonic doctrines were and are. The hostility between Continental Freemasonry and the Catholic Church, however, has caused the latter to institute painstaking researches, and the long article on Freemasonry in the *Catholic Encyclopaedia* throws what appears to be valuable light on Rossetti's views. The account there given is naturally strongly biassed, and the masonic authorities quoted are for the most part representatives of the Scottish Rite organised in 1801 ; but this is only the more to our purpose since in all probability it was according to that Rite, which preponderates in the Latin countries, that Rossetti was initiated. " Masonry propagates no creed," says

[1] See p. 21.

one of the authorities quoted, " except its own most simple and sublime one taught by Nature and Reason.   There has never been a false religion in the world.   The permanent and universal revelation is written in visible Nature and explained by the reason and is completed by the analogies of faith.   There is but one true religion, one dogma, one legitimate belief."   Masonry is defined in the words " a system of morality veiled in allegory and illustrated by symbols," and it is stated as tolerably clear that the essential principle and bond of union of all masons is " the universal religion of humanity." [1] The constitutions from 1717 onwards have laid stress on freedom of conscience ; belief in any particular system of dogmas is not necessarily excluded but is regarded as a matter of secondary importance or even prejudicial to the law of universal love and toleration.   One recalls the celebrated dictum, " Every wise man has the same religion and no wise man will say what it is."

Latin Freemasonry has long diverged from the Masonic body in England, its militant, political and anticlerical bias having raised strong protests in this country and America.   But in any case, during the eighteenth century the association was subjected everywhere to the influence of contemporary scepticism.   The old charges delivered to initiates of the masonic dark ages before 1717, seem to have been definitely Christian in character ; but after the organisation of Grand Lodges and the beginnings of the freemasonry of to-day the old Christian formulae are replaced by requirements of belief in the " Grand Architect of the Universe."   Many of the first masons at the foundation of the Grand Lodge in England in 1717 were members of the Royal Society.   Voltaire was initiated in 1778, receiving his masonic garb from Helvétius.   In accordance with the trend of eighteenth-century philosophy, masonry is said to profess the empiric or positivist method of reason and deduction in the investigation of truth ; and its tenets are said to have been influential among the many confluents which produced the French Revolution.[2] However this may be, it seems certain that " the ancient and accepted Scottish rite " has always stood for the natural rights of man against religious and political despotisms.   " Wherever a nation struggles to gain or regain its freedom, wherever the human mind asserts its independence and the people demand their inalienable rights, there shall go our warmest sympathies." [2]

That all this is in the closest accordance with Rossetti's religious

[1] Compare Aroux's phrase, p. 91.
[2] Again from writers quoted in *The Catholic Encyclopaedia*.

belief and political enthusiasms nobody could doubt for a moment. It may be said of course that he derived them directly or indirectly from the same philosophers who were responsible for the diffusion of such ideas in the eighteenth century, in masonry and outside it. But there is no reason to ignore what could easily have been the most immediate source of them for our poet, especially in view of the fact that masonry with its offshoot Carbonarism were so widely spread amongst his friends.

We make then the tentative suggestion that the religious views expressed by Rossetti in the *Psaltery* were partly derived from his association with the Freemasons ; and the possibility seems all the more likely when we find somewhat similar views attributed by him to Dante and explained by the existence of masonic organisations in the Middle Ages. But since he represents the masonry of Dante as going to lengths of Pagan impiety that he could not himself uphold, it is necessary to add a little more. Some of the older historians of Freemasonry consulted by Rossetti used to trace its descent from the most distant fringes of history. It built Noah's ark, the tower of Babel, the Pyramids, and Solomon's temple. It originated in the Egyptian, Eleusinian, Dionysiac, even the Druidic mysteries ; among the Pythagoreans or the Gnostics. And in France from 1737 at least one masonic body associated itself with the knights of St. John of Jerusalem, i.e. with the Templars. Modern historians are more cautious. It is certain that Freemasonry, speculative as well as operative, goes back to a much earlier date than 1717, and some masonic scholars have made an interesting case for a continuity of signs and symbols from ancient primitive rites once universal. But their conclusions are not yet accepted as proved, and in any case nobody now gives any serious consideration to the old assertions about Nimrod and Noah.

We have spent some time on these considerations because they constitute the best approach to the Dante theories. For while the latter may entirely misrepresent Dante, it is very likely that they represent tolerably well the inculcations of Freemasonry as Rossetti knew them ; and with these preliminaries we may now turn to the theories themselves.

III

The first discoverable exchange of opinions about Rossetti's Dante theories was made with the well-known translator Cary, then an official at the British Museum. He had been reading the first volume of the *Comento*, or part of it, at that time in manuscript, and wrote to the poet as follows : " I find the same ingenuity and acuteness in your commentary as before and the same doubts still in my own mind. After the best consideration I have been able to give your hypothesis respecting the City of Dis, I own myself unconvinced." But he asks nevertheless to be put down as a subscriber. Rossetti replies that what Cary says to him he used to say to himself. His friend is too profoundly learned in the old explanations to be able to give unprejudiced consideration to these new ones. Nobody's criticism ever had the slightest effect on Rossetti's enthusiasm and conviction. He goes on to ask Cary whether his work is worthy to see the light ; and fortunately for his own self-respect Cary said that it was, making at the same time in the politest manner a number of sensible suggestions —the interpretation should not break the continuity of the text, the whole should be published at once, the work should not extend beyond three volumes, and the new interpretation would be most likely to obtain a hearing if proposed in as brief and dispassionate a manner as possible. All this excellent advice Rossetti completely disregarded. Cary remained his friend for many years more ; they were moreover linked by a common grievance against Panizzi, more grounded in Cary's case than in Rossetti's.[1] But Cary never became a convert to the Rossetti system ; a note in his *Dante* states his disagreement ; and on the receipt of the second volume of the *Comento* he offers indeed many compliments, but also the further and very final suggestion that Rossetti should direct his efforts to some object that would be more likely to help him in the support of a rising family.

All through 1825 a vigorous pursuit of possible subscribers for the *Comento* was carried on, not only by Rossetti himself but also by some of his friends, foremost among them Edward Davenport who secured no less than eighty subscriptions, or at least the promise of them. Davenport was ardently enthusiastic about the work. He talked " for ever about it to Lord Lansdowne who thought

---

[1] In 1837 Panizzi was made Keeper of the Printed Books over the head of Cary. Many protests were made, and meetings held, at one of which a speaker complained that Panizzi had been seen in the streets of London selling white mice. Cary himself protested, claiming that age and the state of his health entitled him to " that alleviation of labour which, in this as in many other public offices, is gained by promotion to a superior place."

Rossetti had gone too far." Probably it was he who secured the subscription of Lady Davy who subsequently regretted giving it. "I bought Rossetti and read some but left off for fear I should feel obliged to give way to his theories. I am a devoted admirer of Dante, and should never forgive the man who lessened him in my estimation. There was too much politics perhaps before, but an allegory in every word is horrid. I admire Johnson for saying after all his labours the honest truth, that a person had best read Shakespeare after all quite through, before he looked at a single note, and I advise all to read Dante as I have done three times, and as I mean to do a fourth, before they read Rossetti." *Amica veritas major amicus Dante !*

Among the subscribers appear of course several members of the Frere family, Isaac Disraeli, Henry Hallam, Francis Palgrave, Samuel Rogers, Lord John Russell, Sir Walter Scott, Signor Polidori and his daughter Miss Frances. The work, *La Divina Commedia di Dante Alighieri con Comento Analitico*, eventually appeared at the end of 1825, bearing date 1826. A second volume completing the *Inferno* came out at the end of 1827 ; the commentary on the *Purgatorio* and part of the *Paradiso* was written but never published, although Rossetti's admirers often urged him to bring the work to a conclusion. He had, however, in the meanwhile, started new and alluring hares and was possibly impatient of being tied to the text of Dante ; and besides it had been an unsuccessful and costly venture. The two volumes cost in all £605. About 750 copies were printed, and three years afterwards 400 of them remained on Murray's hands. According to Rossetti, Murray forgot to send copies to a third of the subscribers to Volume I., so that many of them not unnaturally refused to have Volume II. Various others refused to pay their subscriptions—these must have been out of Rossetti's reach, for a curious note on one of his letters gives a list of people who have paid for their copies, and ends with the comment, "All my pupils have paid for Volume I."

It was not of course for the first time that this suggestion of secret meanings in Dante had been raised ; but no one before had made so detailed an attempt to elucidate them. Except for certain small points at the beginning, says Rossetti—with what truth we must leave it to others to decide—"I saw it all by myself without the help of any man." The *Comento* consists of a formidable array of preliminary discourses, comments, prose paraphrases, added notes, reflexions, expositions and examinations, "like a plague of locusts ", as someone said of commentators in general. *The Divine Comedy* itself makes an occasional appearance in tiny gobbets which are immediately swallowed up in new comments, produced by Rossetti as a conjurer produces rabbits out of a hat. " Admirable is this simile, and employed with more than human judgment. Allow me to develop it. . . ."

Explaining so much as he did, it was inevitable that Rossetti should explain some things in the manner of other people ; what was proper to himself was the interpretation of the whole poem as a Ghibelline allegory. The Ghibellines, we are to believe, had a secret society and a conventional vocabulary (*gergo*) by means of which, pretending to speak of one thing they were really talking of something else. They were very extended and included men of *si*, *oc*, and *oil* ; and when they did not wish to be understood by their enemies, they wrote in the vernacular, not in Latin. According to Rossetti, Dante himself belonged to the society, having been received into it at Bologna just before 1300. There were two grades in the sect, known as Men and Women, that is active proselytes and contemplative directors, and so it comes about that the women of the poets are often really men. Attachment to the empire is called by them *Amore*. Divide it, and you get *Amo re*— I love the king. Spell it *Amor* and reverse it, and you get its negative or opposite, *Roma*. Life is Ghibellinism, death is Guelphism. To be dead is to be a Guelph, to die is either to become one, or to pretend to become one for greater safety. The City of Dis is Florence, Hell in general is the abode of the Guelphs ; Satan who rules over Hell is consequently the Pope, for does not Dante state quite clearly,

> Pap'è Satan [the Pope is Satan] ?

(Two other and quite different interpretations of this obscure passage are given in the course of the work.) " This ", says Rossetti, " is what I shall confine myself to saying in final analysis : the Satan of Dante is a satirical allegory which in its entirety offers the image of Guelphism corrupt and corrupting, and above all, its Head, who was according to the poet's claim the cause of misery in this world and of damnation in the world to come." The mysterious *Veltro* who was to bring salvation is the Emperor Henry of Luxemburg, who is shadowed forth in many anagrams and acrostics. Virgil is the monarchic political system, Beatrice is the purified non-hierarchical Christian religion.

All this develops rapidly as Rossetti proceeds, and the second volume is much more daring and reckless than the first. After commentating his way through eleven cantos he remarks, " I perceive a thought taking form in my mind, which may be the germ of no small volume " ; and every thought begets more thoughts. However, the more daring he became the more apologetic he thought it wise to be. " I am more than hundreds and hundreds of miles from approving of these secret furies of the Ghibelline poet." He affirms that Dante, although opposed to the Papacy, was still the best of Christians. At the same time he becomes more and more emphatic and exclamatory. This is the century of discoveries, and literature will lead the way. If anyone should laugh at his promise to make his theory good, he will bet a hundred pounds on it, nay a thousand. " Would that it were so, I can already see the money fall ringing into my hand." He is prepared to teach all Italy to understand her greatest poet, and what is more all her oldest poets into the bargain. For they, he says at the end, " sighed indeed, but not for Beatrice, Selvaggia, Mandetta, Vanna, Pinella, Becchina, Nina and the rest ; the object of their dearest wishes was our sweet Italy, the dearer to them as she was the more unfortunate." Which really brings him back to the point of his departure.

IV

The *Comento* was on the whole not badly received. In some quarters there were of course abuse and ridicule—his methods of exposition had made that inevitable ; but it was met elsewhere with a good deal of respect. It remains the most useful of all his critical work. Rossetti now, however, was fairly lost in the maze. Lyell, who regretted that the rest of the *Comento* was not to appear, declared nevertheless that Rossetti was right to with-hold it—he had opened Pandora's box and then closed the lid just in time. The latter half of this remark was so far from being true that the poet's friends were soon imploring him to go back to his *Comento* as to a relatively harmless occupation, and to leave his later discoveries to rest in safe obscurity. For what he now went on to discover was that Dante was not merely anti-papal but also anti-christian, and going a step further he came within an ace of discovering that there was nothing in Christianity at all ; though exactly what he supposed himself to have discovered is not clearly to be seen through his apologies and denunciations and the reticences which overtake him at the moment of revelation.

By the end of 1831 he had written a new work which was financed by Lyell and published in 1832, with the title *Lo Spirito Antipapale che produsse la Riforma*. An English translation by Caroline Ward, a friend and disciple, appeared in 1834.

Rossetti, as we have seen, was confident enough in the merits of this production to use it as a credential when applying for the chair at King's ; indeed in a letter to Lyell he declares that if the public doesn't like the book it has no soul and no curiosity. The purport of his extraordinary work is to show that a widespread opposition to the Church of Rome was carried on in the Middle Ages by members of a secret society with imperial aims in politics and a naturalistic system of belief. The sectarians' thoughts, he says, were entirely concerned with this world and life. Happiness they conceived to be the fruit of moral conduct and good order in society ; the latter to be secured by the establishment of a world Emperor. They rejected the mysteries of revelation ; the Divine Wisdom was knowable only as manifested in mankind, and in that way the adepts thought themselves avatars of God. They were thus not only anti-papal but also anti-christian. The origins of the sect are lost in antiquity and in the darkness of the east, but the spread of Manichaean doctrines established it in Europe among the Paulicians, Cathari, Albigenses, Patarini. It has had five epochs :

1. The classical.
2. The early mediaeval.
3. The time of Dante, when Templars, Albigenses, and Ghibellines were all branches of it.
4. The eighteenth century.
5. Rossetti's own day.

The modern thirst for freedom is the product of this age-old sect, which has always worked to save men from the tyranny of priests and despots. Sectarians opposing the Papacy as long ago as the time of Frederick II. were preparing, not only the Reformation, but also the French Revolution. Moreover they were closely connected with the history of Freemasonry, Petrarch's Laura indeed being nothing other than a masonic lodge ; and their tradition in later ages was represented by the Puritans and by Swedenborg.

Of this sect which seems to have been so successfully ubiquitous in the development of the modern world, Dante was an important member ; so also was Petrarch and almost all the other early Italian poets. Their writings, entirely allegorical in nature, are concerned with the sectarian organisation and arcana.

Rossetti concludes the book by a series of complaints against his critics, printing extracts from their strictures ; and with an address to Lyell in which he lays out his plans for the future. Many poets are to be brought in for vivisection, " among whom your own most mysterious Chaucer."

His Scottish friend was fully prepared to hear more. " After all ", he wrote in January 1832, " this admirable volume . . . only does the thing by halves. We must have another and the Mysterium Magnum must be revealed." Meanwhile Rossetti sends him a list of compliments received which is reminiscent of Pepys after his speech before the Bar of the House of Commons. " Truth ", says Rossetti, " is now in the market-square and will never look backward."

v

Frere took twenty copies of the *Spirito Antipapale* and offered to pay some of the cost of the new work in hand, meanwhile asking for a brief chronological abstract of the history of the sect. He was never gratified by compliance with this very reasonable request, nor was he at all pleased, as time went on, at what he had heard of the new work's progress. He eventually sent what Rossetti calls " a letter of fire " about it, while his sister implored Rossetti to go on with Dante and to leave those wild surmises alone. At this point the theorist paused in his course, began to be haunted by nightmares, and declared he had better turn novelist. Actually he returned to his *Psaltery*, which was published in 1833. But all the time his spirit yearned towards the figure of Truth, still waiting for him in the market-place. A second edition of the *Spirito Antipapale* was mooted. Frere opposes it strongly in October, recommending him instead to write a life of Dante and a history of the sects. In December, Lyell urges him on to it. Pull devil, pull baker. But it mattered little what either of them said, as Rossetti was now in full spate, rushing on to the 1744 pages of the treatise on Platonic Love which was printed though not published in 1840.

The full title of this book was *Il Mistero dell' Amor Platonico del Medio Evo derivato dai Misteri Antichi*. The work is a mass of undigested and unorganised learning, wandering as mysteriously as its subject from topic to topic, touching on matters which it would require a syndicate of scholars to treat authoritatively. It is divided into five volumes, to provide, as Rossetti explains, resting-places for the tired reader, and given sufficient time it makes curious and by no means uninteresting reading.

Although in these days few of the very few who read the *Amor Platonico* will be at all scandalised by the propositions it enunciates, it is easy to imagine the uneasiness and disgust of some of Rossetti's contemporaries. It is particularly easy to realise why Mrs. Rossetti burnt all the copies she could find immediately after the poet's death. The revelation it contained may be briefly summarised as follows. The gods of ancient times, allegorical and personal, represented differing manifestations of the one underlying and indefinable unity. This may be called Wisdom, God-Man, Man-God, Intellectual Being, etc. Whatever name is given to the ineffable and inconceivable unity will approach more or less to the truth as it is accompanied by a greater or less degree of initiation. Separate manifestations of it have always been necessary at different times to different peoples. The priests, however, in former times enlightened and adept, fully understood the dependent relations of these parts to the underlying whole, and thus the ancient religions were relatively false among the people and true among the priests. Rossetti thought that the hieratic tradition was widely disseminated among the poets of antiquity ; it is to be found in Virgil (*procul este profani*), in Horace (*Odi profanum vulgus*), and also in Homer. " Multos, O juvenes, carmen decepit ", as the wise Eumolpus says in the *Satyricon*. No one, Rossetti tells us, will ever be able to understand the poetry of antiquity who is " unacquainted with the secret *natura deorum*, which Cicero, like Lucretius, reduces to the *rerum natura*."

Plato himself was one of the initiates. His philosophy with its insistence on a single abstract godhead of Wisdom, Beauty, Truth, its assertion of the superiority of the soul to the flesh, and its exaltation of the spiritual or intellectual love of Beauty and Wisdom, is one of the noblest expressions of the secret tradition. Moreover, the Platonic school of thought lent something to Manes, who en-grafting, as Rossetti supposed, Oriental theology, Pythagorism, and Platonism upon Christianity, established the uncompromising dualistic system known as Manichaeism. From this sprang many later heretical sects, such as the Paulicians, Cathari, Albigenses, Patarini. Through them all runs the tradition of what Rossetti calls the religion of love. Thus from Plato to Victor Hugo, taking in Chaucer, Dante, Bunyan and Milton on the way, he sees the initiates of the age-old mystery expressing their devotion in an unbroken succession.

In the Middle Ages, Rossetti asserts, its adherents had their own secret language, or *gergo*, and among the adepts who employed it were most of the mediaeval poets. This brings him to the love poetry of the *trouvères* and to the *Roman de la Rose*. Finally with profound salutations to Sicily and to Frederick II., " first singer of love in Italy ", he begins to consider the early Italian love poetry. Dante's Beatrice, and the mistresses of his fellow poets are all, he says, personifications of the same being or essence which was at the heart of the ancient mysteries. Over against them stood the official church asserting the absolute truth of the Christian revelation and ready to defend it with racks and *autos-da-fé*. " Had I been one of the faithful ", writes Rossetti, " to whom Dante sent his famous sonnet about Beatrice, I should have said, ' Leave these Manichaean monkey-tricks alone ; woe to you if you were understood. Look yonder at those reverend gentlemen around that pile—see how they wave their torches and set fire to it. Those friars have something quite other than brotherly love in their hearts, and they have already burnt thousands and thousands of people alive." For, he goes on to say, the church had set up a reign of hate against which the doctrine of Love was, not unnaturally, arrayed in resolute opposition.

That no doubt existed in Rossetti's mind about the association of the secret tradition with Freemasonry, is shown by the fact that he believed the famous Platonic Academy in Florence to have been a masonic lodge ; he is ready to prove it from the three Pulcis. Landino, Politian, Ficino. What is more, Petrarch's Laura herself stands for a masonic lodge, and the whole of Dante's *Paradiso* represents a lodge too. For after long exercising his pen in the erotic symbolism through which the sect achieved expression, Dante was obliged by sudden danger threatening from the Inquisition to change his manner of writing from the erotic to the theological. The whole of the *Divine Comedy* is thus a parable of masonic initiations, although at the same time it shadows forth " the one primitive and universal religion, which, destroying all the differences of men, is truly the religion of fraternal love." Christianity is only true because it is in fact based on this religion. Had it not been, " it would have been a false belief, for this is the true one." It is the religion of humanity which embraces all, " *le grand tout humanitaire ou franc-maçonnique* ", as one of Rossetti's correspondents called it. As for the *Arcanum Magnum*, much spoken of but never quite revealed, its nature is not hard to guess at

Rossetti is always hinting at it and then withdrawing in a mixture of personal apprehension and simulated horror. It seems to be simply this (though it is a far cry from Plato and Manes)—that there is no god but man, that god is man and man god, very much as Swinburne said so vociferously in *Hertha* and *A Hymn to Man*. The Catholic historians have decided that this was probably the central tenet of Latin Freemasonry ; William Michael states that in his opinion it was his father's *arcanum magnum*. These two entirely independent judgments are significant.

VI

The sad fate of this ponderous and in some respects egregious work may be left for a moment until we have brought to an end the story of Rossetti's investigations. By this time the fairly confined stream of the *Comento* had spread out into thousands of trickling rivulets wandering over a sandy waste and therein disappearing from sight. Further progress was impossible, and Rossetti returns to bank up and deepen one of the most important channels. The enterprise arose out of a request of Lyell's for a preface on the subject of Beatrice for a work of his own, to which Rossetti responded with such alacrity that the result soon exceeded by far the limits of Lyell's design. Eventually Rossetti published a third part of it at his own expense ; the rest is still in manuscript. Its title is *The Beatrice of Dante*, and its author was prouder of this than of all the rest of his work. It will be, he affirms, his passport to a future age ; he assures several correspondents that it is a mathematical demonstration. Certainly it is clearer, less wordy, better arranged and organised, than his other books ; and it has the great advantage of dealing with a theory of considerable antecedent possibility, that is the theory that Beatrice had no objective existence at all. It was of course no new idea. Byron refers to earlier theorists in *Don Juan*, saying that for his part

> I think that Dante's more abstruse ecstatics
> Meant to personify the mathematics.

And the subject had often been touched upon before by Rossetti himself. In 1828 he thought Beatrice existed but served only to veil Dante's real meaning. In the *Spirito Antipapale* she has developed into God, the Holy Trinity, particularised as the second person (i.e. Man-God, or God-Man) ; two pages later she is both Pope and Emperor reduced to a unity, she is the figure of imperial

Rome. In this last of his critical works he attempts to show the identity of the Beatrice of the *Divine Comedy* and that of the *Vita Nuova* with the elusive Philosophy of the *Convito*, and to demonstrate that they are one and all emblems of the secret brotherhood of which he had already written so much. The publication has a curious sequel. A French scholar called Aroux, who was interested in Rossetti's theories, asked for the loan of the complete *Beatrice*, in order, he said, to make and publish a summary of them in his own country. Rossetti willingly lent the manuscript, whereupon Aroux published a book of his own, using Rossetti's material but turning it to purposes a good deal more conciliatory to the Catholic Church. Rossetti was very angry. But it is impossible not to be a little amused at Aroux's rather cynical letters. He reassures Rossetti about his fear of having undermined the Christian religion. " Je vous avouerai humblement que malgré les indications que vous m'avez données, je ne parviens à saisir ni le secret de Dante, ni celui de la franc-maçonnerie. Vous pouvez donc vous tranquilliser quant à la crainte de saper la religion que je crois comme vous nécessaire aux hommes ; car je suis bien assuré que ceux qui liront votre livre ou le resumée que je veux en faire, n'y découvront pas plus que moi pour le plûpart." Aroux's book came out in 1853. It was dedicated to Pio Nono, and all rights of translation were reserved ! He has been arraigned and condemned for all this by a distinguished Italian student of Gabriele ; but for all the latter's anger, one finds with surprise that he sent Aroux a copy of the *Arpa Evangelica* in 1854, and that Aroux asked for any English reviews of the book to be sent at his own expense.

VII

The *Comento* and the *Spirito Antipapale* had a considerable following in Italy, copies of the former, we are told, having been passed round and worn to pieces with constant reading. This of course was rather the consequence of their anti-clerical bias than of their value as historical interpretations. Where readers were not predisposed in their favour by sharing Rossetti's own political and religious sympathies, the manifest faults of his writings were more immediately apparent. His headlong and quite unscholarly self-confidence, the antecedent absurdity of the idea that *all* the poets of Dante's time were members of a secret society and that *none* of their love poetry had anything to do with human love, his often ridiculous verbosity and longwindedness, his reliance on manifestly nonsensical anagrams and acrostics, his incautious quotations torn from their contexts in the writings of philosophers and mystics, and his apparent inability to understand them, his hesitations and disavowals which make it uncertain whether he was truly disgusted with the doctrines he supposed himself to have found, or whether he was unwillingly convinced by them, his constant suggestion that there were many things he could say if they were not too horrible to tell, the complacency and childish pride with which he presents everything—these and other peculiarities could not help but amuse the humorous and annoy the earnest. And no man was ever more sensitive to critical attack. A critic of his theories was for Rossetti a personal enemy, animated by malice and hatred ; and his letters and the conclusions of his books are full of loud complaints against reviewers.

The first volume of the *Comento* aroused comparatively little comment. There was a polite and complimentary notice in *The Literary Gazette* of 7 January 1826 ; *The Westminster Review* in October 1826 pained Rossetti by talking of his " strange fancies " ; in Italy the work was welcomed with interest but with a certain amount of incredulity. But with the appearance of the more daring second volume, critics became more violent. A reviewer in the *Quarterly*, January 1828, was lightly contemptuous. " Secrets are to be got at by piecing syllables together which are scattered throughout a whole line, or even half a dozen lines, when up starts a Ghibelline, or your old friend the Emperor—like Harlequin, whose limbs being collected from different quarters of the stage, combine at once into a perfect and living man." Rossetti was driven to distraction when he saw this paragraph. Lyell tried to control his friend. " Let me advise you to avoid grappling with the enemy at present for his tooth is sharp and poisonous, and he is the very boa constrictor of the *Quarterly*." But Rossetti was not to be held back. He sent a letter to the reviewer, who turned out to be a clergyman called Blunt, and who replied in due course, courteously enough, to the effect that he had had no malice. " There might be some levity in the mode of treating the thing, but certainly no deliberate intention of giving pain." This was small consolation to Rossetti, who drew up and possibly may have sent an agitated reply, bitterly complaining of the levity which the reviewer thought so immaterial. " This levity from one who knows neither Rossetti nor his book has brought both of them into contempt. . . . It has treated with ridicule a writer whom kings have thought worthy of their resentment . . . it takes from a terrified father his children's bread. Levity of a serious kind indeed."

Some comfort may have been derived from the indulgent reviewer in *The Literary Gazette*, 28 February 1828, who thought that Dante would sanction the opinions of his able critic could he read them, but a dreadful blow was in store. *The Foreign Quarterly* came out in October with a notice of some length. It disavows any malice. " Signor Rossetti is a very clever man ; we have no personal enmity towards him, to wish that his credit should in the slightest degree be impugned." The Commentary does much credit to its author's ingenuity ; but he should restrain his fancy and substitute cold logic in its place. In spite of so much politeness the reviewer calls the theory " sublime and perfect nonsense ". Rossetti has invented it without having read Dante, and then has ransacked his writings to find support for it. He tortures grammar, history, criticism and poetry, to prop up his system ; he knows nothing about the Ghibellines or their philosophy. The critic had written these things after the appearance of the first volume but had not published them out of pure compassion. The publication of the second volume " has determined us not to have any more mercy upon him—for he deserves none ; and if we could ever repent of any generous action, we should of the kindness with which we have spoken of him. Did we not think it worth our while not to allow him any longer to impose most shamefully on our countrymen, we should regret the time lost in reviewing his book ; for it is beneath notice. Let not the reader think the expressions too strong. We will advert only to some parts of the second volume of this work, and then we have done with it *for ever*."

Rossetti thought it was the work of a certain Ravina, *corvaccio fetido* as he calls him [stinking raven]. " Oh what calumnies, what a mad dog attack. . . . In comparison, what the *Quarterly Review* said about me was a panegyric. Twenty pages full of scorn, mockery, insults, and every kind of ironic or open ridicule." More than two years later Rossetti discovered that the real writer was the arch-enemy, Antonio Panizzi, and at the end of the *Spirito Antipapale* he gave " that unmannerly ignoramus a blow for which he will grieve all the rest of his life." What had happened seems tolerably clear. Panizzi wrote his remarks on Volume I. and left them unpublished because in the meantime he had become a rival candidate for the university chair. After he had secured it he heard some report of Rossetti's animadversions on his appointment, and immediately got his review into print. That accounts for the delay until October and the venom of the remarks on Volume II.

We may here dispose finally of the life-long quarrel with Panizzi. Rossetti's reply taunted Panizzi into another rejoinder. His original review with Rossetti's answer and further notes was published in Italian at Florence in 1832, anonymously. No attempt is made to confute the *Spirito Antipapale*—" to attempt any serious confutation of such fantastic stuff would be as ridiculous as to believe it. Anybody with ordinary good sense can see its oddity at a glance, and anybody who does not had better have his mind's eye opened by a doctor, not by a critic." This now brought into the quarrel a heated ally on the side of Rossetti, in Thomas Keightley, his friend and an enthusiastic supporter of the Dante theories. Reviewing a book of Panizzi's in *The Foreign Quarterly*, Vol. XV., he succeeded in being more abusive than either of the two rivals had been themselves ; and Panizzi wrote a furious reply to the proprietors of the magazine. This was in 1835. There was now a lull in the storm. Indeed during the year before, Panizzi had mystified Rossetti by marked advances, had recommended him to various families as the best Italian professor, had written a very polite letter, was reported to be going about saying good things about him. But the old suspicion remained ready to spring alive in all its old vigour. When Schlegel attacked the Dante theory in 1836, Rossetti was sure that Panizzi had set him on—he was in Germany two months ago—and was terribly angry. " Let Panizzis in London and Schlegels in Germany and devils everywhere arise in hundreds—I will never lose command of myself," he declares ; and a year afterwards he accuses " this nobody " of egging on against him Hallam, Schlegel, *The Athenaeum*, an English priest, and the whole world. The terrible magician who bewitches everybody cannot be escaped. He reviews the *Amor Platonico* with his customary violence in 1842, goes to the printer of the *Beatrice* to ask if it is true that Rossetti has published another book, and demands the obligatory British Museum copy. " What shall I do," says Rossetti in great distress to Lyell, " if he attacks my *Beatrice* ? " Indeed there was nothing to do except to forgive him ; and forgive him Rossetti eventually does in the *Autobiography*, at the end of a full account of his villainy :

> Perdono a' miei nemici, ed anche al mago
> Ed anche a Ferdinando, a tutti insomma.[1]
> [I forgive my enemies, even the sorcerer,
> And even Ferdinand, in fact all of them.]

But this was in the nature of a jail delivery, and, as we have seen, he hoped to find no Panizzi in heaven.

VIII

We return to mention more briefly other attacks and criticisms. The only one of which Rossetti speaks with any respect, and indeed one of the best, was written by Arthur Hallam, Tennyson's friend ; published first in *The Athenaeum* and later as a pamphlet in 1832 with the signature of T. H. E. A.   Rossetti thought this stood for a certain Adams, but that Panizzi had probably animated it ; nevertheless he says the style is very good and it can be read with pleasure. One can say more of it than this—no clearer objection to the theory and to its modern upholders as well could very well be put forward.   It is altogether admirable in candour, fairness, and relevance.   Hallam admits freely the author's boldness, cleverness, and the rest.   What is more he does not deny that the reasoning is curious and interesting, although not decisive.   The proofs justify a presumption that something beyond what meets the ear was intended by some of the writers whose work he examines.   Some of the obscurer poems brighten up under the new lights sufficiently well—and some meaning is preferable to none.   However, " the world is full of coincidences that mean nothing ; and masonic lodges even in the view of our ingenious author do not occupy the whole of God's earth."   It may well be that metaphors converted into symbolic rites by the initiates of a sect, may have commended themselves to Dante by reason of the same fitness that led to their use in the rites, without any connection between the two.   To say that Dante is a Ghibelline is one thing, and easily digested ; to add to this that the Ghibellines were all infidels is quite another— in this matter Rossetti may make some converts, but there is one who will never come over to his opinion—the Muse of History. As for Beatrice we can maintain a thing to be allegorical in part but not altogether.   " We are not inclined to admit the force of Rossetti's argument founded on the famous scene of the chariot ; because when we have cheerfully granted that the daughter of

[1] This passage is not found in W. M. R.'s translation, where the diatribe against Panizzi is much condensed.

Folco Portinari was never robbed of the Christian Church by a Babylonian harlot, we do not agree with him that we have conceded all that is of moment in the matter." And as for the suggestion that Laura was a masonic lodge it is " the very idiocy of hypothesis." Hallam goes on to show in vigorous terms that mediaeval Christianity was a deep and real thing ; and bound to inspire poets. Now if Dante and Petrarch are not Christian, where *are* the Christian poets ? Two striking passages occur at the end of the pamphlet, one of them in the notes. " Why not ", asks Hallam, " startle the world at once with the information that theology has always been a masonic trick ?—there needs only one bold application of the Professor's principles and the whole edifice of religion comes crumbling to the ground." This of course was what Rossetti was constantly suggesting, and what he practically says in the *Amor Platonico*. And for a final thrust—" We have known many able and worthy Italians both in exile and in their own land, but none who could see a yard out of the atmosphere of their local liberalism. They talk of poetry but they mean politics." He concludes by wishing him well. " Signor Rossetti is very sensitive to criticism ; but we trust he will believe our remarks at least to have been made in fairness and love of truth."

There is so much of the complimentary about Hallam's pamphlet, apart from its general moderation of tone, that at the conclusion of the *Amor Platonico* Rossetti speaks very kindly of its author, describing him as a lover of truth who might quite possibly have been converted by the five later volumes. Very different was his attitude to the only other attack that need be mentioned. In 1832 Lyell had a copy of the *Spirito Antipapale* given to the famous critic A. W. Schlegel, who said at the time that he could not agree with it, but for the moment did nothing more. Lyell's son, calling on the great man and finding him very interested in Rossetti's theories, hoped Schlegel would give his father the benefit of some comments. (The younger Lyell was always pleased to report ill news of Rossetti and his theories, irritated no doubt by what he thought his father's extravagance and credulity.) Eventually Schlegel gave the whole world the benefit of his comments in the *Revue des Deux Mondes*, August 1836. He wrote without mincing matters. He called Rossetti a historian without discernment and a man of letters without any feeling for poetry. He prophesied for his work a speedy oblivion on the dustiest shelves of the libraries, next to Goropius Becanus and Olaus Rudbeckius. Gabriele was

beside himself with anger—it was an infamous article, worse than
Panizzi's own ; Schlegel is " that beast of a German " [*tedescaccio*].
He declared that it was this article that made it necessary for him
to go on with the *Amor Platonico* ; for he was incapable either of
neglecting abuse or of listening to criticism. Any suggestion
of doubt immediately sent him off again in the pursuit of
proof.

There were of course friendly reviewers quite apart from Rossetti's
friends, though no writer of any note accepted his views. Mention
will be made here of only one of Rossetti's converts, and that because
it introduces in a comical way a person of some little importance
in the development of Dante Gabriel's art. A German scholar,
Joseph Mendelssohn, lectured in Berlin on Rossetti's theories and
published his lectures in 1843. A copy of this publication was sent
to Rossetti on Mendelssohn's behalf by a young German called
Dr. Adolf Heimann. In reporting this event to Lyell, Rossetti
calls the young man Hrimann. Within a fortnight the Manichaeans
have been too much for his memory, and in a letter to Frere Hrimann
degenerates into Ahrimann. In January of the next year Rossetti
arrives at the final assimilation ; his new friend is now innocently
referred to as Ahriman.

IX

Not less interesting than the theories themselves, and a good deal
easier to understand, are the relations of Rossetti with the most
sympathetic of his supporters, Charles Lyell and Hookham Frere.
They were both in some degree responsible for the extravagance of
his discoveries. " How true ", says Carlyle, " is that of Novalis,
' It is certain my belief gains quite infinitely the moment I can
convince another mind thereof.' " And not only did they buttress
Rossetti's confidence with their belief—they contributed discoveries
of their own, and those often among the most incredible, Frere for
instance saying that he had been considering Chaucer and had
found him tarred with the masonic brush, and Lyell supplying
the ridiculous anagram of *Veltro—Lutero*.[1] " Who knows ", says
Rossetti on one occasion, " whether you have not put into my hand
a thread which will untie a knot."

These two friends, though very different in character, were both

---

[1] By which Dante in the obscure *Veltro* passages is supposed to
have foreshadowed Luther and the Reformation. Rossetti uses the
anagram in the *Spirito Antipapale*, II, p. 227 (English version).

men of means and leisure, and both endlessly kind to their Italian
protégé. Frere was the better scholar of the two, and much
the better provided with humour. He was consequently the
less deluded ; it is in fact amazing that he took in as much
as he did, but he was himself a Freemason and seems to have
entertained millenary hopes to a degree quite unexpected in so
eminently sane and well-balanced a mind. Charles Lyell of
Kinnordy, the father of the famous geologist, was an enthusiastic
Dantist, immensely proud of his Dante library. He had that
combination of shrewdness with friendly and uncritical appreciation
of other people and their work which is often found in Scotchmen.
He was also growing old and took great pleasure in the position of
Maecenus to a younger and more venturesome scholar ; besides,
he had a real and very generous interest in Rossetti's welfare. To
absurdities he was quite insensitive ; there is a good deal of friendly
jesting in his letters, but no sign of that readiness to see the funny
side of things which makes some of Frere's letters delightful reading. Finally both men were dilettante in their support of Rossetti's
theories. They would and they would not. They supplied a good
deal of money between them, Lyell mainly for the publications,
Frere mainly for Rossetti's personal relief ; but they were restive
patrons and grew increasingly afraid of the result of Rossetti's
publications upon their own reputations, until between them they
ended by suppressing the *Amor Platonico*. All three partners in
the alliance seem to have misjudged the situation. Rossetti was
not aware how far his respect for his patrons was dependent on
their friendliness and their concurrence in his doctrines. He
could not separate in his mind a willingness to help from an
obligation to agree, and was terribly upset when disagreement
was expressed. Lyell went blindly on supposing either that his
reputation as a man of piety and decorum would not be affected,
or that if it were he did not mind ; until he discovered that he
did in fact mind very much. Frere, though more aware of the
possible effects of Rossetti's work, was not less suspicious of the
sidelong light it might throw upon himself. His position was the
more reasonable since for the most part he did not subsidise the
works ; but Rossetti and Lyell never had any clear conception
of the responsibilities and the rights of patrons.

Lyell became known to Rossetti after the publication of the
first volume of the *Comento*, and Rossetti was delighted at finding
so friendly and useful an ally. In what appears to be one of the

earliest letters of their correspondence, Rossetti addresses Lyell in the words spoken by Dante to Virgil—

> O sol che sani ogni vista turbata,
> Tu mi contenti sì quando correggi
> Che non men che far bene errar mi aggrata.[1]

" I will tell you candidly that when you point out my mistakes you give me more joy than when you applaud me : in the second case you delight my heart but you profit me nothing ; but in the first you clear my mind and help me to take a step forward." And so Lyell's doubt—" a very acute one "—about Cavalcanti shall be dealt with in a note in such a way as to clear it away entirely ; and as for the interpretation of *Pape Satan*, Lyell is clearly wrong about that. For Rossetti had a short way with doubts and queries whether from Lyell or from anybody else. However, he will set on record his gratitude in speech and in writing, and will give assurance of it volume by volume.

Needless to say, Lyell and his son appear among the subscribers to the second volume ; by the time it appeared he had become a respected friend and had acted as godfather to Dante Gabriel. At rare intervals he came to Charlotte Street, but for the most part his relations with Rossetti have to be followed in the enormous correspondence preserved in Rome and at Kinnordy. The letters are sometimes of great length, often there are two on one day, and on one occasion even three. Often Rossetti continues in the evening a letter which had had to be hurriedly concluded at the sound of the postman's bell. Lyell for his part could raise queries, but his admiration was unbounded. He is " confident that the world will pronounce it to be the most useful, learned, satisfactory, and unexpected elucidation of Dante that has ever appeared." If the *Comento* goes no farther " the loss to literature will be lament- able and irretrievable. . . . Notoriety is all you want ; fair and exalted fame must follow." He suggests in January 1828 a cheap edition of the *Inferno* of a kind calculated " to excite intense curiosity." He has some doubts about the *gergo* ; " by a mis- application of your key we could make it appear that Petrarch's Laura was the spirit of Ghibellinism." (Rossetti certainly could, and very soon would.) He also discovers an anagram in Canto I. which pleases him mightily. At the same time he knows that the *Comento*

---

[1] " O Sun, who healest all imperfect sight, thy corrections are so pleasing to me that I am no less glad to be in error than to do well." The lines are an adaptation of *Inferno*, xi., 91–3.

will raise opponents, and warns Rossetti that he must expect
attacks in the *Quarterly* and *Edinburgh*. This soon happened and
Lyell had much ado to soothe his wounded friend, even entering
the lists himself ; we find him for some time busy with a review
for which Rossetti himself supplied material, but which he had
great difficulty in getting published. Here is a fair example of
his letters at this time. " No letter upon a literary subject ever
afforded me half the delight of those with which you have favoured
me, and of the many which I possess and have read over and over
again,[1] the two last . . . are perhaps the most convincing . . .
that you possess the keys which unlock all Dante's hidden treasures.
. . . The free press of America . . . and of this excellent country
(with all its faults) . . . will make Truth triumphant and neither
Freemasons nor Dante will have any secrets.

" Your two volumes on the *Inferno* (so infamously and falsely
abused by a *Foreign* enemy, and so slighted and sneezed at by
some English coxcombs who have merely glanced at them with
jaundiced eyes), are the best prelude imaginable to the analysis
that is to follow. But oh *quanto tarda a me ch'altri qui giunga*.[2]
I am becoming so aged that the ability to enjoy your two volumes,
with their most curious *Disamine*, or *Il Purgatorio*, is likely to be
extinguished before Volume the third can appear in print. . . .
The Review in the *F.Q.* will surely provoke some purchasers ; it
has little merit besides, except that the very injustice it does to
your merits will make them more conspicuous . . . when the
truth of your discoveries will put the Foscoli, Ottusi and Corvi to
the blush, for having pronounced them " strange fancies ", harle-
quinades ", and shameful impositions. . . . Editors care not for
Dante or Rossetti. They demand an article which shall amuse
the idle reader and which shall not detract from the character of
their review, and have not hesitated to say that the prejudice against
Rossetti *must* be humoured and that the praise *must* be qualified,
or they should not think it safe to print it. Under these circumstances I trust that you will see a strong proof of my regard for
you in this review, poor and unsatisfactory as it is, and that I have
done my best for you. Give me credit too for having, old as I
am, kept up a fight for you during twelve months, and often an
angry one, and that at last an article which treats your work with

---

[1] Rossetti's letters to Lyell are often carefully underlined and
annotated in red ink.

[2] How long it seems to me ere the other arrive. (See *Inferno*, ix., 9.)

respect, though not with proper praise, has been published in the best of our periodicals, and the one which is·eclipsing the *Q.R.* which has scorned and rejected us. This has been the first warfare of the kind I have ever engaged in, and I would not risk such another."

That was on 1 March 1830. On the 18th we find that Lyell has undertaken to finance a new work and that Rossetti is to make over all the copies to him, an offer that was at first declined but afterwards accepted. In October Lyell offers £25 for the new work and suggests publication in Paris. This was tried and the manuscript sent off. The whole cost will be £50, says Gabriele, for 1000 copies. Lyell shall have 100 which will leave " 900 for me and that is not a few." In April next year the manuscript comes back again and arrangements are made to publish in England. Lyell is flustered by the dedication ; its flattery is more than he can bear. Half a year later it still worries him ; " be modest," he implores Rossetti, " and try to be as cold as a frosty-spirited Englishman." In May he is in London, promises £100 for the work, spends four evenings running with Rossetti talking about Dante until one in the morning. In October Rossetti announces new worlds to conquer. He is about to examine the three Griseldas.[1] An Italian will show the English how to understand their own ancient poetry. He has something to say about Chaucer, and then about Spenser ; perhaps he will leave Milton alone ; but if his arguments are well received he will " tear the mask even from the Secretary of the Protector." Lyell was too cautious to swallow this, and Rossetti says he will not touch the English poets since his friend advises him not to, although " no nation has so many writings of this nature as yours." In November the book is almost printed ; in December Lyell offers to allow an extension to 600 or 650 pages ; but Rossetti surprisingly declines.

Early in 1832 the book (the *Spirito Antipapale*) appeared. Lyell is very pleased with it and is soon wanting a second and fuller edition—" Your husband is a great man, lovely Francesca," writes Rossetti to his wife, " a great man ! we must certainly agree about that." But Hallam's *Remarks* this year gave Lyell as much distress as Rossetti ; he had come to regard the book he had paid for as his own child. He draws up lists of remarks on the *Remarks*, a procedure not adopted with any other review—Hallam must have

[1] I.e. Petrarch's, Boccaccio's, and Chaucer's (Clerk's Tale).

seemed particularly formidable. But Lyell was no more daunted than Rossetti himself. " That your next volume will be a glorious one I would venture to lay any bet, even all my beautiful book-shelves, filled with editions of Dante, against the dirty ungentle-manly pamphlet of Mr. Remarker." And yet it must have been with some relief that he heard at last of another supporter of Rossetti's who would help to share the burden of giving all these great truths to the world. It was Frere, and at this point we may turn to see what that leisurely gentleman was thinking about it all.

Frere and his sister had taken a friendly interest in the *Comento*, and in subsequent years often implored Rossetti to return to it. In 1831 Susan Frere gave a copy of it to two American clergymen, " whose free-born spirit was quite shocked when I explained the caution which would be necessary in order to keep possession of your book when they should land in Sicily." But Frere did not become closely involved in the Dante discoveries until the *Spirito Antipapale* was taking shape. He was not at first prepossessed in its favour. " Mr. Frere and I have conversed together about your *arcanum magnum* and both concur in fearing that your vivid imagination may carry you too far," writes Archibald Murray in July 1830. But Frere had himself written to Rossetti about his doubts on 8 June. First there is the consideration of expediency —how much will the world bear to be told ? Show a continued allegory in Petrarch's sonnets and all the admirers of Laura will be up in arms at once—like the madman in Horace who was angry at being deprived of an agreeable illusion. Then there is the doubtfulness of the whole proposition. Frere believes that " one secret association at least may be found by successive changes and affiliations to be derived from the most remote times," but does not believe that it ever had much power or influence. In any case it is a great mistake to ascribe all effects to one cause, as he thinks Rossetti is inclined to do. Then he takes to laughing at himself for his authoritative tone. " You who have seen something of the modern tone of criticism must be aware that whenever a man devotes his time and talents to a particular pursuit, he becomes liable to be lectured and corrected by those whose total ignorance of the subject enables them in their own opinion . . . to take an enlarged view of it." He will be glad to see what Rossetti has written but has taken the precaution of writing his review before-hand. " Nothing flattens the spirit of a review so much as the previous perusal of the work."

On 5 March 1832 the book was sent to Frere, who, as soon as he had read it, wrote with the most astonishing abandon. Gone are all his doubts and hesitancies. He has applied Rossetti's key to Chaucer and found him a member of the sect. The doctrines of the Paulicians are distinctly asserted in two passages of *Palamon and Arcite*. There are indications of a Pagan sect in the letters of Erasmus. Tristram is the personification of the schismatic system of the Druids of Cornwall. He regrets however that he can find nothing to the point in Milton. He asks for twenty copies, two of which are to be sent to Southey and one to Coleridge. At the same time he is still distrustful of the world's opinion and will not venture to bring such subjects into discussion in Malta. Rossetti replies to this with gusto, sending a statement of his central discovery separately and under precaution. " If it were lost on the way, I should be little concerned ; if you were to put it in the fire, I should mind still less. Born and brought up as I was in a most pious family, religion is to me a cherished sentiment ; and I was distressed when the sight of my mind, without connivance of the will, led me on to that which I should have wished never to see." As for Milton, given up by Frere, he certainly was of the sect, and Cromwell was the head and regulator of it in his period —he was the Christ who was to found the New Jerusalem which was announced to be so near at hand. This however was too much for Frere, who hoped that Rossetti's head was not getting turned like those of some of the discoverers of the Copernican system. But by March he has read the book three times, asks for more copies if there are any unsold, sends £50, and offers to pay for as many copies of the *Amor Platonico* as he has had of the *Spirito Antipapale*. Meanwhile Rossetti had temporarily repented of plunging into such deep and dangerous waters ; his conscience had received a severe shock, and he had reverted to his *Psaltery*. This was now dedicated to Frere, who was assured that he need not hesitate to accept the dedication since some had advised offering it to the Archbishop of Canterbury or the Bishop of London.

Then comes an amusing and very sensible letter from Frere advising Rossetti to be cautious, and not to let himself be led on to his own destruction by admiring friends. They tell him to go on, and confound his enemies ; fame awaits him. " It reminds me of a story which was told me at Lisbon. A Jew was going to be burnt, and the rabble of boys were very anxious to see him burnt alive, and proportionately apprehensive lest he should disappoint them by recanting. They therefore followed and encouraged him with shouts of *Sta fermo, Mose!* *Sta fermo, Mose!* You can reckon at least half a dozen voices all unanimously shouting out to you *Sta fermo, Mose!*

"But all these speculations are foreign to your actual situation. If you were in Italy indeed I have no doubt that the Duke of Modena would be willing to accommodate you with a dungeon; which after you had consecrated it by making it, for twenty years, the abode of persecuted genius, would in future ages be visited by sympathetic tourists; and an Album would be kept there, in which they would each deposit their extempore effusions, composed beforehand at the Inn—moreover, independent of this glorious posthumous prospect, your period of captivity would in the meanwhile be soothed by hearing the known voices of literary friends occasionally shouting ' *Sta fermo* ' under your window." In England, Frere goes on to say, nobody will trouble his head about him. For what then will he sacrifice himself? "When you were going to England I warned you by the example of Foscolo. But believe me the abandonment in which Foscolo found himself would be nothing compared to that which you would experience, if it could be said of you that you were the author of a *dangerous work.*" "There are many things, my dear Rosetti, [*sic*][1] which make me fear the worst for you. Your openness to adulation such as that of Count Segovi—(which my sister, when she saw it, said was an affront to your understanding) and which is just a repetition of the same sort of encouragement which induced you to put yourself forward at Naples. ' They are persuading him ', she said, ' to go forward and set fire to a Mine.' The influence of your brother Exiles — I judge them whether justly or no from a sample or two I have seen here; a young man came as a refugee, he had been obliged to leave Naples, he said, having renounced the Catholic Religion. "What religion then do you now profess?" ' Sono del Methodo.' [*sic*] As he did not look like one of our Methodists, I enquired what the Methodo meant? When I was told in a confidential tone, ' Sono Carbonari.' [*sic*] . . . That you should associate with your brothers in Exile is natural—even the satisfaction of hearing your native tongue spoken is an inducement— and though they may not be so far advanced in their philosophic views as the young gentleman of the Methodo, yet it is not to be imagined that they will advise you to maintain a self-denying

[1] Frere never spells the name correctly.

silence upon subjects *sacro digno silentio*, they would rather
encourage you to go forward and set fire to the Mine. . . .

"The Gentile dispensation is essentially exoteric and the
exception proves the rule ; the Apocalypse is appointed to remain
sealed to the time of the end. At this time of the end, many of
the harmonies of the ancient and primitive world, now prohibited
to profane and impious curiosity, will be developed and revealed,
but in the meantime it is an inexpiable crime to attempt to break
open the sanctuary in which they are concealed, with Engines
borrowed from the Magazines of profane learning. That you may
avoid this guilt, and live to behold this consummation which
(according to the opinions of the best and the most learned
Christians) is not far distant, is the sincere wish of

Your very sincere friend

J. H. FRERE."

What is really in Frere's mind ? A genuine desire to keep his
protégé from ruining his fortunes ; an equally genuine intention
not to incur the odium of impiety himself ; these are clear enough.
But is there not also some suggestion of the Freemason uneasy at a
too free handling of the society's tenets ? This looks more likely
still from a further and more urgent appeal on 31 July. " Pray
think well and consult with conscientious men and with your own
conscience before you venture on the irretrievable step of revealing
one of the two great antagonist mysteries. My firm conviction
and apprehension is that it will be ruinous to your fortune and
future peace of mind. You shall suffer no pecuniary loss by what
you suppress. I have not time to say more, but may God guide
you and preserve you from becoming the instrument of evil."

In the meantime the *Psaltery* had appeared with the dedication
to Frere. Susan Frere, in thanking Rossetti for it, says that it has
given her brother some embarrassment since he cannot now give
it to others to read ; but his feelings were actually stronger than
this. The dedication seemed to him to have nailed his flag to the
mast of a ship of questionable repute ; and his anxiety after a time
got the better of his kindly regard for Rossetti. " The dedication
prefixed to the *Salterio* would have marked me to all the world,
either as a hypocrite, who encouraged opinions which he had not
the spirit to avow openly ; or as an imbecile old dupe, blind by
cajolery."

This closing phrase was a knock-out blow to the good-hearted theorist. He is overcome by such grief that he cannot look at those tremendous words without feeling his heart wrung. He will take to writing novels, he will write grammars and dialogues as others do ; but no more of all these other things. Frere's reproof is a kindness but it is certainly the least of all his kindnesses. A little pacified, his patron replied as follows : " I felt as a man does when by awkward management a gun has been let off accidentally, and the shot has passed within an inch of his nose—but the shot has missed me, the danger is over, I am confident that there was no design and my trepidation and consequent irritation have been long at an end." Meanwhile he is against the proposed second edition of the *Spirito Antipapale*. The extensions would only follow lines laid down by Young Italy and the higher duties laid upon all Italian *literati* at present. However, " it will be printed I feel quite sure—I am not able to engage you to forbearance by outbidding the golden dreams of an anticipated party triumph, nor eloquent enough to persuade you." Poets who meddle in politics never do any good for themselves. Why not write a life of Dante or a history of the sects ? Or why talk of novels ?— " verse is your faculty." Rossetti's reply disclaims all connection with Young Italy, apologises for offending Frere, agrees not to publish a second edition of the *Spirito Antipapale*, and asks Frere to refrain from giving him any more financial help for the present.

The offices of the two patrons now begin to overlap. Lyell's enquiries about the new Maecenas had been answered by an account of Frere and his kindness, and Scotland was now resorted to for consolation after these stern reproaches from Malta. On the 26 November 1833 Rossetti complains to Lyell that Frere has taken a notion that he is making war against the Christian religion, that he has joined Young Italy, and wishes to make an unfair use of Frere's name to accredit himself with the English public. " In the frenzy which thus came over him, he wrote me a letter of fire, five sheets long, in which, now exhorting, now reproaching, now most bitterly complaining, he conjured me to desist from that impious enterprise which would outrage him and ruin myself. . . . Imagine my feelings. Imagine them if you can. Even the assurance of a clear conscience was hardly sufficient to calm me. For several days I remained distracted and stupefied. What was for me the most sharpest sting was the horrible idea that I should be guilty of the black villainy of using a name so highly honoured by me in such a nefarious procedure." Lyell replied in appropriate terms, and was duly thanked by Rossetti for having distilled a certain amount of balsam into the acerbity of his wound.

The storm blew over. Frere and Gabriele resume their discussions of the sectarians; the former offers up Herbert of Cherbury, the latter produces a perfect example in *The Pilgrim's Progress*. "How many masked sphinxes in the literary world! I have come upon so many that it is a true marvel." Even Victor Hugo in *Notre Dame de Paris*. A copy of the *Spirito Antipapale* together with an assurance that Rossetti had understood the real meaning of *Notre Dame* have been sent to Victor Hugo himself, who has congratulated him and said he was not surprised. Meanwhile Lyell inspired by Rossetti's researches engages in a translation of Dante's lyrical poems, and with constant appeals to Rossetti and Mrs. Rossetti for help, he finishes the task and publishes the result in 1835, with due acknowledgments to Rossetti and illustrations from his works. A copy was sent to Frere who according to his sister was much impressed with it.

This publication of Lyell's set Rossetti upon making a new book. Lyell had asked him for a dissertation of a hundred pages on Platonic Love to serve as an introduction to his translations. Rossetti started on this *con amore*, but it had soon gone beyond Lyell's needs, and was never used by him for the purpose stated. By February 1836 the hundred pages have become two volumes; the first parts have been printed and sent to Frere for his approval. And now begins the long struggle over that unlucky book. After reading a hundred and forty pages, Frere is full of "alarm and astonishment; I feel convinced that of those who read what I have been reading, those who draw any conclusion at all (or at least 99 out of 100 of them) will be led to this short inference, that all religions alike are all equally the result of human policy and contrivance, according to the words of the vulgar old infidel song,

> Religion's a politic trick
> Devised to keep blockheads in awe.

Admire, my dear Rosetti, the majestic energy and beauty of the English character and language, which comprises in a couple of lines the enunciation of a proposition which your Petrarchs and Dantes are obliged to develop bit by bit in hundreds of cantos and cartloads of commentaries." He urges Rossetti to consider the times in which they are living. " Upon the verge of the first

Christian dispensation, on the eve of those times in which it has
been predicted that faith should not be found upon earth. You,
my dear Rosetti . . . may live and probably will live to witness
some stupendous development demonstrating that those systems
that your readers had been taught by you to consider as
branches of the same, were essentially the forms of two antagonist
principles. Figure to yourself what will be your feelings of horror
if the events which you may live to witness should enforce that
conviction upon your mind." And he offers to pay Rossetti whatever profit he thinks he would be likely to make on the publication,
were it to be published.

To this new blast of disapproval Rossetti bowed his head ; he
consents not to have the work published in England ; but he does
not yield without grumbling. Had not Cudworth anticipated some
of his conclusions in 1678 ? He had shown the manuscript to his
aged father-in-law, " a very prudent man ", and to Mr. Keightley,
" a religious and erudite man "—both of them gave it their
approval. For a time the work languished, and this made the
other patron impatient. He had already written at the end of
the year before, urging quicker progress. " I would not hurry
you but on this occasion (and indeed on all others) the shortness
of life should be remembered and also that Filodante is sixty-
seven and that his executors might be wicked enough to stop the
press. Remember that between my receiving page 200 and 336,
my beloved daughter was reduced from the bloom and strength of
apparent full health (of 21) and by insensible degrees to a perfect
skeleton and to the grave." In the following September he
enquires anxiously what has become of his friend. The *Amor
Platonico* seems to have come to a standstill, spellbound at page 350.

But the spell-binder now relented for a time, and the work
went on, reached three volumes, its author constantly wondering
whether to publish it or to confide it only to the hands of men of
learning alone. As it neared completion the situation grew more
and more intense. Lyell had been paying for the printing. At
the end of 1838 he is getting uneasy about the length of the book ;
is determined to stop at page 1248 and then to wash his hands of
it entirely. But Rossetti will be well advised to stop at that page
himself and consider whether to print or not. An enemy such as
Panizzi could easily say that if these pages prove anything it is
that all religion is imposture ; and the effect on Rossetti's fortunes
as a teacher would be disastrous. He, Lyell, had never yet ven-

tured to mention the printing of the *Amor Platonico* to any member
of his family. A year later he is horrified at receiving a bill of
£87 12s. for " alterations, very numerous ", and has told the printer
not to expect payment from him for a single page more. He is
very dubious about the whole thing, both as to whether it is true
and as to the effect on Rossetti's affairs. A few days later it is a
wonderful work ; his sacrifices are not regretted ; his apprehensions
were an old man's fears. Yet in June 1840 he can write as
brutally as this :

" To send me your conclusions in manuscript would be wrong.
I am a timid lover of Truth, much in love with orthodoxy and
Ozanam,[1] but so partial to Rossetti that he has almost made me a
heretic, but I do not mean the world to doubt my being a right
good Catholic (like Dante) in the true protestant sense of the term.
Therefore I recommend your sending all your proofs of the
heterodoxy of Dante to the Printer's Devil before you send them to

My dear Sir,

Yours very sincerely,

CHARLES LYELL."

No wonder that the thing was becoming a nightmare to Rossetti
as he tells Frere it was. His sleep is restless and disturbed. Oh
that he had never begun ! It becomes at last a burning question
—a hundred copies must be preserved for Lyell since he has paid
for so much of the printing, but all the rest Rossetti offers to send
to Frere to be given to the flames. He could not do it himself,
but " whether Neptune or Vulcan devour my vigils, I shall not
see it, I shall not suffer." And he will give up his perilous studies
for ever. For he is becoming obsessed ; " my own shadow terrifies
me . . . I have become like one of those people of exaggerated
piety who think that in their most insignificant action they have
committed a mortal sin." Frere accepts the task of burning the
whole edition and asks Rossetti to send at the same time a note of
outstanding expenses. On 27 September 1840, Rossetti writes
that Lyell has paid up to page 1292. The rest, about 450 pages,
" (with confusion I tell you and at the same time with gratitude)
awaits your spontaneous generosity. I think that this imprudence
of mine will cost you about £130." Frere sent £150, but in

[1] Writer of *Dante et la philosophie catholique au 14e siècle*, Paris,
1839, in which he declares that Rossetti had written " pour payer
l'hospitalité protestante."

August 1841 Rossetti writes that £35 are still owing. " Now I
have to confess to you that, ashamed at having to burden so much
generosity, I refrained from telling you that £35 odd remain to
clear off my printer's bill. . . . The cost of printing in England
is truly terrible. Mr. Lyell has paid £400, you £150, and still
there remains a little wound to be healed in the way indicated."
On 19 October he acknowledges the receipt of £35 12s., and the
financial part of the problem was settled. But that was not the
most painful subject of worry and contrivance. Rossetti was trying to play off one patron against the other. He was obliged to
accept Frere's assistance, and protested his desire to follow Frere's
advice ; but who shall blame him for wanting to save the fruit
of so many nightly vigils from utter destruction ? Lyell as usual
vacillates about it. On the last day of 1840, he writes to say that
he will not have the work dedicated to him. " I renounce the
dedication unalterably ; in deference to the aimable prejudices of
one whom I love and honour, and who would be made unhappy
by seeing my name prefixed to a work the early chapters of which
have left a very painful and indelible impression. Therefore, my
dear sir, press me no further." He insists that he has never said
it could be published with safety, and refuses to write to Frere
about it as Rossetti had requested. Nevertheless the next day,
not yet, of course, having received this letter from Lyell, Rossetti
was writing to Frere to say that Lyell had declared there was no
reason why he should not publish the work, and indeed had given
four reasons for doing so. To all these, however, he (Rossetti)
had opposed the peace of his conscience and refused to publish.
Again in January Lyell writes anxiously to say that he has never
sanctioned publication and that he has done with the question,
" though my interest in the author, the fate of the work, and the
subject, will not be less ardent till the twilight of the day when
your old friend C. L. has passed away." Frere's attitude remained
consistent ; he did not like the work, Rossetti had suggested burning it himself—so let the burning proceed. Rossetti's agitation
grew extreme. On one occasion he went to the post with a letter
to Lyell, forgot whether he had posted it or lost it, and had to write
another. He implores Lyell to write to Frere, supplies him with
reasons against burning which he might urge on Frere, sends the
same reasons to Frere himself. Copies, he says, have already gone
to the Continent ; interest will be awakened ; enquiries will be
made for more copies ; there will be none ; and then some printer

will reprint the work and multiply copies, and Rossetti will have no control over the process. A terrible prospect truly ! Lyell sympathises and sends a letter marked " Private," saying " The meditated destruction of the *Amor Platonico* is (between ourselves) most absurd. I protest against it, and claim a right to as many copies of the work as is equal to the proportion I have paid Messrs. R. and J. E. T. of their whole bill for printing the work, *unless* you approve the burning, *then* I may change my opinion—I will write my sentiments and wishes to your good friend Mr. Frere. . . . *I abhor burning*." This letter was immediately reported to Frere with the suggestion that the whole edition should be sent to Lyell instead of Frere, if Frere has no objection. Lyell meanwhile was as good as his word, rising from a sick-bed to send his protest to Frere. He writes that he is anxious about the work ; thinks few will read it, but the conclusion that must be drawn from it is hateful. It might close the doors of all the ladies' schools to Rossetti. " What then is to be done ? He is half distracted, and implores me to write to you, and entreat you to revoke the order which condemns his book to the flames. He pledges himself not to sell a copy in England . . . and as he has already sent nine copies to La Giovane Italia I give consent to his dividing the remainder between her and La jeune France." Frere by this time had heard enough of the matter, and the burning was postponed until Mrs. Rossetti, who no doubt had also heard enough of it, was in a position to undertake it herself. How many copies were left after that holocaust is uncertain. Rossetti must have distributed a number among friends in England and France ; he sent not less than twenty to Italy and two to Germany ; Lyell had fifty copies which in January of 1842 were lying still untouched on Messrs. Taylor's bookshelves, and which possibly remained there to be burnt with the rest of the edition. We may surmise that a considerable number of copies still exist in the unsuspecting world.

Meanwhile its author as a diversion was composing " a little poem on the cholera morbus," clutching vainly at a belated straw in December 1842 when he met a learned Church of England clergyman called Nolan, very erudite in the occult, who thought there was no reason why Rossetti should not publish his work in England. And in spite of his assurance to Frere that he would never again touch these dangerous matters, Rossetti was soon at work on his theories again. Lyell, contemplating a new edition of his Dante translations, had set him on to write a preliminary dissertation on Beatrice for it—was she real or allegorical? Lyell should have known by this time that no one was more unfitted to write preliminary dissertations to other people's books than Rossetti. What might have been expected happened. The dissertation soon extended to impossible lengths and a long correspondence ensued, at times almost acrimonious in tone, into details of which we must not now go. Lyell hesitates and changes his mind ; wants it in English, wants it in Italian ; wants the author's name to appear, then thinks it better not ; finds it too long, finds it unorthodox. Dante has already been so costly a hobby that he is somewhat ashamed of it. When Lyell eventually refuses to have the dissertation, Rossetti is furious. " You say that this fancy for Dante has made you spend too much money and that your friends are laughing at you about it. It is at least some comfort to me not to have to reproach myself with having induced you to do so. We are all instruments of fate here on earth, and perhaps I too may be fit matter for jokes ; for if you have spent much money, I for my part have spent much time, inviting the laughter of contemporaries for the sake of illuminating posterity. . . ." But he protests that his attitude has been misunderstood. " How can my intention of doing you a service be transformed into a hope of receiving help from you ? " Having escaped responsibility, Lyell remained on very friendly terms, and hopes that Rossetti will succeed in presenting his long-delayed treatise to the world, to " floor me and my theory that Beatrice was once as ' pretty a piece of virginity ' as Shakespeare's ' sweet Anne Page ' ; and that Dante, who was a staunch admirer of her and of Papacy, thought the very highest compliment he could pay to her memory was to paint her, in his *religious* poem, as a St. Thomas Acquinas in petticoats. This will be a pleasant little job for your next winter." So far had Lyell lapsed from his old enthusiastic acceptance of Rossetti's theories.

X

However, a new and more forthright ally was now at hand. The dedication of the ill-fated *Amor Platonico*, which could not be given to either Frere or Lyell, was eventually addressed to Seymour Kirkup, an artist resident in Italy, and known in England chiefly as having had a main hand in the discovery of the Giotto portrait of Dante in the Bargello at Florence. He was a friend of Trelawney, totally unconventional and free-thinking ; no polite patron with fears for his reputation, but a wild and intransigent disciple. It is pathetic to see him now descending like a bombshell into the decorous and timid correspondence of Lyell's old age. Up to 1843 all had gone well. Kirkup had written enthusiastic letters to Rossetti, had written about him to his friends as if of a Messiah. He had reported his discovery of the Dante portrait and had sent Rossetti a copy ; he had even sent one for Lyell. He had invited Rossetti to visit him in Tuscany, had asked his brother the surgeon to give the poet advice, and had interested Lord Vernon in the *Beatrice*. His references to Lyell are polite and friendly, as befits one disciple writing of another. Suddenly the whole relationship flares up. On 23 January 1844 Kirkup writes to say that the arrangements with Lord Vernon about the publication of the *Beatrice* are going forward satisfactorily. " Mr. Lyell will be delighted—as he says in his book that both friends and enemies are desirous to see it public. He is of course doubly so. He is both, very double ! A Scotch friend indeed—who runs with the hare and hunts with the hounds—I suspected him, though I could not make him out from your letter. But he has unmasked himself to me without intending to. *Ecco*.

" He wrote to me last June that his book would soon be out . . . and that he did not quite agree with you therein, but that it was written more to suit the taste of an accomplished and religious sister than that of the philosophers of the present day.

" Some time after, he wrote to Lord Vernon (who brought me the letter from Rome) that in opposing you he wrote what he *believed the truth*. These equivocal explanations first opened my eyes, and when the book came I read it very attentively, although I own it was so much time lost, as I did not discover one single new point of information to reward me for the fatigue and nuisance of all the cant and commonplace it contains.

" My indignation was roused then by a letter in which he mentioned with the greatest levity and vanity the jokes that passed between you and him about your surprise at anyone in the present enlightened age believing that Dante could be a Christian, etc.

" I wrote, however, very tenderly to him, for I remembered on my formerly pressing him to come and escape a winter in Florence, he had told me he was 75. The strongest expression that I used was that, as in his book he blew *hot and cold*, I should consider the chill came from his sister, and that it was to please her that he had ranged himself with all the bigots, your enemies etc etc. He took offence and unfortunately his memory is as feeble as the rest. He says my letter is indelicate and offensive, and asks what right I have to attribute anything to his sister. He goes on ' You may reply : the authority of Rossetti. It could only be he, and in mentioning the circumstances he has been guilty of an unpardonable breach of confidence and can hardly have told you as much as I will now. That religious sister whom you place in a category of Fools " *who think themselves models of piety for all mankind* " was in truth one of those *weak* people that in this age of reason believe in revelation, and was the immediate occasion of my composing that essay. She had read all the works of G. R. most carefully and saw their scope, and then wrote to me as follows. " By allowing the dedication to yourself the world has a right to suppose you espouse the opinions of the author, and they might be shown by Panizzi or any other enemy in a very small pamphlet to be such as you would be ashamed of, and the *Commedia* (according to G. R.) to be as revolting a parody as Hone's of our litany. Let me advise you therefore to guard against *a danger to yourself*, and to lose no time in warning G. R. not to provoke his enemy P., for it is in his power to close every school door and every private house against him as a teacher, and thus to deprive him of his bread." '

" What think you, dear Rossetti ? sending me such a defence ! I answered : ' By heaven, the enemy seems to have been in a panic ! and he would have been less dangerous after a good flagellation than after seeing friends slide away, and raise a hue and cry of atheism in a priest-ridden country against Foscolo . . . and la giovane Italia. If P. *can* shut doors, is it from affection that he forbears ? For shame ! an independent man afraid of the *danger to himself* of the world *supposing* his opinions are his friend's.'

" I wrote him a stinging answer, never forgetting his years, and never again mentioning his sister, whom he says is dead, and did not live to see *her* book come out. I ended my letter by letting him know that I was in public and private the declared enemy of priests and priestcraft and no friend of those that supported them. So I hope that the correspondence is closed.

" I reminded him of course of his being the first to mention his sister, as I certainly should not, and that you had not betrayed his confidence, as doubtless you had been duly bound down to keep the important secret of the lady's existence, and Rossetti is no traitor.

" I did not intend to have said a word to you on this subject, but I think it right you should know on what a *bending, booing* reed you rely. I told him : save me from my friends (I was going to say Scotch friends, but I spared him) I can guard myself from my enemies.

" On comparing his letters with his deeds, I determined on telling you all. They are of a piece with his refusing to print the *Beatrice*, after making you give so much time and perhaps weakening your eyesight and general health by the extra exertion. Add to that his holding your hand when you would have touched that scoundrel and then joining him in public and cajoling you in private. I may be wrong, but to me it all bears the stamp of contemptible dirtiness, and if he had been twenty years younger I would have told him so."

Rossetti's tone to his distressed old patron Lyell was at first patronising—" You shouldn't have answered him ; " then reproachful—" Why did you tell Kirkup that I was guilty of a gross indiscretion ? why wish to bring me into ill odour with respected friends, to whom I have always spoken of you with the greatest veneration ? " deeply pained and not in the least regretful. Kirkup returns to the attack in April with much about Lyell's cowardice and Scotch meanness. He has shown the world he is a recreant. " All his gold won't gild that pill—It is a nauseous one, and as dirty a compound as any Scotch old woman ever mixed up. He has found it out by this time—Qualms and gripes will follow."

Rossetti was blown along by these violent blasts and in July 1844 we find him writing to Frere a long series of complaints about Lyell, all based on Kirkup's letters. Lyell has attempted publicly to controvert his system ; urged him on to all his works and left him stranded half-way through the *Amor Platonico* ; asked for the *Beatrice* and then refused to print it ; asked for a list of things which could conceivably be said against the theory and then went and made a book out of them. " And why ? Because a sister urged him to, as he has confessed to Kirkup my friend. And since you have not written in reply to my last two letters, I fear he may have been writing to you too." A month later he writes it all over again in case Frere has not received the last. Frere probably suggested kinder explanations of Lyell's conduct than Rossetti was now cherishing, for the latter next writes to say that he is glad that his fears were unfounded, and that Lyell no doubt had his own reasons for what he has done, and it is not for him to say any more about it.

I

Kirkup was still talking about "that beast Panizzi," and Lyell's shiftiness and Frere's timidity in 1866. But by that time too much learning in the occult had driven him mad, or very nearly so. From a series of letters written to Rossetti's son William, it seems that Dante had begun to appear to him in person. "Did I tell you that Dante has lately drawn part of his own portrait and written his name under it to oblige me? He spells his name with two l's, Dante Allighieri, which is not the common way in Italy." It was a unique opportunity for settling the old vexed question once and for all. "I asked Dante if Beatrice was a Florentine lady—No.—Who was she?—*Era un'idea della mia testa.* . . . Dante's ghost confirms your father's opinion." About the same time, Kirkup asks William Michael to write a biography of his father for Dante's sake, since "my long intercourse (of twelve years) with Dante, and other mutual services, have made me feel a real friendship for him and other spirits." But thirty-five years were to elapse before Dante was to be gratified by the appearance of an English biography of his interpreter, and by that time even the most long-lived of the actors in those old quarrels had laid down their timid or their angry pens for ever.

XI

"Dante Alighieri was a sort of banshee in the Charlotte Street houses; his shriek audible even to familiarity, but the message of it not scrutinised." Such, according to William Michael, was the effect of Gabriele's researches upon the minds of his children; and even in after years, the discoveries so dear to his heart were not accepted by any of them.

Dante Gabriel is said by Watts Dunton to have called his father's theories "absolutely and hopelessly eccentric and worthless." For him the Beatrice of the *Vita Nuova* could be no other than a real woman and the beloved of Dante. In a note to his translation, occurring just after the introduction of the Lady of the Window, he states what he believes to lie "at the heart of all true Dantesque commentary; that is, the existence always of the actual events even where the allegorical superstructure has been raised by Dante himself." If this belief were true, his father's "devoted studies", as he calls them in the *Preface*, were a colossal waste of ink, paper, eyesight, and time; and indeed Dante Gabriel had no sympathy with them at all.

Maria was more respectful but not more ready to accept. Her

book *A Shadow of Dante* is dedicated to her father's memory ; its introduction records her indebtedness to " my late dear Father ; " and there are a few references to him in the notes. But on page 18 she remarks, " The Beatrice of Dante remains to this day the perplexity of scholars and commentators, some regarding her as a personage from first to last purely allegorical. I adopt the view of Boccaccio and the majority."

As for Christina it may be doubted whether she had ever read any of her father's work on the subject. She had in any case less concern with Dante than the others and shows no sign of interest in problems of interpretation until almost at the end of her life. In a magazine article of 1884, she describes the *Comento* as being " to tyros a clew and to fellow experts a theory." But as for hidden lore, such a field is not for her or for her readers—" at least not for them through any help of mine : to me it is and must remain dim and unexplored, even as that *selva oscura* (dark wood) with which the cantica of the *Hell* opens." Certainly she could not have read much of her father's work, since in 1892 she innocently asks William, " Does anyone dispute the *existence* of Beatrice Bardi, *nata* Portinari ? "

William Michael on the other hand had probably read more of his father's writings than any man before or since. But he was gifted, or afflicted, with a chronically open mind, and whenever he discusses his father's work it is with the careful and judicious weighing of possibilities which marks all his writing. In his translation of the *Inferno* he does not enter into any discussion at all. There are one or two references to the *Comento* in the notes, but he does not feel called upon here to speak of theories and inter- pretations. " To take him [Dante] literally is enough and more than enough for most men." Later when the passage of time and the deaths of his relatives had brought him to the sad duty of biography, he was obliged to speak more fully on the subject. He now says in effect that his father's theories were subtle and ingenious, but that he had carried them too far. Panizzi's attacks seemed to him not surprising in view of the extreme nature of Gabriele's theories. One may surmise that working over his father's manuscripts and correspondence for the purpose of the translation of the *Autobiography* published in 1901, he was led to think further over the problems which had bemused his father for so many years. In 1910 he published a study of the *Convito*, " inscribed to the memory of my father Gabriele Rossetti, bold and often helpful as a commentator." It is an attempt to bring the Philosophy of the *Convito* into line with the *Vita Nuova*; but although it discusses many points which throw doubt on the objective existence of Beatrice, and although the evidence of Perez, who thought Beatrice was simply the Active Intelligence of the schoolmen, is brought into consideration, the treatment is tentative and inconclusive. William's mind retained then in 1910 the same openness on the subject as it had shown long ago in Pre-Raphaelite days, when he made a list of the pros and cons which could support or discredit the physical existence of Beatrice, and refrained from deciding between them.

Thus the impression that Rossetti the commentator made upon his family differs little from the impression he made upon the world at large; except that there is lacking that element of enthusiasm that in small but ardent circles he awakened outside. But this could hardly be expected among those who from remotest childhood had been alternately overawed and amused by their father's absorption in his theme.

XII

It remains only to point out that the world has not yet heard the last of the Rossetti system of interpretation. It was revived in various forms throughout the nineteenth century; and has found an energetic exponent in recent years in Luigi Valli, whose death in 1931 was as unexpected as it was regretted. In his book *Il Linguaggio Segreto di Dante* and its sequel he re-presents Rossetti's theories with modern improvements and with a more scientific and economic method of exposition. He has made many converts in Italy and some inevitably in Germany; but none among the recognised Dante scholars, who seclude themselves in dignified silence, not thinking the trouble of replying to be justified by the occasion. We must leave any comment on the matter to those more fitted to offer it; noticing however in passing that to Rossetti's fame as a patriotic poet, as an Italian nonconformist, as the father of Dante Gabriel and Christina, in all of which he has long had his admirers, we must still add also his fame as a Dante commentator. It has lasted against all probability and without any support from his reputation in other capacities for a full hundred years.

CHAPTER SIX

CHARLOTTE STREET AND HOLMER GREEN

I

WHILE Rossetti was engaged on his sensational discoveries concerning Dante and the universal religion, and discussing them in hundreds of long and excited letters, while evening after evening his home in Charlotte Street was invaded by his picturesque and emotional Italian friends, his children were steadily growing up in the quietest and most unsensational way. There are no startling events to record. We are faced by a long chronicle of small and perhaps at first sight trivial things, which are nevertheless interesting, and sometimes significant. The one event which materially affected the life of the family was the weakening of Gabriele's sight, almost to the point of blindness, so that his habitual exaggeration naturally leads him to describe himself as actually blind. His sight had once been exceptionally good, but intense study gradually destroyed it, as it did Milton's with whom he likes to compare himself.[1] Susan Frere expressed some anxiety about his eyes soon after he came to England, and by May 1832 he had begun to see so imperfectly that he bought himself a cheap pair of spectacles, with which he was greatly delighted. " When you return ", he writes to his wife, " you will certainly take me for a president. I will not tell you how much they cost, because you would immediately conclude that my spectacles were bad, and they serve their purpose wonderfully well. . . ." The cheap spectacles probably made things worse. Rossetti had more trouble in 1833, and although the defect did not become grave for more than ten years after this, it must have been a constant cause of anxiety and was eventually to bring about his retirement from King's College and to throw the burden of

---

[1] The disease was the same—amaurosis.

supporting the family mainly upon Mrs. Rossetti and William Michael.

Otherwise affairs followed their normal course. Lessons increase or fall off ; pupils keep sending notes of excuse " with that hateful ' I am very sorry ' " ; wife and children go off to the country leaving Rossetti to work with more concentration, but also to lament their absence. On one such occasion the house is decorated all through to the great delight of Fitch their formidable domestic, who keeps coming and telling Gabriele things he does not understand at all. Meanwhile the sovereigns in the box go up from 115 to 132, and to 151, and the relieved begetter of so much wealth can now regard his children, as he says, with less terror. Maria is beginning to add to her mother's letters little messages in her own writing ; Christina at the other end of the list begins to show signs of fretfulness and unrest. " I am sorry to hear that that angelic little demon of a Christina is so fractious and miserable ; but perhaps when her health is better she will get less restless." It was never destined to get much better. The child is mother of the woman, and this remark about Christina at the age of two and a half is a comment upon her whole life.

A winter visit of Mrs. Rossetti to Holmer Green in January 1834, leaving the children at home, produced the following interesting epistle. It gives a lively impression of the grand descents of Harriet Pearce into the young Rossettis' family life and of the children themselves ; incidentally it serves as an example of the microscopic neatness of Gabriele's writing.

13 *January* 1834.

Dear Francesca,

Everything is going well here : the children are in very good health and good temper. After you left I took Maria and Gabriel to the café to give them the cakes they had asked for, and then took them home. On the way they were delighted at meeting a steam carriage and a squadron of life guards. Maria liked the steam carriage best, and Gabriel the soldiers. William and Christina, when we got back, had their share of the cakes. From then onwards they have been happy all the time, and though they mention you now and again, and speak with pleasure of your return, I haven't seen them at all upset [at your absence] as I feared they were bound to be. I am pleased at that in one way, not at all in another. How quickly children cease to miss even

My dear Madame,

Gabriel William & Robert
Christina, write their
And present their best
Respects to your Grand=
mama and tell her I shall
tell you the things
they arrive
rest in the Case and

REDUCED FACSIMILE OF A LETTER FROM GABRIELE ROSSETTI AND HIS DAUGHTER, MARIA, TO MRS. ROSSETTI, 13 JANUARY 1834

the people they most love ! Mary does her utmost to keep them cheerful and peaceful and to take care of them in every way. On Sunday morning, about half-past ten, your good aunt came in a carriage to see them, concerned at their being left without their mother's care. Coming in, she first found Christina in the parlour (the others were upstairs being dressed by Mary) ; and she thought that Christina was Gabriel. But then when Gabriel, properly dressed, came down in all his radiant beauty (and that morning he was truly dazzling) she was doubly amazed, as she kept on saying, that Christina had grown so much, and that Gabriel was still more beautiful than she had thought him before. . . . A third thing impressed her pleasurably as well ; that is that Maria's appearance had improved a good deal ; and at the mixture of amazement and satisfaction she betrayed, I judged how hideous she must have thought that poor child before. She asked in great detail about many things and especially about Gabriel's foot, declaring that we had done well to put him under the observation of a surgeon of the first standing and to have it attended to at once, for otherwise the boy might have been lame all his life, or so she thought.[1] She stayed about half an hour, and then on going gave them each a bright shilling, at the sight of which they raised a chorus of rejoicing and thanked their great-aunt in their innocent way. I assure you that they behaved very well indeed in her presence. On Saturday evening Henry sent a note asking me to go and help him eat some turkey (the one that was to have been sent to Holmer Green but which, it was thought, couldn't risk any longer delay without seriously jeopardising its eatability— May Polidori get the Crusca to excuse me for that word.) I went at about nine in the evening, finding there also Mr. Boyley who seemed to me a very worthy man. On Sunday a servant brought me a reply from Panizzi. I had written him a very short letter in merely polite terms to thank him for having got me the lesson with the Misses Lock ; and now he overwhelms me with courteous expressions saying that I owed that lesson not to him but to my own reputation ; and that if anyone were to return thanks about it, it should be Mrs. Lock to him for having procured so good a teacher for her daughter's studies in our language and literature. I will give you his letter to read. . . . I have expressed my wonder to Signor Rolandi at politeness so marked and so little

---

[1] In November, 1833, Dante Gabriel twisted an ankle badly enough to keep him on a couch for six weeks.

in accord with Panizzi's earlier behaviour toward me, and Rolandi has told me that recently Panizzi has spoken of me with great respect, calling me a great man of letters and a true gentleman. This metamorphosis is very curious and I don't know what to put it down to. Maria has read the letter you sent her with delight ; she sat down with it and called all the little family around her. She had already written this letter when she received yours ; and to supplement her excessively laconic epistle, it occurred to me to insert between the enormous lines of her letter the microscopic lines of mine.

Although I thought it was a good idea for you to make the return journey in your father's company, I don't at all approve of your staying more than a week. So I am certainly expecting to see you on Friday at latest. I don't need to remind you that you have left your four poor children here. It is late and I must close this letter and post it. A thousand good wishes to Polidori and sincerest good wishes to your mother—you know how much I am concerned about her health. Give my compliments, and the children's, to Robert and Eliza, and believe me,

Your affectionate husband,
G. ROSSETTI.[1]

Towards the end of the year Rossetti seems to have been in poor health. He had bronchitis, and his eyesight troubled him. Kirkup the surgeon had been called in. In addition, he suffered agonies from his old enemy, the gout. For nine days, he says, " I have measured with terrified eyes the space between my study and my bedroom, and every time I have set out on that seemingly interminable journey, I have found it a very road to Calvary : every step was a scourging, a crown of thorns, and when at last I have reached my bed, the night has been a crucifixion." He eventually got the better of his old enemy in 1836 by giving up beer.

In 1835 there is little to record. Maria, the most precocious of the children, had evidently begun to produce verses—Ferretti

---

[1] See facsimile. Transcription of Maria's copperplate letter is unnecessary. *Mary* was probably a nursemaid ; W. M. R. says that they had one in very early years (*Reminiscences*, I. p. 9). The children always called Harriet Pearce *Granny*, hence the term in Maria's letter. The pencil marks on this letter are W. M. R.'s, who at one time had some intention of publishing it.

sends his respects to her from Rome, " *Bacia per me la tua figlia poetessa.*" [Give your poet-daughter a kiss from me.] Gabriel, like Christina, was showing increasing signs of independence, so that Lyell hopes that his godson " has ceased to be rebellious when turned out of the drawing room." All the children were taken to see the portrait of their father done for Lyell by Wright, and all demonstrated its excellence by saying *Papa !* at once. But perhaps the chief event of the year was the death of Deagostini who left Polidori £220 a year, thus enabling him to retire and rest in the country. "Poor old man," says Rossetti, " he badly needed a rest." (The full incongruity of this remark appears nearly twenty years later, when Gabriele, afflicted and almost blind, was to comment wistfully on his father-in-law's spirits and energy.) Deagostini's legacy seems to have had a reversionary interest for Rossetti himself. After telling Lyell about it he goes on, " At the death of Polidori a thousand pounds will come to me by Deagostini's will, and my wife will have about two thousand from her mother. So that if when I am old I retire to some corner of the continent, I shall still have a piece of bread to put on my table." However, the two old Polidoris lived on to 1853, when Rossetti was himself too ill to enjoy whatever worldly wealth they then relinquished.

II

1836 was an anxious and comparatively eventful year for the Rossetti family. To begin with they moved from 38 to 50 Charlotte Street. "The new house", Gabriele writes to Lyell, " is not far from the old one, and is bigger and more comfortable ; but who can tell you all the inconveniences and annoyances and expenses I have been put to in this change of abode ? Enough to drive anyone to madness and despair ; uprooting so many little things, transporting them, setting them up in their new places, big and little and medium and tiny, the accumulation of ten years, mending broken things and providing new ones either useful or necessary. . . . But I was obliged to make this change ; my family has got to such a stage that it is necessary at all costs to separate the boys from the girls, and in the old house we couldn't do so." 38 Charlotte Street looks big enough from the outside view to have held them all comfortably, but apparently was less capacious than it looks. No. 50 was a good deal bigger, having two rooms on the ground floor (the front one constantly used by the whole family), two on the first floor, five or six bedrooms on the second and third, besides a kitchen in the basement. The front windows looked across Charlotte Street at a quiet public-house, the back windows into a small yard.

A worse disturbance than moving house was immediately to fill Gabriele with grave anxiety. Mrs. Rossetti was ill. The letter quoted above goes on, " On top of this serious disturbance comes another of the gravest kind which makes me very unhappy and the future terrible to contemplate, unless Providence takes pity on me. Dear friend, my wife has become unrecognisable—nothing but skin and bone. Everybody is astonished and troubled about it, and her relatives share with me the most well-founded fears. She had begun to lose flesh when I hurt my head badly, and it took a long time to get better ; and then came the dangerous illness of my son,[1] and then the disagreeable inconveniences of the removal, all helping to hasten on that dangerous tendency. The worst of it is that no doctor can discover or guess the cause of it. . . ." She has gone off into the country and will stay till she is better. " God bring that to pass, but I am in great fear . . . unhappy I if such a disaster were to befall me." She was at Holmer Green for a good deal of that year and gradually improved in health. Frere sent £50 as soon as he heard the news of her illness, while Lyell sent three dozen bottles of port and sherry ; whereupon Rossetti, who had called Holmer Green " Epidaurus, famous abode of Aesculapius ", transfers these epithets to Scotland and Lyell. The latter's letter on the subject is a good illustration of his friend-liness and rather laborious humour. " I can answer for the satisfaction of her new physician in having hit her taste in what he has recommended, and can assure her he is a man who wishes for no fee nor reward, nor even thanks, but merely the pleasure of thinking he has been instrumental to her recovery. The efficacy of the prescription depends much upon the goodness of the drugs, and the two that he has sent are of the very best quality. Whether the red or the white is preferable in her case, doctors differ as much almost as your Bianchi and Neri . . . but all the disciples of Dr. Jephson of Leamington (the most popular ladies' physician in Britain) advocate the superior virtues of the white, or Spanish Elixir, vulgarly called sherry. Dr. Jephson's uniform advice is this (in cases of debility and a weak stomach), ' avoid

---

[1] William. " Before the close of September 1835, I had a dangerous gastric illness." (*Memoir* of D. G. R., p. 59.)

soup, fish, and vegetables, but live generously, and take two glasses of rich brown old sherry.' Commend me to such a doctor. Upon the strength of this high authority Dr. Scott has ventured to offer Mrs. Rossetti the sherry without meaning to dispute with Dr. Bull in the least the great excellence, as a tonic, of old port. His maxim is that both may be loved—and taken,

> Che amar si può Bianco per diletto
> E'l Nero puossi amar per alto sperare.[1]

And he finds that to wash the one down with the other is so safe and pleasant that he recommends Mrs. Rossetti to try it whenever it is agreeable to her ; and has nothing further to advise, or add, but his hearty wishes for her perfect convalescence." One of the very few remaining letters of Mrs. Rossetti thanks Lyell for this present.

[13 *December* 1836]

My Dear Sir,

As Rossetti has left this space, I cannot refrain from repeating my thanks, though in a former letter he has expressed them so much more adequately, though not more sincerely than I can do, for your kind and handsome present, which cannot fail entirely to re-establish my health, already so considerably improved, that I scarcely look or feel like my former self. Assuring you that neither Rossetti nor myself can ever forget your delicate attention and extraordinary kindness,

> I remain, dear Sir,
> Yours truly obliged,
> Frances M. L. Rossetti.

This is not of much interest in itself ; but it forms a curious and characteristic contrast to Rossetti's own epistolary style.

Sometimes Mrs. Rossetti had two of the children with her at Holmer Green, sometimes she left them all in London, and she was so much away during the year that we have in her husband's letters a fuller account than usual of family affairs. The first spell is from early January to the middle of March, when a separation is made between the sheep and the goats, Dante Gabriel and Christina being with Mrs. Rossetti, William and Maria with their

[1] " For White may be loved out of delight, and the Black out of high hope." I cannot find the reference for this ; it cannot be an exact quotation since the second line is not metrical.

father in Charlotte Street. Here we begin to notice the first effects of budding genius. Maria and William in London are very good and quiet ; Gabriel and Christina at Holmer Green are entirely the reverse. " If you would like to exchange two storms for two calms, I would leave you William and Maria, and would take Gabriel and Christina back with me ", Rossetti writes to his wife in February. But no doubt the two storms had been taken to Holmer Green for the express purpose of leaving the writer of the *Amor Platonico* in peace.

" Everything here goes well," writes Gabriele on 16 January. " You wouldn't believe how good and quiet and lovable Maria and William are. Your substitute [1] never tires of praising them every day, and is always telling me that she has never seen children more docile, obedient, and peaceful. . . . Maria has taken it upon herself to record my lessons daily, and thinks she has risen to greater importance and dignity. I can't tell you how attentive and alert she is. In the morning before I go out she asks me about the lessons I have to give and immediately takes her pretty book and writes them down. . . . What a dear little interesting girl our Maria is ! She is like her mother in spirit, as she is like her father in face." Margaret, he says, is looking after them well, while Betsy the maid is giving satisfaction and has cooked an excellent veal pasty. " Write to me," he goes on, " don't keep anything whatever from me, either good or bad : I want to know the truth and nothing but the truth about you. For if the air of Holmer Green doesn't suit you, we will think of some seaside place if it seems better for you. I am ready to spend all I have, to sell all I have, to do indeed everything that in me lies to get back your precious health. It is the best thing I have in the world and I am ready to sacrifice everything for it. If ever (Heaven prevent it) you feel worse, write to me at once and I will come immediately to take you home, or wherever the doctors may advise. I never knew how much I loved you until now that you are not well ; you have never seemed so precious, so necessary to my existence, as you do now. I love above all your lovely soul, and ten years of possession and scrutiny have only shown me its worth more clearly. That morning you left, I felt as if my heart was torn from my bosom . . . but enough, don't let us speak of sorrows, I will speak only of my hopes and think only of the joy I shall have when I hear you are better and when I see you completely recovered."

[1] I.e. Aunt Margaret.

Meanwhile the children are absorbed in their own interests. William has coloured a lovely theatrical print that he intends to give to Gabriel, Maria has cut one out that she intends to gild for her mother. Their father promises to send Gabriel a packet full of them if he will write a letter. And in sending his wife some writing-paper, he suggests that she should give Gabriel some of it so that he can vent some of his energy in making those scrawlings of his, and so leave her in peace at least for some part of the day. Dante Gabriel's drawing at this time must have been very promising ; the sketch of a rocking-horse reproduced by Marillier was done two years earlier in 1834. What with writing and drawing and even composing verses, the two older children now seemed very elevated beings to William and Christina who could not yet read. Maria, as William says, was to the younger two " an inspiriting Muse in a pinafore (or as they called it pincloth) ", while Dante Gabriel was " a familiar spirit—familiar but fiery and not lightly to be rebelled against."

Margaret was now trying to teach William to read, but he goes on " very slowly," and although he never refuses, it is clear that it gives him a good deal of trouble. Unlike Gabriel, " who used to show his dislike for it with scornful resolution, [William] expresses his distaste sometimes with a yawn, sometimes in a weary voice, and sometimes even by crying." Rossetti fears that he will be a long time in learning and in that resembles himself ; but it is high time he learnt, he is getting a big boy now. And once he has overcome the initial difficulties he will go on joyfully in double quick time. Christina is also learning from her mother. Rossetti hopes that she is not having so much difficulty as William—" I think she is better gifted than he is to overcome the initial difficulties." Dante Gabriel at this time was well advanced. He " does nothing but read ; this is his greatest passion, the second is for drawing. He knows many passages of Shakespeare by heart and recites them with spirit. He devours a volume with more appetite and perhaps more quickly than I do myself." And on his return from Holmer Green in March, he began to learn Latin " with attention and pleasure." The backward William caught his brother's enthusiasm for Shakespeare, and could also be heard declaiming passages from that poet, but his father reports that " he is more inclined to arithmetic and, young as he is, knows more about it than I do at my age."

One of Rossetti's letters, 20 January 1836, gives us an amusing glimpse of Maria. He had taken her to a café with William, where they sat eating some cakes he had bought them, while he himself was reading the paper at a little distance from them. In came Count Pepoli, and after a polite phrase or two to Gabriele, his eye fell on Maria, who noticed it and blushed. Pepoli, not knowing that she was Rossetti's daughter, said in a low voice, " Look what an Italian face that girl has ! and what perfect and unusual beauty ! " To further extravagant remarks Rossetti replied that it was enough for him if there was nothing wrong with her, and that he hoped she would be good. When Pepoli knew that she was his daughter, he broke out into wild congratulations—she was the *bello ideale*, she resembled the Fornarina of Raphael, etc. He was now talking so loudly that Maria heard him, and on leaving the café she said to her father, " Papa, I don't believe what that gentleman said. Christina is much prettier than I, everybody says so." Poor Maria. Rossetti told her that she was right and that the Count was not wrong ; but William himself in later years added a note to this letter to the effect that Maria could not be termed either pretty or beautiful at any period of life. That her appearance was Italian, the most so of them all, is, however, true. Rossetti used to say that she took after the Pietrocola side of the family.

" Poor William ", says Rossetti on the same occasion, " could not attract as much as one look from this enraptured admirer of Maria. And yet the boy has regular features, a gentle appearance, and very pleasant manners."

Admired or not, they were both behaving so wonderfully well that their father was quite touched at the spectacle. " If only the other two who are with you were the same! but it is foolish to hope for long calm on the sea. Polidori tells me that not seldom they quarrel and fight and cry and yell at each other."

III

The quiet uneventfulness of our poet's life at this time may be gauged by the disturbance he felt at the sad lapse of Betsy the maid. This is a trivial episode but in its way as interesting as revolutions. Betsy was Irish, the maker of delicious potato puffs she had recently been well reported on by Rossetti, and, as we have seen, her veal pasty commended by Rossetti. But on 2: January Polidori received a short note from Rossetti marked " *Read this alone*," telling him that Betsy has been observed on two or three occasions to let a policeman into the house—a six in the morning. This morning she admitted two! What is to be done? Francesca mustn't be told. Ought the police to be called in? "How much we have done for the minx! Medicines, medicaments, another servant to help her with her duties; and this is the way she rewards us." Polidori apparently came to the poet's help in the terrible dilemma, and a few days later a full report was sent to Mrs. Rossetti, from which it appears that Betsy's injured innocence and Irish ways nearly won the day, and were only defeated by the abiding presence of Francesca's high standard of respectability and decorum. The policeman was Irish; Betsy knew him and his wife. He came first to give a message from his wife, and then the next day to get an answer[!] Rossetti thinks her defence very just. The second policeman was invited so as to avoid suspicion of ill conduct. The workmen who had given her away were bad men who had threatened to ruin her, and if she had given them a pot of beer as they demanded she would never have suffered this disgrace. " She weeps and laments herself enough to touch the heart, and to tell the truth she affects me greatly. In a word, dear Francesca, I have grave doubts about the reality of her offence. . . . We shall have to send her off to justify ourselves in the eyes of the world, but in sending her off we ought to pity and not disgrace her. If you had only seen her at the moment when, in the presence of Mr. Marshall and Polidori, I directly accused her of her misdemeanour! She trembled and wept, got confused in her words, seemed more indignant than humiliated: in the midst of her weeping she had a smile of indignation on her lips which revealed to expert eyes an exasperated innocence. If on further investigation we discover anything to justify her, we shall be obliged in conscience not to abandon her, and perhaps after some time to have her back again. She keeps on saying that if only her mistress were here, she would know her to be innocent.

" I advise you not to be misled by the studied submissiveness of that Fitch; perhaps for some time she will succeed in repressing that hateful bad-tempered character of hers; but be assured (and you ought to know her well enough) that her natural self will get the upper hand again, and you will have the same insulting behaviour from her which has so much distressed you before. Even though we shouldn't think of going on with Betsy (and perhaps that is our right course), we ought to look out for something quite different from Fitch. What use to us is her honesty, when it is always

accompanied by insolence ? Honesty is essential, but not everything ; something more is needed to make a good servant." **Mrs.**
Rossetti should write to Charlotte and say what there is to be said
for Betsy, for it would be a very ill thing if her sister were to lose
her place as well ; he would be very sorry indeed if this unfortunate
affair were to take the bread from both of them. " Poor luckless
creatures ! " Betsy is getting her things ready to go ; Rossetti
and Polidori have both given her ten shillings.

It would be interesting to know the ultimate fate of this Betsy,
who so touched the soft hearts of the two Italians with her very
improbable story. It may be presumed that her exile was permanent. The hateful Fitch was certainly installed soon after, for
in October Rossetti writes ". . . I hear a noise on the stairs like
windows being broken. . . . *Pazienza !* it's Fitch, at it again.
She has broken one of the four windows in the door that leads
to the yard. Good-bye three shillings."

IV

By the end of August 1836, Mrs. Rossetti was away again, leaving
all the children in London, storms as well as calms. A letter written
at this time offers evidence about the children's knowledge of
Italian. Their father, it is said, used to address them in Italian
and was answered by them in the same language ; but if that
were always so, it is surprising that he should here comment on
their ability to understand a letter in that language. " At the
postman's well-known knock the three children ran shouting with
joy, and crowded round me to hear what their dear Mother had
to say. Incredible and yet true. I read your letter with them about
me hanging upon every word . . . although it was in Italian they
understood it, and afterwards gave an account of it in English."

Christina now begins to appear in a less fretful character. Indeed
" she hasn't shed a tear since you left, and you know that when
you were here, you could have filled little bottles with the tears
she used to shed." Aunt Margaret for her part reports that
" Christina has taken Maria's place in performing the office of
dressing me, which she does not do amiss for so young a tyro in
the art. I fancy she feels no small degree of awe, whilst in the act
of hooking her Aunt, and her Aunt is obliged to stand like patience
upon a monument." She can now read moderately well. Rossetti
promised her a red book as a reward for her application and
progress ; " it has to be red because she wishes it so. What a

curious girl!'' Maria continues to show prowess in the writing of letters, and her father asks for them to be in Italian to keep her in practice with the language of "the beautiful land". "Tell Maria that her letter was as welcome as a bill of exchange. She is the true brilliant among the four gems of our crown." William is given a six-volume Shakespeare on his birthday, an old edition with illustrations and rather well bound—it was promised to him a year ago when he began to learn to read. The oldest of these children is now nine, the youngest not yet six; yet here they are writing letters, reading and declaiming Shakespeare, and collecting prints, their literary and artistic bent determined from the start.

On 24 September Rossetti sends his wife some wine and a German sausage, or at least part of one. "I was assured by the man in the shop that it was of the best quality, and to make sure I have tried a little and find that he told the truth. Gabriel, who is beginning to be a meat-eater,[1] and William and Christina who were so already, have decided that it is good. Margaret has confirmed the judgment and Sangiovanni has sealed it with his authority. Nevertheless I say (and I too have a discerning palate) that it is not so good as the one that German bookseller gave us." With such aids, and after swallowing "half a shopful of medicine," Mrs. Rossetti grows better, and the time of her return approaches. They are counting the days, Christina more assiduously than anyone else. They are going to meet her at the coach-house and bring her home in triumph, "outbidding the most pompous ovations of ancient Rome. . . . Oh that I had two arms as long as from here to Holmer Green! . . . you would then be gently seized and deposited in Charlotte Street, saving you the trouble of the journey by road." And at the beginning of November Rossetti can report to Lyell that she is back, quite recovered.

Only at such abnormal times as these, and perhaps but little even then, had Rossetti anything to do with the children's education. His activities with them were confined to offering rewards, encouraging them by the presents of books, admonishing them when necessary, sometimes taking them for a walk, occasionally taking them on his knee and doing *Pat-a-cake* or singing them some Italian rhyme, bringing them home the sweets his wife so strongly deprecated. He thought whatever a child liked was good for it.

[1] W. M. R. in *Memoir* of D. G. R., p. 42, remarks that Dante Gabriel would scarcely touch meat until turned of eight years.

Indirectly his own recitations of verse to the friends who called will have had something to do with the boys' declamations of Shakespeare. He was undoubtedly a kind good-natured father, proud of his children, taking an interest in them in his spare moments, and allowing them to romp around him while he was at work. But he was teaching nearly all day, and often came home very tired to his dinner ; after which he had a habit of lying stretched out on the hearth-rug before the fire, falling asleep there for an hour or two and snoring vigorously. Later on there were his guests to talk with, or Ahriman called him to his beloved *libri mistici*.

The process of education therefore fell mostly to Mrs. Rossetti's part ; the girls indeed had no other education at all. Naturally it was of a limited nature, mainly religious and literary. She was an adept in the telling of stories, which must have been a valuable gift in their early years and was remembered gratefully by Christina when writing *Speaking Likenesses*. Discipline was enforced by affection rather than by violence ; of corporal punishment there was next to nothing. The two most gifted members of the family suffered in some degree from the gentle austerity of their training, and the dominance over them of their mother's personality, Christina's strongly suppressed nature and Dante Gabriel's confused instincts showing clear signs of it ; the other two, less strongly individual in bent, took the stamp more easily and were gainers by it in most ways ; all of them no doubt would be said by the modern psychologist to have been affected by a pronounced " mother fixation ".

There were plenty of relaxations of course, and any suggestion of gloom in the household atmosphere would be very wide of the mark. Both Rossetti and his wife were cheerful by nature, and the children delighted in each other's company. Dante Gabriel and William were inseparable companions until the former started upon his career as painter ; they shared a bed in childhood, they went to school together, collected prints and read books together, Gabriel always taking the lead in their pursuits—William late in life confesses that had it not been for his brother he " might never have attempted anything in the nature of literature, art criticism, and the like." This ascendancy was at its most marked in childhood, when two years make a world of difference. Nearness of age tended at the same time to throw Christina and William together in sympathy, and many traces of this are left in Christina's letters ; she seems to have loved her younger brother best in later life too, although he had nothing to say to her on the subjects she most liked to contemplate. As for Gabriel, she understood some aspects of his character better than William did, and the link of genius brought understanding between them, but Gabriel was bohemian and incalculable, whereas the steady and reliable William was perpetually at hand, a pillar of help and strength.

The Rossettis saw little of other children and felt little need to do so. They would in any case have been lucky if they could have found other children to share their tastes. Outdoor games were little indulged in, but they went for walks in Regent's Park,[1] with Mrs. Rossetti, or their father, or Aunt Margaret, sometimes getting as far as Primrose Hill. Indoors, besides their literary and artistic occupations, there were the usual childish diversions—tops and a rocking horse, ninepins, blindman's buff and puss in the corner (these last no doubt on particularly festive occasions). Later there was the simpler kind of card game, such as *Beggar my Neighbour*. Their mother played these with the children, but never for any kind of stakes. Gambling in any form was abhorrent to her Puritan mind, and all the more no doubt because of its connection with her brother's untimely death. The aversion persisted in all the children. Gabriele never played cards, but he liked chess and taught the children ; this is never mentioned in later days, and it is difficult to imagine that any of them except William ever took much interest in it.

Music was of all the arts the worst represented. The Rossettis, as we have seen, occasionally went to an opera, but nobody at home was proficient in any form of musical expression. Gabriele had a pleasant tenor voice when he chose to use it ; Mrs. Rossetti for her part used to play the piano, after a fashion. Her favourite piece was *The Battle of Prague*, one of the more memorable effects of which was the groans of the dying. She also sang to the children occasionally. Here again early years shape the later—none of the Rossettis seem to have had any special liking for music, Dante

---

[1] Regent's Park was first opened to the public in 1834. In 1830 it abounded with " hares, pheasants, partridges, and various kinds of wild fowl, all of which are being vigilantly preserved by the keepers, who are on the watch night and day. Last year the Commissioner of Woods and Forests, accompanied by members of the Government, were very successful in their shooti.. of partridges there on September 1." (*Evening Standard*, 13 September 1830.)

Gabriel practically none at all, in spite of the quantities of odd musical instruments which he owned at Tudor House and painted in his pictures.

Curiously enough a casual visitor might have supposed that the art of painting was hardly less likely to find a representative in 50 Charlotte Street. The pictures were few and uninteresting—two views by Smargiassi the Vastese painter and a friend of Rossetti's, *The Marriage Feast of Tobias* in oils, thought by its donor to be a Veronese, a self portrait of Wright of Derby, and to crown all, an engraving of Queen Victoria in her opera box, the gift of Harriet Pearce. It was understood, however, from very early years that Gabriel was going to be a painter and his sketching was encouraged by his father who had himself some skill in the art ; but his inspiration in his earliest efforts was literary, and literary it remained to the end. For the one art which was cultivated and understood by all members of the family was that of literature.

Of his promising young brood, Gabriele was inordinately proud. " Princes," he says grandly, " ye have persecuted me in vain ! "

VI

We have paused at the end of 1836 to take stock of the situation, because the next year is one of the turning-points in the history of the family. It is the point at which the development of the boys began definitely to diverge from that of the girls ; the point at which influences quite other than those of the home began to shape the minds of Gabriel and William. At the beginning of 1837 they started going to school together—" with transport " as Rossetti tells Lyell. " They study Latin as if it were a fairy tale." They went first to a small school kept by a Rev. Mr. Paul, and after the summer holidays to King's College School ; Rossetti as professor had the privilege of sending one son without payment of fees, and the other at a reduced charge. William was the youngest pupil in the school.

There is no need to repeat the information given by William in the *Memoir* of his brother about their school experiences, but we may quote what he says about the general effect on their minds. " It would be too true to acknowledge that Dante Gabriel rapidly deteriorated here. I would add the same very emphatically of myself. . . . At home he had witnessed nothing but resolute and cheerful performance of duty, and heard nothing that was not pure, right, highminded and looking to loftier things. School first brought him face to face with what is common and unclean. . . . His regard for veracity, the strictness of his sense of honour, his readiness to brave inconvenience for principle, were subject to daily undermining ; for the moral atmosphere around reeked too perceptibly of unveracity, slipperiness, and shirking." Dante Gabriel's experience was probably little different from that of other sensitive and well-trained children since schools began ; nevertheless the closer the seclusion and the refinement of home life, the greater must be the shock of contrast. In any case the harmful effects of school life on Dante Gabriel could only be commensurate with the failure of home principles to hold him. It seems probable that having felt the restraint of home to a degree beyond what William's more orderly nature would experience, his reaction when opportunity came would be proportionately noticeable. William, although he associates himself with the same process of deterioration, really suffered less ; the whole tenor of his later life may be said to have remained in keeping with his earliest training, except in the one matter of religious belief ; and even there his position was essentially little different from his father's.

Neither William nor Gabriel was particularly happy at school ; this could hardly be expected. They took no part in athletic exercises and had a considerable distaste for the rough-and-tumble side of school life. They made no intimate friends. The effect at first was to throw them more closely into the familiar seclusion of the family life and occupations ; while at the same time their minds were sending out independent shoots of their own in response to the new stimuli. In the case of Gabriel the conflict between self-will and duty, between the inbred idealism and the instinctive realism was already beginning, only to end with his death. His life one might say was a battle-ground over which his mother fought a long battle with the world, an indecisive engagement which left the field badly scarred and disfigured. He was at this time a very handsome child with auburn hair, bright and engaging in manner and a general favourite ; imperious and self-willed, but very good-natured and placable like his father. He seems to have been considered difficult from an early age and to have caused his parents considerable anxiety. The fiery Kirkup, however, did his best to allay parental fears : " Take care, my dear Friend, how you root up the *cattivo germe* [bad seed] which you complain of in your son. That *immerso tutto* [complete absorption] is the surest sign of genius. The rarest of all gifts in the present day." Kirkup was right. They could only let their difficult and promising son take his course, and hope that his wilfulness would eventually be justified.

VII

But the children as yet are still very young, and the chief causes of anxiety for the present are their childish complaints. A few days after the boys started going to school, the whole family went down with influenza, Gabriel getting a worse attack than the others. Three months later they have all got whopping-cough ; Christina this time most severely, vomiting blood for two days running. " The poor children ", says Rossetti, " are making a goat chorus [*armonia caprina*] of terrible coughing which touches my heart." By the end of May they were all a good deal better, and the two girls went off into the country.

Meanwhile it had been a good year for Rossetti. There had been so many private students that at times he had seven or eight lessons a day. On the other hand, he lost about £30 in a theft by an Irish carpenter called Mullins, for whom he seems to have been almost as sorry as he was for Betsy. He was very unwilling to proceed against the man, as appears from the following letter.

G. R. to Mr. Rawlinson, Police Magistrate.

6 *December* 1837.

Sir,

Having heard the account of Mullin's examination before you yesterday, I feel pity for him, and a disinclination to prosecute for the following reasons. His being an industrious man ; his having a respectable wife and four little children ; and a conviction I feel from his foolish confession and his having passed the notes so near his home and to persons well acquainted with him, that He [*sic*] is probably unaccustomed to crime. I am the more confirmed in this opinion from having heard from various persons who imployed [*sic*] him for many years that he was considered perfectly honest.

Begging you to excuse me for troubling you,

I remain Sir,

Your obedient servant,

GABRIEL ROSSETTI.

P.S.—I wish to add in Mullin's favour that he stole only a part, when he might have taken the whole of a larger sum.[1]

[1] This letter, of course, is in English.

But the appeal was in vain. The unlucky Mullins was prosecuted and sentenced to ten years' transportation. The terrible severity of the sentence must have troubled our humanitarian with four little children of his own ; but he had done his best to avoid it.

This loss of money was soon followed by others. Lessons in 1838 grew few. It was the coronation year, and the ladies, Rossetti told Lyell, were determined to have a year of diversion. One of them went abroad in March owing him £38 ; two schools went bankrupt, one owing him £50, the other £16. By the theft and other misfortunes he had lost more than £150 by the middle of June. Another school had collapsed by March of the next year, when Rossetti tells Frere that in three insolvencies he has lost upwards of £150. (Frere of course came to his help with his usual generosity.) What was worse, in August he was so ill that he thought he would not get better ; " if my last hour has come," he writes to Lyell, " *paratus sum*." Then the children began with scarlet fever, first the boys and then the girls. " My poor eldest daughter has had a cruel attack of it, very violent and dangerous. For two weeks she hovered between life and death ; during the third she was attacked by another affection, this time of the throat, which made it difficult to breathe or swallow." Only a few months elapsed before he was writing to Lyell, " Illness has entered my house again. After the scarlet fever which laid them all four low, and from which they had so happily recovered, measles has taken possession of them. The two boys are now quite better but the girls are much upset by it at present."

VIII

In the latter part of 1839, which we have now reached, the family lost its convalescent home at Holmer Green. The Polidori family had decided to transplant itself to London. Rossetti, delighted in the prospect of having Gaetano so close, set about the search for a house with great enthusiasm and perfect success. " Our children ", he writes to his wife, " will frequently be able to kiss their grandparents' hands." The house, or cottage, he has found is near the Regent's Park canal. There are four bedrooms, an attic, two receiving rooms, one up and one down, two kitchens, a beautiful little garden. The rent is £63 and both Janer and Sangiovanni approve. A day or two afterwards he has taken Margaret to see the cottage and likes it better than ever. " If you could only see how clean it is, how neat, what lovely rooms, what magnificent white marble mantlepieces, what fireplaces of polished steel! Our house is a sepulchre in comparison with it." There is a plentiful supply of water in the kitchen, bells in almost every room, and drains so good that the landlord says there are no better in the kingdom. The taxes are about £12 and the only drawback is the absence of a copper. This was on 25 August. By 5 September nothing has finally been settled, for on that day Gaetano writes to ask his wife if he should take the house. There is no coalshed, nor pantry, but there are plenty of coal merchants near at hand, and as for the pantry, she could make do with some kind of wooden cupboard outside in the garden. The situation would be sure to please her, " in front being the railway, at the back the canal with a wide sloping bank, and not far away the cavalry barracks, so that on one side you would sometimes see boats going to and fro and would hear from time to time the sound of the martial trumpet, and on the other you would see a train running preceded by a cloud of smoke, but too far away to reach your window. Between the house and the railway is the road which leads to the Zoological Gardens nearby. On both sides, and in the front, there are pretty little houses with plots of garden, trees, and shrubs, so that you could imagine yourself to be either in the town or the country." The kitchen is small it is true, but still tolerable, and " better a little kitchen and a deep purse than a little purse and a big kitchen." The attractions specified may not seem now so seductive as they did then; but Gaetano is evidently much in favour of taking the house, and since his wife never left her bedroom the deficiencies of kitchen and pantry were not likely to worry her. And naturally the more she could see from her window the better. The barracks were thought an especially desirable entertainment. Rossetti writes again to his wife, after another visit, that he has seen soldiers doing their drill there. " This will be a novel daily amusement for your mother, since she (according to Polidori who was much pleased with this martial spectacle) was born with a strong and warlike spirit; and if she had belonged to our sex, she would have achieved some kind of greatness, and perhaps history would already have consecrated some page to her deeds."

The house had no name; Maria was asked to consult her repertory of Greek lore and to find some " sonorous Hellenic vocable " to put on the wall. Polidori favoured the name of *Tuscan Cottage*. But whether anything was put up on the wall or not, the house in fact was always known as No. 15 Park Village East. It took about a quarter of an hour to walk there from Charlotte Street, no doubt longer for Mrs. Rossetti, who visited her parents almost every day, taking Maria and Christina, and frequently the two boys. Polidori's books were more attractive to young minds than Rossetti's, for among them were to be found The *Newgate Calendar*, Hone's *Every-Day Book*, *Legends of Terror*, and the like.

To contend with the difficulties of kitchen, pantry, and copper, Polidori installed a charwoman (called Eliza Catchpole) ; and in the back garden he set up his famous private printing-press, for which he had as assistant a Sicilian compositor called Privitera, who insisted on making soup of the garden snails, to Eliza's great disgust. Aunt Margaret subsequently joined her parents in the house, later Uncle Henry went to live there too ; and this Polidori centre became a place of great importance in the Rossetti family life.

About this time we have an opportunity of judging how far William (aged ten) had proceeded in the art of writing, from the following letter written to his mother at Holmer Green on 21 August 1839.

MY DEAR MAMMA,

I hope that Grandpapa's plan of settling in London will succeed, and that it will suit Grandmamma. If you please tell Maria that I have not begun the Greek verbs, as we are now in the substantives, and also that I have not seen any more of Flaxman's Illustrations of the *Iliad*. We have made a new volume of the Brigands as well as the dramatics. We have given them to Byers telling him to bind the former like " *Tales* " and the latter in calf.

Sept. 2nd.

Papa and Christina were nearly arrived at Hungerford Market, on their way to Richmond, when the former recollected that he had forgot the directions for finding out the house of Mrs. Jervis, and was obliged to return to get the paper where there are the particulars, and that he might not be too long was obliged to take a cab. When they were in the Steam Packet, it began to shower, and Papa to escape the rain went in a cabin where there were several people. Among whom there was a Gentleman and a Lady, who hearing Christina talk Italian to Papa began talking to Christina on several subjects. After arriving safely at Mrs. Jervis's house they had luncheon. A little time after Papa, Christina, Mrs. Jervis, and her family took a walk which both Chi. . . and Papa liked very much. Just when they had come to a turnpike it began to rain, they all began to run, in which Miss Jane and Miss Agnes took the lead Mrs. Jervis and Christina followed. Christina went into the Drawing Room where she conversed with Miss Florence. At 4 o'clock Christina took her tea. After which Sir Thomas and another Gentleman came. Papa came back in an Omnibus and arrived here after 10 o'clock. I have now no more to say, so

Believe me

Your affectionate Son,

WILLIAM MICHAEL.

This catalogue of events is not wildly exciting ; though it is interesting to know that at 4 o'clock Christina took her tea, and to notice the obvious feeling which runs through it that Christina was having an altogether distinguished time. She was apparently staying with the Jervis family. Maria had been there earlier and had made a great impression with her precocious learning. " I have heard from Polidori," writes Gabriele to his wife on 5 September, " that Maria has been reading with rapture a Greek tragedy by Euripides, translated into Italian, and the *Theogony* of Hesiod, and now intends to read the expedition of the Argonauts in search of the Golden Fleece. Bravo, bravo indeed ! Everybody is afraid that too much application may injure her health, but I have no such fear, for when voluntary application produces so much pleasure it cannot do any harm ; rather, it becomes food for the mind which in its turn does the body good. Mrs. Jervis herself mentioned her concern at it to me, and I made the same reply, with which she partly agreed. She told me that when Maria was with her she interpreted some print or picture . . . of a mythological kind, speaking of it with great knowledge and self-possession. Mr. Jervis was present on the occasion, and he, hearing that she had read Mr. Keightley's *Classical Mythology* several times, seemed astonished at it, since, knowing that book, he thought it to be above the intelligence of a child as young as Maria. Christina behaved with great discretion that day, but I don't know whether I shall go again with her on Sunday at eight. She wants to go and asks me to take her, but it seems to me a long way and besides it costs a good deal to get there ; for coming and going I spent seven shillings. And what is more I lost the whole day, and was unable to read or write a line. Probably I shall send a note of excuse. If I go, it will only be out of regard for the friendliness those good folk have for me and my family." Rossetti was very proud of Maria's prowess—she was undoubtedly the quickest and most assiduous of them all. " My two boys who go to King's College ", he writes this year to Lyell, " are making considerable progress in Latin and Greek, and in the other branches of instruction. But I am particularly pleased with my oldest girl Maria Francesca, who has been gifted by nature with a quite uncommon intelligence. She is a comfort to us and to all her relations. You cannot believe with what ardour she has set herself unaided to the study of Greek and what progress she has made in it." Lyell replied that if she had not already the prettiest of names, she ought to be called Corinna.

From this her last sojourn at Holmer Green Mrs. Rossetti returned in September, bringing flowers and an instalment of the Polidori household effects. " If it has occurred to you to gather a good bunch of marjoram from the hedge sides you will have answered my silent prayer," wrote Gabriele ; to which Aunt Margaret added, " If not too inconvenient, will you bring my Canary, if not, leave it alone."

IX

About this time Rossetti received two desperate appeals for help from his brother, the unfortunate barber of Vasto.[1] Gabriele was

[1] In earlier days Antonio had written a description of himself, which may be roughly represented as follows :

> Not tall, not little, my face offended
> With pock marks, nose not much extended ;
> Hair thick and black, the shoulders bending ;
> Luminous eyes, an open air,
> Cheeks ruddy in hue, mouth debonair ;
> A chin just covered with growing hair ;
> Sensitive heart ; in converse kind ;
> Not proud, not flattering, undesigning ;
> Deafish, faithful, humble in mind ;
> Born by the Adriatic's shores serene,
> An expert actor on village scene,
> Tragic and gay my parts have been ;
> Ever on fire with warmth Thebean ;
> No cultured poet but bard plebeian,
> For wicked fate was ever my foe ;
> A writer of masks desiring glory
> I am a barber and that's my story,
> A maker of wigs, O Reader, and glad to be so.
>   (See the original poem in the Appendix.)

a little ashamed of him, judging from a letter to Lyell in 1841 where Antonio is euphemistically described as a " doctor and poet, but an unhappy and unfortunate old man." Antonio had kept in touch with his brother, writing at considerable intervals. Probably he thought that so popular a poet as Gabriele, befriended by great men, author of works important enough to be proscribed by the Church, and professor in the University of London, was a good deal better provided with worldly goods than was actually the case. He had written in 1834 asking for news and assistance, and his miserable condition had been described to Rossetti in 1836 by the painter Smargiassi. " I found your brother very much aged, deaf and paralytic, and for that reason unable to go on exercising his profession. His son-in-law, D. Cesare Pietrocola, supports him as well as he can, for he himself is burdened with children, ten in number, six boys and four girls." Rossetti's other brother, Andrea, died at Christmas 1833—Antonio had looked after him for three years and three months and then buried him. His sister Maria Giuseppe had died in 1822, and her husband a few months after her, leaving three children whom poor Antonio had also helped as much as he could. " I tell you all this so that you may recognise the heroic heart of your worthy brother Don Antonio. He often exclaims, ' I declined to get married so as to avoid having to shoulder a heavy cross, and yet every kind of cross has been mine.' He congratulates you and wept with tenderness when he heard from me about your glorious position." Rossetti writes to Antonio in August 1838. Very painful circumstances have prevented an earlier reply ; he has lost much money in a theft and through the bankruptcy of debtors. " Would that I were what you think me. I have acquired no little fame, but very little money." He sends £10 (60 ducats) and hopes to do the same every year, but emphasises the word *hopes*. He has a wife and children ; and the day in which he spends as little as six ducats is a day of great economy.[1] He has heard with great grief of the family's woes. He himself has passed great perils but at present is fairly secure. He has a wife cultured and virtuous in the highest

---

[1] Rossetti himself supplies the equivalent 60 ducats for £10. According to this, six ducats were £1 ; so that if his expenses on " a day of great economy " came to that amount, his expenditure in a year must have been over £365. He was exaggerating. Generally his income was between £220 and £280. A year in which he could make £300 was considered good. (W. M. R., *Reminiscences*, I., p. 2.)

degree, in whom Antonio has an effective advocate, and four
children. At the end he says with a gesture of great generosity,
" I renounce in your favour every right to the olive garden, our
mother's wedding portion, and to anything else on which I may have
a claim. Would that I might give up something more valuable
to you, as I only too willingly would."

In August 1839 Antonio wrote again.

" MY KIND-HEARTED AND BELOVED BROTHER,

After the help you sent me, I wrote you two other letters, but
did not have a reply. I thanked you in them for your generosity
and said that if it had not been for your goodness I should have
died of hunger ; for my son-in-law fell ill in September of last
year and almost knocked at the gates of eternity ; his illness lasted
several months. Imagine a father with ten children and entirely
destitute—in such a state was this family. However, I am still
alive, my estimable and charitable brother. My indispositions are
very distressing and get worse day by day, all my discomforts
increase with advancing age, and I cannot live much longer. If
you could see what I am reduced to you would be obliged to weep
with compassion. . . . Send me more help for love of our worthy
and virtuous parents and on behalf of all our dead brothers and
sisters. . . . Through having a human heart, as you know, I am
among the number of the indigent, but I do not repent of what I
have done ; I would do it a thousand times again if Providence
gave me the means to relieve necessity like my own, and it grieves
me that I am no longer able to do so. Oh, what a comfort there
is in doing good to one's unfortunate neighbour." He proceeds
to send his greetings and kisses to the children and hopes they will
be a credit and consolation to Gabriele ; also to " your heroic
companion their mother. You told me that she is an effective
advocate with you . . . and in witness of my gratitude for her
kindness, I send her the following weak sonnet, and flatter myself
that it will give her real pleasure. Her name is unknown to me,
for although you told me all the names of your children, you did
not mention hers.

To the most virtuous Signora N. N.

SONNET.

Oh worthy sister, sensitive and kind,
My kinsman, thy dear husband, writes to me
That thou on my behalf didst speak thy mind ;
And here I thank thy heart's nobility.

For all the goodness thou to me designed
A heavenly guerdon thou wilt surely see.
A soul elect is in thy breast confined,
A heart like his that thou didst take to thee.
Without the timely succour that he gave,
Thanks to thy pity, my protectress dear,
I should have passed already to the grave!
Ah, in thy chaste caress remind him still
Of an old man both poor and full of fear,
A very Job, laden with every ill.

Another desperate appeal was sent on 23 October. Antonio transcribed again the sonnet to Mrs. Rossetti in case it should not have arrived, and adds this "extemporised *strambotto* addressed to your gentle sons, my dear nephews."

My little nephews and my nieces dear,
To your most worthy father often say,
" Dearest Papa, our wretched Uncle dies
Of hunger if you turn your face away.
O dear Papa, some help to him extend!
You in your bosom close a pitiful heart;
Dearest Papa, some kindness to him do.
He is our Uncle and your kinsman too."
If speaking often thus you take my part,
You of yourselves will help my fortunes mend;
Because, thus urged by you, his sympathy
Will find some way to succour and amend.
So with a kiss I leave you; may you be
Blest by just heaven itself for helping me.

"There," might Rossetti have said, on contemplating these letters, "there but for the grace of God goes Gabriele Rossetti." And yet later he could ask in public, "Is there anyone in the world more to be lamented than I?"

A good deal of the correspondence which passed between the two brothers is presumably lost. Gabriele could hardly be expected to do much for his brother's chronic distress, but he seems to have kept his promise with regard to an annual present, at least for a few years. In 1843 Antonio is very anxious for news, as the promised 60 ducats for last Christmas have not arrived; is Gabriele ill? "Ah! I live in doubt, I die continually of apprehension. . . . I await your answer as the Jews await the Messiah." But this was a bad year for Gabriele, the year in which he broke down and went to Paris. Antonio writes again on 10 August, saying it is the seventh letter he has written, and asking whether his brother has sent those ducats yet.

Our portrait shows him looking very much as he would be expected to look from the poems and letters we have just printed —old, poor, and as he says himself always humble. He died in extreme poverty at the age of eighty-two, two years before Rossetti himself, and his poems are piously preserved in the Museum of Vasto. He seems to have been a well-known figure in his native town, and in his youth had about him an infectious light-heartedness which it is touching to remember when reading the pathetic appeals of his old age.

CHAPTER SEVEN

DECLINING YEARS

I

AT the age of fifty-six Gabriele had passed his prime, and was never again to know perfect health. " For more than three months ", he writes to Lyell on 16 December 1839, " I have been feeling very unwell : I am tired in every limb, and feel a general lack of interest amounting to apathy—hence the inertia which has overtaken me and made me so late in replying to other people's letters, even when concerned with the most urgent affairs. And yet my head is still clear and capable of production. I fear that my days will be few. Be it as it may." By April of the following year his condition is worse. He complains of having had diabetes for the last ten months, which makes life nauseous. His end will be a blessing and he thinks it not far distant. At this time he was much harassed over the *Amor Platonico*, and his anxiety must have aggravated the weariness of the flesh. Polidori meanwhile, now seventy-six years old, continues in enviable good health and spirits. " Signor Polidori thanks you for your very courteous letter ; he told me of it with indescribable delight. His avidity for fame is marvellous at that age : as for me I have now hardly a thought for it."

There is little information to be gleaned about Rossetti's activities or the affairs of the family between 1839 and 1842, except with regard to the *Amor Platonico*. His letters, however, contain occasional references to the children who are now getting old enough to be thinking about their professions. It had long been determined that Dante Gabriel was to be a painter, and in October 1841 Rossetti reports to Frere that he has " started him on pursuing the profession he covets ; if he succeeds, he will assist my old age." " My second son ", writes the poet at about the same time, " will probably apply himself to the medical profession." But unkind circumstances prevented this, and

148

William stayed on at King's School after his brother's departure, growing, according to his own account, " audaciously lazy ". He remained there until 1845. Meanwhile the family fortunes had gone from bad to worse, and the children in whom genius did not establish its prerogative had no option but to set to work to remedy matters. Thus William, disappointed but uncomplaining, began as a clerk at Somerset House, where he remained throughout his life, working industriously, like many others a civil servant by day and a man of letters by night.

II

1843 is a central year in the story, the black year in which Rossetti's health broke down. In April the poet was invited to Putney Hill by Temple Leader, who had been urged to this friendliness by Kirkup. Other guests present were " the famous liberal Roebec (I don't know whether that is how you spell it) " and Sir William Molesworth. An interesting letter exists, containing a full account of the visit. It appears that although he would have preferred to stay in the house, having been ill with bronchitis, Rossetti was taken for a walk round the estate—" as big as from our house to Piccadilly ", he writes to his wife, giving her a detailed description of the fields and orchards, cows, horses, sheep, fowl, lakes, and so on. At dinner he seems to have forgotten his ailments with the greatest recklessness. " The table was sumptuous ; I ate twice as much as usual ; first a calf's head soup ; then salmon with lobster sauce ; then a good portion of roast lamb which was delicious ; then a very good sort of blanc-mange of which I had two helpings ; and I left all the rest alone except for some fruit and a little salad which I liked very much ; I also took an anchovy, two potatoes and a little boiled broccoli with the lamb. I was astonished at my appetite, at the amount I ate and how much I enjoyed it." Unfortunately this repast was followed by an uncomfortable night. He coughed a good deal, and did not want much breakfast, ingenuously complaining that there had been too many blankets.

The following month Rossetti's health gives cause for grave anxiety. On 20 May he writes to Lyell to excuse himself for a long delay in writing. He has been seriously ill with what seems to be consumption. " I say *seems*, since none of the doctors I have consulted has called it that with any assurance. The symptoms, however, tell me only too clearly that my judgment is right.

Oh, if you were to see your Rossetti I am sure you wouldn't recognise him. I am grown so thin that if the process continues I shall soon be nothing but a walking skeleton." His stomach is out of order, five teeth have fallen out, four others are loose ; he has a constant pain in the back which often disturbs his sleep ; and until recently had entirely lost his appetite. The doctor having advised a change of air, he is thinking of going to Boulogne at the end of June. A postscript by Mrs. Rossetti adds, " I seize the opportunity to tell you that he has been and still is in such a state of health, as to produce serious apprehension in my mind and that of our friends. . . . He varies from day to day, sometimes feeling and inspiring the brightest hopes, and then again awakening all my fears. I make no apology for troubling one of his best and kindest friends with these particulars and requesting the favour that you will not allude to what I have said in any letter to him,

I remain my dear Sir,

Your truly obliged,

FRANCES R."

Instead of going to Boulogne, however, Rossetti went first to Hastings and soon after to Paris. Kirkup invited him to go on to Florence, but he does not appear to have thought seriously of this. He did however contemplate going to Marseilles for the winter. Very slowly his condition improved. Three doctors have agreed that he is suffering not from consumption but from persistent bronchitis. By August he is much better, and feels as though he is coming back from death to life again. On 18 October he is again in London, very much better but having lost the sight of the lower half of his right eye. " One of my eyes ", he writes to Frere, " was totally darkened. . . . For three or four months I remained afraid for the other, but thanks to God it regained strength and now I read, write, walk, teach, do anything." After this time he often writes of himself as blind, as in the *Veggente* ; but he never actually was so, and it is not until the last year of his life that his writing markedly declines from its minute neatness and legibility.

The generosity of Frere pulled the family through this calamity. On the receipt of a letter from Lyell, he immediately sent £42, in return for which Rossetti wished him forty-two more years of life. Before the end of 1844 £58 more were received. Never was Frere's help more opportune. When Rossetti stopped working he had forty-five lessons a week ; when he was able to begin again he had only twenty-six. " All my anxiety ", he told Frere, " is now directed to the education of my children as good English men and women."

III

At this time Gabriele was busy with the composition of *Il Veggente in Solitudine*, [*The Seer in Solitude*] the manuscript of which seems to have been written in turn by all the members of the family, and which was published in 1846. It is a long and uneven work concerned mainly with Italian affairs and embodying many of the more successful of Rossetti's lyrics from past years ; it had an enthusiastic reception in Italy. The Seer's own life of course often comes into the foreground, though in terms so poetic that they can hardly be taken literally. There are some interesting passages about the children—

> She who the first a father's name bestowed
> On me, with rosy lips and childish grace,
> For eighteen years hath been upon life's road ;
> Her hair is darkest brown, and brown her face ;
> Within the eager pupil's dazzling ray
> Her father's ardent spirit shines alway.

> Maria heads the list, Christina endeth,
> Her mother's very self in duplicate ;
> Who not alone her form has here renewed,
> So that she seems with second youth endued,
> But even her spirit that the muse attendeth
> In both our daughters dwells inviolate ;
> And mine perhaps with hers uniting there,
> A double torch doth make that shines more fair.

Of his sons he says that he has always wished them not to forget that Italy languishes and that they have Italian blood in their veins.

> When in the glimmer of a day that dies
> I sit encircled by my family,
> Depicting Italy who for sorrow sighs,
> Whilst the two-headed monster claws at her,
> I see in each now wrath, now ruth, arise,
> A tearful look, or sparkling happy eyes,
> And their disturbed affection is express'd
> By louder heart-beats in a troubled breast.

" Fervid Gabriel," he says, has seen the harvest grow golden sixteen times ; " good-tempered William " is a year younger ; in both burns an Italico-British fire :

> How many times at closing of the day
> As suppliants we prostrate ourselves in woe,
> And the four innocent pledges of our love
> Kneeling about us, make a circle so ;
> Six fervent prayers from six hearts do ascend,
> Which being alike, in one sole prayer have end.

There is here, no doubt, a good deal of Gabriele's customary heightening of effect ; there are few signs, if any, of so strong a love for Italy or so deep a pity for her wrongs in what we know of either William or Gabriel, but that they were sometimes moved by their father's fluent and ardent conversation is not impossible. The girls' interests and occupations would lie more out of the sphere of their father's influence. Christina we may be sure responded little to the story of Italy's woes, being early concerned with woes of a more intimate and at the same time more general nature. As for Maria, we do not at any time of her life hear enough about her, and cannot tell what she thought of such matters. She seems to have been the most Italian in temperament of them all as well as in appearance ; the most ardent and enthusiastic ; the most frequently employed by Rossetti as amanuensis, though whether this would be a stimulant or a sedative it is difficult to say. In any case her ardour from an early age was directed into religious channels, and the devoted admirer of Keble was little likely to be a very enthusiastic adherent of the Italian cause.

Rossetti's references to them all by this time tend to fall into stereotyped phrases. Mrs. Rossetti is always his *ottima moglie* [excellent wife], the others are *carissima Maria*, *ingegnoso Gabriele*, *saggio Guglielmo*, *vivace Christina* [dearest, clever, wise, vivacious]. The last epithet may seem surprising to some readers of Christina's poetry, but is well supported by details of her youth supplied in William's writings. She had the liveliness of her own Maude, and like Maude's it was not incompatible with a highly precocious seriousness and melancholy of mind. They are all described again a year or two later in the *Autobiography*—but there is little variety and no subtlety at all in anything that Gabriele says about them. He was no analyst of character either in the home or outside it.

My loving girls, in whom my soul descries
A heavenly mind in virgin modesty,
Of intellect and ethics you have given
Already a shining proof in prose and verse :
You from a double looking-glass, it seems,
Reflect upon us all your mother's soul.

As from a twin-branched fountain-source there spurt
Rills of fresh lymph to inundate a mead—
[As from a double torch there shine bright rays
Which, mingling, shed a double light abroad—]
So sometimes sister-like do poetry
And painting beautify the selfsame mind :
And both unite in you, my Gabriel,
And fertilise your soul, and give it fire.
These like two fountains both in you upflow,
Both in you like two torches are alight ;
And while you make them brightly manifest,
They both prepare in you exalted work.
Run and attain the duplicated goal,
Though yours is the most early dawn of life :
As able poet I hear you already hailed,
Already as able painter see you admired.
Now onward, and the double race-course win !
You will be doing what I could not do.

If 'tis not vanity, almost reborn
I feel in person, even in countenance,
[In you, good William, beardless Plato mine]
Thought in your eyes and on your lips a smile.
[In you, beloved son, I live again,
And gazing on you contemplate myself.
But such a mind as yours exerts its power
Among the thinkers, not on Helicon.]
In two dead languages and four that live
Already Truth converses with your mind ;
[Already, speaking of you, more than one
Entitle you the young philosopher.][1]

[W. M. R.]

With regard to the languages mentioned above, and often referred
to with pride by Gabriele—the children all of course knew English
(their native language Rossetti called it), Italian and French. The
boys and Maria knew Latin and a modicum of Greek. The

[1] The passages in brackets are supplied from the Italian text.
W. M. R. omitted them, as being " representative of fatherly fondness
more than of myself." (*Autobiography*, p. 90.)

fourth modern language was German, which they all learnt up to a certain point from Heimann, the "Ahriman" of the Dante correspondence, who exchanged lessons to the children in his own language for lessons in Italian from Gabriele. He married a Jewish lady in 1843, and became professor of German at University College in 1848. The young Rossettis saw a good deal of the Heimanns for some years, and though he was apparently a miracle of courtesy (he is the friend referred to by Christina in *Time Flies*, 24 May), the atmosphere of his home seems to have been lacking in delicacy, as Christina felt at the time of her engagement to Collinson. Heimann is said by the historian of University College to have been remarkable for nothing but his connection with the Rossettis ; but that connection left a tolerably deep mark on Dante Gabriel's work, if it may be supposed that without Heimann's intervention he would not have met with Bürger and Hoffmann, and other German romantics.

IV

In 1847 the breakdown of Gabriele's health obliged him to resign his appointment at King's College. The letter of resignation, addressed to the Principal, Dr. Jelf, may still be read among the archives of the college. It is in English.

REVD. SIR,

God has seen fitting to afflict me with a terrible calamity and I resign myself to his supreme will. After repeated vain attempts under the first oculists to procure the restoration of my nearly lost sight, I am compelled to acquiesce in the conviction that I have no longer the power to be of active service as Professor o Italian Literature in King's College. I must therefore request the Council of the College to accept my resignation in order that the College may not suffer detriment from the want of an effective Italian Professor. Having had the honour of being chosen as Professor at King's College at the time of its foundation, I trust that I have given satisfaction by my conduct and zealous endeavours to promote the advancement of my pupils in the knowledge of my native tongue. I have ever considered it a high honour to be connected with so noble an institution, and shall with pride entitle myself to the day of my death late Professor of King's College.

With a sincere desire that my successor, if not more zealous, may be still more adequate to the advancement of his pupils ; and requesting you to have the goodness to lay before the Council this communication, with my thanks for a long period of courteous consideration, and for the kind indulgence of the last four years ; with the most sincere wishes for the continued prosperity of King's College, I remain

Revd. Sir,
Your obedient Servant,
GABRIELE ROSSETTI.

April 28th 1847.

P.S.—If the Council of King's College would wish to hear my conscientious opinion concerning an Italian worthy to succeed me in this Institution, I will give it ; and am sure that my wishes for the well-being of the College will guide me to a right decision.

GABRIELE ROSSETTI.

He supported the candidature of Gallenga, later Professor at University College, a doubtful person who had distressed Mazzini by repeated offers to assassinate Charles Albert of Piedmont, but who had never quite been able to bring himself to the point of doing so. He had some reputation among liberal men of letters ; but little experience as a teacher of Italian. The Council passed him over, preferring the more respectable reputation of Valerio Pistrucci, son of Rossetti's old friend, whose appointment was less gratifying to the poet than might have been expected ; he thought it was not a good choice.

Jelf acknowledged Rossetti's letter the next day.

29 *April*, 1847.

MY DEAR SIR,

I have received your letter with great regret and I shall feel very much the task which it imposes upon me of communicating to the Council your resignation of the office which you have so long held with high credit to yourself and with advantage to the College.

I have personal feelings, arising out of my relations to the Crown Prince of Hanover, which make me sympathise most sincerely with you in the calamity with which it has pleased God to afflict you. Like my beloved pupil, however, you resort for consolation to the only source of comfort, and there you will, I doubt not, find it abundantly. I remain

Dear Sir, with sincere respect,
Your very faithful servant,
R. W. JELF, *Principal.*

V

While fate was using Rossetti thus hardly, the cloud hanging over Italy seemed about to lift. The events of 1848 filled him at first with delirious joy, and with renewed hope of returning at last to his beloved country. " In a few weeks' time," he writes to an Italian correspondent, " I expect to receive letters from friends calling me back to my country ; but I do not think it will be possible for me to go until about August. If I were young I should leave at once ; but old and almost blind as I am, I must wait until the situation is stable and secure." Pepe's letter of invitation, dated 26 April, has already been quoted.[1] But the situation showed no sign of becoming stable. In May Rossetti is all impatience. " I cannot tell you how uneasy my heart is over the delays and the uncertainties of Italy's fortunes. She has forgotten the adage : Strike while the iron is hot. . . . I fear, if things do not take a turn for the better, that I shall die in the land of mists and shall not give back my spirit to the bright sun of Italy from which I first received it. *Pazienza !* It will be something if I do not die of hunger." He had at first great faith in Charles Albert and wrote an ode when he heard that that prince had taken the field. Later he celebrates the Milanese ' five days ' in various poems. The liberal pronouncements of Pio Nono again raised high hopes ; he dreamed of an Italian federation under the Pope. But that potentate was to become " Pio ? No ! No ! " and the subject of endless execrations in Charlotte Street ; for Gabriele's soaring hopes soon fell to the ground. Constitutional government again collapsed in Naples and Ferdinand's barbarity broke out anew—" Now I shall not return until I hear that he has committed suicide or taken flight," says Rossetti. He writes despairingly to his wife in August about the latest Italian news, " horrible, horrible ! Even that hope has failed me ! I had clung to it as a raft in the miserable shipwreck of my life : but Providence will take care of us. . . . Every one of our children, upright, well-educated, and old enough to be independent, will be able to do something to mitigate the calamity which has fallen upon me. My premature old age, my misfortune and not my fault, should make them all determined to take serious thought for themselves." Soon he was thankful that he had not gone to Italy earlier in the year. " It was providential that I resisted the repeated persuasions

[1] See p. 69.

of my friends to return to Naples. Although I was offered the office of Councillor of State as a bait, I was not tempted. All Italy, indeed all Europe, except this happy England, is a tempest-tossed sea and I see no prospect of future calm." His country's woes, added to illness and personal misfortune, left him little to live for, and by the end of the year he is writing to Ricciardi in great dejection. " I am so disheartened that I have lost all my energy ; poverty, *turpis egestas*, is knocking at my door and threatening to make a violent entry, and I see no means of driving it away." When the portrait painted this year for Lyell by Dante Gabriel was finished, Rossetti wrote to warn his old friend " that between the Rossetti you used to know and the Rossetti whose image you will see, there is all the difference between robust health and declining age. . . . I seem the father of myself. Quite white-haired, fleshless and toothless, and although I am not yet blind . . . you will see eyes so dim and cloudy that you will hardly know them again. I can truly apply to myself the Virgilian saying *Quantum mutatus ab illo*. But enough of that ; it is something that I am not in my grave."

VI

He had now of course given up going out to teach but still gave a few lessons in his own house.[1] He had in October an idea of getting together a class of about twenty and intended to advertise it, but there is no news of this having materialised. Meanwhile the other members of the family were doing what they could. From 1844-5 onwards Mrs. Rossetti had put her own knowledge of French and Italian to some use in teaching. In 1844 Aunt Charlotte had obtained for Maria her first post as governess, with Lord and Lady Charles Thynne ; subsequently she went to another family where she was better appreciated. Later she lived at home, and went out to give lessons. By 1850 William was receiving £110 a year at the Excise Office. Thus the family never reached the limit of absolute poverty, although they were certainly passing through a time of very great anxiety. Rossetti was often left lonely and unhappy at home. " I am always alone," he writes to Ricciardi, " for everybody in this house has undertaken work

[1] One of his pupils at this time was Charles Bagot Cayley. Christina consequently must have met Cayley and Collinson for the first time within the same year.

of one kind or another to earn a living. And yet all of them put together cannot make the half of what I used to make myself."

There are two descriptions of Rossetti as he appeared about this time, which, although well known, are too vivid to be passed over. William Bell Scott visited the house for the first time in December 1847 or January 1848. " I entered the small front parlour or dining room of the house and found an old gentleman sitting by the fire in a great chair, the table drawn close to his chair, with a thick manuscript book open before him, and the largest snuff-box I ever saw beside it conveniently open. He had a black cap on his head furnished with a great peak or shade for the eyes, so that I saw his face only partially. . . ." Frederic Stephens, visiting the Rossettis a few months later, is fuller and more eloquent. " As might be expected of one possessing so many accomplishments, and whose career had been marked by so much courage, the professor was a man of striking character and aspect, so that when I was first introduced to him in 1848, and his grand climacteric was past, and, as with most Italians, a life of studies told upon him heavily, I could not but be struck by the noble energy of his face and by the high culture his expression attested, while a sort of eager, almost passionate, resolution seemed to glow in all he said and did. To a youngster, such as I was then, he seemed much older than his years ; and while seated reading at a table with two candles behind him and, because his sight was failing, with a wide shade over his eyes, he looked a very Rembrandt come to life. The light was reflected from a manuscript placed close to his face, and, in the shadow which covered them, made distinct all the fineness and vigour of his sharply moulded features. It was half lost upon his somewhat shrunken figure wrapped in a student's dressing-gown and shone fully upon the lean, bony, and delicate hands in which he held the paper. He looked like an old and somewhat imperative prophet, and his voice had a slightly rigorous ring speaking to his sons and their visitors. Near his side, but beyond the radiant circle of the candles—her erect, comely, and very English form, and face remarkable for its noble and beautiful matronhood, and but half visible in the flickering glow of the fire—sat Mrs. Rossetti, the mother of Dante Gabriel. He too, leaning his elbows upon the table and holding his face between both hands so that the long curling masses of his dark brown hair fell forward, sat on the other side, his attenuated features sharply outlined by the candles' light."

VII

Among Rossetti's friends at this time were a group of Italian evangelicals, some of them being unfrocked or relapsed priests of the Roman communion. The family in general appears to have disliked them, William speaking distastefully of their influence over his father in these declining years. Among the more reputable members of the group was Salvatore Ferretti, a Florentine priest, cousin of Pio Nono, who fell in love and absconded to London, where he arrived in October 1842. He and his wife founded a refuge for children in 1844. Camillo Mapei was another of their leading figures. Less worthy was Giacinto Achilli, although he established a church of an evangelical character; while another, Raffaele Ciocci, was eventually convicted at Brighton for house-breaking. These and others published a *Confessione di Fede di Londra* [London Confession of Faith], which raised a cloud of Catholic witnesses. Wiseman himself entered the conflict in the *Dublin Review*. Subsequently, in 1847, the group established a monthly magazine called *L'Eco di Savonarola*.[1]

To this seemingly innocent periodical our notoriously anti-clerical Rossetti was induced by Mapei to contribute. The ostensible object of the magazine was to call Italians to the study of the Bible. Actually, however, it combined a good deal of evangelical moralising and haphazard theology with a strong animus against Pio Nono and the papacy in general, and was put on the *Index* as soon as it appeared, while all its contributors were excommunicated. Rossetti joined in the theologising and the objurgations with gusto, contributing a number of poems, some of them violent in tone, and various prose articles in which he attacks indulgences, the belief in purgatory and transubstantiation, and the practice of confession and celibacy, using arguments as literal and rationalistic as those which he used to employ in his Dante interpretation. Rome is the Synagogue of Satan; the Papacy is a fulfilment of 2 Thess. ii. 1–4: " . . . that man of sin . . . the son of perdition; who opposeth and exalteth himself above all that is called God, or that is worshipped; so that he as God sitteth in the temple of God, showing himself that he is God." And in *The Mystery of Babylon* he goes so far as to say

[1] The first two numbers were translated into English and published under the title of *Light for Italy*, with an introduction by an English minister, W. H. Rule.

that if there were no other form of the Christian religion than that which Rome teaches, he would say without the least hesitation that it was false and worse than many Pagan religions, and would abjure it at once. His writing was never lacking in emphasis. On the occasion of a refusal by the editor to print one of his poems, Rossetti complains that the paper is colourless and that when anyone attempts to lend it a little colour he is not welcomed. At a public meeting organised by the evangelicals at this time he made a speech against the Pope, and no doubt his efforts would have been still greater if his health had been less precarious. But possibly, as William Michael suggests, if the old poet had been less weak and ill, it would not have been so easy for his evangelical friends to draw him on to these excited declarations. While they are not inconsistent with views expressed in earlier years, Rossetti had always refrained from identifying himself with what he thought to be Dante's own belief that the Pope was no other than the Devil in disguise. By this time, partly through illness and the irritability of old age, partly through time and disuse, his old Catholic habits of thought were no doubt weakened. It is in any case a pity that his feelings should have found such violent expression, and that he did not content himself with the composition of hymns —an occupation to which he had recently turned with much fervour. His *Arpa Evangelica* appeared in print in 1852, and consists of hymns and lyrics of a religious though mainly undogmatic nature. It had in its day a considerable reputation in Italy, although in most parts of the country prohibited by the Government. Some of the hymns are still sung to-day in Italian protestant churches. They are not particularly interesting or beautiful, but they have at all events some of the qualities which are most essential in compositions of this type—simplicity of conception, clarity of style, and easy versification. Carducci has praised them in a guarded way, calling them " true poems, beautiful and useful civil poems." They have been credited with some influence over Christina, who certainly translated one of them, and who addresses her father in one of her earliest and most beautiful religious poems.

In a letter to Lyell at the end of 1849, Rossetti states that he has already written a hundred and five of these poems, adding that according to his wife, Polidori, and the children, he has never written with " such enthusiasm and so much unction as in this [his] sacred period."

VIII

There is indeed one thing for which the gentlemen of the *Eco* may at least be thanked ; it is that they gave Rossetti a good deal to think about at a time of enforced inactivity when his spirits had sunk to a level hardly sufficient to keep an interest in life alive. On various occasions from 1843 onwards he had expressed a desire for death which was perfectly genuine ; his usefulness was over, his health broken, and there seemed no part in life left to play. Polidori continues to be a marvel to him ; in August 1849 he tells Lyell of his father-in-law's great joy in life, contrasting so deeply with his own feelings ; life to Rossetti appears a disaster, death a great blessing. But of course he could still take a pride and interest in the achievements of his children, and he writes about them to his friends in England and on the Continent. Dante Gabriel has exhibited his first picture amid a chorus of praise. A rich lady of the provinces, who has not even seen it, has offered £60 for it, and on finding that its price was £80 has paid the higher amount without question.[1] What is more, her bill of exchange was cashed at once by the banker. Gabriel has also written much verse of which some has been published ; William is not less fertile and has an even greater poetic reputation ; Christina too has written beautiful poems, some of which were published three years ago ; Maria is a great scholar and possesses a knowledge of five languages, but she has little inclination to compose. They are all now, he thanks Providence, in the way of making an honourable subsistence for themselves. " They will complete their pilgrimage like their father, obeying the imperious command ' In the sweat of thy brow thou shalt eat thy bread.' "

Whatever their promise of future greatness, however, the Rossettis were still poor, and reduced circumstances at last made it necessary for them to leave Charlotte Street. At the beginning of 1851 they moved to 38 Arlington Street, Mornington Crescent, where Mrs. Rossetti opened a school, and where the dutiful Christina reluctantly lent a hand with the teaching. The house had a small garden at the back in which Gabriele was able to take a little exercise ; except for this and occasional visits to Polidori,

[1] The picture was *The Girlhood of Mary Virgin*. The " lady of the provinces " was not so detached as she appears in Rossetti's letter— she was the Marchioness of Bath, in whose family Aunt Charlotte had advanced from the position of governess to that of companion.

he practically never went out. "My excellent wife", he says,
"has opened a school there for young ladies of good family."
But although it may have been opened for young ladies of this
kind, it was actually attended by "a few daughters of the local
tradesfolk, the hairdresser, the porkbutcher and so on," and could
hardly be counted a success.

A new friend appears upon the scene at this time in Teodorico
Pietrocola-Rossetti, Gabriele's nephew, who later became a protestant minister.[1] To him Rossetti wrote some melancholy
letters, full of the expectation and the desire for death. "I
am so tired of life that I shall bless my death when it comes ; and
thank God it is not far off : might it only come to-day ! The
state of our wretched Italy weighs upon my heart. . . . My aged
father-in-law . . . is tolerably well in spite of his 88 years. I
am 66 and seem older than he. . . . My time is past." "An
habitual melancholy has taken possession of me ; I wish to die,
but God will not yet concede so great a benefit." A little later,
in April of 1851, he was very ill with a stroke of paralysis and
afterwards with influenza ; he expected to die, but nevertheless
recovered. It is not surprising that about this time a report of
his death circulated in Italy.

It was in the Arlington Street house that Dante Gabriel sketched
the well-known and very delightful portrait of his father reading
in his study with a great peaked cap pulled down over his eyes.
There is nothing melancholy about his appearance here ; the
artist has caught with affectionate observation the most appealing
aspect of his father's old age. Contrasting with the portrait is
the word picture left by Pietrocola of the old man in these last
years. "I seem still to see him with his cap pulled down to shield
his eyes from the bright sunshine which tortured him, and I
seem still to hear him ask his loving children to draw the thick
curtains. . . ." "He had lost all his teeth, his hair was scanty
and white, his shoulders were bent, and it was as much as he could
do to walk." He used to get up early, and shut himself up in his
study ; he read reflectively and wrote very slowly. "He rarely

---

[1] Francesco Pisarri, in an article in *Noi e il Mondo*, November 1923,
quoting Carlo Zanini (*Cenni su Teodorico Pietrocola-Rossetti*, Ales-
sandria, 1895), says that Teodorico did not become an evangelical
until between 1853 and 1855 ; possibly therefore after his uncle's
death. At all events he was certainly not a minister when he first
appeared in London. (See *Autobiography*, p. 72.)

took a walk, so feeble and burdensome to himself he had become. The only visits he ever paid regularly were to his father-in-law Polidori. I used often to accompany him, offering him an arm, but the poor old man had great difficulty in bestirring himself." One evening he spoke of his desire to die and recited some verses :

> Into the sea the drop
> Falleth and disappears.
> Life is a little drop,
> Lost in the sea of years.

It must have brought some alleviation of Rossetti's sadness to receive in 1852 such a letter as the following, which illustrates the esteem in which he was held in Italy.

ROME, 6 *August* 1852.

DEAR SIR,

The story of our affairs has had an echo for which no one could have hoped. It struck your imagination and you turned our misfortunes into song. A mother deprived of her son and condemned for lamenting him, gives you thanks ; so also do three young women plunged into the horror of public prisons for having prayed for peace by the graves of brave men who died for Italy's freedom ; so also does Rome herself, for, to the free people among whom you live, you have told the story of the iniquities in which our oppressors vent their madness. Nevertheless if we have suffered and suffer still, the hope of a day of liberty and of peace comforts and exalts us. On that day we shall await your hymn : the hymn of redemption.

With the highest esteem and respect, we have the honour to call ourselves your obedient servants and friends,

TERESA NARDUCCI
and the three sisters CARLELLANI.

CHAPTER EIGHT

THE YOUNG ROSSETTIS

I

IF two of the young Rossettis had not been endowed with greater genius than that of their father, this book (like how many others ?) would not have been written. And although to anyone approaching their work as we have done by way of the family and a vast correspondence, a few poems and pictures seem small things in face of the quiet and inexorable revolution of human generations out of which they rose, it is nevertheless for their sake that the story is told. Having attempted to give some idea of the Rossetti children's early life and training, it is our purpose now to carry forward separately the account of their individual development within the space of their father's lifetime, that is to say up to 1854, and to show that Gabriele lived long enough to know not only the nature of his children's genius but also the best of which they were capable.

Few lives have been so fully documented by the preservations of family piety as those of the Rossettis, so that only with difficulty is the danger avoided of establishing a quite illusory familiarity. These were greatly gifted and complex minds, and if it has been truly said that no dramatist ever successfully presents a soul greater than his own, in how much worse a plight is the wingless critic ? It would be an impertinence to suppose that with whatever apparatus of letters and diaries and contemporary records he can make consistent to a later and stranger day what was problematic even to the closest relations in minds so richly endowed. No such pretence is to be made here ; all that can be hoped is that the most important influences and effects of environment, training, and reading may be thrown into a clear light and the main channels of inspiration accounted for.

The Rossettis remained to the end, in spite of various temperamental divergences, a closely united group bound together by many links of thought, feeling, and habit of mind. Secluded from the ordinary English life as they were, they had all felt the effects of their mother's teaching (and she remained long among them, to keep them in mind of it), their father's excitability, their grandfather's solid puritanism, the conversation of the family's Italian visitors, and the general atmosphere of literary culture which filled the home. Moreover, the family absorption in intellectual pursuits, together with their Bloomsbury environment, prevented the young Rossettis from acquiring that love of physical exertion in the open air by which the normal British child is characterised.

At Holmer Green they were all very much town children in the country. They are never to be heard of making hay, loitering about the farms, or even bird's-nesting. On the contrary they were no less secluded there than in London, and far more is heard of Polidori's garden than of the country round about. There might not have been a farmstead within walking distance. What does Gabriel like doing there ? " He loitered about a little, doing nothing in particular. His chief amusement was to haunt a pond in the grounds and catch frogs." And William ? Of course he helped Gabriel catch frogs. As for spiders, earwigs, and slugs, " they were viewed with repulsion (though I was not brought up to have any foolish prejudices against animals harmless though possibly uncouth.") By Gabriel, however, " even a blackbeetle was regarded with a certain indulgence ; it was an animal, much like another." To Christina, Holmer Green meant more than to either of her brothers. She liked to talk about it late in life, and references to things seen there are numerous in *Time Flies*. The garden was her " familiar haunt " and " inexhaustible delight ". However, she had never seen a good sunrise until near the end of her life, and as late as 1883 she discovered the existence of a flower called " love in a mist ". She shared the general interest in frogs ; and a lasting impression was made on her mind by discovering a dead mouse in the garden—she buried it, and removing its covering of moss a few days later, saw a black insect emerge. " I fled in horror, and for long years ensuing I never mentioned this ghastly adventure to anyone." Of course she saw many other pleasanter things and took delight in them ; but although throughout her life Christina loved to see flowers and watch animals, she never had any real intimacy with them. Watts-Dunton said that she spoke of wild animals sometimes as though they were human beings and sometimes as though they were fairies. He also says she loved the beauty of this world as symbolic of

M

another world beyond it. As human beings, fairies, or as symbols —but not for themselves. Perhaps this would be going too far. There are many delicate touches of observation in her poetry and passages of pure delight, sufficient to justify those who have declared that her power as a poetess of nature used to be underestimated. But there is now a danger of the other extreme. She noticed this and she noticed that, with the charming freshness of one seeing things for the first time, but nature never drew her into its own life. When she wanted flower descriptions for symbolic purposes in *Called to be Saints* she had recourse to a botany book. Indeed the charm of many of her passages about flowers and animals often arises from her very detachment and unfamiliarity, as when she describes the attractions of the cow in this manner : " Her person is comely and motherly, ample, unhurried ; her broad blunt nose seems ever bedewed with the moisture of grass-blades and flower-cups ; her eyes are lovely and her breath is sweet." When she is less inspired she can write as she does of the honeysuckle. " Its flowers are elegant and by combination rich. . . . Choice beauties grace it ; nothing of gorgeousness or strong contrast, but tender tints of pink or straw yellow, with white for a scentless variety." She has clearly seen the honeysuckle flower and liked it—one could say no more. The " scentless variety ", without doubt, was supplied by the botany book.

Both she and Dante Gabriel seem from the first to have liked animals. William is always comically philosophic on the subject, and Maria seems to have regarded nature as a heaven-sent collection of object lessons. But Dante had animal pets, a dormouse and a hedgehog, and he loved the Zoo, while it was Christina who first introduced him to the charms of the wombat, a beast of whom one hears a good deal in biographies of Dante Gabriel. Later she became an ardent antivivisectionist, turning to her brother on one occasion for his signature to a protest, and subsequently thanking him for the " personal kindness to myself which has led you to sign though without thorough agreement "—a highly characteristic procedure. One of the first favourite books of the family, especially with Dante Gabriel, had been Peter Parley's *Natural History* ; it was the beginning of an interest which ended in the Tudor House menagerie.

Whatever enjoyment the Rossetti children may have derived from their visits to the country came to an end in 1839. After the Polidoris moved to London, the children saw little of the country at all. Meanwhile their home amusements were plentiful and varied, growing more and more intellectual as the years went on. We have seen that they sometimes played cards, first simple games such as *Patience, Beggar my Neighbour*, the *Duchess of Rutland's Whim*, which later gave way to *Whist* and *Tre Sette*—with the latter Dante Gabriel and William would at one time amuse themselves for hours. They identified themselves with the four suits in a way which now seems crudely symbolical, except in the case of Maria. Dante Gabriel's suit was of course hearts ; Christina's was diamonds ; and what suit could have been more fittingly appropriated by William Michael than spades ?

Friendly rivalry in artistic activities soon took the place of table games, and a select brotherhood existed in Charlotte Street long before the days of Pre-Raphaelitism. With regard to literature William remarks that there was never a time when, knowing what poetry was, they did not also recognise a correct line ; and their earliest efforts in verse either English or Italian have at least the merit of metrical accuracy, whether it is Dante Gabriel's message to Maria at the age if eight,

> l'amabile Maria
> ringraziata sia
> de' due biglietti suoi
> mandati ad ambi noi

or Christina's birthday lines to her mother at the age of eleven,

> To-day's your natal day ;
> Sweet flowers I bring :
> Mother, accept I pray
> My offering.
>
> And may you happy live,
> And long us bless ;
> Receiving as you give
> Great happiness.

Whatever effusion was written by any one of them was sure of appreciation and sensible criticism from the others, as well as from father, mother, or grandfather. Both facility and ingenuity were encouraged also by the practice of writing to *bouts-rimés*, usually in the sonnet form, a pastime in which William, Christina, and Dante Gabriel indulged a good deal in 1847–8. Gabriel was the most ingenious contributor, but all three were " dexterous practitioners ", the time taken in completing the sonnet being five to seven minutes ; ten to twelve was considered somewhat long. Then there were family magazines and scrap books to which they all contributed ; *The Blessed Damozel* was itself written for one of them. All this joint literary activity within one family is paralleled only, if at all, by the childish story-telling of the Brontës ; but " the three sisters on their lonely moor " had no such advice and sympathetic encouragement as that which was always at hand for the Rossetti children if they required it. Their long and emulative training in the way of amusement accounts for the perfection of some of the earliest published work of Dante Gabriel and his sister. When they entered the guild of poets their apprenticeship had already been served.

They were all of course great readers ; except Christina, who at all times read much less than the other children and never possessed many books of her own. Maria was easily the most precocious—at the age of five she " could read anything in either English or Italian, and read she did with tireless persistency." The things they all read in common and enjoyed in various degrees were of very diverse quality. Their mother naturally provided them with the current examples of improving fiction, *Sandford and Merton* and others. They all delighted in Keightley's *Fairy Mythology*, as well as in his *Classical Mythology*, which led them on to the *Iliad* (in Pope's translation) ; the latter was Maria's chosen hunting-ground. Shakespeare was discovered at an early age ; strangely enough all the children at first preferred *Henry VI.*, but other plays soon followed ; they were reading the text of Shakespeare and enjoying it long before most children have got as far as Lamb's *Tales*. A very natural favourite since almost anything may be found in it, was Hone's *Every-Day Book*. In this storehouse of information and entertainment Christina, and presumably the other children too, first met with Keats. Finally a great deal of their early reading was romantic and macabre. Poe was the delight of them all, though at what date they began to know him it is difficult to say. Scott, his poems first and afterwards his novels, Maturin with his terrific *Melmoth*, Monk Lewis and his *Tales of Terror*, with other literature of the chivalric, Gothic and supernatural kind, all fed the morbidly excitable tracts of Dante Gabriel's and even Christina's imaginations ; and are undoubtedly one of the chief sources of the horrific features of their work. This is of course more noticeable in the case of Dante Gabriel whose inspiration is always more literary and derivative than that of Christina ; but her second best verse does not escape it, as for example in that much-praised poem *Amor Mundi*.

Divergencies of taste soon, however, made themselves felt. The boys, Dante Gabriel taking the lead, grew more and more interested in painting, while their reading wandered into paths where the girls would hardly tread. Byron pleased Gabriel at an early age ; and in 1844 both he and William were swept off their feet by the bold and iridescent idealism of Shelley. This is an important landmark. William's admiration of Shelley was lifelong—he published an edition of his poems in 1869, helped Furnivall to establish the Shelley Society in 1866 and remained Chairman of Committee until its dissolution in 1895. As for Gabriel, traces of Shelley are discoverable in *The Blessed Damozel* and a good deal later in *The Stream's Secret* and *Love's Nocturn*, and while his genius was too diverse in type from that of Shelley to take strong colouring from the older poet, his indifference in religious matters may well have been encouraged by Shelley's hostility to Christianity. Aunt Margaret was perturbed when she heard he was proposing to read a poet so indecent and wrote to his mother about it ; bringing forth an indignant protest against her interference and a declaration that he proposed to read Shelley " for the sake of the splendid versification and not for any love of his atheistical sentiments." But when in 1849 Coventry Patmore disapproved of the attitude to death expressed in some of William's sonnets, Gabriel encouraged his brother with the jocular remark that Shelley was with him " and watches (perhaps) from his grave."

In the meantime closer association with their mother as well as the special peculiarities of their own temperaments had taken the girls in the opposite direction, so that in 1843 Dante Gabriel is amused at Maria's love of Keble. Maria's enthusiastic nature turned early into religious channels ; and her influence combined with her mother's in directing Christina's less naturally devotional temperament into the same course—for Christina, religious rather than mystical, dutiful rather than devotional, had neither the unquestioning simplicity of her mother nor the ardent faith of her sister. All the children had of course attended religious services regularly with their mother from the beginning ; going first to Trinity Church, Marylebone Road ; from about 1839 to St. Katherine's Chapel, Regent's Park ; and finally to Christ Church, Albany Street. Soon after they began to attend the services in Albany Street, the church was invaded by the flood of High Anglicanism, and before long the incumbent and his three curates all went over to Rome. A high church tone remained after their departure, and by the middle of the 'forties Mrs. Rossetti and her daughters had ceased to be evangelical in their religious practices. Writing of a service he had seen in France in 1844, Gabriel remarks that if Maria had been there it would certainly have made her a Catholic ; and indeed considering her Italian origin, her great love of Dante, and the somewhat dogmatic nature of her mind, it is strange that she never became one. Many too have thought that Christina would have been happier in the older communion, and it is very possible that this would have been the case ; but despite the associations of her Italian heredity, her engagement to Collinson, not to speak of the influence of High Church doctrine and ritual, never once does Christina show any sign of desiring to cross the line. Perhaps her father's anti-papal bias was not without effect, perhaps the early evangelical training was not easily outlived, perhaps her essentially unmystical nature never drew her that way at all—certain it is that she thought the Catholics were " in error on some points," and that both she and Maria resisted the attempts of their Uncle Henry to convert them. Perhaps above all the actual form of Christina's religion was due simply to the lifelong dominion over her of her mother's example.

For many years the boys were also regularly taken to church, but they went without any enthusiasm. " I do not think I shall go to church on Sunday, for in the first place I do not know where I can sit, and in the second place I find that we are so stared at wherever we go, that I do not much relish the idea of sitting for two hours the lodestone of attraction in the very centre of the aboriginees, on whose minds curiosity seems to have taken a firm hold." So writes Dante Gabriel in 1842—they are not the words of an enthusiast. William had ceased to attend by 1846 or 1847, and it is hardly likely that Gabriel attended regularly any longer, although he was never so definitely agnostic as William and for some years would occasionally accompany his mother to church to please her. Neither he nor his brother was ever confirmed.

But we must now leave these considerations in which all the children are concerned, to follow their development separately.

II. MARIA FRANCESCA

I

Not much light is thrown upon Maria's childhood by her father's letters. Her early cleverness is a frequent theme, but her character never comes under discussion at all. The same is true of William, and the reason is probably the same in both cases—that they did what was expected of them and called little attention to themselves by any development of unexpected peculiarities. Maria was the quickest to read and the most indefatigable reader ; in the acquirement of knowledge she easily outstripped them all, and being as ardent as she was clever, she cherished in childhood a great number of enthusiasms. The British Navy, the heroes of the *Iliad*, Napoleon, all attracted her in their turn. They were the expression of a lively and active mind, eager to find something on which to exercise itself, but lacking that strong and purposeful bent in some one direction that is often found in the childhood of the greatly gifted. Her nature was decided and dominating, and not without a touch of jealousy. When Gabriel and William began to learn Greek at school, thus taking a step beyond her purview, Maria insisted on learning Greek by herself at home, and this she accomplished with considerable success. Over Christina she seems to have established a complete ascendancy from the first. " To this hour," Christina writes in *Time Flies* (July 17), " I remember a certain wild strawberry growing on a hedgerow bank, watched day by day while it ripened by a little girl and by my yet younger self. My elder instructed me not to pluck it prematurely, and I complied." However, after a few days they found that " a snail or some such marauder " had passed that way, and exercising no such restraint had left the strawberry half-eaten and good for nothing. But though self-confident and not a little domineering, Maria's disposition was warm and loving and lively ; while she compensated for her lack of inventiveness not only by quickness in learning but also by strong common sense. She herself used to say that she had the good sense, William the good nature, Gabriel the good heart, and Christina the bad temper of their father and mother—no doubt she also had better things to say about her sister, but Christina forbears to quote them. And with Maria's good sense went likewise cheerfulness. When she was about to immure herself in her convent in 1873, Gabriel wrote to their mother, " She will indeed be a great loss, being much the healthiest in mind and cheeriest of us all, except yourself. William comes next, and Christina and I are nowhere."

In spite of the enthusiasm of Count Pepoli,[1] Maria was not good looking. Indeed in the photograph of Mrs. Rossetti and her two daughters, reproduced in this book, her appearance would demand a more definitely negative description. Even as a child in Pistrucci's miniature she is far from pretty. Her hair was thick and black, her complexion southern, her eyes large and dark, her mouth full and wide, revealing when amused, according to her elder brother's uncomplimentary description, " a neatly-paved thoroughfare between her ears." " Her features ", says the other brother, " were not more than moderately good, nor was her figure advantagious." Christina and Gabriel both saw a strong likeness to her face in Fra Bartolomeo's portrait of Savonarola.

The very expansive writings of William Michael give no full account of Maria's activities, for he is either telling the stories of Gabriel or Christina, or that of his own life, but here and there from him and others we get little glimpses of her in the background. She helps Lyell with his translations from Dante, and keeps him informed of her father's progress while he is in Paris. She acts as amanuensis for Gabriele when his eyes are weak, and sometimes writes letters for him. The execrated Aroux takes to adding messages to her in a hand so small that Gabriele will not be able to read it. She listens open-eyed to the conversation of the Italian visitors ; but has sufficient presence of mind to make other guests feel at home. We conceive her taking a motherly interest in all, ready, confident, cheerful, admonitory, and preserving among all excitements the most precise sense of what was right and what was not.

In about 1844, at the age of seventeen, Maria emerges for a moment from her obscurity to become a governess in the Thynne family. She did not like the family, but appears to have endured her exile among them for at least two and a half years. It must have been from the Thynnes that she wrote to her father in January 1846, when apparently there was some prospect of her being able to return to her home. " I am anticipating with the greatest pleasure

[1] See p. 130.

the day of my return to the ' bel nido natio ' where certainly it would be very pleasant to remain always. However, I thank God for having given me talents which enable me to assist my dear father by removing the burden of my maintenance which he has borne for so many years with so much loving care. Might I only remove as easily all the anxieties which weigh upon his heart, and all the vexations that oppress his mind. Never will I cease to pray God to bless him in this world and in eternity ; and let us comfort ourselves with the thought that ' He doth not willingly afflict the children of men.' " [1] She was herself, it seems, suffering from the usual affliction of governesses—the unruliness of spoilt children. " I hope you told Lady Charles ", writes Gabriel to his mother, " that poor Maggie is not to be bullied and badgered out of her life by a lot of beastly brats ; and that Lady C. fully understands the same, and has already provided the said Maggie with a bamboo." From the Thynnes, Maria went to a Mrs. Read, where she was much happier ; and, at a date not discoverable, returned to her home, thenceforward taking no more resident posts but going out teaching in various families.

II

Although Dante Gabriel and Christina soon outstripped their sister in inventive pursuits, Maria did her best to hold her own, and appeared in (semi-public) print before any of the others. In 1847 Rossetti writes to Ferretti thanking him for his introduction to Cavalier Campana, for whom he has the greatest admiration. " Not the least of his gifts is that with which the Muses endowed him : his ode on the death of the Princess Borghese is extremely beautiful, magnificent, imaginative, tender, moving, most elegant. Two editions have been made of it, in which it is preceded by an English translation, the work of my young fourteen-year-old Sappho ; and a third is in preparation." This translation had been done by the young Sappho in 1841, and was printed (very badly) by Polidori on his private press. It is not an impressive performance. There is no attempt at rhyme, the stanzas of the original being reproduced in blank verse of a stiffly faithful kind, from the opening " Lived Gwendolina ! " to the " long tract of road " which figures in the notes at the end as a translation of " lungo tratto di via ". *Not on sale*, the title page announces ; and though Rossetti's pride was natural, the information was perhaps unnecessary.

[1] This letter is in Italian.

Maria's next production, more ambitious, was priced at a shilling. This was the *Vision of Human Life*, which ·Gabriel announces she has written for one of the family scrap-books in August 1843. It was published in 1846 under the title of *The Rivulets, A dream not all a Dream*, with a motto from *The Christian Year*. It is said that in the course of time Maria came to disapprove of the theological implications of this little story, and so suppressed it. What exactly she can have found objectionable in it is difficult to determine, but certain it is that only two copies of it are now extant, possibly only one. *The Rivulets* is a short allegorical tale in prose about four children, each of whom is set to guard a rivulet from pollution—the four rivulets representing the human heart, as a very convenient catechism explains at the end. The children, somewhat oddly, have German names—Liebe, Selbstsucht, Eigendünkel, Faule (i.e. Love, Selfishness, Conceit, Laziness)—and attend to their duty in ways corresponding to these labels. Liebe's devotion is eventually rewarded by assumption into heaven ; even Eigendünkel and Faule come off more favourably than might have been expected. Only the unforgivable Selbstsucht is lost, his mysterious end making perhaps the most vivid passage in the story and recalling in a crude way the eerie effect of some of Christina's poetry, as in the *Ballad of Boding*. The story altogether is the product of a deeply religious and earnest young mind, without much fertility of invention.

The Rivulets is the only piece of Maria's original composition which seems to have been preserved ; probably she wrote little else. Her father, as we have mentioned, accounted for this deviation by saying that she had no inclination to compose. Christina loyally chose to think that her sister was only prevented from achieving fame by religious scruples and domestic care ; but she herself, no less burdened in either way, could not be suppressed, and it is easy for a mind like Christina's to mistake strength of mind and character for genius. She thought Maria so much her superior in all things, that it was natural that she should attribute her manifest inferiority in this respect to her general superiority in devotion to duty and in religious faith.

[1] When Maria turned to other kinds of composition Christina was

---

[1] It has seemed worth while to carry the account of Maria to the close of her career, since little is ever said about her, and since there is in any case very little to say.

delighted. In January 1865 she writes to Dante Gabriel, " Have you heard of Maria's astute plan for an Italian Exercise Book ? I am doing some of the subordinate work for her down here in my hermitage. Truth to tell I have a great fancy for her name endorsing a book, as we three have all got into that stage, so I work with a certain enthusiasm." *Exercises in Idiomatic Italian through literal translation from the English* was published in 1867, together with a key called *Aneddoti Italiani*. The system of this ingenious work is to present anecdotes in a highly grotesque English which when translated literally may become very good Italian. For example, a lion has seized a child and gone off with it. " The mother at such a spectacle, forgets herself, pursues the wild beast, and having come up with it, throws herself at its feet, outstretches the arms, and the bosom panting and with the flames in the eyes, ' Return me,' she cries, ' return me the son.' The lion which had suspended the step, looks at her, and as if it venerated in her the love of mother, lays down softly the prey without the slightest injury and continues its steps. The artists have taken the care to transmit to the posterity this memorable event." It must have been amusing and easy for Maria's pupils to do their Italian compositions out of this book ; it certainly would have the effect of imprinting Italian idioms on the memory. It is not easy to forget the use of the verb *precipitare*, once you have translated the passage about a captain who detached himself from the paternal arms and precipitated into those of some one else. It is to be hoped, however, that no Italian has ever used the *Aneddoti* for English composition, and relied upon the *Exercises* for the key.

The number of students who found this book useful was sufficient to make it pay, though modestly and at some distance of time. At the end of the first year only eighty copies had been sold, and fifty of the key. But twenty years later, after Maria's death, the *Exercises* began to yield an unexpected profit, and in 1892 Christina was suddenly surprised by a payment of £12 6s. 6d., perhaps a not inadequate reward for her labours in 1865.

The hereditary task of Dante discipleship had of course been shouldered by Maria through the long years of her governessing and tutoring. She knew the poet through and through and talked of him with greater pleasure than of any other subject. Indeed a curious sidelight is thrown on Sir Edmund Gosse's joke at her expense that " the name of Dante was usually required to awaken her from a certain social torpor," by her own strictures on the general ignorance of the poet in England as elsewhere. " If in cultivated society we start him as a topic of conversation, how far is our interlocutor likely to sympathise with our vivid interest ? " Her enthusiasm eventually produced her best piece of writing, published in 1871, and called, after the passage in her fathers *Veggente*, *A Shadow of Dante*. It is a clear and able exposition of *The Divine Comedy*, still capable of being useful to beginners, although not free from a desire to improve the moral for Dante. Maria dedicated the book to her father, and there are occasional references to his work, though it would be wrong to call *A Shadow of Dante* the " child of the *Comento*," as an Italian writer has done, in any but a very general way. The family link is strengthened by her use of William's very flat translation of the *Inferno* and the incorporation of some of his notes on the poem. Strangely enough, when she quotes from the *Vita Nuova*, she translates for herself, disdaining for some reason the assistance of Dante Gabriel's version, the finest piece of work on Dante that the family produced. For the *Purgatorio* and the *Paradiso* she uses the blank verse rendering of Longfellow, which she calls " eminently faithful and beautiful."

The book was the fruit of a lifetime's devotion, and met with the success it merited, going through several editions. Swinburne complimented her warmly upon it, Dante Gabriel thought highly of it, and Christina's admiration was unbounded. It is quoted three times in *The Face of the Deep*, and to her niece Christina spoke of it thus : " It is indeed a work written from a fund of knowledge far wider and deeper than could be compressed into its pages, eloquent and elegant, the fruit of a fine mind and a noble soul. And to me, though not to you, it is graced with the endearing charm of resembling its beloved author by being full of goodness, and with no insignificant touch of greatness." Christina even thought it desirable that the book should be made accessible to Italian readers, and declared that were she a rich woman she would commission Teodorico to make it so.[1]

[1] There is in the British Museum a copy of another book by Maria Francesca, not mentioned by W. M. R., *Letters to my Bible Class on 37 Sundays*. Published by the S.P.C.K., London, n.d. According to the *Preface* the letters were addressed to a Friendly Society of girls and young women in a London parish. The first letter, dated 1860, 3rd Sunday in Lent, explains that ill-health had forced her to give up the class. The letters are easy and colloquial in manner, and though they no doubt adequately served their purpose, they are not now of any particular interest.

III

In spite of this success and of Christina's devotion, it would hardly have been surprising to discover in Maria some remnant of that jealousy which is said not to have survived the days of her childhood. She had much to envy. Not only were her brothers and sister gifted to a far greater extent with literary ability, but in grace of person and charm of mind they quite outshone her in the early days. It is perhaps possible that, conscious of her disadvantages in these respects, she unconsciously betook herself with more ardour to a religion in which they are mercifully ignored. Far harder to bear must have been the fact that such close personal contacts as came her way seem to have been both transitory and painful. Thus Ruskin appears to have had at one time a great esteem for Maria. When in a letter to Dante Gabriel he sends " deep and sincere respect to your sister," he does not mean, as might have been supposed, Christina, for whom he seems to have had little regard, but Maria. But his warm feeling for her soon died away ; and the monument of it remains in *Time Flies* in the words, " One of the most genuine Christians I ever knew once took lightly the dying out of a brief acquaintance which had engaged her warm heart, on the ground that such mere tastes and glimpses of congenial intercourse on earth wait for their development in Heaven."

Like Christina, moreover, she seems to have fallen in love with a Pre-Raphaelite Brother. This was Charles Allston Collins, brother of Wilkie, the only member of the group who was definitely High Church in sympathies. About 1855 Maria saw a good deal of him and his widowed mother. " The nearest approach to a ' preference ' that I knew her at any time to entertain was bestowed upon Collins." Whether her feeling was at all returned, or what happened to the relationship, it is impossible to say, since nothing but this solitary piece of information is forthcoming on the subject.

Towards the end of the 'sixties Maria formed the intention of entering a religious community. William's announcement in the summer of 1873 that he was to be married the following year gave his sister the opportunity of putting her desire into effect. It was proposed that Mrs. Rossetti and her two daughters should continue to live with William under the new régime ; they did not need Maria's help, and she would be a further incumbrance in the new household—the occasion seemed propitious, and Maria took the final step. She became a novice in the All Saints' Home, Margaret

Street, and after considerable delay, a professed sister. It is not until 3 November 1875 that Rossetti writes to Allingham; " Poor Maggie is parting with her greyish hair next Sunday, and annexing the kingdom of heaven for good."

At the time of entering upon her novitiate she was ill, which predisposed the family to anxiety. Even an Anglican convent, from which the novices seem to have been let out to spend Christmas with their families, is not the most comfortable place for an invalid. Two months after her admission Gabriel writes to William, " I have really felt very sincerely anxious about Maria since what you tell me of no fires in this blessed place. I simply could not exist on such terms —it would be a novitiate for another world ; and I view the matter as most serious for her." It is worth passing outside our prescribed dates to draw in this characteristic remark. He could have said nothing more unconsciously appropriate. For Maria it was in very truth a novitiate for another world, and she herself no doubt regarded the place as " blessed " ; whilst the whole matter was of course " most serious ". After all, she had not gone there for a holiday. It will be readily believed, on the other hand, that on such terms Dante Gabriel simply could not have existed. However, when Maria took her final vows, Dante Gabriel sent her a message through their mother to say how much he felt with her " in this great change to which her lifelong tendencies have pointed from the first."

Maria " delighted beyond measure in the religious life " ; but her health, far from robust when she entered upon it, grew worse very rapidly, until it was obvious that she could live little longer. Dante Gabriel was very attentive to her to the last. " It is terrible indeed," he writes to her mother a few days before her death, " to think of that bright mind and those ardently acquired stores of knowledge now prisoned in so frail and perishing a frame. How sweet and true a life, and how pure a death, hopeful and confiding in every last instant ! Her expressions to me as to the relation she felt herself to bear to her Lord, and her certainty of seeing him in person, were things hardly to be counted as intercourse with a soul still on earth." Maria died peacefully on 24 November 1876.

William wrote to Swinburne soon afterwards, " If Maria's beliefs were correct, she is certainly at this moment a Saint in Heaven— she having been of all persons I ever knew, the most naturally religious-minded, and the most (perhaps the *most*) undeviating in doing exactly what she perceived or assumed to be right." And describing her more fully in his *Reminiscences* years afterwards, he says, " Her Christian faith, conviction, and personal confidence, were of the most absolute kind ; she viewed with solemn gladness her inevitably approaching death, longing to be with Christ. . . . She would I believe (though born rather timid than otherwise) have gone to the stake with the greatest intrepidity for any religious tenet which she held precious—such for instance as the real presence of Christ in the eucharist."

IV

About Maria, the least known and at first glimpse perhaps the least attractive of Gabriele's four children, two very different opinions have been expressed. Mr. T. J. Wise says " Maria Rossetti was the most humanly attractive of the Rossetti family. In my estimation she holds, in character though not in performance, a similar position to that held by Emily in the Brontë circle." Sir Edmund Gosse, on the other hand, in his essay on Christina, has a paragraph in which he describes Maria as a woman of strong but narrow mind and of poor imagination, quite unconversable except on the subject of Dante, and acting upon the sensitive mind of her sister as Newton acted upon Cowper. Her influence, he says, was " a species of police surveillance," which " starved the less pietistic, but painfully conscientious nature of Christina." Of these two opinions, the second, harsh though it is, is perhaps the more accordant with the impression made upon the mind of a close student of the Rossetti records. But both are misleading. Maria did not at all resemble Emily Brontë ; and the parallel with Newton is inappropriate because Maria, as a sister, loved deeply, and was most deeply beloved, and also because Christina's conscientiousness never approached the border-line of insanity. And even a literary critic may sometimes remember that literature is not everything, nor even the better part of everything. Christina's love and veneration for Maria was lifelong. She quotes her sister's most casual words like an oracle, both in her family letters and in her books. " I remember our dear Maria used to say . . ." or " I have never forgotten the courageous reverence with which one who . . ." The influence of Maria over her mind must have been considerable ; she herself would have said that her debt was infinite. The might-have-been is the most futile of speculations in the sphere of criticism as elsewhere. Without Maria it may be that the mind which produced Christina's poetry would have been quite different ; in that case the poetry also would have been different, but it is beyond the power of Sir Edmund Gosse or anybody else to know if it would have been better. Indeed that peculiar inner tension which gives her religious verse so taut and clear a poignancy, which gives it in fact most of its power, might as reasonably be laid to Maria's credit as the overscrupulousness of which the critics complain. For the latter of course she may well have been partly responsible. Maria was afraid to look at Blake's designs for the book of Job because of the second commandment; she would not go into the mummy room at the British Museum for fear the last judgment should take place while she was there. At the same time she was capable of enjoying a wedding feast, and had a strong aversion to sad funerals; while we have already quoted Dante Gabriel's opinion that she was the most cheerful member of the family except their mother. Christina's habitual melancholy—to avoid the use of a much defined and much disputed epithet—could certainly not have been approved by her sister.

The last thing which it seems proper to remember is that Christina loved and admired Maria for qualities which she thought lacking in herself, and which in truth were lacking. How she felt toward her sister may finally be suggested by the poem she wrote about Maria in 1886 :

> My love whose heart is tender said to me,
> " A moon lacks light except her sun befriend her.
> Let us keep tryst in heaven, dear Friend," said she,
> My love whose heart is tender.
>
> From such a loftiness no words could bend her ;
> Yet still she spoke of " us " and spoke as " we ",
> Her hope substantial while my hope grew slender.
>
> Now keeps she tryst beyond earth's utmost sea,
> Wholly at rest tho' storms should toss and rend her ;
> And still she keeps my heart and keeps its key,
> My love whose heart is tender.

III. DANTE GABRIEL

Watts-Dunton said of Dante Gabriel Rossetti that the English strain in the family found expression in him and in him alone; he speaks of "the hearty ring of his voice that drew Englishmen to him as to a magnet." (To this he adds, with an unconscious lack of national pride, that of the sense of duty which was so strong in the other members of the family, Dante Gabriel had but little.) Similarly William Michael declares that while Maria, Christina, and himself all felt themselves to be aliens, Dante Gabriel liked to think of himself as an Englishman and cherished English prejudices; he "liked England and the English better than any other country or nation," and "was quite as ready as other Britons to reckon to the discredit of Frenchmen and generally of foreigners, a certain shallow and frothy demonstrativeness." Ruskin, on the other hand, would have us believe that he was all Italian. "He was not really an Englishman, but a great Italian tormented in the Inferno of London, doing the best he could and teaching the best he could; but the 'could' shortened by the strength of his animal passions, without any trained control or guiding faith."

Without venturing here into the difficult question of racial propensities, it may be observed that one of the most obvious characteristics of Dante Gabriel—his habit of laughing at things which he knew to be serious—is equally proper both to Englishmen and Florentines. There was nothing about which he was ever deeply in earnest, about which he did not at one time or another write or speak jestingly or even flippantly. His painting, his poetry, his depression and Christina's melancholy, Maria's entering the religious life, even his love for Lizzie Siddal, are all included. Possibly his mother is the only exception. It is a characteristic that makes little appearance in his poetry or painting, but is scattered everywhere in his letters. Had his personality achieved complete expression in verse, it might have resembled Byron's more closely than that of any other English writer. He had no religion, and practically no reverence.

For the rest Watts-Dunton's remark about the sense of duty is obviously true. Nothing marks Dante Gabriel off more clearly from the rest of the family than his irresponsibility, wilfulness, self-indulgence, and total lack of self-discipline. " What I ought to do is what I can't do," he once said. The most richly endowed in genius, he was the most weakly framed in moral quality ; and the defect is not only at the root of all that is best passed over in his life, but also of all that will least bear scrutiny in his art.

II

We left Dante Gabriel in childhood, defiant, spirited, handsome, and attractive, a general favourite, and much encouraged to take his own way. A cabman later in life called him a " harbitary cove ", and such he was from his earliest years. He was not less fond of his mother than were the others, and not really less affected by her inculcations ; but he was more demonic than they, and felt a stronger impulse to follow his own path. By the time he was leaving school and beginning to paint, a sharp contrast appears between his letters to his parents and to William Michael. A letter to William in November 1844 begins thus : " I received yesterday evening your unsightly missive containing the two *Chuzzlewits*, which were much admired." A few days later he writes to his father, " I fear you must have thought me remiss in not writing sooner. I should have done so, had I had anything to say which I thought would interest you." After ten more lines he goes on, " After much racking of brains I am sorry to find that this first piece of news is likewise the last." But it is followed a week later by a long and lively letter to William about his purchases and the books he has been reading ; then by a letter to his mother which concludes, " Being afraid, dear Mamma, that any news I might have to tell would not be of a nature to interest *you*, I shall address it instead to William."

As he reaches manhood the anxieties his parents felt in his child-hood grew greater. All had been to some extent sacrificed to his career ; and yet there seemed to be grave doubt whether he was making the best of his opportunities. Their distress reached a climax over the portrait of his father that Lyell had commissioned him to paint in 1848—his first picture in oil. Dante Gabriel had many friends by this time, and many delightful ways of spending his time. Besides this, Lyell had sent him £10 on account. On 8 August Gabriele writes to his wife, who is at Brighton with Polidori and Christina, " Here everything is going well, except that

Gabriel seems to think as much about doing my portrait for Mr. Lyell as I do about making a journey to the moon. He has begun it three times, and every time he has torn up the sketch. So I have lost about eight hours and even more patience, sitting as still as a post. For three days running now he has gone out, and he never says a word about the picture. To-day he is going to Gravesend with a friend of his, and so he will do to-morrow and the next day, and good-bye to work. What shall we say to Mr. Lyell ? I blush to think of it. You did not do well to let him get those £10 from you ; the money should not have been given to him until the work was finished. I say nothing to him for fear of some insulting reply. You know him well enough. The money has simply led him astray, not reconciled him to his work. But I will write no more about it. Why should I worry you ? . . ." Four days later finds the situation unchanged. " Gabriel continues to carry on in the way which it gave me so much pain to describe. For the work to which conscience and honour should impel him he does nothing, nothing, nothing. He goes out all day long and only returns very late at night. I hope that when the ten pounds have come to an end (and I hope it will not take long) and he has nothing left to squander, he will begin to do what he ought to do. This is the tenth day that he has given no thought to it."

Some idea of the counter-attractions which duty and the Lyell portrait had to contend with may be gathered from the young painter's letters to his brother in the month of August. " Hunt and I went the other night to Woolner's where we composed a poem of twenty-four stanzas on the alternate system. I transcribe the last stanza, which was mine, to show you the style of thing :

> ' 'Twas thus, thus is, and thus shall be :
> The Beautiful—the Good—
> Still mirror to the Human Soul
> Its own intensitude ! ' "

" *Apropos* of death, Hunt and I are going to get up among our acquaintance a Mutual Suicide Association, by the regulations whereof any member, being weary of life, may call at any time upon another to cut his throat for him. It is all of course to be done very quietly, without weeping or gnashing of teeth." " I went the other night to see *Lucrezia* at Covent Garden. . . . At the end of the first act . . . Grisi screamed continuously for about two minutes and was immense."

It is very obvious that Gabriele had no influence over him at all. The result of his father's complaints was that Mrs. Rossetti herself wrote from Hastings, with much more success. " I thank you for writing to Gabriel. It seems that your letter has produced a good effect. He read it yesterday evening on his return home at about 11.30, and this morning, coming down to breakfast at about ten, he told me that he was going out for a couple of hours, and that on his return he would again take up work on the portrait, of which he made an outline at an earlier sitting. Pray God he may persevere in this purpose, for his own good which is hardly to be separated from our own." All now went well. " I have the satisfaction ", writes his father on 21 August, " of informing you that this (Monday) morning our Gabriel has for an hour and a half been working at my portrait in colours, which appears to me to come very like, if I can trust my poor eyesight and the exclamations of our emphatic Maria. Moreover I asked Gabriel whether he would go on to-morrow, and he said that he would. If he takes a fancy to it, he will not leave off until he has finished the work ; you know his character as well as I do. I now trust that all I wrote you in my recent letter was only the outcome of the excessive anxiety of a father who gets distressed at any appearance of evil in what concerns a beloved son. You did well not to communicate what I said to anybody. We have perhaps saved Polidori an anxiety."

It is curious to turn from this correspondence to the diary of Madox Brown, Dante Gabriel's master, during the years 1847-8 ; and to read there the account of this aspiring and energetic man carving his way to fame, working at times, twelve, fifteen, or even eighteen hours a day, a man who, after a day's toil till dusk on one occasion, could make the entry, " Am a very swine—shall never get the painting done in time—am a beast and a sleepy brute." Or to read of Millais, to whom Fortune turned a more smiling face, unimpeded in his tireless industry by all the prosperity of his home.

At last on 27 October Gabriele is able to tell Lyell that the picture is ready. " I announce to you with joy that our Gabriel-Carlo-Dante has now finished the portrait that is to have the honour of a place in the library of one of the most distinguished men of letters in Scotland. And I tell you this with greater satisfaction since in the judgment of all who have seen it, it resembles me exactly. The day before yesterday my friend Count Pepoli saw it and praised it to the skies, both for its perfect resemblance and for its pictorial quality, which he called *masterly* ; and Pepoli is a great connoisseur of painting, and has been a painter himself." On 3 November he acknowledges with effusive gratitude a payment of £15 " which you have been pleased to add to the ten pounds, already a munificent reward for his work. . . . He may be considered a certain hope of his noble profession, and I trust that England will have its Gabriel as Italy has its Raphael." The painter of the picture, however, by no means approved of his father's superlative expressions. He writes to his godfather on 14 November, and the difference of tone is amusing. " It has been a subject of much regret to me that a picture upon which I am at present engaged (and some parts of which, requiring natural objects, it was necessary to paint before the winter came on, has so long delayed the completion of the portrait which this letter accompanies. Of your kindness and generosity as regards that portrait I need not here express my deep sense ; I will only beg you to believe in its sincerity.

I was much annoyed on hearing my father's letter to you, that he should so have raised your expectation of the picture as I *know* that now you cannot but feel disappointed upon seeing it. But to induce him to let slip any opportunity of praising his children would be impossible ; and though the affection thus displayed is very gratifying, its result is sometimes far otherwise. As for Conte Pepoli, friends *will* be polite, as I told him when he was bestowing his commendations. The real fact is that the only merit of the portrait is its resemblance, which all pronounce to be striking, and which I myself can also perceive. I endeavour to persuade myself that its unsatisfactory character in other respects is owing in a great measure to its being my first attempt in oils of the size of life. Believing this to be the case, I have commenced a likeness of my father on a smaller scale (more corresponding with the size of the heads I generally paint), of which I intend to beg your kind acceptance from your grateful godson. I had hoped to send it with this, but could not get it finished in time, and was unwilling to occasion any further delay in the transmission of the larger portrait."

Gabriele's anxiety about his son was not stilled by the happy end of this vexation. Toward the end of his father's life, Gabriel occasionally calls him " the governor ", which can only mean that affection might still be alive, but that respect was not. It irritated his father not only to see him apparently wasting his time, but also spending time in reading and writing which Gabriele thought he should give to his profession. Sometimes, risking the " insulting reply ", he " found occasion to reprehend Dante sharply, and even severely ; and to reprehension ", says William, " my brother was at all times more than sufficiently stubborn. These rifts in cordial family affection were always distressing when they occurred, though they soon healed over again." His father's reproaches remained upon his conscience to his dying day, and had power to distress him deeply in moments of illness and depression. With reference to some correction which must have been more than usually bitter, Christina writes to William in 1881, " Thinking about what you said of poor Gabriel's distress, I seem to recover a shadowy recollection of the incident, and if I am right, Mamma used her influence successfully to get the words unsaid. . . . No wonder that in weakness and suffering such a reminiscence haunts weary days and sleepless hours of double darkness." It was a year before the death of his father that Gabriel wrote the sonnet *Known in Vain*.

> . . . So it happeneth
> When work and will awake too late, to gaze
> After their life sailed by, and hold their breath.
> Ah ! who shall dare to search through what sad maze
> Thenceforth their incommunicable ways
> Follow the desultory feet of death.

Dissatisfaction with his own progress towards independence together with the precarious situation of the family almost drove Dante Gabriel into becoming a telegraphist on the North Western Railway, a project the speedy collapse of which, as William suggests, was lucky for the passengers. But eventually, yielding to parental entreaty and the common sense of his position, he decided in 1853 to concentrate his energies on painting and to leave poetry comparatively alone. Thus our closing date is fixed approximately at a real turning-point in his career.

III

The work of no writer is more full of literary inspiration than that of Rossetti. His memory was very retentive, especially for things that appealed to him, as is the way with most men of genius ; and his reading was so wide and various as to make it futile to attempt to follow in detail the effects of it all upon his mind. William Michael having recorded its main elements in some fullness, we need only refer to the chief names on his lists. Dante Gabriel's earliest enthusiasms were for Shakespeare, *Faust*, Scott, *The Arabian Nights*, and fiction of the Gothic and macabre kind. Byron followed Scott as first favourite (next to Shakespeare) in his schooldays. Dickens was read as he appeared. And about the same time came a good deal of what may be called boys' fiction, *Tales of Chivalry*, *Brigand Tales*, *The Seven Champions of Christendom*, *Legends of Terror* ; as well as *Gil Blas*, *Don Quixote*, and some romances of Bulwer. Hone's *Every-Day Book* and *The Newgate Calendar* were constant favourites. In Italian a little Ariosto was read ; in French *Notre Dame de Paris*. Byron yielded to Shelley in 1844, and was followed by Keats, the old ballads, and Mrs. Browning. De Musset, Victor Hugo, Dumas, Poe, Tennyson, Coleridge, Blake— all these were read and enjoyed in the years following 1844. In the literature of the wonderful he read Hoffmann's *Tales*, Chamisson's *Peter Schlemihl*, Lamotte-Fouqué's *Undine*, the romances of Maturin (which he took in with breathless excitement), and Meinhold's *Sidonia the Sorceress*. Surprising as it may be, after such a list, Thackeray was highly appreciated by Dante Gabriel even before the appearance of *Vanity Fair*. His last important discovery was made about 1847, when Browning came into his orbit and carried all before him. Informative books, of the historical or even less of the scientific kind, he hardly read at all ; his knowledge of history according to his brother being mainly derived from Shakespeare and the historical novelists. His father objected to this and used to say, " When you have read a novel of Walter Scott, what do you know ? The fancies of Walter Scott." Though whether the fancies of Walter Scott are less reliable as a source of historical information than the fancies of Gabriele Rossetti may well be doubted.

All these books and many others were in some degree admired, and some of them contributed a good deal to the formation of the poet-painter's genius. Leaving out of account the Bible with which Mrs. Rossetti had ensured his acquaintance, and in which he was particularly affected by the books of *Job*, *Ecclesiastes*, and *Revelations*, two names always stood for him above all others (as the P. R. B. might have said, in Class I. of the Immortals, with four stars). One was Shakespeare ; the other, not so far mentioned, was Dante. All Gabriel's earliest reading was in English ; and French books seem to have made a more frequent appearance than Italian, in which language his youthful reading does not appear to have been at all wide. Of Dante he could not fail to hear a great deal at home throughout his childhood, but if he did not read him for many years there are obvious reasons. Children rarely take easily to books which are the constant preoccupation of their elders, especially a

child so addicted to making his own discoveries as Dante Gabriel
was. Another and very sufficient reason is that Dante is not
adapted for a child's reading. Becoming adolescent, and with
his mother's training behind him, Dante Gabriel found that
the much talked of Dante spoke to him directly. In 1841, when
he was thirteen, Kirkup's copy of the Bargello Dante came
into his father's hands, and must have given some reality to the
" banshee " for the children ; all the more because this was not
the stern, ascetic, laurel-crowned Dante of *The Divine Comedy* but
the young poet of the *Vita Nuova*, the singer of Beatrice. At sixteen
Gabriel was reading the poet for himself, with an absorption and a
delight which grew greater with years. His coming under the
shadow of Dante has been described by himself in a well-known
passage of the preface to his translations. " In those early days, all
around me partook of the influence of the great Florentine ; till from
viewing it as a natural element, I also, growing older, was drawn
within the circle."

IV

Considering the great variety of Dante Gabriel's reading in the light
of his later work, both in painting and poetry, it is clear that its most
fruitful parts fall into two classes, the Dantesque and the Gothic,
Dante standing sublime amid a host of very minor satellites,
over against the glamorous array of dealers in magic and spells.
Among the latter is Keats with the two *Eves* and the *Belle Dame*,
and Coleridge ; Scott and the old ballads ; Poe and Maturin and
Monk Lewis ; Meinhold and the *Wandering Jew*. The fusion
and confusion of these two elements in his mind gives the key to
almost all his work. It is no doubt necessary to go beyond them to
account for subsidiary features, a touch of Shelley here and there,
more than a touch of Browning in *A Last Confession* (a not very
characteristic piece of work), a good deal of Shakespeare, and perhaps
even of Milton, in the style of his sonnets ; but in the conception
and spirit of his work there is no doubt that our two main classes
of reading account for the greater part of Dante Gabriel's inspiration.

Consider the first direction in which his childish compositions
turned. His first effort, a dramatic poem written at about the age
of six, was called *The Slave*, and appears to have been primitively
Shakespearean. The characters were Don Manuel, a Spanish Lord ;
Traitor, an Officer ; Slave, a Servant to Traitor ; Mortimer, an

English Knight ; Guards, Messengers, etc. These gentlemen abuse each other and fight throughout the poem ; Traitor kills himself, Mortimer slays himself in sympathy, Don Manuel kills Slave, and thus is left the only survivor. There was, needless to say, no love interest. At about the same time he was drawing subjects from Shakespeare's plays.

The Slave was followed in the same notebook by the beginning of a collection of the *Beauties of Shakespeare*, not carried any farther than the speech of Portia on Mercy, and a few lines of a story called *Aladdin*. After these no other composition is recorded until 1840, the young poet being then twelve, when all the children began to write a romantic tale, only Dante Gabriel's being preserved. We are now in the full tide of chivalric romance. The tale was called *Roderick and Rosalba, a story of the Round Table*. It concerned a lady who was captured by a " marauder " who wanted to wed her perforce, but who was of course rescued by her affianced knight. The story opens thus :

It was a dark and stormy night in the month of December when a figure, closely wrapped in the sable folds of his cloak, and mounted on a jaded steed, was seen hurrying across a bleak common towards a stately castle in the distance, whose lofty towers and time-worn battlements frowned over the wide expanse beneath.

At about the same time, perhaps a little later, he composed a poem in a similar vein. This was *Sir Hugh the Heron, a Legendary Tale in Four Parts*. Almost all written at the age of twelve, it was finished two years later, at the persuasion of Polidori who wished to print it. This was his first printed work. His father sent a copy of it to Frere, to its author's regret since he was already ashamed of it ; later in life he hated to hear it referred to. It certainly has no great merit, but one or two points are worth a moment's pause. The subject was taken from one of the stories in the *Legends of Terror*, while the manner is that of Scott. The poem starts in ballad metre, telling how Sir Hugh, discovered in a chapel, hears a noise of arms outside, and sallying forth, disperses a pirate band of which no more is heard than their presence and defeat, kills their leader on his own ship and rescues a " lady bright " called Beatrice, surely a very unusual name for a lady of romance. He took her to his castle ; but soon, following his knightly duty of fighting in foreign lands, he leaves her in the care of his brother Sir Aymer.

> Thus saying, from the fortalice
> His footsteps quick he wound :
> " He's gone," sobbed Lady Beatrice,
> And fainted on the ground.

At last a minstrel comes to the castle, telling in a song about the death of Sir Hugh on the " fatal field of Barnet." And here a note explains, " I have caused the minstrel to commit the mistake of representing Hugh as falling in this battle, in order to apprise the reader that his tale is a fabrication ; our hero being in France at the time." The minstrel says he was met on the way to battle by an old bard who rose before him and gave him a warning :

> Wildly sounds that old man's lyre,
> Touched by some unearthly hand

But he would not turn back, and so was killed,

> Sorely through his rash rejection
> Of that prophet minstrel old

—just as King James was to reject the warnings of the mysterious old hag much later in *The King's Tragedy*. And *Rose Mary* is recalled by the next episode, where a necromancer sitting mysterious by the embers of a fire shows the hero, in a magic mirror, a vision of what is going on at home.

> What he saw that wizard knew,
> But no mortal soul beside.

Sir Hugh rushes back to England where the heroine is in great distress. Sir Aymer is breaking his trust, but Sir Hugh arrives just in time to rescue her from his brother's " powerful grasp ". Childish though it may be, this spirited production has in obvious embryo the mind which was to delight in " stunning words " (cf. fortalice), and to excel in mysterious and romantic balladry.

At fifteen, soon after he had begun to learn German from Heimann, Dante Gabriel wrote a shorter ballad called *William and Marie*, in which William Michael thought that, in addition to the still admired Scott, there may have been a touch of Bürger's *Lenore*. It is about a wicked knight who having killed a good one, threw his lady love into a moat, and was killed for his pains by an avenging flash of lightning. A prose tale, *Sorrentino*, written about the same time is not content with mysterious evils, but embodying another strain of German origin, introduces the Devil in person, the poet's interest in whom is further attested by his sketch of Mephistopheles at the door of Gretchen's cell (1846), and the sonnet *Retro me Satana* (the subject also of an oil in 1847, afterwards destroyed). Finally to 1846 belongs the grotesque ballad *Jan van Hunks*, which was finished on the poet's death-bed. The story, founded on one of the *Tales of Chivalry*, is about a Dutchman who was challenged by the devil to a smoking match, was of course beaten, and carried off to Hell to be turned into a pipe for the devil's use in perpetuity, a fate he had thoroughly earned by cruelty to his family. The poem is humorous in a grim way, and has some strikingly eerie phrases, but the general effect is juvenile and amateurish. Examples of the humorous grotesque treatment of fantastic subjects may be found in the *Tales of Terror*, which were perhaps in Rossetti's mind when he began the poem, as well as the story in *Tales of Chivalry* ; but treatment and theme lie outside the beaten track of the poet's work and are linked to it only by slight suggestions. The stanza is that of *The Blessed Damozel*, rather more carelessly managed. Jan's son knocking at the door while the smoking is at full blast within, and then his daughter knocking too, and telling that her mother is dead vaguely recall the supplicants outside the window in *Sister Helen*, while the expedient of showing a vision in a mirror, already used in *Sir Hugh the Heron*, appears with the substitution of a beryl in *Rose Mary*.

So much for the juvenile work which preceded Dante Gabriel's important compositions. It is all romantic and leaning to the mediaeval, the sombre, and the supernatural ; with streaks of the macabre. Meanwhile the young poet was also serving his apprenticeship as a translator. About 1844 he made a version of Bürger's *Lenore*, which he already knew in the *Tales of Terror*, and subsequently he embarked on a translation of the *Nibelungenlied*. This ambitious venture was not carried through and the manuscript was subsequently lost. To the year 1846 belongs the translation of *Der Arme Heinrich*, which appears in the collected works. But before this he had begun to translate Dante and the old Italian lyrists.

V

Dante too was mediaeval. Unless Rossetti the elder was right, he and his fellows wrote of love, and often of distressed or bereaved love. There was clearly a bridge between Dante and Dante Gabriel's other favourites which he crossed and recrossed in those years of emotional adolescence. But it is a bridge between two very different lands. Between Dante and the old ballads there are possibly certain resemblances ; between Dante and the romantic mediae-valisers of later ages there is no resemblance at all. Rossetti as we shall later see tended to merge them together in a dreamy and erotic mist which obscured the outlines of both ; for the present it is sufficient to remark that the path from Scott to the singer of Beatrice was easy for him in 1844.

Books were plentiful and always ready to hand. His father quotes profusely from Dante's contemporaries and certainly possessed the works of many of them ; and once his interest was aroused, Dante Gabriel sought for what he could not find at home in the British Museum library, now in process of transformation under the skilful hand of his father's supposed arch-enemy, the magician Panizzi. What is more, on his father's bookshelves was a translation of Dante's minor poems—his father, mother, and sister had helped in its composition, his own godfather had written it. Lyell's version of the lyrical poems of Dante, which had first appeared in 1835, was reprinted in 1840 ; and again with additions in 1845, this being the year in which Gabriel began to concern himself with the subject. Was he possibly moved by Lyell's very wooden efforts to see what he could do himself ? Writing to Lyell in 1848, he says, " I need not say of how much benefit your works have proved to me in my undertaking, as regards the literary portion of it." But actually he could have had little to gain from them, unless it were the impulse to enter the lists himself.

The dates of his translations are a little obscure. William Michael says that most of them were made between 1845 and 1849 and that the *Vita Nuova* was probably done first ; his evidence is not lightly to be put aside, but there is no other to take us back as far as 1845. The earliest data outside William's recollections are to be found in the letters to Lyell, late in 1848. On 27 October Gabriele tells Lyell that his son has that day finished his translation of the *Vita Nuova*—no other poems are mentioned. In a letter of July 1854, the poet himself says that he made the translation " some five years ago ", which comes a little short of fact and very much short of William's suggested date. In November 1850 he is " translating *canzoni* at a great rate of evenings ", and returns the same month from Sevenoaks bringing with him " a great quantity of translations from the old Italian." Altogether it is safest to assume that he made some tentative beginnings as early as 1845, when Lyell's republished translations had come to hand ; that he grew absorbed in the task in 1848 when working hard at the *Vita Nuova*, and that in the next year or two he made the majority of the remaining translations. By this time the idea of making a book of them had developed but did not at first materialise ; he then contemplated publishing them in some periodical, perhaps *Fraser*, but gave up the project. Eventually they appeared, his first book, in 1861.

It would be interesting to know whether Dante Gabriel solicited his father's help with this enterprise. There is no evidence at all that he did ; while it is psychologically improbable. The translation of the *Vita Nuova* was obviously intensely felt ; the poet was working with Dante's loss of a real Beatrice in mind, full of a young man's sympathy for love in gentle hearts. To consult his father's advice would have been to invite an altogether unwelcome disquisition on the *gergo* and the Freemasons, with all of which he evidently had little patience at all. His father on the other hand could hardly fail to be aware of his son's complete disregard of his theories, and it is surprising that he makes no mention of it to Lyell. Let us hope that neither William nor Gabriel passed on to their father the comment made on the translations by a famous friend of the Pre-Raphaelites, " Patmore says they are the only true love poems he ever saw."

The quality of these translations has been closely examined only by Mr. R. L. Mégroz in what is certainly the weakest chapter in his suggestive book on Rossetti. He asserts that the poet's style suffered from the effort to render both metre and sense of sometimes complicated originals, that he acquired from the exercise a habit of otiose phrase and tortured syntax. But the argument is made to proceed from a letter to Norton in which Rossetti is represented as saying that the obscurities are " a thousand times more murky *than* in the originals." What the poet actually said in that letter was that the obscurities are " a thousand times more murky in the originals ", and there is lacking in Mr. Mégroz's chapter any evidence of resort to those originals which would have shown that Rossetti's remark is strictly true.

The translations have been so much loved and praised that there is no need here to dwell upon their marvellous recreation of the Italian poems in spirit and in form. They are by far the finest tribute to Dante paid by the Rossetti family. Benson remarks that the translation of the *Vita Nuova* is not always faithful, the infidelities occurring not wilfully but in the attempt to avoid verbal difficulties ; and that the general effect is " to screw Dante's note up a little higher." To the first of these criticisms Rossetti himself supplies the answer in his preface to the printed collection ; a strictly literal translation was not his aim.   In spite of this, the degree of closeness he achieves is amazing, and only to be appreciated by one who has compared the translation and the original line by line.   In the prose parts, the slightly archaic English is a perfect re-embodiment of Dante's Italian ; in the verse more freedom has naturally been taken, and the fidelity to the sense varies from poem to poem.   The famous canzone, *Donne ch'avete intelletto d'amore*, is an example of triumphant fidelity.   Elsewhere it is true that an empty phrase is sometimes used to fill up a line or to supply a rhyme—as for example *in very sooth* (Sonnet 4), *Love fills up the space* (Sonnet 8), *verily* (Ibid.), *in somewise* (Sonnet 11) ; and it may be that in this way the poet acquired a habit that persists in his original work.   A stanza in the earliest version of *The Blessed Damozel* ends weakly with *Yea verily* ; Sonnet 96 of *The House of Life* has a deplorable *I ween* ; and Sonnet 101 ends with a line which owes its existence more to the fact that a sonnet must have fourteen lines than to any other reason—

> Not less nor more, but even that word alone.

As for the heightening of Dante's pitch, it is true that some expressions in the translations have a definiteness and a vigour which in the originals they did not possess and do not require. Dante's ninth sonnet ends *There begins a trembling in my heart which makes the soul leave my pulses*.   This appears as

> the blood seems as shaken from my heart
> And all my pulses beat at once and stop

which is excellent in itself, but too arresting in its context.   Other examples are easy to find—Death's *crudele adoperare* (Sonnet 2) becomes a *leaden sleep*, *appressarsi* (Canzone 2) becomes *bending themselves over me*, the sighs which *disconsolati vanno via* in Sonnet 17 are rendered by *mark how they force their way out and press through*, *che non sospiri in dolcezza d'amore* (Sonnet 16) becomes *Without a passion of exceeding love*.   That such divergences occur and that they are to some degree unfaithful to the gentle sweetness of the *Vita Nuova* cannot be denied.   But they are not frequent enough to justify so strong a phrase as Benson's, particularly since they do not occur at all in the prose and some of the most suave and peaceful poems are free from them.   The rendering for instance of *Tanto gentile e tanto onesta pare* (Sonnet 15) is altogether admirable.

My lady looks so gentle and so pure
When yielding salutation by the way,
That the tongue trembles and has nought to say,
And the eyes, which fain would see, may not endure.
And still, amid the praise she hears secure,
She walks with humbleness for her array ;
Seeming a creature sent from Heaven to stay
On earth, and show a miracle made sure.
    She is so pleasant in the eyes of men
    That through the sight the inmost heart doth gain
    A sweetness which needs proof to know it by :
    And from between her lips there seems to move,
    A soothing essence that is full of love,
    Saying for ever to the spirit, " Sigh ! "

These remarks apply as well to the rest of the poems by other authors. But here Rossetti was often translating obscure and eccentric work, altogether lacking in the clarity and ease of Dante's. The inspiration of the translation rises naturally with the beauty of the original ; the loveliest of all these poems has the most perfect of all the renderings, and becomes almost as marvellous a poem in English as it was in Italian—

    Al cor gentil ripara sempre Amore
    Come alla selva augello in la verdura

loses nothing at all in Rossetti's

    Within the gentle heart Love shelters him
    As birds within the green shade of the grove.

If in other poems the translation sounds awkward and obscure, the fault should not be laid to Rossetti's charge without resort to the original. One example will illustrate this. Mr. Mégroz complains of the " long and tortured sentences " in the rendering of what he calls Pisano's canzone, *Of his change through love*. This poet, Pannuccio del Bagno (certainly Pisano but no more so than all the other inhabitants of Pisa), is one of the most obscure and artificial of the Pisan poets. The opening stanza of the poem in question can hardly be less difficult to Italians than Rossetti's version to Englishmen ; and the first line of the fifth stanza, to which Mr. Mégroz has a particular objection,

    Without almost, I am all rapturous

is nothing but a faithful attempt to reproduce

    Senza alcun quasi par son' in gran gioia.

At the same time the tendency to strengthen the original noticed in the *Vita Nuova* is here and there still apparent, giving a faint tinge of Rossetti colouring which at one point at least is inexcusable. Giacomino Pugliese has a beautiful poem addressed to Death, noted by Rossetti as being the first Italian poem concerned with a dead love. One of its stanzas in Rossetti's translation runs :

> Where is my lady, and the lovely face
> She had, and the sweet motion when she walked ?—
> Her chaste, mild favour—her so delicate grace—
> Her eyes, her mouth, and the dear way she talked ?—
> Her courteous bending—her most noble air—
> The soft fall of her hair ? . . .
> My lady—she to whom my soul
>   A gladness brought !
> Now do I never see her anywhere,
> And may not, looking in her eyes, gain there
>   The blessing which I sought.

We shall not here transcribe the original of this ; but whoever chooses to consult it will find that the latter part of the stanza is admirably translated while the first half is very much Rossetti's own. There is nothing in Giacomino about her *sweet motion when she walked* ; nothing about *bending* ; and above all there is no authority for the very Rossettian *soft fall of her hair*. The passage as it stands recalls what William Michael terms the " female figures with floral adjuncts " of his brother's painting. And notice that the falling of hair is to appear again in an original poem of Rossetti's about this time, a poem also concerned with a dead love, *The Blessed Damozel*.[1]

It is comparatively immaterial that the poet follows his guides into certain mistakes which later scholarship have exposed. Of the canzoni of Cavalcanti, for example, which he found very difficult to translate, he gives neither of the two now recognised as authentic, while the four he does give are all spurious. There is also one comical mistranslation which changes the purport of a whole sonnet. It is by Cecco Angiolieri.

> Dante Alighieri in Becchina's praise
> Won't have me sing, and bears him like my lord.
> He's but a pinchbeck florin, on my word ;
> Sugar he seems, but salt's in all his ways ;
> He looks like wheaten bread, who's bread of maize ;

[1] See also Sonnet 21 and *The Stream's Secret*.

He's but a sty, though like a tower in height ;
A falcon, till you find that he's a kite ;
Call him a cock !—a hen's more like his case.
   Go now to Florence, Sonnet of my own,
   And there with dames and maids hold pretty parles,
   And say that all he is doth only seem.
   And I meanwhile will make him better known
   Unto the Count of Provence, good King Charles ;
   And in this way we'll singe his skin for him.

This is vigorous abuse, but unfortunately it was not in the original
directed against Dante.   A correct translation of the first two lines
would read, " Dante Alighieri, I will stop singing about Becchina,
and will say something about the Marshal "—that is a certan
Diego della Ratta, who commanded the Catalan mercenaries in
Florence in the name of the King of Naples.   Old Gabriele himself
had been mistaken about this sonnet.   " This Cecco (Angiolieri)
wrote to Dante a sonnet, ' Dante Alighieri, I intend no longer to
sing about Becchina ; call me Mariscalco if you will ; for this
Becchina is outwardly a golden florin, but inwardly brass. . . .' "
So now Becchina receives the abuse, but that is of no consequence,
seeing that in the eyes of Gabriele the whole sonnet is a blind,
threatening to reveal the secret of the *gergo* to King Charles.
We cannot believe that a poet would go to the King to accuse
his mistress ; this is one of the " incongruities which a knowledge of the allegorical language clears away " !

VI

One is tempted to say that the *Early Italian Poets* is finer than
anything else Rossetti produced, except *The Blessed Damozel*.   At
all events it was the finest fruit of the family's absorption in Dante.
And yet, faithful as these translations are, it is clear that Dante
Gabriel could receive from the great poet only what he brought
to him ; and what he brought was mainly a young man's idealisation
of passion.   This is evident enough from the poem called *Dante at
Verona*, written between 1849 and 1853.   Here is he concerned
with a sterner Dante than that of the *Vita Nuova*, and though
with great care he versifies the traditional legends and is faithful
enough to the facts as he knew them, the poem is not successful.
It has been a good deal praised, but it is not easy to see why.   His
imagination did not glow at the task ; it is a cold and uninspired
piece of work.

With the austerer, more abstractly spiritual Dante, with Dante
at his greatest, Dante Gabriel had no affinity. His mind was
decorative, pictorial, romantic, rather than searching and philo-
sophical—altogether unlike the mind of Dante. It was moreover
as much unlike the mind of his father, who had resolved everything
in Dante into abstractions while Dante Gabriel sought almost
exclusively visual images and the accent of romantic passion. So
that material, in its origin Dantesque, was assimilated to the lan-
guors and the excitements of Gothic poetry and fiction. Ford
Madox Hueffer has remarked with truth, though maybe with too
much bluntness, that Dante Gabriel evidently thought Paolo and
Francesca " happy enough in Hell with their mackintosh of swoon-
ing passion all round them " ; and Mr. T. S. Eliot has warned
English readers against approaching the *Vita Nuova* before *The
Divine Comedy* because of the danger of doing so under Pre-
Raphaelite influence—which chiefly means the influence of Rossetti's
painting.

The inappropriately languorous effect suggested above is certainly
more obvious in Dante Gabriel's painting than in his poetry.
The translation of the *Vita Nuova* had at once suggested to Rossetti
a series of subjects for treatment. They are set forth in the letter
to Lyell already in part quoted, and all of them, though provided
with an apparatus of Dantesque symbolism, clearly pursue the
theme of his romantic love for Beatrice to the disregard of that
spiritual aspiration which alone led Dante to write. " Ever since
I have read the *Vita Nuova*," Rossetti says, " I have always borne
it in mind as a work offering admirable opportunities for pictorial
illustration : a task which I am now resolved to attempt." Three
of these, he says, are already completed.

1. Dante overhearing the conversation of the friends of Beatrice
    after the death of her father.
2. Dante interrupted while drawing an angel in memory of
    Beatrice.
3. An emblematical frontispiece. " In this last I have intro-
    duced on one side the figure of Dante and on the other
    that of Beatrice : while in the centre Love is represented
    holding in one hand a sun dial, and in the other a lamp
    the shadow cast by the lamp upon the dial being made to
    fall upon the figure nine. At the same time Death, stand-
    ing behind, is drawing from the quiver of Love an arrow
    wherewith to strike Beatrice."

Ten further subjects are named, and though he never executed more than five of them, he drew or painted many others both from the *Vita Nuova* and *The Divine Comedy*. Paget Toynbee's list of Rossetti's Dante designs has 96 items—377 is the total number of sketches and paintings listed by his brother. They go on all through his life, alternating with pictures of a purely romantic kind such as *The Merciless Lady* or with the mysteriously allegorical *Astarte Syriacas* and *Sybilla Palmiferas*; but the later Dante subjects are mainly replicas of earlier pictures of the period of *King Arthur's Tomb* or *King René's Honeymoon*, and have usually much the same mediaeval accessories. The earliest version of the Paolo and Francesca subject was the water-colour of 1851 in three compartments, representing the fateful kiss, and the two lovers in Hell, separated by dark figures of Dante and Virgil and the words " O Lasso ! " But the most carefully finished and most beautiful work on the subject was the elaboration of the first compartment made at some uncertain date before 1861. Here the two lovers might as well be Launcelot and Guenevere, or Tristram and Iseult, or any other pair of mediaeval lovers. It was the glory of passion that held the mind of Dante Gabriel ; for Dante it was its fatality. There is a curious design of 1860 called *Dantis Amor*, in which the face of Christ looks down upon that of Beatrice across a figure of Love dressed as a pilgrim and carrying an array of symbolical appurtenances derived from the love mythology of the *Vita Nuova*, while from left to right diagonally runs the inscription *Amor che muove il sol e l'altre stelle*, which, it is hardly necessary to say, is the last line of *The Divine Comedy*. It may be that for Dante the Love of the *Vita Nuova* was gradually transformed into the divine love of the *Commedia*, but they were nevertheless different and distinct things. In Rossetti they are dissolved into a romantic haze which is essentially unlike either of them.

If this blending of Dante with the spirit of mediaeval or nineteenth-century romance was far removed from the original tone and spirit of Dante himself, it was hardly less removed from the tone and spirit of 50 Charlotte Street. On the one hand was love, a thing of wonder and of wild delight, wrapped around with mysteries and strange circumstance ; on the other there was the poet's constant recollection of, or habitual instinctive recourse to, his early training, the noble purity of his mother's daily life, and the almost cloistral spiritual beauty of Christina's.

The two could not be reconciled, yet neither could be denied. Had his mother's work been done less thoroughly, or had there been nothing at all in him which responded to it, he would have acquired that complete paganism which some have thought was his by nature. As it was a fundamental disharmony arose, which affected the whole of his life and a great deal of his work, and affected it very curiously.

Another factor is to be borne in mind. Holman Hunt's description of Rossetti at about 1848 has the following significant passage. " In these early days, with all his headstrongness and a certain want of consideration, his life within was untainted to an exemplary degree, and he worthily rejoiced in the poetic atmosphere of the sacred and spiritual dreams that then encircled him, however some of his noisy demonstrations at the time might hinder this from being recognised by a hasty judgment." But what determined the nature of these spiritual dreams ? William Michael tells us, and other evidence is not lacking, that by 1848 Gabriel was a decided sceptic. He remained so throughout life, sometimes expressing himself on the subject with juvenile flippancy, while at the same time retaining a good deal of imaginative and inbred sympathy with the forms of Christian faith. His remark on his death-bed is characteristic —" I can make nothing of Christianity, I only want a confessor to give me absolution for my sins."

VII

However, up to the time of his meeting with Miss Siddal in 1850, his imagination, undisturbed by the experience of love, was free to weave what patterns it pleased from these various and ill-assorted threads. Throughout his life, when he was writing either out of literary reminiscence or out of pure imagination or both, his work achieves some effectual wholeness. But when he is concerned with the expression of personal passion his conflicting mental equipment only makes for confusion by supplying terms and conceptions that are really irrelevant to the subject of his experience. His poetry fails as " a criticism of life ", whenever it deals with the stuff of which life is made, because he never had any critical standard of his own to apply.

The poems written by Dante Gabriel before 1854 reflect variou influences and interests. Some, of little importance, are politic or ethical in theme, such as the sonnet *At the Sunrise in* 1848 *Wellington's Funeral* (1852), *The Burden of Nineveh* about the sam time ; the three sonnets called *The Choice* (1848–9), and *Retro Me Satana* (1847). Three sonnets on *Old and New Art* (1848–9), deal directly with the Pre-Raphaelite aims, while two poems of greater importance can be associated with the Pre-Raphaelite interest in contemporary subjects. *My Sister's Sleep*, written possibly before *The Blessed Damozel*, has always been noted for the quiet and sad realism which is one of the marks of the school, although if William is right about the date of its composition, it was written before the group was formed. Is there a possible reminiscence of Hood's maiden ?

> We thought her dying when she slept,
> And sleeping when she died.

She also died during the night ; she also " had another morn than ours ". There is some similarity of subject, and of religious simplicity ; as though Rossetti had supplied the central fact with a setting of circumstance, and with an emphasis on the psychological state of the onlookers. Hood was one of his earliest favourites ; and if there is any link of reminiscence here, there might well be also in the subject of *Jenny*, the first draft of which, dealing with Jenny herself without mention of any second person, was written about the same time as *The Blessed Damozel*.

> Touch her not scornfully ;
> Think of her mournfully,
> Gently and humanly ;
>
> Sisterly, brotherly,
> Fatherly, motherly
> Feelings had changed :
> Love, by harsh evidence,
> Thrown from its eminence,
> Even God's Providence
> Seeming estranged.

As Rossetti says, " it makes a goblin of the sun." He had recently too found a human treatment of a similar subject in W. B. Scott's *Rosabell*, which Scott declares was in Rossetti's mind when he painted the unfinished *Found*. William Michael denies the association ; painting as well as poem may go back to Hood. Both of them at all events show a refined and untested nature viewing the world's ugliness from a distance, and consequently with the more pity. The realistic touches of the setting, in the poem as it now stands, were added much later.

Apart from these two, and the Browningesque *Last Confession*, the more important of the early poems are either mediaeval-romantic or Rossetti-Dantesque ; the latter are the more memorable. The sultry and overloaded *Bridechamber Talk* (a good deal of it written 1847–9 and later called *The Bride's Prelude*) is sombrely Keatsian, *Stratton Water* (1849–53) imitates the simpler kind of mediaeval narrative ballad, while the powerful *Sister Helen* (1851–2) combines the effect of such energetic dramatic ballads as *Edward, Edward*, with the love of gruesome mediaeval enchantments. *The Staff and the Scrip* (planned in 1849, written ? 1853), though a less effective poem, has a more unique quality, linking with its mediaeval accessories, the Pre-Raphaelite dreamy repose and ' pictorial quality ', and the pale-faced languorous womanhood which the early Rossetti delighted in, and which is to be found alike in his representations of Beatrice, his sonnets concerned with Miss Siddal, his early Madonnas, and *Jenny*. Its source was doubtless both in the Beatrice of the *Vita Nuova*, whose paleness is as the pearl and who is wrapt round in melancholy, and the delicate pensive gravity of the poet's sister Christina, his model in various early pictures and subject of a number of portraits. It is wrong to assume as some have done that it came from Miss Siddal—since it was present before he met her, and no doubt he fell in love with her very largely because she corresponded to his preconceived ideal, being likewise pale, remote and mysterious.

The remaining poems of the early phase, disregarding sonnets, are three in number, *The Blessed Damozel* (1847), *The Portrait* and *Ave* (both a little later). As to the first of these we shall resume briefly what we have written more fully elsewhere. Its first conception arose from Poe's *Raven*, where the poet has dealt with the sadness of a lover left alone on earth ; Rossetti set out to represent the other side of the theme, the longing of the maiden in heaven. After that preliminary impetus, he forgot Poe in the thought of Heaven, as depicted in the *Apocalypse* and Dante's *Paradise*, and even in Shelley's *Queen Mab*. The theme is the theme of the *Vita Nuova*, love separated here but to be renewed hereafter. The Damozel, like Beatrice, has " gone up into high heaven " ; her lover sees her in a vision after ten years of separation, as Dante saw Beatrice in a vision after ten years. Associations from Dante from the poets of his circle, and even from Petrarch, crowded into the poet's mind as he contemplated the theme, and his stanzas are full of obvious reminiscence, sometimes clearer in the earlies version of the poem than in the later ones.

The total result of course is not in the least Dantesque. The marvellous and harmonious clarity of the vision, the wholeness of its spellbound peace are all Rossetti's own. What he took from Dante and the *Apocalypse* have been subtly assimilated to the dream of young and ideal love, spiritual in feeling and symbol but only so because still virginal. The Damozel may be in Heaven, but she is not a disembodied spirit like those in the *Paradiso* of Dante ; she is human, longs for her human lover, and gazes down towards him out of her heavenly peace. She smiles at her lover as Beatrice smiled at Dante from the Rose of Paradise ; but having smiled,

> She leant her head against her arm
> And wept ;

while Beatrice " turned back again to the eternal fountain," in blissful contemplation of the Divine Light.

In this famous poem, the idealistic conception of love which is too good for earth, but nevertheless retains its human warmth in heaven, foreshadows discord to come. The poem is not religious and yet it has spiritual aspiration ; it is not a poem of love, but of imagined love ; and it owes its harmonious perfection as much to its writer's youth as to his genius.

Ave again has a Dantesque association, recalling at first the hymn of praise to the Virgin raised by St. Bernard at the end of the *Paradiso*. Compare

> Mother of the fair delight,
> Thou handmaid perfect in God's sight,
> Thou headstone of humanity,
> Groundstone of the great Mystery,
> Fashioned like us, yet more than we

with

> Vergine madre, figlia del tuo figlio,
> umile ed alta più che creatura,
> termine fisso d'eterno consiglio ;
> Tu sei colei che l'umana natura
> nobilitasti sì che il suo Fattore
> non disdegnò di farsi sua fattura.
> [*Paradiso*, xxxiii., 1–6.]

For the rest Rossetti's poem passes into a graceful and tender legendary vein, to return to a more ecstatic paradisal note at the end.

The Portrait [1] is a quite different matter, and complicated by the fact that it was retouched at a later date, the additions and changes being now only a matter of guesswork. This poem too is concerned with a dead love, and for the most part is conceived on the plane of earthly passion, shot through with that suggestion of the supernatural in which Rossetti was always an adept. But nevertheless it shows very clearly the clash between the romantic and the Dantesque qualities of Rossetti's inspiration. *The Portrait* is a poem of wistful love recollection; its strange ghost-haunted loneliness depends largely on the inscrutable finality of the imagined loss, culminating magnificently in the desolation of

> And as I stood there suddenly
> All wan with traversing the night,
> Upon the desolate verge of light
> Yearned loud the iron-bosomed sea.

That, one would confidently guess, is one of the later additions. But it is immediately followed by a stanza which not only breaks the atmosphere by its suggestion of mystic Christian hope, but also inconsequently telescopes Dante's tenth heaven with a Rossettian heaven of perfected human love:

> Even so, where Heaven holds breath and hears
> The beating heart of Love's own breast,—
> Where round the secret of all spheres
> All angels lay their wings to rest,—
> How shall my soul stand rapt and awed,
> When, by the new birth borne abroad
> Throughout the music of the suns,
> It enters in her soul at once
> And knows the silence there for God.

It is a shameful thing, says Dante, " if one should rhyme under the semblance of metaphor or rhetorical similitude, and afterwards, being questioned thereof, should be unable to rid his words of such semblance, unto their right understanding." Had Rossetti been questioned about the last two lines of this otherwise very beautiful stanza, could he have explained them in terms either of literal

[1] Earlier called *Jane's Portrait*, and *Mary's Portrait*. This poem, like *The Blessed Damozel*, seems to foreshadow Rossetti's future; but both were entirely imaginative conceptions. *The Portrait* should be compared with Jacopo da Lentino's poem, *Of his Lady, and of his making her Portrait*, in *The Early Italian Poets*. The association is slight but certain.

belief, or of metaphorical imagination ? [1]   There is no wonder that
Christina once said to an admirer of her brother's work, " How
earnestly do I hope that what you see is truly there to be seen,"
or that she made a reserve in admiring *The Blessed Damozel*—
" beautiful indeed . . . even whilst I agree with you that it falls
short of expressing the highest view, which yet (I hope) it does
not contradict."

This eerie poem with its quasi-Dantesque conclusion recalls for
the first time in Rossetti's work his sonnet *Dantis Tenebrae* (i.e.
The Shadow of Dante) which is addressed to his father's memory,
and which attributes to his reading of Dante an effect which was
really more the product of quite other literature.

> And didst thou know indeed, when at the font
>   Together with thy name thou gav'st me his,
>   That also on thy son must Beatrice
> Decline her eyes according to her wont,
> Accepting me to be of those that haunt
>   The vale of magical dark mysteries
>   Where to the hills her poet's foot-track lies
> And wisdom's living fountain to his chaunt
> Trembles in music ? This is that steep land
>   Where he that holds his journey stands at gaze
>   Tow'rd sunset, when the clouds like a new height
> Seem piled to climb. These things I understand :
>   For here, where day still soothes my lifted face,
>   On thy bowed head, my father, fell the night.

What has Beatrice to do with the vale of magical dark mysteries ?
For most readers of Dante nothing ; for Rossetti much. It is a
curious link between Dante Gabriel and his father that as out of
the Beatrice of the *Vita Nuova* came for one the *arcanum magnum*,
so for the other came eventually *Astarte Syriaca* and unfathomable
mystery.

Did not space and the prescribed limits of this book forbid, it

[1] Perhaps the only possible explanation is that Rossetti, reversing
the procedure of the mystics, many of whom have used the vocabulary of human passion to express divine love, is here using the
divine to express the human, as he clearly does at times in *The House
of Life* (see particularly Sonnett iii., *Love's Testament*, and compare
its earlier form, 1870, under the title *Love's Redemption*). The
passage quoted from *The Portrait*, in that case, may represent
nothing more than the sexual embrace writ fairer in terms of
heaven, and made altogether ineffable.

would be easy to demonstrate the continuity and the effect of Rossetti's twofold inspiration on the one hand in the ballads where one side of it is obvious, and on the other in those " devious coverts of dismay " the sonnets of *The House of Life*. An American scholar recently edited the series without attempting to deal with their Italian relationship—which is as if some one were to edit *The Spanish Tragedy* without reference to Seneca. For *The House of Life* is not only full of Dantesque echoes, but its radical quality was deeply affected by the Italian poet. The mythological symbolism of the *Vita Nuova* is scattered through the sonnets ; and the sacramental conception of love as an initiation to the infinite mystery is there also. There are Dantesque phrases, personifications, and visions ; and when to the old love succeeds the new, Dante's sophistries about the Lady of the Window are at once recalled.

Francis Hueffer once said that Rossetti wrote the thoughts of Dante in the language of Shakespeare, an extreme remark which is only partially true. But certainly what he wished to say was frequently alien to the forms in which he chose to express it. Some of the sonnets are exempt from such a criticism : all those not concerned with love, and those which directly express what Rossetti called " the passionate and just delights of the body." The latter are the easiest to understand. But usually he is dominated by old habits of thought. There is Body's Beauty and Soul's Beauty—and yet the sonnets show an uncertainty about the soul which accounts for the vagueness with which he often writes about it. *Still-born Love*, graceful as it is, must seem puzzling and insincere to any careful reader of the other sonnets. The sincerest expression of Rossetti's erotic experience will be found either in the uninvolved sonnets already referred to, or in those in which there is a very modern sense of love's mystery, the uncertain apprehension of the sceptic deeply stirred by beauty, and endeavouring to express some shadowy aspiration for which he can find no satisfaction in established creeds.

> Sometimes thou seemst not as thyself alone
> But as the meaning of all things that are.

In a significant comment on the last line of his Giorgione sonnet, " *Life touching lips with immortality*," he says, " It gives only the momentary contact with the immortal which results from sensuous culmination, and is always a half-conscious element of it." The remark throws light on the famous lines

Thy soul I know not from thy body, nor
Thee from myself, neither our love from God.

This vague apprehension of the divine through the body is widely disseminated in the modern agnostic poets, but it is not definite enough to give any meaning to phrases like " some heavenly solstice hushed and halcyon," or " the last relay and ultimate outpost of eternity." For these represent the compromise of a mind at war with itself, not sure whether those " passionate and just delights of the body " might, with their mysterious penumbra, be sufficient in themselves, or whether there might not after all be something in

The love that moves the sun and the other stars

in which Dante, and in their way, Dante Gabriel's mother and sisters so deeply believed, and with which the delights of the body seemed to have only the vaguest concern.

The warring elements within him which brought his life to such depths of misery and remorse as few poets have plumbed, are symbolised by the opposite poles of his literary inspiration, which complicate the thought and the expression of his sonnets. The mind turns sadly from them back to the early days,

When life ran gaily as the sparkling Thames,

to the painter of the *Annunciation*, the writer of *Hand and Soul*, the young poet of *The Blessed Damozel*. His fate indeed was not unlike that of the Lady of Shalott. He lived in a world of shadows and reflections, and happily wove them into his web, until maturity took him down to Camelot and broke the web for ever. But still the shadows haunted him, and mocked his attempts to come to terms with life. The most famous, the most gifted, the most admired of all the Rossettis, Dante Gabriel alone among them was unable to master his destiny. Woe unto him " that goeth on the earth two ways." But perhaps we should leave Christina to add the last word on her poet brother, " who," she says, " whatever he was not, was lovable."

IV. WILLIAM MICHAEL

William Michael Rossetti was in some ways to Dante Gabriel what Maria was to Christina. Although the poet was older than his brother and had little of Christina's self-distrust, he must often have felt in William, as Christina felt in Maria, a steady power and serenity which went far to compensate for the lack of genius. When William was about to be married, Gabriel wrote in no mere spirit of formal congratulation, " I wish I were worthier to be her brother and yours."   Their affectionate relationship was never broken by any misunderstanding, and what the one gave in inspiration, friendships, and interest, the other repaid fully in sympathetic comprehension, ready assistance, and eventually in affectionate and scholarly commemoration.

William is much better known than Maria. In the long series of lives and editions which he so painstakingly compiled, he not only supplied the world with all it needed to know about his relations ; he also drew, sometimes without realising it, a full-length portrait of himself ; so that nothing unexpected or surprising was revealed when he gathered up the residue of his long memories in his own autobiography. He was obviously a Polidori rather than a Rossetti ; contemplating his life and activities one is constantly reminded of Gaetano, hardly ever of Gabriele. His habitual and undisturbable calm, his admirable, almost oppressive, good sense, his steady reliability, his industry, his longevity, these are all clearly enough a Polidori inheritance. At the same time certain acquired habits of mind came naturally from the circumstances of his home and from the influence of his father.

William as a child was " the good boy of the family " ; never from childhood to old age did he willingly give anybody any offence, nor did he ever do anything sensational or astonishing. He was slow in learning to read ; Aunt Margaret, he says, coerced him into the craft—it was as we have seen during his mother's long illness of 1835 that the opportunity of doing so arose.[1] Subsequently his more detached and more widely curious intelligence, which earned him the epithet of " beardless Plato " from his father, carried him much farther afield in his reading than his more gifted brother and sister ; he and Maria became the scholars of the family.

As we have seen, William and Christina, the two youngest members of the Rossetti family, were a good deal thrown together in their early years ; and a special intimacy and sympathy between them continued into later life. The great advantage of the calm and sympathetic mind is that while it may not awake the strongest enthusiasms, it can always be resorted to for help and comfort in distress. Christina often wrote to William on subjects she would not for the world have broached to Gabriel—as in the matter of Collinson. And yet genius called to genius in its own way. Her letters to Gabriel are almost always much livelier than those to William ; and in the appreciation and criticism of her poems, her poet brother was of course a more stimulating and helpful friend. Similarly she probably understood Gabriel better than William did, in spite of her very natural reserve on the subject. Still, William remained her " brother of brothers ". " You and Gabriel are my resources," she writes on one occasion, " and you are by far the more agreeable."

Allowing for this close relationship with Christina, William's amusements and pursuits as a child always followed those of Gabriel. With Gabriel he caught frogs, with Gabriel he collected prints. He tried unsuccessfully to draw, and with more success attempted literary composition, Gabriel always suggesting his subjects but giving him no help subsequently in working them out. William himself goes so far as to say that he who wrote so much and knew so many of the notable figures of his time, might probably have written nothing and made few friends if he had not been driven on by Gabriel's inspiring energy. So while Gabriel wrote about Roderick and Rosalba, William told the story of Raimond and Matilda, and while Gabriel wrote of William and Marie, William turned to the subject of Ulfred the Saxon. Their imaginative reading went on *pari passu*, Gabriel here still leading the way. Together they revelled in Scott and Shakespeare, and together they discovered a new world in Shelley. By the age of sixteen, moreover, emulation had set William, with the minimum of poetic talent, upon the writing of verse. A lyric of his called *In the Hill*

[1] See p. 129.

Shadow was printed in *The Athenaeum* in 1848, before anything of
Dante Gabriel's or Christina's had achieved the dignity of public
print, to the great delight of his father who proudly reports the
occurrence to Lyell.

II

Early in 1845, in order to eke out the scanty resources of the
family, through the good offices of Sir Isaac Goldsmid, Rossetti
secured for his younger son a clerkship in the Excise Office. The
man of letters as civil servant is a well enough known phenomenon
in the past as to-day ; nevertheless the appointment must have
seemed to William the end of his hopes rather than the beginning
of a career. He had wished all along to be a doctor ; and apart
from that, the spectacle of Dante Gabriel, from whom he had
learnt all his chief interests, gaily pursuing his own course as a
student of art, must have been a somewhat bitter one. Nevertheless with characteristic persistence he stuck to the post throughout
his life, eventually rising to a position of some importance. If it
always fell to William to be primarily useful to others, it must have
given him some satisfaction to know that his clerkship was for
several years the most stable point in a very insecure situation.
For the rest, he managed with his brother's help to have interests
and acquaintances that any young man might have envied.

Dante Gabriel's friends were his ; and it was Dante Gabriel who
in 1848 hoisted him into the Pre-Raphaelite Brotherhood where
otherwise he would have had no right of way. We may here
notice that if William had not been introduced into the Brotherhood with so much high-handed brotherly affection, the P.R.B.
would not have seemed to the world so largely a creation of Dante
Gabriel Rossetti's as it has been thought. William was neither
painter nor poet ; he was not even a first-class critic ; but he was
a very devoted brother, a Rossetti, and a very prolific writer, so
that whatever others may have contributed to the movement, Dante
Gabriel's part at least could not escape public attention.

William was delighted at this opportunity of taking a share in
the revival of the art of painting, and threw himself into the proceedings of the Brotherhood with enthusiasm. As its secretary he
drew up the regulations, edited its journal, and wrote reviews, as
well as that very awkward sonnet " in a rather aggressively Gothic
type " which stated the Pre-Raphaelite aims, and which according
to Bell Scott would require the united intellects of a Browning

Society for its elucidation. He rarely missed a meeting, kept a diary of their work and proceedings very regularly up to 8 April 1850, and when Millais caused a resolution to be passed that every member should set down in writing the meaning he attached to the name P.R.B., only William did so. It is amusing, though not unnatural, that the collapse of the Brotherhood should have been most regretted by its two literary members—William Michael who never attempted to paint, and Stephens who was already declining into a critic. The spectacle of the former's enthusiastic exertions in the cause of British Art seems to have amused Christina, who pokes gentle fun at him in some verses on the Brotherhood :

> D. G. Rossetti offered two
> Good pictures to the public view ;
> Unnumbered ones great John Millais,
> And Holman more than I can say.
> William Rossetti, calm and solemn,
> Cuts up his brethren by the column.

Amateur contributions to *The Germ* led to professional journalism. In the summer of 1850 William became art critic for *The Critic*, and from November of that year for *The Spectator*, drawing from this occupation a small yearly income which figures triumphantly in his father's letters. From Pre-Raphaelite associations sprang also his blank verse poem, *Mrs. Holmes Grey*, printed in *The Broadway*, 1868. It belongs, in intention at least, to the class of *Jenny* and *Found*, treating a contemporary subject with strict regard for truth of detail, a class better represented no doubt in Pre-Raphaelite painting than in their poetry, and thus often forgotten. It purports to give a conversation " about the death of a lady, a surgeon's wife, who had died suddenly in the house of another medical man for whom she had conceived a vehement and unreciprocated passion ; and a newspaper report of the coroner's inquest occupies a large space in the composition." The unpretentious and prosaic style was deliberately adopted because of the theme and the purpose, although it would probably have been inevitable. The pursuit of realism to its utmost extreme brings poetry within the powers of the most prosaic ; and certainly produces the only variety of verse which William was capable of writing. For like his sister Maria, William Michael had not been befriended by the Muses.[1] He says himself that he knows

[1] Mr. F. M. Hueffer (now Ford) in his monograph *The Pre-Raphaelite Brotherhood*, 1906, p. 50, has declared that a poet of some

the " pacific temperament has congenital defects perhaps as serious as those of the contentious temperament," and such a fundamental calm as his makes creative work in art impossible. Nothing ever seems to have moved William Michael from his posture of judicious repose, unless it were politics, in which he had derived libertarian principles from his father and the revolutionary poets. Even his critical work is more remarkable for scholarship and careful judgment than for the sensitive response which gives the soul of a certain kind of critic its adventures among masterpieces. Through all the quarrels of the Pre-Raphaelites he preserved his unemotional demeanour, " the most unutterably calm of men."

The equanimity of Gaetano Polidori, from whom William derived many of his characteristics, was considerable, but nothing compared with his grandson's ; and Polidori was much more readily stirred by natural beauty. In one of his poems, describing the snowy silence of a winter landscape, he concludes :

> But most sublime of all, most holy,
> The unfathomable melancholy
> When winds are silent in their cells ;
> When underneath the moon's calm light,
> And in the unalter'd snow which veils
> All height and depth—to look thereon,
> It seems throughout the solemn night
> As if the earth and sky were one.[1]

While William having arrived at Davos Platz with his daughter, remarks that " Snow is a natural phenomenon which, from an aesthetic point of view I can enjoy as well as other people ; but I have not much relish for it as a daily environment."

III

In *Letter and Spirit* Christina observes that " Even were the Scriptural fool to prove his point [i.e. that there is no God], filial

importance was lost in William; but for the fact that he devoted all his earlier life to his family " he would assuredly have been a poet as considerable as his more celebrated brother, and only less great in degree than Christina Rossetti." William himself, however, knew better. " I have never supposed myself to be authentically a poet. . . . I have no ambition to swell the densely crowded ranks of the well-meaning in verse who are also the mediocre." (See D. G. R.'s *Family Letters*, p. 375.)

[1] Translated by D. G. R., *Collected Works*, 1890, II., p. 418.

piety would remain to us as the last holy trace of a vanished something holier even than itself." Was she here wistfully thinking of her two agnostic brothers ? Neither of them of course had gone so far in blank denial as the " Scriptural fool " ; but William had soon found that " among the examples of religious belief offered for [his] inspection " he most agreed with that of his father and Gaetano ; and he was barely fourteen when, as he puts it, " the Christian faith became inoperative " on his mind. The reading of Shelley in 1844 is described by himself as making an epoch in his life. Without any painful spiritual conflicts, and without any unpleasant wrangling at home where his defection was nevertheless deeply felt, he became an agnostic and necessitarian of a pronounced Victorian stamp. Gabriel was " on the whole less definitely alien from the faith than myself. His fine intellect dwelt little in the region of argument, controversy, or the weighing of evidence ; it was swayed by feelings." Religious experience was indeed entirely outside William's sphere ; he pursues the feeling of Christina's poetry with friendly but clumsy strides, hoping to catch up with it, but never in fact quite doing so. His attitude remained unchanged throughout his life. In 1883 he declared that he found little alteration in his opinions on the matter since he was eighteen ; he thought it a mistake to erect a cross over his brother's grave, though he realised in time that his mother's feelings were more important than his opinions ; he refused Christina's dedication to the *Verses* of 1893, " on the ground that poems so intensely devotional ought hardly to be dedicated to anyone who did not share the same beliefs in full." And yet he was " less disinclined to believe in ghosts than most people are." There is something indescribably touching about the relationship of William and Christina Rossetti ; their love and trust were so complete and uninterrupted, and yet so deep a gulf lay between them, which William was powerless to cross, and of which at times he seems even unaware. Discussing the story of *Maude*, in the heroine of which Christina had embodied some of her own worst deficiences, he cannot see " that the much reprehended Maude commits a serious fault from title page to finis." He offers the following irrelevant remark about Christina's renunciation of Cayley's love : " She would have been far happier, and might have become rather broader in mental outlook, and no one would have been any the worse for it." She on her side was painfully conscious of the abyss that separated them. " It seems unnatural to love you so much and yet never say one word about

matters which colour my life." She pathetically asks on one
occasion for his prayers, and doubts whether his unbaptised
children can in any real sense be happy. The story ends with the
image of William, earnest and baffled, trying to console the last
moments of his dying sister : " I endeavoured to show her that
according to her own theories, she was just as safe as they [Maria
and her mother] ; but this—such was her humility of self-estimate
—did not relieve her from troubles of soul." On her gravestone
he had inscribed the line from Dante,

> Volsersi a me con salutevol cenno
> [They turned to me with welcoming gesture]

" as suggesting (though not with such a degree of definiteness as I
do not personally believe) the reunion of the other tenants of that
grave with Christina in the spiritual world."

Of his own philosophy, as well as of his poetic powers, the
following sonnet may serve as an indication.

THE PAST

A purpose in the ages. Protoplasm
Grows polypus and fish and ichthyosaur ;
The molten fire-mass shrinks to cliff and scaur ;
Successive chasms leave Nature free from chasm ;
Vine-tendrils shall festoon the earthquake's spasm ;
Mammoth and mastodon and ape to more
And more of man progress ; and on the floor
Of earth vast rivers drain the swamp's marasm.
  Last History unveils her world of dreams.
  Savages slaughter and gorge on savages ;
  An Aryan here, a Mongol there we see.
  Egypt and Israel, India, Persia, Greece,
  Italy, Spain, France, England, Germany,
  America, scud fast in louring gleams.

In view of the last thirteen and a half lines, a question mark seems
necessary after the first phrase. The rest appears to be beyond
dispute, but is scarcely an answer. William Michael was never
able to give one, and was never able to accept those of other people.

IV

The period between 1848 and 1853 was probably the happiest in
William Michael's life ; during those five years he had at least every
reason for contentment. He was young, able, and enthusiastic.
A sketch of him at the age of eighteen, by his brother, shows him

to have been nearly as handsome as Dante Gabriel himself—his general appearance less romantic, but his features more regular. At the age of twenty-one he was gravely instructing the British public on matters of art in one of the leading periodicals. Surrounded in his leisure hours by some of the most attractive creative spirits of the time, all young, all ardent, and all optimistic, he was at the same time conscious of being the mainstay of his family. Add to all this the fact that in 1851 he fell in love, and the picture of happy busy youth is complete. But youth stays for no man, and hopes will fade. In 1850 William Michael had the misfortune to lose nearly all his hair. His romance, which declined into an engagement by 1856, faded completely away in 1860 through the opposition of the lady's parents and her own vacillation ; William then resolved to remain a bachelor, a determination he kept manfully for some twelve years. Meanwhile Gabriel had long since left the home, their father had died, and life was daily becoming graver and more responsible.

But it is unnecessary to prolong the story of William Michael beyond our closing date, as we did in the case of Maria. His life was long and uneventful, sadly punctuated by the deaths of near relatives, and sometimes deeply disturbed by their misfortunes. He was grieved that his wife did not get on with Mrs. Rossetti and Christina as well as he had hoped, and that his marriage likewise separated him from several of his most valued friends. " Few things could have been less to my liking than this. . . . But the rule ' therefore shall a man cleave to his wife ' represents a genuine practical requirement in life, as well as a genuine conception of what ranks highest in the affections, and therefore I accepted my position as it came." A normal man treading a normal path from childhood to old age, and cheerfully accepting the burdens that fall upon the shoulders of the world's pedestrians, William Michael was rewarded with a life of calm and fruitful industry and with the distinction of handing on a famous name to later generations.

The centre of his life was always fixed in that devotion to the home which some one has rashly declared to be a markedly Italian feature of his nature. As historiographer to the Rossetti family, William constituted himself the repository of its members' honour no less than the historian of their careers ; habitually, and very properly, presenting the good, diminishing the bad, and concealing the disreputable. Even in the case of his father, whose cupboards had no skeletons, he was generally careful to suppress details which he thought too **extremely** indicative of vanity or unfounded resentment. He is often prolix (in the *Reminiscences* to the point of garrulity), and his style is cumbrous with a formal informality, as may be judged from the many quotations scattered throughout this book. But these are small faults to set over against his virtues of great loyalty, an almost religious thoroughness, and the most scrupulous and scholarly care. His life, one may say, falls into two parts deserving equal admiration, the first spent in helping his family and the second in writing their stories.

V. CHRISTINA

I

The personality of Christina Rossetti is, and will probably remain, enigmatic. The quietest, most reserved, and most self-effacing member of the family, her essential life was all inward. " In a roomful of mediocrities ", says William Michael, " she consented to seem the most mediocre as the most unobtrusive of all." Her letters, for the most part curiously uninteresting, reveal only the merest fragments of personality, and though her poetry is almost entirely lyrical, its personal reference is usually veiled and problematical. In what has recently been written about her, two features are noticeable. One is the tendency to rank her achievement higher than her brother's on account of its sincerity, consistency, and (when at its best) its exquisite melody ; which preference seems now to have become established as the judgment of posterity. The other, more disputable, is a habit of regarding her as being by nature a passionate Italian, crushed and numbed by the exigencies of a narrow and hostile environment. Into the first of these assumptions it is needless to enter ; the second which is almost certainly a false conception, may possibly appear so in the course of these pages.

Like Dante Gabriel, Christina was regarded as a difficult child, but it is important to notice that while he was obstinately determined, she was restless, tearful, capricious, and often irritable. Of her childish irritability she once wrote to a correspondent, " Ask William, he could a tale unfold." Such qualities in childhood may or may not betoken embryonic genius—they certainly indicate some degree of physical weakness ; and although the long tale of Christina's serious ailments does not begin till she is fifteen, there are constant references in her father's letters to the childish affections from which she was suffering, and there is every reason to suppose that from the first she was most delicately and precariously constituted. At the same time Christina as a child was lively, affectionate, and engaging ; she was generally liked, being much prettier and more graceful in mind and person than Maria. In appearance, and probably in physique, she favoured the maternal side of the family. On one occasion Gabriele says that her mother seems reborn in her, while he mentions several times that she has her grandmother's eyes. (Her maternal grandmother, it may be remembered, was for years a confirmed invalid, a woman of determined will and of somewhat gloomy mind.) In temperament she developed the Polidori reserve and steadiness of will, their careful capacity in matters of daily routine, their industry and their comparative lack of humour. She was strongly drawn to Gaetano himself, whom she loved, according to William, perhaps even better than her father. He loved her too, encouraged her writing and printed her earliest verses. Polidori had, in fact, formed high hopes of her future—" She will be the cleverest of them all," he said, a remark that she was later to apply to one of William's daughters, with the addition which she no doubt thought Gaetano should have made, " allowing for the inborn preponderance of man over woman." And her grief at her grandfather's death was profound and desolating. But into the quiet depths of the Polidori-Pearce inheritance had slipped a livelier element of poetic sensibility, the breath of the muse blowing where it listeth, fostered by her general literary environment and intensified by great nervous activity working within a sub-normal constitution.

If Christina was probably Polidori-Pearce by inheritance, she was certainly so by training. From her mother and the Polidori aunts she acquired her breeding in the old-fashioned Victorian tradition from which she was never able to escape, her education, and above all her instruction in Anglican Christianity. Without any difficulty or doubt she accepted the traditional pieties and preserved them through life, with no greater change as time went on than that from the simplicity of evangelical worship to a greater care for saints' days and ritual and a belief in the value of confession. Her beliefs, though formal, were not in any way insincere ; but they were accepted without criticism, and long acceptance, strengthening her fidelity, increased her absorption. At the same time they seem to have been accompanied by no direct sense of the supernatural ; the life of this world, its beauty at times, but more often its sorrow, constitutes Christina's chief concern, and her vision does not extend beyond the confines of a wistful hope. The " better resurrection " which comes in perfunctorily at the end of so many of her poems is an article of belief rather than a leaping of the frontier, and does not delude the reader, who knows very well that her hope and expectation are mainly for the quiet of the restful grave which at all events

is bound to be hers at last. " Rest remains when all is done."
She believed that death was not an end, but felt towards it as she did
towards the frozen snowdrops and the wintry birds :

> Sing, Robin, sing ;
> I yet am sore in doubt concerning Spring.

Certainly she was not one who could say with Francis Thompson
" O world invisible we view thee." Her religion was the object of
lifelong fidelity and self-surrender, and yet it often seems a little
traditional and impersonal. She could write, without noticing their
absurdity, lines such as

> Lo in the room, the upper,
> She shall sit down to supper,

and

> I would get quit of earth and get robed for heaven,
> Putting on my raiment white within the screen ;

apparently thinking of her heavenly garment as a sort of nightdress.
Very little of her best verse is directly inspired by her religion,
although of course a distinction should be made between such poems
as those quoted or her graveyard poems with the formal trump to
follow, and her finer religious work, as for example in *Gifts and
Graces*, where she shows a good deal more insight into the human
spirit with its faith and needs :

> If thou be dead, forgive and thou shalt live ;
> If thou hast sinned, forgive and be forgiven ;
> God waiteth to be gracious and forgive,
> And open heaven.

It should not be too readily assumed that her mother and her
sister Maria with their serenity and untroubled belief bound her in
chains which she longed unconsciously to break. It is a mistake to
think of Christina as a passionate nature strongly curbed. The
damned-up stream will exert its power in some way or other, but
one may seek in vain in the work of Christina for any indication
of the reaction which would have been bound to follow such
a suppression. Energy is not lost though its nature may be
changed. It is impossible to understand Christina Rossetti at
all unless one begins by realising that she was not in middle
age " too late for joy," but was hardly born to it at all. She
never had any firm hold on it, it lay always just beyond her
grasp. Her nature was too tentative ever to impose terms on the

world around ; hence her fear of it, and her renunciation. Her
mother and Maria confident, unswerving, happy in their faith
and in the management of their lives, not only seemed, but were,
models to her, or not models perhaps so much as firm supports
on which she could lean. They did not need to compel her
nature in such matters. She most deeply loved and admired them,
finding in them examples of what she would choose to be herself ;
and with fine persistence of will and intention she attempted to
follow their path. Thus she attached herself to Maria's convent,
wearing the significant title of *Outer Sister* ; she became an associate of the St. Mary Magdalene Home, wearing the dress at times,
though refusing an invitation to be its superintendent. It may
no doubt be surmised that had Christina been born into circumstances free from religious or puritanic restrictions she might
have written happier verses ; and that if she had been a Roman
Catholic she might have had one of her chief causes of tribulation
removed—that is to say her belief in the perfectibility of human
nature at war with her experience of its frail and imperfect state.
But it is impossible that she would ever have been either a great
religious poet or a modern Sappho. Her poetry in any case, as we
know it, is the product of a sensitive and beauty-loving mind striv-
ing to accommodate itself to an accepted formula and beloved
guides ; without the physical and mental stamina required to
lift her above

> A world of change and loss, a world of death,
> Of heart and eyes that fail, of labouring breath,
> Of pains to bear and painful deeds to do.

II

Let us imagine her, however, in 1848 at the age of seventeen, a
young woman of average height, grey-eyed and chestnut-haired,
quiet, unobtrusive, and self-effacing ; in face beautiful with an
expression of pensive sweetness, as she appears in her brother's very
lovely oil-painting of that year, or with a look of inward brooding
as she appears in the *Annunciation* (*Ecce Ancilla Domini*), or in the
earlier *Girlhood of Mary Virgin*, who

> like an angel-watered lily
> Grows and is quiet.

Life is already a perplexity to her. There are so many things to
enjoy, and yet it is difficult to enjoy them when they come ; they

are very disappointing, better to think about than to experience. Besides she is never quite well.   At fifteen she was supposed to be suffering from angina pectoris ; this in due course passed off, but in its place symptoms appeared that distressingly suggested a consumption which never actually developed.   Death was already become so near a neighbour and so familiar to her thoughts that even in December 1847 she had written,

> The roses bloom too late for me ;
> The violets I shall not see ;
> Even the snowdrops will not come
> Till I have passed from home to home.

Meanwhile there were duties in the home needing attention, and they were dutifully performed ; and brothers busy with exciting schemes demanding sympathy, and her interest was not withheld.   And all the time the inward life goes on, the dreaming, the wistful yearning for joy, the hopelessness of finding it, the self-scrutiny, the self-condemnation.   Now and again she slips away to fill up another page in one of her neat little notebooks, and on her return no one has so much as noticed that she had left the room.

It was about Christmas time of 1847 that W. B. Scott paid the visit recorded elsewhere.[1]   " By the window was a high narrow reading desk, at which stood writing a slight girl with a regular serious profile, dark against the pallid wintry light without.   This most interesting to me of the two inmates turned on my entrance, made the most formal and graceful curtsey, and resumed her writing."

Some idea of the narrow range of her interests and of her own opinion of herself may be derived from *Maude, a Story for Girls*, intended as an exemplary tale and composed between 1848 and 1850.   It was not published until after her death—she may have decided against publication either because she supposed it to be somewhat dull (it is indeed " not dangerously exciting to the nervous system," as Dante Gabriel said about *Commonplace*), or because it is too personal ; for its main object had been the exhibition of what she regarded as defects in her own character. With William's assurance that Maude is the shadow of Christina herself, the little tale becomes highly revealing.

It is about this Maude that William says that he cannot see that she commits any serious fault at all, but Maude's sense of sin is strictly relative to her own experience.   The story takes us into the

[1] See p. 158.

realm of young ladies' parties, autograph albums, invitations to tea, and Christmas decorations. Maude is a highly introspective and delicate young woman given to the composition of melancholy verses, and varying between lively animation and complete abstraction. " ' A penny for your thoughts ! ' . . . This observation remaining unanswered, the mother, only too accustomed to inattention continued. . . ." Maude was then engaged in writing. " Touching these same verses, it was the amazement of every one what could make her poetry so broken-hearted as was mostly the case." For outwardly her friends can see little cause for so much melancholy, or little sign of it in her demeanour. At her birthday party all look naturally to her for amusement. " A general appeal was made to Miss Foster [i.e. Maude] for some game, novel, entertaining and ingenious or, some of the more diffident hinted, easy." She will not let them play the " common games ", such as *Proverbs*, and *How do you like it ?* but have they tried *bouts-rimés* ? Expostulations follow, but Maude is unbending : " ' Indeed I have nothing else to propose. This is very much better than the more common games ; but if you will not try it, that ends the matter ', and Maude leaned back in her chair." When the game has been played, she makes unsparing comments on the efforts of her friends, and then, appeased, consents to suggest other games more within their capacity. In these her good humour and animation are infectious.

Certainly Maude has a substantial share not only of Christina's occasional liveliness, but also of the intellectual pride and aloofness of which she accused herself. When, for instance, Maude goes to visit the amiable Mrs. Strawdy she finds it impossible to talk to her ; worse still, other visitors arrive, and Maude is pestered and complimented about her verses. Will she be so good as to recite some of them ? She will not. Finally she returns home dissatisfied with her circumstances, her friends, and herself. If Christina ever behaved like this one would not be surprised ; she was ill-adapted for such diversions, yet she would be right in accusing herself of a certain lack of generous humanity. Her Maude and she were alike victims of ill-adaptation ; the inward mind refuses to move with the outer observances condemning these for their insincerity and artificiality, while condemning in themselves their half-hearted acquiescence. And even the inner life itself becomes tarnished by publicity. " How I envy you who live in the country," says Maude, " and are exactly what you appear, and never wish for what you do not possess. I am sick of display, and poetry, and acting." Hence the reserve, the living more and more to herself, the endless private composition.

But all other vexations and self-reproaches are as nothing compared with Maude's religious troubles. On Christmas Eve she complains of headache and goes upstairs. There, soon after, she is discovered by her friend Agnes, with a manuscript book before her into which she has just copied something, looking pale, languid, and as if in pain. She is now struggling with religious griefs. " I shall not receive to-morrow. . . . No, at least I will not profane Holy things ; I will not add this to the rest. I have gone over and over again, thinking I should come right in time, and I do not come right. I will go no more." In answer to remonstrations she says that she is beyond hope, because she is not even trying. " No one will say that I cannot avoid putting myself forward and displaying my verses. Agnes, you must admit as much." Agnes at last goes away, sympathetic but puzzled, leaving Maude in bitter tears. At last sleepy, she undresses ; thinking of her prayers unsaid, the idea of beginning them frightens her ; yet she cannot settle down without saying something. At last she lay down, " harassed, wretched, remorseful, everything but penitent." Eventually she is slightly injured in an accident, sickens and dies ; and Agnes buries the manuscript book unopened in her coffin, " with all its words of folly, sin, vanity : and she humbly trusted of true penitence also."

Maude in the story cannot be acquitted of vanity, lack of consideration for others, selfishness, intellectual snobbery, and no doubt of other sins as well. The fact that other people would hardly take so serious a view of her delinquencies as she does herself, does not turn them into delusions. Christina's self-reproaches were concerned with offences no less real, no less over-emphasised. The narrowness of her self-scrutiny is well known ; she was worried on her death-bed about some paints that she had promised William in childhood but which she had never in fact given him. Daily she said to herself in effect, " I have gone over and over again, thinking I should come right, and I do not come right." It is obvious that a good deal of her melancholy was the result of the inevitably futile pursuit of human perfection ; and yet again, are not the purity of her mind and the intensity of her utterance just as much the result of it too ?

III

Maude's literary preoccupations are of course a direct reflection of Christina's, to which now we turn. Christina had been as precocious a versifier as the rest of the family and her mind had been nourished to some extent on the same reading, though she certainly read a good deal less than the others at all times of her life, and never possessed many books of her own. For the most part her inspiration is inward or biblical, her best poetry being remarkably underivative. Therein, of course, lies one source of her great superiority over her brother, who rarely wrote so directly out of the heart and without artifice as she invariably did. If one is to look for evidences of her reading in her poetry, they will be chiefly found in her earliest work. It has been remarked, for example, that in the *Verses* privately printed by Polidori in 1847, a number of the poems are concerned with the theme of parted, or unhappy, or deserted love. There is nothing remarkable in this. The same is true of Dante Gabriel's early work ; and in both cases it is a matter of literary mode. Christina seems to have in mind not Dante and Beatrice so much as the forlorn ladies of old romance or of revivalist balladry, such as those found in the ballads of Mrs. Browning, or the afflicted maidens of Maturin, an author she liked and was still echoing as late as 1856. Dante she did not study until 1848 ; from then onwards he was well known to her and very highly regarded. She once remarked that a wise man might well choose to be born an Italian, " thus securing Dante as his elder brother, and *The Divine Comedy* as his birthright." On another occasion, at the end of her life, when she felt herself being at last " sucked into the Dantesque vortex," she declares that " perhaps it is enough to be half an Italian, but certainly it is enough to be a Rossetti, to render Dante a fascinating centre of thought." However, although Christina knew *The Divine Comedy* well and sometimes quotes it, it would be difficult to find any clear trace of the Dantesque in her own work.

Among other poets, she had an early liking for Tasso, whose gravity no doubt commended him to her above the more kaleidoscopic Ariosto whom she liked only in parts. Keats, whose work she much admired, can be heard now and again in the *Verses* of 1847, and both Shelley and Coleridge have made their contributions to *The Song of the Star* in that little volume. But her constant companion among poets in her childhood and girlhood, from nine to fourteen, was Metastasio. Her great love for this poet may seem at first unaccountable, his graceful artificiality being so remote from anything we associate with Christina in mind or character. But her father had exploited a Metastasian vein in his early poems ; while the graceful and easy clarity of the Italian poet may have

appealed to and encouraged Christina's own instinct for those qualities. He wrote moreover of love in all its guises, and of virtue in
almost as many, in both of which subjects Christina was predisposed
to be interested ; while his great gift of inexhaustible melody
naturally delighted the mind which later was to write *Dream Land*,
and *When I am dead my dearest*. One or two Italian love poems in
the *Verses* are obviously Metastasian, and from him she took the very
appropriate motto with which she dedicated the book to her mother :

> Perchè temer degg'io ?   Son le mie voci
> Inesperte, lo so : ma il primo omaggio
> D'accettarne la Madre
> Perciò non sdegnerà ; ch'anzi assai meglio
> Quanto a lei grata io sono
> L'umil dirà semplicità del dono.[1]

A very obvious trace of her Italian ear, and habituation to Italian
versification, is the abundance of double rhymes in this volume, an
excess which she soon learnt to control.

One other book had penetrated to every part of her consciousness ; that was the Bible. The resemblances which some have
found between her verse and Swinburne's are strengthened by the
frequency with which Biblical phrase and imagery are woven as if
unconsciously into the texture of their work. Like Dante Gabriel
she had a special love for the *Apocalypse*, eventually to be the subject
of her last and finest prose work.

IV

If Polidori had waited a year longer before printing his grand-
daughter's verses, they would have contained some of her most
famous poems. As it is, the *Verses* of 1847 sound most of her
characteristic notes without anywhere reaching her highest level of
excellence. Some of them were written as early as 1842, when
Christina was only twelve years old ; the best of them belong to the
year of publication when she was sixteen.[2] The marvel is not that
they are not better, but that they are so good as they are, and it
is easy to sympathise with Polidori's enthusiasm : " Though I am

---

[1] Why should I fear ?   My songs, I know, are inexperienced ; but
my Mother will not for that reason refuse to accept their first homage;
for indeed the lowly simplicity of the gift will tell her all the better
how grateful I am to her.

[2] The book was published before her birthday in that year, when
she became seventeen.

ready to acknowledge that the well-known partial affection of a grandparent may perhaps lead me to overrate the merit of her youthful strains, I am still confident that the lovers of poetry will not wholly attribute my judgment to partiality.''

The volume opens with an ethical allegory called *The Dead City*, directed against pride and luxury, but not written apparently so much for the moral, which is neither clear nor enforced, as for the story of wandering in the wood and finding the strange city, the pleasure of describing the birds, the blossoms, the luscious fruits, the golden vessels and the like. A good deal of Christina's capacity for sensuous enjoyment is apparent in this poem of 1847. The idea of the city of stone is borrowed, of course, from *The Arabian Nights*; and one remembers with foreboding that the same story later was to seize the imagination of the arch-pessimist Thomson, who first made it into the poem called *The Doom of a City*, and later transformed it into *The City of Dreadful Night*. No heavy shadow, however, lies over Christina's poem, though through the riot of gorgeous description one discerns clearly enough in the distance that grim spectre who was to preside so ruthlessly over her art, the Preacher's *Vanitas Vanitatum*.

Polidori seems to have chosen the most brightly coloured of the poems for the opening of his little book. *The Dead City* is followed by *The Water Spirit's Song*, *The Song of the Star*, and *Summer*, all of them full of delight in simple natural things, moonlight and scaly fishes, ripe seeds and berried bushes, finches and thrushes and nightingales,

> Tulips like a glowing fire,
> Clematis of milky whiteness,
> Sweet geraniums' varied brightness,
> Honeysuckle, commeline,
> Roses, myrtles, jessamine.

And yet there is in them all a strange virginal detachment, a remoteness as of the Star itself or of the Water Spirit among the green fishes of the sea depths, where

> the cold bright moon looks down on us
> With her fixed unchanging smile.

And even summer comes but to pass away—

> She pushes away her pall,
> And she leaves the dead behind her :

And she flies across the seas
To gladden for a time
The blossoms and the bees
Of some far distant clime.

For a time and for a time only. One would imagine from the poems of this book that Christina never gave herself up to enjoyment so completely as to be even momentarily unconscious of its inevitable end. She foresees the end at the beginning, and when she delights in the passing moment it is with the true epicurean sense of the eternal flux. And this before she was seventeen.

Earthly joys are very fleeting,
Earthly sorrows very long ;
Parting still succeeds to meeting,
Night succeeds to evensong.

she says rather obviously in *Present and Future* ; and two or three pages farther on she repeats the commonplace in another poem :

Life is fleeting, joy is fleeting,
Coldness follows love and greeting,
Parting still succeeds to meeting.

In *Charity*, a palpable imitation of Herbert, she praises

the myrtle and the rose
At sunrise in their beauty vying ;
I passed them at the short day's close,
And both were dying.

though her antithesis in place of Herbert's Virtue is Love—

All, all, save Love alone, shall die.

So much despair of happiness at the age of sixteen might in some be merely the yearning of adolescence ; nobody can suppose it to be so in Christina. She had already accepted sorrow as her life-long companion. " For there is no remembrance of the wise more than of the fool for ever ; seeing that which now is in the days to come shall be forgotten ; and how dieth the wise man ? As the fool. Therefore I hated life ; because the work that is wrought under the sun is grievous unto me : for all is vanity and vexation of spirit."

These poems are the first notes of her constantly recurring theme, *Passing away, Passing away, saith the world.* She found it in the Bible —" For the world passeth away and the lust thereof."—" The earth mourneth and fadeth away, the world languisheth and fadeth away ; " she found it in Thomas à Kempis " Why dost thou gaze about, since

this is not the place of thy rest ? In Heaven ought to be thy
dwelling-place, and all earthly things are to be looked upon as it
were by the way ; all things are passing away, and thou together with
them ; " she could find it daily in Christian writing and sermons.
So doubtless do many others, who nevertheless forget it all in the
heat of the pursuit ; but for Christina's temperament there could be
no pursuit hot enough to absorb her, violent enough to break down
the walls of that pale retreat whence she so wistfully watched the
passing of the seasons and the pageant of nature's beauty.   She sees
it all and knows that it is good ; but at sixteen she also knows that it
is all vanity and emptiness :

> " Ah woe is me for pleasure that is vain !
> Ah woe is me for glory that is past !
> Pleasure that bringeth sorrow at the last ;
> Glory that at the last bringeth no gain ! "
> So saith the sinking heart.

" Dreary with a cureless woe," sick of " earth's misery or tainted joy
at best," whither at sixteen is the resort of her sad mind ?   We shall
find in the *Verses* of 1847 many references to " that river Blest "
and the " perfect bliss " which " shall be our lot on high," but we
shall not find any evidence of that direct and all-containing love of
God, which can make a Julian of Norwich cry, " O God of thy goodness give me Thyself, for Thou art enough for me . . . and if I ask
anything that is less, ever me wanteth."   The only note of consolation we shall find (and what reader of Christina will not at once
recognise it ?), is this :

> He resteth ; weep not ;
> The living sleep not
> With so much calm :
> He hears no chiding
> And no deriding,
> Hath no joy for sorrow
> For night hath morrow,
> For wounds hath balm,
> For life's strange riot
> Hath death and quiet,
> Who would recall him
> Of those that love him ?
> No fears appal him ;
> No ills befall him ;
> There's nought above him
> Save turf and flowers
> And pleasant grass.

The themes of " Passing Away," Rest, and the vanity of the world are represented by three poems, *Gone for Ever*, *Resurrection Eve*, *Vanity of Vanities*, which are not only the best poems in the book but are also the most characteristic of the poetess.   Here clearly was no youthful romantic melancholy, but the most real inspiration Christina was to know.

There remains, however, a group of poems on another subject which under a veil of close reserve was to supply themes for some of the most personal poetry of Christina's later years.   A number of love poems, none of them happy, some of them mournful, some of them narrative and others lyrical, represent what the poet had so far made of the passion from her reading and imagination.   We may at once dismiss those which owe their origin to recognisable literary models ;   the Metastasian lyrics in Italian, attempts at romantic balladry such as *The Ruined Cross* and *Fair Margaret*, so juvenile that even William Michael omitted them from his collected edition, echoes from Maturin such as *Zara* and *Eva*.   In the more personal poems of this class, love is one of the sweet things which vanish :

> Love is sweet, and so are flowers
> Blooming in bright summer bowers . .
> Flowers soon must fade away :
> Love endures but for a day.

That was written in 1845.   A year later, love is arraigned more sternly :

> Like breath of summer breezes
> Gently it sighs,
> But soon, alas ! one ceases,
> The other dies :
>
> And like an inundation
> It leaves behind
> An utter desolation
> Of heart and mind.
>
> Who then would court Love's presence,
> If here below
> It can be but the essence
> Of restless woe ?

To this attack Christina writes a reply which, mere imaginative exercise as it was in 1846, is pathetic in view of the sequel :

> But the face of heaven and earth,
> And the murmur of the main,
> Surely are a recompense
> For a little pain.

It could safely have been assumed that the writer of these verses would before long herself hear " the murmur of the main," and it might no less have been surmised that if so frail a vessel were to put forth at all on that perilous sea it would be soon forced to return to port.

Meanwhile we may pause to notice another aspect of Christina's mind. The conviction that " vanity is the end of all our ways " did not preclude a certain degree of self-assertiveness in some directions. When some one had criticised the *Verses* unkindly, Dante Gabriel wrote, " As to the nonsense about Christina's *Verses*, I should advise her to console herself with the inward sense of superiority. . . ." The advice, as we gather from *Maude*, was not altogether necessary. Fame no doubt was vanity and emptiness like the rest, but she was by no means superior to it. Sending some verses to the editor of a magazine in 1854, she explains that she knows there is " something above the despicable in them ", and says that she would be gratified if they were printed. She had the natural pleasure in effective self-expression, her verse being the most direct outlet for the inner power she was conscious of possessing ; and she was pleased at any kind of recognition, whether from simple folk who loved her religious verse, or from Swinburne, who was capable of being moved to tears by Christina's penetrating melodies. Yet her justifiable pride never overstepped the line. Much of her verse upheld the virtues and the hopes she lived for ; others with a less exalted aim she sometimes suppressed, even when they were as beautiful as *The Triad*. When Dante Gabriel suggested that her association with the S.P.C.K. as publishers might be harmful to her reputation, she replied that she did not think so, and that if it was, she would still " be glad to throw [her] grain of dust into the religious scale." And anything in the nature of a publicity sufficient to disturb the personal obscurity in which she liked to lie hidden was abhorrent to her. When she was informed after the death of Tennyson that there was a feeling in some quarters that she should be Poet Laureate, Christina shuddered and was filled with real horror.

v

Some time in 1847 or 1848 the young poetess met, for the first time, an artist called James Collinson. In the latter year he was twenty-three years old, Christina eighteen. William Michael describes him as " a small thick-necked man, chiefly a domestic painter, who began with careful and rather timid practice, in demeanour, modest and retiring." Ardently religious in mind, he first came to the notice of Mrs. Rossetti and her daughters as an assiduous attender at Christ Church, Albany Street ; but the Rome-ward movement there apparently carried him off, and at about the time when the Pre-Raphaelite Brotherhood was formed, Collinson himself became a Roman Catholic. The exhibition of his picture, *The Charity Boy's Début*, had commended him to Dante Gabriel, who declared he was " a born stunner " and in his arbitrary way insisted on his being admitted to membership of P.R.B. Millais appears to have been amused at the suggestion, and Hunt (recollecting the correspondence years afterwards) wrote to him, " It appears that the Rossettis are much attached to him . . . and Collinson himself has been pressing me to get him accepted. I like the meek little chap." He seems to have been a very reluctant Bohemian and a general joke among the Brethren. According to Hunt he invariably fell asleep at the beginning of the monthly meetings and had to be wakened at the end. " He could never see the fun of anything and I fear we didn't make his life more joyful. . . . Even in the day he was asleep over the fire with his model waiting idle, earning his shilling per hour all the time." No wonder that he " did not rise to any distinction in the pictorial art."

This very unlikely young man fell in love with Christina Rossetti, which is in no way surprising ; and in 1848 he asked her to be his wife. There is no record of her feelings about the proposal. She must have liked his quietness and modesty, and his piety was common ground. But her first instinct was evidently one of retreat ; and she appears to have told Collinson that his Catholicism was an insurmountable barrier. Much in love, he examined the barrier, and to his great relief saw it vanishing away. Once more a Protestant, he again proposed and was this time accepted.

Comments altogether too light and unsympathetic have been made on Collinson's part in this now well-known story. Fortunate above most men, he had met with great beauty of mind and person, had become entirely subject to it, and for a time valued nothing in comparison. But he was a small man now launched into close relationship with a highly cultured and gifted family ; his own mind was undistinguished, his origin humble and bourgeois. He soon, no doubt, began to feel a certain uneasiness and misgiving. Meanwhile Gabriel at least must have been pleased with the course of events, for as late as 25 October 1849 he writes Collinson an emphatically affectionate letter, full of liveliness and fun. William, the

" brother of brothers ", had paid a visit to the Collinson family at
their home at Pleasley Hill, near Mansfield, toward the end of 1848.
Christina wrote to him there, a letter in which anxious modesty
appears through a veil of great decorum. " I am glad you like Miss
Collinson, but have a notion that she must be dreadfully clever. Is
either of these ladies alarming ? not to you of course, but would they
be so to me ? . . . You probably not only profusely banqueted but
surfeited your victims with my poetry, but in this you may not have
been the sole culprit." She ends by asking to be remembered
" most particularly to Mr. Collinson." In the summer of the next
year she is at Pleasley Hill herself, and from her letters to William
in London the impossibility of the relationship begins to appear.
" Local converse wearies me somewhat ; yet this advantage it possesses—I cannot join in it ; so may, during its continuance, abandon
myself to my own meditations. My dreary poem is not completed,
but a few appropriate stanzas have been added since my leaving
town. . . . The talk of *beaus* is as perpetual here as at Mrs.
Heimann's : however, fewer jokes (?) have been passed on me than
might have been anticipated ; and of these Mary is entirely innocent. Do you know, I rather like Mary ; she is not at all caressing,
but seems real. . . . In my desperation I knit lace with a perse-
verance completely foreign to my nature. Yesterday I made a dirt-
pudding in the garden wherein to plant some slips of currant. . . .
Ah Will ! if you were here we would write *bouts-rimés* sonnets, and
be subdued together." There is such a thing as being unfortunate
in the very goodness of one's family ; certainly the Rossetti family
made it almost impossible for any of the children to be entirely easy
in marriage—even for William Michael. For Christina, whose
feminine dependence linked her more firmly to the family, it became
impossible to make the attempt. When Mary Collinson prophesied
that Christina would be a *favourite* with her other brother Charles on
account of her unalterable self-possession, the compliment provokes
this remark to William : " Fancy the inflated state in which I shall
re-enter London, should this flattering preference result from my
visit." She asks William to send her a copy of " As I lay a-thinking," and having received it mentioned " its sweet prettiness " to
Mary ; " but she does not appreciate it ; at least not as we do."
     Five weeks later, in London again, she writes to William, " My
correspondence with Mary Collinson has come to an end by her
desire. Do not imagine we have been quarrelling : not at all : but
she seems to think her brother's affairs so unpromising as to render

our continuing to write to each other not pleasant. Does not this sound extraordinary ? We are much surprised." It was indeed extraordinary ; but no doubt Mary was better acquainted with her brother's feelings at the time than even Christina herself. Soon after this the betrothal came to an end. Very probably Collinson was unable to bear the burden of conscious inferiority. He announced that he was going to return to the Catholic Church, and thereupon Christina herself broke off the engagement. But it is sufficiently obvious that the religious difference, generally accepted as the reason for Christina's decision, could not have been the main issue.

The break came in May—June of 1850, and shortly afterwards Collinson resigned also from the P.R.B., saying that he felt uneasy about its activities. " I love and reverence God's faith, and I love his Holy Saints ; and I cannot bear any longer the self-accusation that, to gratify a little vanity, I am helping to dishonour them, and lower their merits, if not absolutely to bring their sanctity into ridicule. I cannot blame any one but myself. . . . It was for me to have judged beforehand whether I could conscientiously, as a Catholic, assist in spreading the artistic opinions of those who are not." In a P.S., he adds : " Please do not attempt to change my mind." Collinson now betook himself to a Jesuit seminary, but left it again in 1854—and was subsequently married. When he and his sister Mary died in 1881, within a few months of each other, Christina noted the event in her diary.

What was the effect of all this on Christina's mind ? William Michael says in his ponderous way, " I cannot say that she was in love with Collinson in any such sense as that she would, before knowing him to be enamoured of her, have wished him to become so ; " but he goes on to say, she had " bestowed her affections and would have been faithful to her promise." Taking all the scanty evidence into consideration, it seems likely that Christina was more in love than her brother thought ; probably she was as much so as her nature would ever have allowed her to be. A false idea of her feelings is at once produced if Collinson is thought of as altogether egregious and unreliable. He cannot have been by any means a despicable person, and on him Christina had hung all her hope of joining in the life and joy of the world. When that hope vanished, it left her feeling *Shut Out* (that significant poem was called in manuscript *What happened to me*). The impression on her mind was permanent. Four or five months after the end of their engagement, she saw Collinson in the street and fainted away. She continued surreptitiously to ask news of him from William, of his health and his painting ; she recommended a poem of his which appeared in *The Germ* to the editor of a biblical anthology in 1881 ; and she reproduced from memory a sonnet by him, which she calls " devotional ", in *Time Flies* (24 January).

> " Give me thy heart." I said : Can I not make
> Abundant sacrifice to Him who gave
> Life, health, possessions, friends, of all I have,
> All but my heart once given ? Lord, do not take
> It from its happy home or it will break.
> " Give me thy broken heart." Can love enslave ?
> Must it be forced to look beyond the grave
> For its fruition ? Lord, for thy Love's sake
> Let this thing be : as two streams journeying on
> Melt into one and widen to the sea,
> So let two souls love-burdened make but one,
> And one full heart rest all its love on Thee.
> " Alas, frail man, for thine infirmity !
> Thy God is Love."—Then, Lord, Thy will be done.

Thirty years' recollection in the mind of a great poetess may very likely have improved this attempt at apology or explanation ; but taking it as it stands, it is not the expression of an ignoble mind.

It is to be noticed that when writing to William to enquire about Collinson's health, Christina was anxious to hide her concern from her mother. Nor did she care to confide in Gabriel. It is very probable that Mrs. Rossetti had little respect for Collinson, and would certainly have had no more liking for Christina's brooding over the matter than she had for her " unhappy little fragments " of verse. Her attitude may very well have been that of one of the characters in Christina's own *Commonplace* who says, " Very well ; do one thing or do the other ; only do not become ridiculous." It is altogether unlikely that Christina talked much about it to anybody ; and when one looks into her verse to find its effects, there is nothing very definite to find. It is impossible to be sure when the poetess is utilising her own experience impersonally, and when she writes in direct expression of her own feelings. Nor does it in the least matter to anyone who reads her poetry for its own sake ; and yet the natural curiosity which will not let the secret of Shakespeare's sonnets rest in peace might equally be led to the examination of Christina Rossetti's verse from 1848 onwards. It is indeed well nigh impossible to avoid the biographical reference. Like her brother in *The House of Life*, Christina is often too enigmatic to escape questioning ; and yet unlike him too reserved to yield any reply. We do not propose to pursue such an enquiry, but it ought to be observed that either Christina herself had despaired of her engagement before ever she visited the Collinsons at Pleasley Hill, which seems very improbable ; or that her love for Collinson had been singularly unavailing to lift the cloud of melancholy from her mind. In February 1848 she wrote *A Pause of Thought*, the first of the *Three Stages* printed by William Michael among her general poems. Here she longs for " that which is not, nor can be ",

> And hope deferred made my heart sick in truth ;
> But years must pass before a hope of youth
> Is resigned utterly.

And it is here that she admonishes herself,

> Alas thou foolish one ! alike unfit
> For healthy joy and salutary pain :
> Thou knowest the chase useless, and again
> Turnest to follow it.

In the second *Stage*, written 18 April 1849, we find

> Oh weary wakening from a life-true dream !
> Oh pleasant dream from which I wake in pain !
> I rested all my trust on things that seem,
> And all my trust is vain,

which recalls the end of a poem which there is the authority of Mr. Mackenzie Bell for taking to refer to Collinson, *What ?*

> A bitter dream to wake from,
> But oh how pleasant while we dream !
> A poisoned fount to take from,
> But oh how sweet the stream !

Now the first *Stage* was originally called *Lines in Memory of Schiller's Der Pilgrim* and so may be regarded as semi-dramatic in nature. The second, and the third of 1854, were never published by Christina because of their intimately personal nature. There is little doubt that they refer to Collinson—and the second was written while she was still engaged to him. This now gives meaning to its fourth stanza :

> Now all the cherished secrets of my heart,
> Now all my hidden hopes, are turned to sin.
> Part of my life is dead, part sick, and part
> Is all on fire within.

With such a passage in mind, is it not difficult to believe that Christina could have been happy in love, with Collinson or with anybody else ?   Does it not call for sympathy, not only with her, but also with the unkindly judged man who had the incredibly difficult task of making happy a woman much greater than himself and who, when he met her, was already foredoomed to unhappiness ?

Echoes of this melancholy episode go on in her verse for many years ; they are to be heard in *What ?* (1853), in *A Pause* (1853), in the beautiful *Echo* itself (1854), in *Shut Out* (1856), probably in the terrible *Introspective* (1857), and the even more terrible fragment called *Nightmare* (1857),

> I have a friend in Ghostland—   '
> Early found, ah me how early lost !—
>
> .   .   .   .   .   .
>
> If I wake he hunts me like a nightmare :
> I feel my hair stand up, my body creep :
> Without light I see a blasting sight there,
> See a secret I must keep.

She writes frequently about her " secret " that " none must know ", that none indeed are ever likely to know.   From the first part of *Memory* (1857), a very significant poem, the conclusion is unavoidable that the breaking of the engagement had little to do with Collinson's catholicism, or with Collinson at all.

> None know the choice I made ; I make it still.
> None know the choice I made and broke my heart,
> Breaking mine idol : I have braced my will
> Once, chosen for once my part.

" There is only one process ", she says in *Time Flies* (November 3), " to make water stable—the process of freezing " ; and she steadily applied the process to herself from 1849 onwards.

And yet Christina retained throughout her life a certain youthfulness of temperament, which breaks out here and there in happier notes of song.   Only ten days distant in date from *Memory* is *A Birthday* which is a spring of pure joy, showing that the unforgotten experience of the past could still stimulate her imagination to a great diversity of moods.

Some of her best known and most perfect verse was written during the time of the engagement itself, which seems to have quickened Christina's poetic activity even when not intruding itself as a theme. For the subject of these poems is not the joy and the hope of love, but death and the grateful quiet of the grave. *When I am dead my dearest* (December 1848) was probably addressed to Collinson ; the sonnet *Remember* (July 1849) almost certainly was

> Remember me when no more day by day
> You tell me of our future that you planned :
> Only remember me ; you understand
> It will be late to counsel then or pray.

The sonnet *Rest* was written in May 1849, and a month earlier one of the most memorable of all her poems, the exquisite *Dream Land*. Her dreamland is the grave

> Where sunless rivers weep
> Their waves into the deep,
> She sleeps a charmed sleep :
>   Awake her not.
> Led by a single star,
> She came from very far
> To seek where shadows are
>   Her pleasant lot.

These last two poems end with the thought of arising to an eternity of joy, paying the inevitable debt to the requirements of piety ; but the feeling of the poems stops short of that close. A truer cry from the heart at this time is no doubt furnished by the close of a sonnet written before the engagement :

> . . . The peace of heaven is placed too high,
> And this earth changeth and is perishing.

One hears a great deal about the early mastery of Dante Gabriel ; no critic ever mentions *The Blessed Damozel* without saying that it was written when the poet was nineteen. But that fact is not nearly so impressive as that these poems of life-weariness and infinitely sad acquiescence, with all their perfect happiness of phrase and music, should have been written by a poetess of only eighteen years. *The Blessed Damozel* is a young man's poem ; these lyrics of Christina's are more personally genuine and more mature, as well as being in no way inferior in artistic beauty.

The third of the *Three Stages*, written in July 1854, tells that at last the chill and numbness had passed away ; she " felt the sunshine glow again, and knew the swallow on its track ; " and with the new pulse of life,

> Ah too my heart woke unawares, intent
> On fruitful harvest-sheaves,

and the longing for happiness begins again. The sonnet *After All* (1852) could be conceived as an imaginary dialogue with Maria about this vain pursuit :

> " I thought your search was over."—" So I thought."
> " But you are seeking still."—" Yes, even so :
> Still seeking in mine own despite below
> That which in heaven alone is found unsought :
> Still spending for that thing which is not bought."
> " Then chase no more this shifting empty show."—
> " Amen : So bid a drowning man forego
> The straw he clutches : will he so be taught ?
> You have a home where peace broods like a dove,
> Screened from the weary world's loud discontent :
> You have home here : you wait for home above.
> I must unlearn the pleasant ways I went :
> Must learn another hope, another love,
> And sigh indeed for home in banishment."

And this internal disjunction and dissatisfaction, this constant seeking and never finding " that something which I never had ", accentuated in the meantime her renewed delight in the simple and unsolicitous joy of all nature, as in *To what Purpose is this Waste?* (1853) where she stops only a little short of a pantheistic communion with the creatures of earth and all their joyous life in hidden places.

VI

This broken romance was the only important event in Christina Rossetti's life during the period under consideration. Outwardly, when she was not too ill to do anything, she was usually teaching either at home or abroad. In due course she succeeded Maria as governess in the Thynne family, but how she fared or how long she was with them is not recorded. To the best of her ability she assisted her mother in the little schools Mrs. Rossetti tried to establish at Arlington Street and Frome. Both were failures, and from Frome Christina brought back no very happy memories. She was probably as glad as her father to leave it and return to Bloomsbury, both of them having been left there a good deal without the support of Mrs. Rossetti, on whose continual presence they both so much depended. We do not need William Michael to tell us that Christina " had no propensity for educational drudgery " ; a more unsuitable temperament for the care of children can hardly be imagined. Children were for her very much like birds and flowers —she liked their innocence and prettiness and gentle ways, but apparently she had no special sympathy with them. It may be judged from *Sing-Song*, her nursery rhyme book, with what success she might hope to enter into a child's mind. Ten of its hundred odd rhymes deal with death, suitably illustrated with its material appurtenances by Hughes. For example,

> My baby has a father and a mother,
>   Rich little baby !
> Fatherless, motherless, I know another
>   Forlorn as maybe :
>   Poor little baby !

The emblem represents a classical-looking figure lying in the sleep of death, with a live little baby clutching at her breast. She has a pillow and a bolster, but for the rest appears to be on a sepulchral slab. And even supposing that children could benefit by an early acquaintance with mortality, what could any young mind make of the following :

> I planted a hand
> And there came up a palm,
> I planted a heart
> And there came up balm.
>
> I planted a wish,
> But there sprang a thorn,
> While heaven frowned with thunder
> And earth sighed forlorn.

To this echo of Blake, Hughes contributed the picture of a dejected old man on a bank, a sickle by his side, a briar at his feet.

These quotations are of course quite unfair to *Sing-Song* as a whole, some of its rhymes being very graceful and entirely suitable for children. But they do serve to illustrate how difficult it was for the poetess to free herself from her orbit of clouded melancholy, and from her habitual contemplation of the death of the body, with all the mournful paraphernalia which seem so much more real and more imaginable to her than the life of the spirit. Equipped with coffin, grave, and tombstone, the dead sleep on in peaceful silence, awaiting the resurrection. In winter a pall of snow will lie above their tired eyes, in spring the snowdrops and an occasional robin will provide a little outward cheer.

The last one hears of Christina's attempts at educational work is in November 1855 when she is away from home apparently as a governess. She writes to William, " I hope you are glad to know that I am very comfortable in my exile ; but at any rate I know I am rejoiced to feel that my health does really unfit me for miscellaneous governessing *en permanence*. For instance, yesterday I indulged in breakfast in bed, having been very unwell the day previous : now I am very tolerable again, but do not feel particularly to be depended upon."

Thenceforward her life was spent in attendance on her much beloved mother, and on her aunts when their illness made it necessary, in church observances and in good works ; moments of retirement added their contribution to the little notebooks, as neatly kept as her books of household accounts.

She had of course considerable opportunity for intercourse with her brothers' friends. It is a great mistake to suppose that her life was of necessity narrow and restricted. Christina Rossetti had better opportunities of knowing the world of men than had, for example, Elizabeth Barrett, or the Brontës. The hosts of strange Italian visitors were present by the fireside almost every evening ; a great range of personalities came at least within her horizon among her brothers' associates. If she did not make more of these opportunities, it was because she could not, or did not, choose to do so. She was of course extremely shy. Nevertheless Christina took a good deal of interest in the P.R.B., contributed poems to *The Germ*, and wrote playful verses about Pre-Raphaelite affairs. This humorous vein she was able throughout her life to exercise happily on occasion ; and sometimes on more serious subjects where its charm is very appealing, as in the very human *Sketch* of Cayley. (*The blindest buzzard that I know*.) The sadness of her verse—" the legitimate exercise of anguish " as Dante Gabriel called it—was distilled from her inner life, and not usually visible on the surface. She considered cheerfulness to be " a fundamental and essential Christian virtue," and it was no doubt one which her mother would not fail to urge upon her. In a characteristic remark she once made to William Sharp, she spoke of " the blithe cheerfulness which one can put over one's sadness like a veil, a bright shining veil." But there were times when cheerfulness was not altogether so perfunctory.

Deeply attached to her own family, Christina was uneasy when brought into contact with alien personalities. Later in life it was only with a good deal of mutual forbearance that she was able to get on with Lucy Madox Brown, the wife of William Michael. What she thought of Gabriel's concerns can hardly be surmised, but within the period we are considering she already meets with some difficulty in this respect, being unable to appreciate to an appropriate degree the charms of Miss Siddal. Jealousy must at all times have been very far from her nature ; and yet it was surely bitter to be replaced in her brother's pictures by this strange woman whom she was forbidden playfully but quite tactlessly to rival. " I find ", Dante Gabriel writes to her, " that you have been perpetrating portraits of some kind. If you answer this note will you enclose a specimen, as I should like to see some of your handiwork ? You must take care however not to rival the Sid, but keep within respectful limits. Since you went away, I have had sent me, among my things from Highgate, a lock of hair shorn from the beloved head of that dear, and radiant as the tresses of Aurora, a sight of which may perhaps dazzle you on your return." How much, not of jealousy, but of family pride and affection, of clear-sighted and wistful sympathy, is there in the sonnet on *An Artist's Studio* which she left unpublished :

> He feeds upon her face by day and night,
> And she with true kind eyes looks back on him,
> Fair as the moon and joyful as the light :
> Not wan with waiting, not with sorrow dim ;
> *Not as she is, but was when hope shone bright ;*
> *Not as she is, but as she fills his dream.*[1]

It is of some importance to remember that throughout Dante Gabriel's feverish life he had always close at hand the clear-eyed sympathy of his mother and sister watching his career from their pale and cool seclusion, and reminding him constantly, as Mr. Mégroz has said, of that Eden from which he had been shut out, or as one would prefer to say, out of which he had gradually shut himself. And if nothing could destroy their love for him, his affection and sympathy was likewise theirs. He reads Christina's volume of 1875 " with that intense sympathy which your work always excites in me." He moved in a man's world and she in a woman's, but far from each other as their paths diverged, their common starting-point was never forgotten by them nor can be long forgotten by their readers.

Taking leave of Christina Rossetti in 1854 we shall not follow her to her second entry into the courts of love, the second event of her quiet life. Some may think that we have already dwelt too long on the first. But so much that is essential to an understanding of the prevailing moods of her poetry is revealed in a scrutiny of poems written at such times that the subject can scarcely be avoided. It is

---

[1] The italics are **not** mine.

easy to blame Collinson for his " successive tergiversations " or Cayley for his " ineffective faithful aloofness ". Is it not obvious that the gentleness of both these men was a necessary part of their attraction for her ? Had they been more robust and unwavering they would never have disturbed her life at all. She was not an Elizabeth Barrett to be carried off by a vigorous gentleman who would not take no for an answer. Her life went on with a kind of gentle tentativeness, a timid wooing of joy both earthly and heavenly, in which she never entirely lost herself. She could never abandon her inner self to God, to nature, or to love ; and that is why her life and her letters are grey, her religious poetry so unjoyous, and her general poetry so melancholy ; and it is why her imagination was most at home in the quiet dreamland which was consequently the inspiration of her best work, for it left in untroubled possession of the field the instinct for retirement which was from the beginning the leading feature of her beautiful and unobtrusive personality.

CHAPTER NINE

PASSING AWAY

I

EARLY in 1853, despairing of her school at 38 Arlington Street, Mrs. Rossetti courageously launched forth into new waters. A certain Rev. Dr. Bennett who had had to leave his London parish on account of his High Church practices, had recently been presented with the living of Frome Selwood, Somerset. Mrs. Rossetti and the girls having by this time risen from their early evangelicalism to an ardent High Anglicanism, it was thought that under the wing of Mr. Bennett they might do better than they had done in London. It was a bold and trustful gesture, but doomed to failure. Mr. Bennett appears to have been unable to help them, the pupils were few and of the same kind as before. Christina went with her mother ; William and Maria remained at Arlington Street until Christmas. Dante Gabriel had left the bosom of the family during the preceding year and was henceforward always separated from his home.

Hardly had Mrs. Rossetti settled in Frome, when her mother was taken seriously ill, and she was obliged to return to London. Mrs. Polidori had long been a confirmed invalid, and died soon after her daughter's arrival. Her painless end, however saddening, could hardly have been a cause of great distress to the younger generation. Christina came to join her mother in London, having expressed a characteristic wish to see her dead grandmother. Afterwards they returned to the new school, taking with them Gabriele, who announces to Ferretti on 2 May that he is about to go to Frome " to leave there these weary bones."

From Frome he writes thus to a friend in Italy. " Do you know that I am seventy years old ? My birth certificate has just arrived from my native town and assures me of it. . . . My wife, excellent woman, has come here to set up a school for young ladies and I hope it will succeed. My two sons have stayed behind in London ; one is an able painter and makes a good deal of money ; the other is employed in the Customs Office with the fine salary of £250 a year, in addition to which he makes £50 more by writing very fine articles on the arts for a periodical (*The Spectator*). . . . To earn so much at so early an age makes a good entry into life. It alone would be enough to support the whole family, but it is my wish to share the feelings of my wife in the matter—she desires to leave the children in possession of all they earn. Even my two daughters can already support themselves. The older of them earns about £80 a year, and the other assists her mother. Alas ! what a change has come over everything since I was attacked by my long series of illnesses. What I used to earn alone, my wife and the four children cannot earn by their joint efforts." If this remark seems both untrue and ungrateful, one can nevertheless sympathise with the stricken old poet, afflicted in self-esteem as well as in body, and writing to the country where the fame of earlier years was still bright.

The *Arpa Evangelica*, printed the year before, had now come to his hands, and is the subject of a good deal of his correspondence. He gives instructions to William in September for distributing copies among his friends, and says he would very much value the criticisms of both his sons. The letter ends sadly, " I started this letter with the idea of filling the four little pages, but having got half way down the second I cannot see to write any more." Dante Gabriel sent his father some appreciative comments on the book, only to receive in reply this grave letter of admonition.

MY DEAREST GABRIEL,

For some while past I have been feeling a strong impulse to write to you, my dearly beloved son ; and to-day I will obey this imperious inner voice.

I am glad that you have undertaken to read the *Arpa Evangelica*. . . . You should, however, always bear in mind that this book is the outcome of only three months' work, and was written with the intention of its being amenable to every grade of intelligence.

I am extremely pleased at the progress which you are making in your beautiful art, and at some profits which you are earning from it to maintain yourself with decorum in society. Remember, my dearly loved son, that you have only your abilities to rely upon for your welfare. Remember that you were born with a marked propensity and that, from your earliest years, you made us conceive the brightest hopes that you would become a great painter. And such you will be, I am certain.

At this moment I have received a letter from Genoa, from my friend Di Negro. He rejoices at the arrival of the *Arpa*. . . . He says that throughout Piedmont, and in Liguria and Sardinia, it is well received and generally admired ; but that in the other parts of Italy the governments prohibit its entry, on account of the author's name, which has become a veritable scarecrow to Kings. If you had to go to Italy, I would recommend you, my dear son, always to call yourself Dante Rossetti. But, before a time comes for that, I trust that affairs will have changed.

I beg you frequently to visit your worthy grandfather. What an excellent old man ! [I have always loved him dearly, but never as I do now. What he wrote to me recently about the *Arpa* is vividly impressed upon my heart.]

Good-bye, my most lovable Gabriel, and believe in the constant affection of

Your affectionate father

GABRIELE ROSSETTI.[1]

P.S.—I perceive that I have not spoken to you at all about the state of my health. And what can I say of it ? It is the same as it was in London ; betwixt life and death, but more tending to the latter than the former.

Dante Gabriel knew what was meant by the tone of his father's letter, and his reply was unusually affectionate. " In your letter, my dear Father, you speak of my profession. I can assure you that now I am not negligent in that respect. With me progress is, and always will be, gradual in everything. Of late also health has not been favourable to me ; but now I am well and at work, and also I find purchasers, and I can see before me, much more clearly than hitherto, the path to success. How much do I owe you, and how much trouble have I given you dearest Father, in this and in all matters ! Needless were it to ask your loving heart to pardon me ; but I must always beg you to believe in the real and deep affection with which I remain,

Your loving son,

DANTE GABRIEL ROSSETTI." [2]

[1] This letter is quoted from W. M. R.'s translation in *Pre-Raphaelite Diaries and Letters*, p. 38 ; except for the passage in brackets, which is supplied from the original in Rome.

[2] This letter is in Italian. Translation quoted from *D. G. R. Family Letters*, p. 123.

II

Polidori, whose spirits had survived the loss of his invalid wife in April, carried on a correspondence with Rossetti during the summer months, in an incredibly myopic hand, not to be read at all without a magnifying-glass. In August they are both concerned with a poem called *Losario*, the work of Gaetano's uncle. In September Christina sends her grandfather a poem called *Seasons*—he is adding a few passages about the seasons of human life and will then return it to her. In October and November follow a number of appreciative letters about the *Arpa*. At last in December, in his ninetieth year, Polidori is taken ill, and Mrs. Rossetti is again called up to London.

On the 15th Rossetti writes her a very pathetic letter. "Things with me are but so so. And you, my love, how are you ? I am looking forward to the day of your return as a great event. I envy you because you are seeing our three eldest children and dear Polidori. I hope you will come back on Monday. Am I wrong ? Pray tell me I am not.

To-day will make the third night I shall sleep without you. Dear Christina does everything she can to make me happy ; but you are not there. The thought makes existence bitter to me. Come back my soul, come back to your Gabriele. How are our three children, Gabriel, William, and Maria ? . . . Pray tell dearest Polidori that I am expecting a letter on the series of the *Arpa* he has had, and then another on the sixth, and then on the seventh, and finally on the eighth. . . . Your sister Charlotte came here yesterday and to-day ; she is welcome, but she is not Francesca. Dearest Francesca mine, greet your two dear sisters, and your brother, and good Sara too ; but above all others dearest Polidori who becomes dearer to me every day. Tell him that if he finds it difficult to write to me, not to do so ; but let him know that his letters are a great joy to me. . . .

But on the same day Mrs. Rossetti was writing to her husband as follows :

DEAREST GABRIELE,

Christina will have told you that my father was so ill yesterday that little hope for him could be entertained. He has never recovered for a moment from that stupor, and now we have the sorrow of hearing from the doctor that he is dying, but that he may last a few hours more. He does not speak, and neither hears nor recognises us ; but thank God he seems to suffer no pain.

You will easily understand that situated as I am now I cannot say exactly when I shall return, but it will be as soon as possible. My heart calls me back to you, but on the other hand bids me fulfil the duty of a daughter about to lose a very loving father. Christina gives me a good report of you, and I thank you very much for your very affectionate letter. I will attempt to comply with your requests. Good-bye, dear Gabriele, I am always

Your loving wife,

FRANCESCA ROSSETTI.[1]

Christina saw this letter before her father and was overcome with grief, crying, " Oh my dear grandfather, oh my dear grandfather," with so much anguish that Gabriele thought he had already died. The next day brought news of the end, and Gabriele wrote, " Your last letter filled me with indescribable desolation. I had deluded myself into supposing that my dear Polidori would shed tears for my death ; and now I find myself shedding them for his. My dearest father-in-law and friend ! Oh what a wretched thing is life, ending always with the grave !

Dearest Francesca, when you are here, you must tell me his last words ; I wish to write them down as an eternal record. But I shall survive him by very little, very little indeed. I shall soon join him, and I hope to embrace him again in the kingdom of happiness I envy Teodorico, William, and all those who were present at his last moments. Dear old man ! They were able to listen to his last words.

Good-bye, O dearly beloved Francesca,

Your affectionate husband,

GABRIELE ROSSETTI."

At the death of her parents Mrs. Rossetti inherited an income which, though small, was sufficient to make further school-teaching unnecessary ; and knowing that they would not be financially a burden to him, she acquiesced in William's plan of uniting the family again under one roof in London. Their lonely father at Frome was delighted when he heard of this intention. On 22 December he writes to his wife, " When are you going to return, when ? . . . Christina and I await you with open arms ; but as yet in vain. Have you then decided to abandon Frome and to return to London ? Hurrah ! Our good William is earning enough to persuade you to do that ? If that excellent young man

[1] The letter is in Italian.

wishes to get married to carry on his race and perpetuate the name of Rossetti in England, I shall give my consent with pleasure. Please tell him so. How is my dear Maria? and my beloved Gabriel? Oh how much I love my four children! But they will not believe it.

Please take care to obtain a good house and of sufficient size, so that our loving Gabriel can join us as well. Oh, what a joy it will be if I can have all my children around me, as we do in Italy."

By Lady Day of 1854 they were all installed at 45 Albany Street—all, that is, except Gabriel, who, whatever the size of the house, would not now have felt able to join them.

III

Thus we approach the dark door through which one after another of Gabriele's old friends had silently preceded him. Frere had died in 1846. When his death was announced to Rossetti, " with tears in his half-sightless eyes, and the passionate fervour of a southern Italian, my father fell on his knees and exclaimed, ' *Anima bella, benedetta sii tu, dovunque sei* '." [*Noble soul, blessed be thou, wherever thou art.*] Frere's old fellow-patron Lyell followed not long after. He had continued a warm-hearted friend although a less than lukewarm supporter of the Dante theories up to the year of his death, and had lived long enough to see the great promise of his godson and to give him his first commission, the portrait of Gabriele to which we have already referred. With this he was much pleased. " It is a work of power and calls every eye to it in my library. The artist of twenty who could do it, may (if Providence grant him health), not only defy want, but command a competency, and even affluence. Always assuming that he has great industry, and a modest confidence in his talents, that he despises flattery, and feels more obliged by an exposure of his artistic faults than his merits ; and is humbled when he contemplates the colouring, taste, and finishing of the great works of our National Gallery." The portrait itself, he says, portrays " faithfully the many cruel furrows which Time and Sickness have worn on your physiognomy since the happy days when you partook of my beefsteak and porter in Norfolk St. and enraptured me with your beautiful articulation, and recitation of *Tanto gentile e tanto onesta pare*. Happy days ! when you infused into me your passion for the study of Dante, the source, to me, of our long correspondence and of years of my greatest literary pleasure."

This is the last letter from Lyell to Rossetti preserved with the rest of their vast correspondence in Rome. A sudden silence follows, and then the following sad postcript of 13 December 1849, being a letter from Charles Lyell Junior : " I have great pleasure in informing you that since I last wrote to you I have found a codicil to my father's will in which he leaves you a legacy of £50.0.0, and another of £10.0.0 to your son. As soon as I can wind up the affairs of executorship which will unavoidably take some time, I will not delay to send you this money."

Rossetti must have felt the loss of his old friend deeply. Nobody had been so closely associated as Lyell with the theories and researches which had taken up so much of his life, and now Lyell had disappeared with the theories into the shadowy past.

IV

Among the letters received by Rossetti in this wintry period preceding his death, some of the least encouraging are those of Keightley. In July 1846 he had written : " John Taylor has brought me your last work. . . . Thank you most sincerely. . . . Dante himself is not more Italian. . . . There is no doubt that it will exert a powerful influence on the minds of the Italian youth ; yet I almost doubt if you are benefiting them by it. The recovery of freedom and independence for Italy seems to me almost hope-less. . . . Political unity does not seem natural to the southern countries. As to religion I think too that is nearly hopeless. I never knew an Italian but yourself and Dr. Romani that had any real religion, but it may not be so bad for I remember Niccolini once said to me, ' There are many Catholics who are Protestant without knowing it.' . . . It is I fear useless for me to enquire about your eyes. I long ago remarked the resemblance between you and Milton and this increases it. Could you not write a poem that could be less personal ? Is there any hope of the rest of the Comento appearing ? " This admiring but disconcerting friend is still writing in the same tone to Rossetti at Frome in October 1853. He has now read all Rossetti's published works and thinks it no fallacy to say that he is the greatest poet that Italy has produced since Tasso, thinks he could have succeeded in any kind, and that he could have written noble sacred dramas if he had taken up some of the subjects Milton had selected for that purpose. " I hope if you are reprinting the Amor Platonico that you will abridge it considerably. Could you not manage to dispose of, even at a very moderate rate, the copies that are lying in R[ed] L[ion] Court to some foreign bookseller? You know there is not the slightest chance of selling any in this country. . . . Is there any chance of the entire *Comento* being printed? I do not expect that you will be any very great gainer in a pecuniary way, but you will enable your descendants to repose under the shadow of a great name. It has often struck me that you were by far the happiest among all the exiles who have sought our shores, for you alone seem to have enjoyed domestic happiness and your children are all talented and amiable. Could you have hoped to enjoy this bliss under the brilliant sky of Naples? . . . It gave me great pleasure to learn from William that your health was improved by the climate of Somerset. You must, however, feel rather lonely as you have not your countrymen to drop in as in London. I fear you and I are not destined to meet any more, and I could not help saying to my niece as we were coming away the last time I called to see you, ' I have now spoken Italian for probably the last time.' " But Keightley lived to speak Italian for many years yet, although not with Rossetti. He was still persuaded of the truth of his friend's Dante interpretation in 1865.

The happiest of the exiles. Rossetti would probably not have thought it true, and yet there was good reason for Keightley's remark. The domestic happiness which he mentions was envied at least by one other of the exiles, who, as he says himself, had not had his family around him for thirty-three years. Filippo Pistrucci, with one son in the thick of Mazzini's conspiracies, and another married and on the high road of English respectability, had betaken himself to Brighton and was teaching there. He was a year older than Rossetti. He writes early in 1846, telling Rossetti of the death of a fellow exile, and saying that he would not mind dying himself, if there were not so many other people to think about. " Let us take comfort then, and try to live as long as we can. My friend, nothing matters but God and Christ; putting them before all things, and having them in our hearts, we cannot die." Next year he has the pleasure of telling Rossetti about the medal which was to be struck in the latter's honour in Florence, one of the fruits of his *Veggente in Solitudine*. Then there is a gap in the correspondence until 1853 when Rossetti was at Frome. " If I can," writes Pistrucci, " I will certainly come to see you before I die, and I hope to remain in this world until the Christmas holidays; although indeed my health at present might lead me to expect to

live as long as Polidori ; and if I do I shall love you until the
end, as I have loved you to this day." A few days later a longish
letter in a gravely religious tone follows, in the course of which
Pistrucci shows serious concern about Rossetti's health, and concludes " You must be very pleased with your children ; I was
extremely glad to get the news you gave me of them. Signora
Francesca must be very busy ; greet her from me ; of course she
would not please her pupils, she has too many virtues, or rather
there are never too many, she has them all." There are a number
of his letters from this time onwards, not very striking in content
but full of the November mist which has long settled over Rossetti's
life and friendships. They are the melancholy and pious letters of
one old man to another, both of them little concerned to go on
living. Very often Pistrucci writes appreciatively of Rossetti's
family. William is " a fine young man " ; he wishes Dante Gabriel
a fortunate career, and thinks he may have a better one than they
expect, if he has judgment. As for Rossetti, " you are alone with
your wife and Christina, but *corpo di Baccho*, those two are worth
two hundred." The death of Polidori in December calls forth the
melancholy remark, " We shall soon go and find him. It is our turn
next ; and I feel it near."

V

Five days after receiving this letter Gabriele died. He had
weakened rapidly on his return to London, and from the beginning
of April the old man lay in almost complete physical prostration,
having lost his sense of touch, and being hardly able to move.
Sometimes his mind wandered, and friendly ghosts came to him out
of the hiding-places of the past. On the 23rd he said to his wife,
" How did Pepe come to be in bed with me ? " and again, " Where
is my mother ? " She replied, " Don't you remember she died
long ago in Italy ? " to which he said, " But she was with me."
On the morning of the 24th he was so anxious to get up that Mrs.
Rossetti dressed him and led him in to breakfast. On entering
the room he said, " How I have longed for this moment ! " In
the night of the 24th–25th, William being present, Mrs. Rossetti
said, " Do you know who it is ? It's William." He replied, " I
see him, I hear him, he is written on my heart." More than once
when Maria asked him, " Where do you feel pain ? " he replied,
" Where do I not feel it ? " At one moment he said, " What a
consolation it is to have all my children around me ! And yet

not to be able to see them." His last distinct words were "*Ah Dio, ajutami tu*" [Oh God, help me].

On 12 May 1854 Maria reported her father's death to the friend in Italy who had been the recipient of so many of his letters during his last years.

DEAR SIGNORA,

Your heart will tell you, without my attempting to describe, what grief we felt at receiving your last kind letter. My dearest father had ceased to live some days before. Since last Christmas he had made up his mind to return to London and did so on 22 March. We feared that he would be too weak to stand the journey of five hours or more : and yet he bore it without very ill effects. However, on Easter Day Mamma thought she ought to call in a doctor, because of certain painful symptoms that had appeared ; and these grew so much worse that on the Saturday following a second doctor was called in, who gave us little hope. On Monday morning my dear father appeared a little stronger, but at 5.30 in the afternoon a terrible change appeared in him ; he was put to bed, and we had at least the consolation of seeing that he recognised us all, and that he listened to the prayers offered for him ; among other things a hymn from his own *Arpa Evangelica* was read to him, a book which, with the Bible, was almost all he read for many months before his death. The two doctors were summoned again, but they could do nothing ; and after two days of extreme languor, though retaining his senses almost to the last moment, he expired without a struggle on Wednesday the 26th at 5.30 p.m. Mamma and all the other children were about his bed ; Teodorico Rossetti was there too, his nephew, and a very affectionate and good young man. A week later he was buried in the cemetery at Highgate, one of the London suburbs ; and we are going to raise a stone there.[1] But perhaps before getting this letter, you will have heard the sad news of our irreparable loss from some newspaper ; still I expect that these details will be of interest to you.

We send our good wishes ; and I remain,

Yours sincerely,

MARIA F. ROSSETTI.

[1] Teodorico, in a long letter to his brother in Vasto, reports that " Germans, Italians, Frenchmen, Englishmen, all wanted to make I know not what display of empty funeral celebrations, but the family would not accept their offers."

P.S.—I cannot omit to tell you of the indescribable patience and gentleness with which my dear father bore his great sufferings up to the end.

With this may be compared the letter written to Allingham by Dante Gabriel about the same event. " We lost my father to-day at half-past five. He had not I think felt much pain this day or two, but it has been a wearisome, protracted state of dull suffering, from which we cannot but feel in some sort happy at seeing him released."

In 1871, after the triumph of the cause he had had so much at heart, and when it had been arranged to re-inter the remains of Ugo Foscolo in the Church of Santa Croce at Florence, it was proposed in the Italian parliament to do the same for Rossetti. All members of the family except one strongly opposed the suggestion ; Dante Gabriel thought it ought to be done, but told W. B. Scott that his mother would never be induced to give her consent. There can be little doubt at all that Gabriele himself would have desired it. Writing to Lyell on one occasion, he blesses every English sod and prays for one to cover his remains, but that is an isolated piece of rhetoric. At least twice he refers to his last resting-place in other words. " When my ashes ", he says, " come to rest in their native earth, all good Italians will come to say their requiems over one who never despaired of their cause." In 1850 he had written emphatically to Ricciardi, " If ever our dear country is redeemed, I implore you to see that my ashes are restored to their own land. This desire I leave to you as a legacy." But it was not to be. Gabriele Rossetti, poet and patriot, does not lack memorials in his native land. There is a tablet in Santa Croce, and in Vasto the monument to which our eyes were turned at the opening of this book ; but his mortal remains still lie in that resting-place to which the final document in the Rome collection refers. Protests to Museum Directors, speeches to Carbonari, learned letters to Lyell and Frere, drafted replies to reviewers, loving messages to his wife and admonitions to his children, those abundant records carry the student through the busy, ardent, affectionate life of Gabriele Rossetti in all its phases, to end at last with a receipted bill from the Trustees of Highgate Cemetery :

For a private grave 7 ft deep ($6\frac{1}{2} \times 2\frac{1}{2}$) . . . £4.9.0

THE END

NOTES

ABBREVIATIONS USED IN THE NOTES

Aut.	*Gabriele Rossetti. A Versified Autobiography.*
CGRFL.	*Family Letters* of Christina Rossetti.
CGRPW.	*Poetical Works* of Christina Rossetti.
D.C.	*La Vita Mia.* Ed. Domenico Ciampoli.
DGRFL.	*Family Letters* of D. G. Rossetti.
Epist.	Epistolario of Gabriele Rossetti in Biblioteca del Risorgimento in Rome.
Kinnordy	Letters of G. R. to Lyell in possession of the Lyell family at Kinnordy (see Bibliog.).
Mem. DGR.	*Memoir* of D. G. Rossetti by W. M. Rossetti.
PRDL.	*Pre-Raphaelite Diaries and Letters.*
Remin.	*Reminiscences* of W. M. Rossetti.

Other works, when named in the Bibliography, are referred to by the name of the author.

NOTES

2. *Now I* etc.] *Opere Inedite e Rare di G. R.* Vasto, 1929.
I., p. 4.

3. *Six other children*] See family tree and details about Antonio
in *D.C.*, pp. 307–11.

men of letters] See *Aut.*, p. 8. Letter to Charles Lyell,
27 March 1830 (Kinnordy). " Ho avuto illustri letterati in
mia famiglia (che fu traslocata da Rimini in Abruzzo fin da
tre secoli passati)." Same letter gives details about family,
and the history of the seal and motto *Frangas non flectas*.
This seal was often used by D. G. R. ; see *Aut.*, p. 7.
The Rossetti house in Vasto, in the eloquent description of
Ciampoli (*D.C.*, p. 311), " elevasi sugli alti sproni che cingon
la incantevole città della parte onde guarda l'azzurra immensità
dell' Adriatico come un fortalizio sugli spaldi. Vi si giunge
per viottole selciate, odoranti di fieno, e vi si sale ne' vari piani
per ripide scalette cadenti. Ma giunti nella vasta stanza, ove
nacque il poeta, e dove resta ancora tarlato e vacillante l' antico
impiantito di cerro, l' occhio abbraccia quasi tre quarti della
rosa de' venti : l' orizzonte da' sottostanti giardini d'oleandri,
di palme e d' aranci, da' poderosi e densi oliveti, che paion
fitte boscaglie di betule, da' fertilissimi vigneti, sino al remoto
confine del mare che fondesi al cielo, ha così prodigioso incan-
tamento, che si rimane assorti come in una visione di sogno
luminoso, nel quale le rocce della Punta della Penna si coloran
d' oro e le isole diomedee han parvenza di ninfe oceanine
sornuotanti nell' opalino dell' onde. Passan le sanguigne
veliere, le gialle paranzelle, i piroscafi frementi, verso la Dal-
mazia, che lievemente disegnasi lontano lontano. E nella soave
freschezza degli effluvi campestri e marini, nella luce diffusa
che quasi idealizza il paesaggio, si comprende come la città
feconda d' ogni bellezza, abbia dato vita e ispirazione, in ogni
tempo, a poeti, come il Rossetti, a pittori, come i Palizzi e il
Laccetti."

4. *drowning*] He was saved by a certain Chiappini to whom he
addresses a poem. See Benelli, p. 3.
Benedetto Betti] See Bedetti, p. 14, and *D.C.*, p. 307.
pen sketches] See *Aut.* and *D.C.*
cuttlefish] See letter to his wife, 8 August 1848, Epist. 278,

where he asks her to bring some calamarelli back from Brighton.
This he is said etc.] Pietrocola, p. 9.

5. *source of lyric poems*] Pietrocola, p. 12.
soul from childhood etc.] See preface to *Versi*, 1847.

7. *Oh ! if only* etc.] See Pietrocola, p. 16.
Mary Queen of Scots] This libretto may possibly be a copy of Giannone's *Maria Stuarda* which was performed in London in 1827. Pasta took the part of Maria, and both Rossetti and Foscolo were present. See Manzoni, p. 61.
None of Rossetti's librettos were ever used by important composers. He knew Rossini—there was a saying which joined their names

Rossini, Rossetti, Divini imperfetti (*Mem. DGR.* p. 7)

and I have read that on one occasion Rossini supplied a pianoforte accompaniment to one of Rossetti's improvisations, but I cannot find the reference.
Rossini was in London when the poet arrived. See p. 30.
Salary and grievances] See *D.C.*, pp. 315-16. At the Teatro San Carlo his salary had been exactly twice as large.
Letter to an Eccellenza] (ministro dell' Interno) 1811. Epist. 323. It is possible that this letter was never sent.
reduced to thirteen] By fines exacted by Arditi. The latter made R. serve as Secretary, and made other demands so exacting that the poet refused to meet them ; Arditi retaliated by stopping his pay for all hours when he was absent from the office. (*D.C.*, p. 315.)

9. *letter to Frere*] 4 Dec. 1827, Epist. 323 ; Festing, p. 304.
minor office] For about seven months he held " a provisional post in the Secretariat of the Provisional Government, being the post which concerns Public Instruction and the Fine Arts." *Aut.*, p. 36.

10. *Letter to Lyell*] 18 March 1830 (Kinnordy).
Carbonaro activities] See *D.C.*, pp. 326-7.
Chair of Eloquence] Details in *D.C.*, p. 338. There were twenty competitors, and Rossetti came fifth in order of merit.

11. *Veggente in Solitudine*] Novena II, Giorno i.
Dream I yet etc.] See Appendix. These two lines, forming a chorus throughout the poem, are taken from one of Metastasio's best known lyrics, the canzonetta *Grazie agl' inganni tuoi*.
Sei pur bella] In *Aut.*, p. 177, W. M. R. gives this the title *Aurora del* 21 *Luglio del* 1820. But it celebrates the 9th, and in *Odi Cittadine* it is called *Il Dì Nove di Luglio del* MDCCCXX.

15. *As Frere suggested*] See p. 106.
In this world etc.] Quoted from Countess Cesaresco, *Italian*

Characters in the Epoch of Unification. III. Luigi Settembrini.

For Rossetti's part in the affair of Rieti, see *Aut.*, pp. 49–52, and further details in *D.C.*, pp. 324–32.

16. *Decree of exile*] Benelli, p. 23.

the Moores] Some of Lady Moore's letters to G. R. may be read in the Epistolario. They are altogether admirable for their sympathetic kindliness although not particularly informative or notable from a literary point of view. Rossetti celebrated the birth of the Moore's first child, a son, in a poem of some length called *La Gioia di Melita*. Letter and poem, with Lady Moore's answer (7 Nov. 1822) may be seen in Epist. 323.

portrait and some manuscripts] See Pietrocola, p. 33. The portrait was the miniature by Marsigli, reproduced in this book. Miss M. E. M. Rossetti, who kindly allows the reproduction to be made, in a letter to me about the miniature, says : " I remember my Father [W. M. R.] used to laugh about it and said he expected the artist had never seen his subject, but imagined that was what a poet *ought* to look like."

17. *Farewell land of misery* etc.] See Appendix. From Rossetti's well-known lyric, *Nella notte più serena.* (24 June 1821.)

one of his Italian critics] Perale, p. 47. His arrival is described in the *Veggente*, Novena II. Giorno ii.

18. *the poem he then improvised*] G. R. embodied it in the *Veggente*, Novena II. Giorno ii., 11.

Frere] See *Memoir* of him by Sir Bartle Frere, 1874.

undated letter to Rossetti] Festing, pp. 299–300. The letter is in French, and belongs to the Malta period, probably to its earlier part.

19. *Cum in meo* etc.] In Rome, *Autografi*, IV.

letter to Ferretti] 26 October 1815, Epist. 323.

Undated letter, 1823] Addressed to a correspondent unnamed, in Malta, and recommending the bearer, Henry Smith. Rossetti states in it his intention of leaving for England in two months. Epist. 323.

20. *letter to Ferretti*] Epist. 323.

W. M. R. on beginning of Dante studies] *Aut.*, p. 65.

a beautifully written copy] This, together with MS. of the *Veggente* and two autograph notebooks, was presented to the Biblioteca del Risorgimento by Signora Agresti in 1931.

21. *Letter to the Consul*] Epist. 323.

writes to Inspector General] See *D.C.*, pp. 334–5.

22. *Odi Cittadine*] *Di sacro genio arcano* and *Sei pur bella* were published together under this title, Naples, 1820.

Sire, wherefore do you wait ?] Quoted from Pietrocola, pp. 30–1, where the circumstances of its composition are described.

" Il Nasuto e il Reggente non poteano perdonare al poeta un sonnetto da lui improvvisato nel Caffè d'Italia, mentre il popolo fremente ed irrequieto aspettava il re che doveva andare a Santo Spirito a giurare la Costituzione, e che indugiava oltre i limiti di ogni convenienza."

Arrivabene] See Atto Vannucci, *Martiri della Libertà Italiana del* 1794–1848, 7th ed. 1887, I., p. 392.

Ugoni] *Ibid.*

Giannone] *Ibid.*, I., p. 557.

Frere's letter to Mr. Hamilton and reply] Festing, pp. 297–8.

23. *Does he who kills* etc.] *Veggente*, Novena II., Giorno vii., 7.
a hundred spies] See *Aut.*, p. 81. It is there said that in spite of police precautions, messages were sent to the poet. The passage does not appear at all in the Italian text.

Journey and letter to Freres] Dated only 1824 ; Epist. 323.

letter to Lady Moore] Dated April 1824. Must be before 5th, on which day Lady M. replies. Both letters in Epist. 323.

some sheets of notes] Rome, Bib. del Ris., *Autografi*, III.

24. *Letter to Lady Erroll*] Dated 1824. Late March or early April. Epist. 323. (Lady Erroll of course was Frere's wife. She had been married before and kept her title in her second marriage.)

27. *Henry Munro*] 3 April 1824, Epist. 323. The lodgings suggested were at 21 Bruton Street.

I am afraid you will be etc.] 5 April. In Italian. Epist. 323.

First lodgings and illness] Letter to Miei cari amici (probably the Freres), 16 April 1824, Epist. 323.

I rely on it etc.] Letter to Lady M., not dated. Certainly in May.

the radiant torch of day etc.] *Veggente*, Novena II., Giorno v. Mazzini's first impressions were not dissimilar. " We have lost even the sky, which the veriest wretch on the Continent can look at." But Mazzini liked the London fogs. " When you look up, the eye loses itself in a reddish, bell-shaped vault which always gives me, I don't know why, an idea of the phosphorescent light of the *Inferno*. The whole city seems under a kind of spell, and reminds me of the Witch's Scene in *Macbeth*, or the Brocksberg, or the Witch of Endor. The passers-by look like ghosts,—one feels almost a ghost oneself." Bolton King, *Mazzini*, London, 1902, pp. 73–4.

London, or rather England etc.] Letter already quoted, 16 April (to Freres).

28. *exiles' committee*] See full detail in Manzoni, pp. 55 ff., 66–7.

Rossetti's visits] Letter already quoted, 16 April.

Menechini] is perhaps the same as that Minichini, praised by G. R. but remembered by W. M. R. as being in personal appearance " anything but prepossessing." (*Aut.*, p. 45.)

only too many of the worst] When Gaetano Polidori left the service of Alfieri to set up as a teacher in London, the dramatist supplied him with introductions and this piece of advice : " Bear yourself well, and have a care for the cleanliness of your person, for the English look for this above all things : and be as cautious as you possibly can with whatever Italians you find there, for they are almost all a scum of rogues (schiuma di ribaldi)." D'Ancona, *Varietà*, p. 178.

Italians, Spaniards etc.] Letter already quoted, 16 April.

the great plethora etc.] 2 May 1824. Translation quoted from Festing, p. 302. Original in Epist. 323.

Davenport] Festing, p. 303.

29. *various distinguished men*] Letter to Frere already quoted, 2 May 1824.

Campbell] Letter to Lady Moore, not dated but probably about 2 May.

three pupils] Letter to Lady Moore, 4 May.

lost them all] Letter to Lady Moore, dated 1824 (replied to, 13 July), Epist. 323.

so that the author etc.] Letter to Frere, 2 May (*v. supra*).

Murray] Letter to Lady Moore, April 1824 (*v. supra*, p. 23 n.). This letter seems to belong to an early date in April so that the poet had lost very little time in approaching Murray.

Davenport's suggestions] were made in a letter of ? June 24.

expressed to Frere] Festing, p. 303.

Coleridge] Letter from Cary, 26 Jan. 1825, Epist. 323.

30. *Turkish Ambassador*] PRDL., p. 6.

Benelli] See letter to (? Frere's), 16 April 1824.

Rossini] Ibid., and letter from Lady Moore, 13 Jan. 1824. Rossini was in great favour in London when G. R. arrived. *The Times*, 5 April 1824, records that *Zelmira*, *The Barber of Seville*, *Il Fanatico per la Musica* (by Magee, but adapted by Rossini), *Ricciardo and Zoraide* were performed about this time at the King's Theatre. The last named was performed on 3rd and 6th.

Pasta] Letter to Lady Moore, 1824: (replied to 13 July 1824). All these letters in Epist. 323.

Cipriani Potter and librettos] See *Aut.*, pp. 117, 121.

31. *Pasta*] *v. supra*.

received £200] It is pleasant to notice that Pasta was less miserly than Paganini ; she figures among the subscribers to the *Comento* (list in Vol. II.).

32. *thought of going to Liverpool*] End of letter about Pasta, *v. supra*.

invited him to Cobham] 11 June 1824, Epist. 323.

Rose and Davenport] Letter about Pasta, *v. supra*.

Thomas Witby] (? Whitby) Letter to G. R., 26 Nov. 1824.

(Epist. 323, but only a copy.)

Spies] See *Aut.*, p. 98, and compare letter to G. R. from Dom. Abatemacco, Paris, 29 Sept. 1824, warning Rossetti to " stare in guardia con un tal Sigr. Aulisio napoletano che si porterà fra giorni in Londra ad oggetto di spiarvi tutti ed in particolare il buon generale G.Pᵉ. [Pepe]." Epist. 323.

established in London] The poet seems to have lived at four addresses before his marriage. The first was 37 Gerard Street, Soho ; the second was 24 Oxenden Street, Leicester Square ; the third 15 Church Street, Soho ; and the fourth 23 Lower Thornhaugh Street. All these addresses may be found in the Epist.

Details about Gaetano Polidori] *Mem. DGR.*, pp. 25 ff., and *Remin.*, pp. 6–7.

Secretary to Alfieri] See the very amusing account of his experiences in this office, in D'Ancona, *Varietà Storiche e Letterarie*, Prima Serie, (1883). Polidori declared that the great dramatist was " proud as Milton's Satan and more irascible than Homer's Achilles," and in a *capitolo* addressed to Charles Lyell in 1844, describes him as

> un signore
> Stravagante, collerico e scortese,
> E più altier del chinese imperatore.

His father] From details given by Gaetano in a copy made by himself of his father's poem *Osteologia* and presented to his daughter Frances ; kindly shown to me by its present owner, Signora Angeli-Rossetti.

34. *Details about the Polidori family*] All from *Mem. DGR.* and *Remin.*

Dante Gabriel on John Polidori] *Letters to Allingham*, pp. 115–16.

Eliza's letter to G. R.] At end of a letter from Polidori to G. R., 20 Sept. 1853, Epist. 278.

35. *Crimea*] Christina wished to go too, but was considered too young. *CGRPW.*, p. lvi.

consoling thought etc.] See *Time Flies*, Oct. 12, and Bell, p. 160.

If you do not think it etc.] From 15 Church Street, 18 July, Epist. 323. Polidori's reply is on blank pages of same sheet.

Pape Satan] See letter to G. R., 11 Nov. 1825, Epist. 323.

Christina on G. P.'s love of Dante] *CGRFL.*, p. 184.

But at no time etc.] unless exception should be made for his translation into Italian of Lyell's *Catholic Spirit of Dante* which dissents completely from G. R.'s theories. *Dello Spirito Cattolico di Dante Alighieri opera di Carlo Lyell . . . tradotto . . . da Gaetano Polidori, tra gli Arcadi Fileremo Etrusco* London, 1844. The book defends Dante's orthodoxy against the disintegrators who, whether by allegorical interpretation or otherwise, would make him anti-Catholic. There are many references to Rossetti, always respectful and sometimes admiring, but never for one moment agreeing. Polidori addresses a rhymed letter to Lyell at the beginning and end of the book. The one at the end gives an interesting account of the writer's own life.

will mention Gaetano in a note]　See *Comento*, I, pp. 275–6. (Among the notes to Canto ix., 61.) After quoting at some length the comment of " un recentissimo espositore ", he goes on :　" Filosofico insegnamento è questo, e il più morale che da intelletto sano trar si potesse dall' azione che Dante qui ne presenta : ed è del tanto dotto quanto modesto Signor Polidori (e dal suo stesso labbro l'udii), della cui amistà mi fo pregio e delizia. Ei che al fondato studio del poema unisce un guidizio retto, e a chiara mente alto cuore, mettendo quasi in pratica il precetto che da Dante apprendea, non solo col consiglio ma pur con l'opera mi sostenne nell'arduo mio lavoro, poichè mi ha aperta la sua scelta bibblioteca [*sic*] con lungo sudore e squisito gusto raccolta, e ricchissima di classica letteratura Italiana ; lo studio della quale mi la sempre più nelle mie scoverte confirmato."

You are the only man]　24 Oct. 1825, Epist. 323.

36. *I cannot thank you too much etc.*]　G. P. to G. R., 23 Oct. 1825, Epist. 323. This letter is addressed to 23 Lower Thornhaugh Street, Bedford Square.

I have stopped a moment etc.]　At back of a letter in Epist. 323, labelled to Polidori, date 1825. Addressee not named by G. R. The note to Frances undated, and obviously not sent. Address on back of sheet, " Al Sign. Ornatissimo Il Sigr. Matteo Ponssielgue, Malta, Valetta." This was the friend who made the MS. copy of the *Salterio* in Malta, see p. 20 ; it is unlikely that the first part of this double letter was meant for him.

37. *Verses to Fanny*]　Rome, *Autografi*, I.

That is to say etc.]　17 Feb. 1826, Purves, p. 111.

Baldacconi]　A card in Epist. 280 reads " Dr. Baldacconi No. 54 Lincoln's Inn Square will be at home any time after six and marry Frances Mary Lavinia Polidori to Gabriele Rossetti." On this card Christina noted " I believe Dr. Baldacconi performed the R.C. marriage of our parents. C. G. R."

The date observed by Christina]　*CGRFL.*, p. 194.

38. *ff. Mrs. Rossetti*]　All based on *Mem. DGR.*, *Remin.*, *Aut.*

39. *At the touch etc.*]　See *Veggente*, Novena II, Giorno v, where he also says,

> Nè mai, dal dì che all' ara amor ci scorse,
> Verme di pentimento il cor mi morse.

40. *Her inculcations* etc.] *DGRFL.*, p. 329.
    My dearest mother etc.] *CGRFL.*, p. 213.
    Christina's conversation with William] *Remin.*, p. 541.
41. *Discords*] See *CGRFL.*, p. 43 : " Of course Mamma is in
    grief and anxiety ; her tender heart receives stabs from all
    sides."
    I send you etc.] *DGRFL.*, pp. 200–1.
42. *Income*] *Remin.*, p. 2.
43. *Fortune of £2000*] *Ibid.*, p. 39. This was under the will of
    her maternal grandfather.
    Offspring of love etc.] Rome, *Autografi*, I.
    University College] See the history of that institution by H.
    Hale Bellott, 1929.
    Recommendation to Campbell and his opinion] *Ibid.*, p. 45.
    Brougham supported Panizzi ; see p. 44.
    Note] Bellott, *op. cit.*, p. 46. " Among the unsuccessful
    candidates were both Foscolo and Gaetano Polidore [*sic*] one
    time secretary to Alfieri."
44. *W. S. Rose*] Letter to G. R. ? 1828, Epist. 323.
    W. S. Rose's translations] Rossetti must have helped in par-
    ticular with the translation of the *Orlando Furioso*, 8 vols.,
    London, 1823–31.
    Cary and Davenport] Letter to Frere, 4 Dec. 1827, Festing,
    p. 304.
    Panizzi] See Louis Fagan, *Life of Sir Anthony Panizzi*, 1880,
    and Constance Brooks, *Antonio Panizzi Scholar and Patriot*,
    1931.
    225 fr. 25] This included the usual fee for the hangman. It
    ought to be added that the execution was actually performed
    in effigy. Panizzi replied to this demand in an amusing letter
    addressed from the " Realm of Death, Elysian Fields " and
    signed " The Soul of Antonio Panizzi." (Fagan, I, p. 51.)
    Mazzini disapproved] Quoted from Luzio, *La Massoneria e il
    Risorgimento Italiano*, 1925, I, p. 250.
45. *Rossetti's hatred of Panizzi*] See his diatribe in *La Vita Mia*,
    pp. 134–6, 159.
    stolta invidia] *La Vita Mia*, p. 134. In the Panizzi MSS. in
    the British Museum there are some letters from his friend De
    Marchi (Add. 36714, ff. 84–8). De Marchi was in Edinburgh
    in the middle of 1827 when the appointment at University
    College was being considered. He had recently met Horner,
    the Principal and apparently a close friend, who wished him
    to submit himself as a candidate. De Marchi however declined
    to do so and recommended Foscolo. Soon after, he heard
    that Panizzi was a candidate and, meeting Horner again, found
    difficulty in recommending Panizzi after his recent praise of
    Foscolo. " La sola cosa che mi cadde in acconcio di dire fu

diretta a scemare l'eccessiva buona opinione che il Sign. Horner pareva avere dell' opera incominciata del Rossetti, uno dei principali candidati—siccome spero queste osservazioni erano meramente accidentali e cagionate dalla produzione del libro, di cui pare che il Rossetti abbia recentemente fatto dono al Sign. H." 1 Aug. 1827 (f. 88). The remark is ingenuous, but De Marchi is little to be blamed in the matter, Panizzi not at all, especially since in all probability he held back a very damaging review until after the appointment was made. See pp. 95-6.

The Council etc.] 20 Feb. 1828, Purves, p. 112.

It grieves me etc.] 23 Feb. 1828, Epist. 323.

46. *To make memorable* etc.] Purves, p. 112.

47. *Impromptu Toast*] *Ibid.*, p. 114. The translation is my own.

I am glad to hear etc.] 31 July 1828, Epist. 323.

I have just come back etc.] 1 Aug. 1828, Epist. 323.

48. *Panizzi has no intention of serving* etc.] P. did not enter upon his duties till autumn of this year, and certainly was not over-pleased with either the pay or the conditions. See Brooks, *op. cit.*, pp. 47-8.

49. *Maria ill.*] Letter to Lyell, 24 Feb. 1829 (Kinnordy), and letter to Frere, Dec. 1829, Epist. 323. (Probably a note of letter, not sent ; full of corrections.)

Coming home etc.] Dated only 1829, Epist. 323.

My daughter etc.] Dated Dec. 1829. (See note to p. 49.)

50. *references to Dante Gabriel*] In Kinnordy letters of the year, in Purves, and Epist.

Expenses of printing the Comento] Letter to Lyell, 9 March 1830 (Kinnordy).

If God thought etc.] *Ibid.*

Polidori's library] Letter to G. R. from Archibald Murray (brother to the publisher), 20 July 1830. " I am truly sorry at your account of Signor Polidori's declension as a teacher. It seems to me a proof that your own diminution of scholars proceeds rather from the calamities and contingencies of the time than from any injury to your reputation effected by these cani arrabiati [the critics]. . . . I feel very much for the sacrifice of Signor Polidori's library and would be almost tempted to be the purchaser of it myself." Epist. 323.

Letter to Miss Polidori] 6 Dec. 1830, Epist. 323.

51. *Lessons in April*] Letter to Lyell, 15 April 1831 (Kinnordy).

reassuring news] 4 May 1831, Epist. 324. Also in *Aut.*, p. 118

8 May] In Epist. 324.

52. *21 May*] 1831, letter to Lyell (Kinnordy).

Eventually etc.] Letter to Mrs. R., 27 May 1831, Epist. 324.

Notice of appointment] Epist. 324. The appointment was

reported by *The Times*, 8 June 1831, together with others made at the same time. G. R. is here styled " M. Gabriele Rossetti, LL.D.".—I have not seen the title elsewhere ; if held at all it must have been honorary.

Acknowledgment] In King's College library.

All the professors etc.] See F. J. C. Hearnshaw, *The Centenary History of King's College, London*, 1828-1928.

When it appears further etc.] Quoted by permission of the authorities of King's College, from documents relating to appointments in the College Library.

Gallenga] Antonio G., a man of marked ability but doubtful character, who gave Mazzini a great deal of trouble, not only opposing his political aims, but implicating him in the unpleasant charge of having desired the assassination of Charles Albert. Gallenga had fanatically and against Mazzini's persuasion set out to accomplish this in 1833, but his courage seems to have failed him. Subsequently, says Mazzini, he " occupied himself in writing books and reviews. He wrote for and against the Italians, his friends, and me." He was later well known in radical circles in London—his application for the Chair at King's College was supported by Carlyle. Eventually, however, he developed reactionary views, became Italian correspondent to *The Times*, and aroused strong indignation among his former fellow-conspirators. He published *Episodes of my Second Life* in 1884. See a discussion of his conduct in *Mazzini's Letters to an English Family*, ed. E. F. Richards, London, 1920. Vol. i., pp. 288-92.

Beolchi] Carlo B. A less distinguished figure, an exile and friend of G. R.'s ; returned to Italy in 1832 (see p. 56) ; published *Reminiscenze dell' Esilio*, Turin, 1852. He was a recipient of help from the exile's committee (see p. 28) in 1823-4. Manzoni, p. 66.

53. *Professor Hearnshaw*] *op. cit.*, p. 91.

major chairs etc.] Hearnshaw, p. 86.

Inaugural] *Discorso Inaugurale per la cattedra di lingua e letteratura Italiana, nel Collegio del Re in Londra.* Londra, 1831.

number of students] See letter to Lyell, 16 Nov. 1831 (Kinnordy) ; letter to Mrs. R., 7 May 1832, Epist. 324 ; letter to Mrs. R., 11 Oct. 1836, Epist. 275 ; letter to Lyell, 30 Oct 1840, from copy in Taylorian Institute, Oxford.

William Michael] *Mem. DGR.*, p. 9.

54. *Panizzi at University*] He had five pupils in 1828, eight in 1829, five again in session 1831-2. In 1828 £200 a year was guaranteed to the language professors ; a year later guarantees were abolished. See Brooks, *op. cit.*, p. 48. Panizzi was then in the same position as Rossetti, but was less successful in securing pupils ; he was spared the necessity of finding them

by his appointment to a minor office in the British Museum in April, 1831.

I spent Saturday evening etc.]   Letter to Mrs. R., 7 May 1832, Epist. 324.

I see from your letter etc.]   27 May 1831, Epist. 324.

Christina]   See *Aut.*, p. 120, and letter to Mrs. R., 21 May 1832, Epist. 324.

55. *What you say about William* etc.]   In last-named letter.

Every word that you wrote etc.]   Letter to Mrs. R., *Aut.*, p. 121.

When his wife writes etc.]   See letter to Mrs. R., 4 June 1832, Epist. 324.

56. *petition*]   See letter to Mrs. R., 29 May 1832, *Aut.*, pp. 124–5.

Curci]   Letter to G. R., 3 April 1833, Epist. 324 ; and another 29 April 1833 from which it appears that Rossetti's petition was supported by " Welincton and Aberdin ".

Yesterday evening etc.]   Letter to Mrs. R., 4 June 1832.

57. *Proposal to adopt W. M. R.*]   *Remin.*, p. 5.

59. *Foscolo*]   See Viglione, *Ugo Foscolo in Inghilterra*, 1910.

Mazzini himself]   See Luzio, *La Madre di Mazzini*, 2nd ed., 1923, pp. 164, 200, 204, 226, 228.

heroes at the time of their arrival]   Count Pecchio (in *Osservazioni Semi-serie di un Esule sull' Inghilterra*, Lugano, 1831) complains that he and his fellows were extravagantly lionised for a few days, and then completely neglected. Pecchio, however, did not stay in London, but went to seek his fortune in the northern counties, teaching for some time in York.

60. *These poor devils work*]   and to end of paragraph, from A. de R. Jervis, *Mazzini's Letters* (a selection translated), 1930, pp. 78–81.

carpet slippers]   4 May 1831, Epist. 324.

Prati]   G. R. to wife, 18 Aug. 1848, Epist. 278.

61. *Among others*]   Epist. 275.

She talked for ten etc.]   6 Sept. 1836, *Aut.*, p. 126.

Carducci]   *Poesie di G. R. ordinate da G. Carducci*, p. lxii, where G. R. is called the " cantore che, nonostante i suoi difetti, più consente al gusto poetico e alla facoltà armoniosa del popolo italiano. Non lusso di tenebrose invenzioni o di forme recondite e strane o di versificate disquisizioni o di nebbiosi velami ; ma fantasia ardita e serena, ma impeto di affetto, ma copia e talora sovrabbondanza di colorito, ma facilità armonia melodia, fanno propriamente italiane queste poesie, le fanno cantabili." For the passage referred to in the text, see *Ibid.*, p. iv.

Galli]   In Epist. 276.   He is probably the same person as the " Florent Gatti " a copy of whose letter to G. R. from Bethlehem, 23 April 1833, is to be found in Epist. 324.   The writer certainly sounds crazy : " Il s'agit de substituer l'empire de

l'amour à celui de la force dans toute l'étendue de l'univers
Tel est mon plan."

62. *this bird of ill-omen* etc.] See *Rivista Europea*, Vol. XIII.
Fasc. 3, 11 June 1879, p. 465.

Galanti's end] Account quoted from *Mem. DGR.*, p. 52 ; but
see also letter to Lyell, late 1849, copy in Taylorian, No. 128 ;
letter to an Italian correspondent (Signora Monti-Baraldi) in
Bedetti, p. 53 (original of account in *Mem. DGR.*) ; letter to
Ricciardi, 11 Sept. 1849, *Riv. Eur.*, Vol. XIV., fasc. 1, p. 121.

Perhaps you do not know etc.] *Riv. Eur.*, XIII., fasc. 4, p. 653.
The letter is dated " Il 2 di aprile del nefasto 1849."

Anichini] From three letters, kindly put at my disposal by
Professor Rébora of this University, it appears that, although
obviously uncultured, Anichini had friends among men of
letters, and had more reading himself than might be supposed
from G. R's description ; and that in all probability he was
not an exile, the first letters being of 1819. All three are
addressed to William Roscoe, biographer of Lorenzo de'
Medici. The first, 3 Feb. 1819, addresses Roscoe as *Amico
dilettissimo*, and opens with a shower of flowery compliments ;
goes on to rejoice in the advances made by freedom everywhere
but in Spain, and to denounce priests ; and is subscribed
Il Suo amico di cuore. The second, 29 May 1819, opens with
various remarks concerned with Roscoe's historical work ; subsequently announces with pride : " Io sto terminando un opus-
colo sulle Femmine Inglesi, che mi lusingo farà molto strepito
in Inghilterra, e fuori, perchè è una plausibile confutazione
di tutte le calunnie che i forestieri hanno detto di quelli
Esseri interessanti." This work he proposes to dedicate to
Roscoe. The third and most interesting, 5 Aug. 1823, is concerned with Panizzi, being a letter of introduction. It is in
English.

" MY DEAR MR. ROSCOE, Allow me to introduce to your acquaintance Advocate Panizza [*sic*], an Italian Gentleman dignified
with the high honor of a sentence of death, to which he has
been condemned by the Lilliputian Duke of Modena, one of
the family of the Tyrants of Italy. The character of that
legitimate will be pourtrayed to you by Mr. Panizza and I am
sure that your sensible heart will burn with hatred towards the
Duke. M. Panizza's purpose in visiting Liverpool is to settle
there as Professor of the Italian Language and Literature ;
and I am confident that you will lend him your powerful
assistance towards the attainment of his aim. You cannot
put, in a more efficient way, to the text [i.e. test] your so often
expressed detestation of any sort of Tyranny than by protecting
its victims. Besides in so doing you will confer a signal service
on me. Believe me, my dear Sir, that my Esteem for and

affection to you are equal to the horror that pervades every one
of my sinews for Despots, and Legitimates—I am

My dear Mr. Roscoe
Your sincere friend and
warm admirer
B.˙ ANICHINI."

Janer came yesterday] Epist. 275.

63. *a month later*] G. R. to Mrs. R., 7 Sept. 1836, Epist. 275.
The father arose etc.] Holman Hunt, *Pre-Raphaelitism*, 1905,
I., pp. 154–5.

64. *Luigi Angeloni*] was a literary purist, described by Manzoni
as an " uomo di tempra antica ". He was a Tribune in Rome
at the time of Napoleon's fall ; soon he went to Paris where
he was closely associated with Pietro Giannone and his circle.
Driven out of Paris because of his republican ideas, he sought
refuge in London early in 1823. (Manzoni, p. 61.)

65. *In May*] See G. R. to Angeloni, 26 May 1836, ? June 1836,
13 Aug. 1836 (quoted entire by Carducci, *op. cit.*, pp. xv ff.),
in Epist. 275. Angeloni's book was *Alla Valente ed Animosa
Gioventù d'Italia, Esortazioni Patrie così di prosa come di verso*,
London, 1837. It was apparently a private publication—" Si
vende (a pound sterling) appresso l'autore, 18 Wardour Street,
Soho." The attack on Rossetti begins on p. 345 and continues
for nine pages. G. R. is not mentioned by name, but there
are references to the *Comento* and the *Salterio*. Apparently
the cause of Angeloni's anger was that G. R. had tried to
dissuade him from printing part of his book, had laughed at
him, said that what Angeloni had written was to be found in
a hundred books and that everybody knew all about it.
" Questo sere ", says Angeloni, " è sì gonfio del suo sè, che
si è pur fitto in capo che ogni uomo creder debba, lui essere
in ogni cosa maestro." He accuses G. R. of attempting to
attract foreigners for his own profit by degrading the most
prized works of the Italian Parnassus. " E del resto tanto
nelle astrazioni si delizia cotesto sere, che alcun dì potrebbegli
intervenire ch' e' fosse ratto alle empiree regioni, là dove, a
detto de' teologanti, è posto il seggio della sua prediletta aerea
profittevol favola [i.e. the Bible]. A dover potere però fuggire
sì fatto pericolo, farà egli gran senno se avrà sempre alcune
pietre nelle tasche acciochè sia da quelle bilanciata l'evaporazion
del corpo pel soverchio arzigogolare." Among other bad-
tempered but amusing sallies is the following : Angeloni used
to visit G. R. every Sunday evening. On one occasion G. R.
asked if A. had any new sheets printed and was given the
latest : " e postosi quasi come in cattedra nella sua soffice
bracciuta scranna, diè di piglio incontanente al moccichino, e
si forbì innanzi tratto il naso, e poi assorta su una sollucherante

presa di tabacco, pausò alquanto per pigliar fiato, siccome talvolta fanno i predicatori "—and then began a long sermon, attempting to persuade Angeloni not to print his work.
Pistrucci has been to the printer's etc.] G. R. to Mrs. R., 24 Sept. 1836, Epist. 275.

66. *Since you wish to offer*] ? Oct. 1836, Epist. 275.

67. *other Italian impostors*] G. R. to Lyell, 17 Jan. 1838, Epist. 276. In a letter to Lyell, 17 Aug. 1841, Epist. 277, attempting to show the harmlessness of the *Amor Platonico*, G. R. says, " Un vecchio quasi nonogenario, chiamato Luigi Angeloni, ha qui pubblicato due anni fa un volumone in 8° grande, nel cui frontispizio si permette di provare che ' La Bibbia è una favolaccia ebraica.' Nessuno ne ha fatto conto, nessuno l'ha comprato, quantunque quello stolido vecchio si fosse tanto adoperato a farlo conoscere e strombettare ; in somma quel volumone di circa 900 pagini è morto nel nascere." G. R puts this forward as a good reason for not suppressing his own work of 1744 pages.
Death of Angeloni] See Todeas Twattle-Basket [Tommaso de Angelis], *Note di Cronaca*, 1897, p. 16.
Sangiovanni] Details from *Mem. DGR.*, pp. 50–1. D. G. R.' remark on him *DGRFL.*, p. 109.
high praises of D. G. R.] See G. R. to Lyell, ? (end of) 1849 copy in Taylorian, No. 128. There are several letters from him to G. R. in Epist. 278.
His death] Pistrucci to G. R., 12 May 1853, Epist. 278.
I knew that Sangiovanni etc.] G. R. to Ferretti, 22 April 1853 in Perale, p. 208.

68. *Epitaph*] Pistrucci to G. R., 12 June 1853, Epist. 278.
Pistrucci] (Filippo) See *Mem. DGR.*, pp. 48, 50 ; and *Aut* several references from p. 122 onwards. There are a numbe of letters from him to G. R. in Epist. 278. His brother Bene detto was medallist in the Mint, and designed the St. Georg and the Dragon of the English sovereign. Filippo came England at some time before 1824, perhaps to join his brothe perhaps having been exiled. He left behind him in Mila his wife and his sons, one of whom, Scipione, became th devoted friend of Mazzini. Pistrucci was at first secretar to Mazzini's Italian school, later its director ; some of h lessons on history, literature, and moral subjects were collecte and printed in volume form. He painted a large oil portra of Mazzini in 1837–8. (See *Mazzini's Letters to an Engli Family*, I., p. 42.)
Pepoli] *Aut.*, p. 161.
His marriage] See G. R. to Mrs. R., 31 Aug. to 2 Sept. 18 (on same sheet as letter from W. M. R. to his mother) ; a G. R. to Mrs. R. undated (Sept. 1839). Both in Epist. 27

69. *Ricciardi*] *Aut.*, pp. 91, 169, 155 ff. See a collection of G. R.'s letters to him in *Rivista Europea*, Vols. XII–XVI., April to Dec. 1879. The letters are of the period 1848–52.

introduced to R.] See Pepe to G. R., 4 March 1833, Epist. 324.

Pepe is coming] *Riv. Eur.*, XIV., fasc. 1, p. 121.

Health, wealth, etc.] When introducing Ricciardi, *v. supra.*

All agreed etc.] Pepe to G. R., 26 April 1848, Epist. 278.

his Memoirs] See Pepe to G. R., 5 June 1850, where he complains of a notice in *The Standard*, 30 May, which speaks well of his book but not of the Italians. He wishes Rossetti to write another article for some well-known paper giving due praise to the Italians and mentioning their courage at Milan, Brescia, Bologna, Venezia, and in Piedmont. The notice in *The Standard* had said he was over 70—he asks Rossetti to say that as he was born in 1783 he could not be more than 70 and so is still able to serve his country. He began to fight, he says, when he was seventeen.

70. *Mazzini*] See the group of letters from him in *Aut.*, p. 155.

great regard for him] See *Rossetti Papers*, 1862–70, p. 231.

disagreement on the subject of Dante] See the essay on the *Minor Works of Dante.* " There have been loud disputes, from the days of Canon Biscione down to Mr. Rossetti, about the real existence of such a person as Beatrice. How . . . learned men have been able to bring themselves—in spite of the most positive evidence to the contrary—to doubt the existence of ' Bice ', or to admit two distinct beings, the Beatrice of the poet and the Beatrice of the theologian—thus destroying that progressive continuity which is the peculiar characteristic of the genius and the love of Dante—I cannot imagine." (Quoted from *Essays*, edited by William Clarke, London, N.D., pp. 195–6.)

It is the fate etc.] *Riv. Eur.*, Vol. XIV., fasc. 3, p. 531.

71. *graver complaints*] See *Riv. Eur.*, Vol. XII., fasc. 4, p. 700 ; Vol. XIII., fasc. 4, p. 649 ; Vol. XIV., fasc. i, p. 125.

72. *Is this thing known to thee*] W. M. R., *Democratic Sonnets*, 1907 ; sonnet on G. R.

I am passing my days etc.] *Riv. Eur.*, XIII., fasc. 3, p. 469.

73. *I am a republican* etc.] *Inedite*, p. 7.

republic a dream of maniacs] Festing, p. 340.

good-bye for ever to despots etc.] *Riv. Eur.*, XIV., fasc. 3, p. 532.

In one of the poems.] *Inedite*, pp. 483–91, *L'Inghilterra.*

74. *Reform Bill*] Festing, p. 320 ; G. R. to Mrs. R., 31 May 1832 and 8 June 1832, both in Epist. 324.

age quod age] See *Remin.*, pp. 12–13.

76. *Rossetti relates*] See *Veggente*, Novena II., Giorno iv.

77. *Do tell me* etc.] Susan Frere to G. R. (in Italian), 30 Sept. 1824, Epist. 323.

78. *Frere's copy of the* Amor Platonico] In the British Museum.
the work of ten men] G. R. to Frere, 8 May 1832, Epist. 324.
bishops] *Mem. DGR.*, p. 71.
He regarded etc.] See G. R. to Lyell, 20 Feb. 1841, Epist. 277.

79. *That is why* etc.] *Riv. Eur.*, XV., fasc. 2, p. 265.
Puseyites] *Ibid.*, XIV., fasc. 2, p. 356 (end of the letter).
new gunpowder plot] See Perale, 202. A stroke prevented
Rossetti from presiding at a great meeting of Italians 3 Feb.
1851, to protest against the Pope's designs on England. " Per
illuderci ha decorato il successore di Guy Fawkes del magnifico
titolo di Sua Eminenza."
warning to Englishmen] See letter to Lyell, 24 Jan. 1841
(Kinnordy). He asks Lyell if he would care to translate the
pamphlet.
One of the alleged causes] G. R. to Frere, 3 March 1840,
Epist. 276.
Catholic priest] This rests on the authority of Francesco
Pisarri in *Noi e il Mondo*, November 1823, *Come morì G. R.*,
where the complete text is published of a letter from Teodorico
Pietrocola-Rossetti to his brother in Vasto, 26 July 1854.
After G. R. went to Frome, he grew very ill. " Fu visitato
dal prete Bumett e fece i sacramenti da buon cattolico." This
letter was published earlier by Domenico Ciampoli in *Per il
cinquantesimo anniversario della morte di Gabriele Rossetti*, 1904,
pp. 36–7, but in a truncated form and with variants in the
text. The sentence quoted above does not appear at all. It
seems that a number of copies of the letter used to exist in
Vasto ; Pisarri claims that his is the authentic text, on what
seem to me to be reasonable grounds. It is a point of some
interest, and it may seem strange that W. M. R. has nowhere
mentioned the visit of this priest ; but since it apparently
happened at Frome, W. M. R. may not have known of it.
Salvation of Mapei] Letter to Ferretti, 2 May 1853, in Perale,
p. 208.
one Italian critic] Perale, p. 183. Perale says quite truly that
Rossetti did not know what he was himself.

80. *If I had been Abraham* etc.] *Remin.*, p. 64.
The texts he chose to give] For these and for a general dis
cussion of G. R.'s religion, see Luzzi, *Le Idee Religiose d*
G. R., 1903.

81. *Look at that sun* etc.] Perale, p. 91.
Psaltery presented to Pope] Leopoldo Curci to G. R., 3 April
1833, Epist. 324. " Domani parto per Roma per dedicare a
Santo Padre la vostra Salmodia, e spero con questo mezzo
ottenere una raccomandazione per voi presso il nostro Re."
Freemasons] See Luzio, *La Massoneria e il Risorgimento Italiano*
1925. Luzio argues that Freemasonry and its affiliations wer

of less importance than is commonly supposed in the inspiration of Risorgimento activity ; but names Rossetti among the men whose membership of the association proved a help to them on their arrival in England.

83. *some masonic scholars*] See, for example, Albert Churchward, *The Signs and Symbols of Primordial Man*, London, 1910.

84. *I find the same ingenuity*] Cary to G. R., 12 Jan. 1825, Epist. 323.
G. R.'s reply] ? 1825, Epist. 323.
sensible suggestions] Cary to G. R., 26 Jan. 1825, Epist. 323.
note in his Dante] See *Inferno*, i., 45, note. " Whether his acute and eloquent interpreter, Rossetti, may not have been carried much too far in the pursuit of a favourite hypothesis, is another question ; and I must avow my disbelief of the secret jargon imputed to our poet and the other writers of that time in the *Comment* on the *Divina Commedia* and in the *Spirito Antipapale*."
final suggestion] Cary to G. R., 18 Nov. 1827, Epist. 323.
eighty subscriptions] Festing, p. 304.
talked for ever about it] See *Life, Letters, and Journals of Sir Charles Lyell*, 1881, II., p. 135.
Note] Fagan, *Life of Sir Anthony Panizzi*, 1880, I., pp. 134–7.

85. *Lady Davy*] *Ibid.*, I., pp. 180–1 (in a letter of Apr. 1828).
commentary on Purgatory] MS. preserved in the Museum, Vasto.
cost of Comento] Purves, p. 112.
750 copies] G. R. to Lyell, 22 March 1830 (Kinnordy).
400 remained] G. R. to Lyell, 25 April 1831 (Kinnordy).
Murray forgot etc.] G. R. to Frere, ? Dec. 1829, Epist. 323.
All my pupils] At back of letter from W. S. Rose, ? 1828, Epist. 323.
I saw it all by myself] . *Comento*, I., p. 19.

86. *Admirable is this simile* etc.] *Comento*, I., p. 52.
Pape Satan] *Comento*, I., p. 189 (resplendeat facies Satani primarii) ; I., p. 379 (Al Papa Satanno Principe questo impero è sacro) ; II., p. 465 (Pap' è Satan !).
The Satan of Dante etc.] II., p. 486.

87. *I am more than* etc.] II., p. 382.
Would that it were so etc.] II., p. 364.
Sighed indeed etc.] II., p. 555.
Pandora's box] Lyell to G. R., 9 Nov. 1832, Epist. 324.

88. *if the public* etc.] G. R. to Lyell, 19 Dec. 1831 (Kinnordy).
English translation] There is a respectful notice, a column and a half in length, in *The Times*, 15 Nov. 1834.

89. *After all* etc.] Lyell to G. R., 24 Jan. 1832, Epist. 324.
Truth etc.] See G. R. to Lyell, 10 March 1832, Epist. 324.
history of the sect] Frere to G. R., 21 March 1833, Epist. 324.
turn novelist] G. R. to Frere, 14 June 1833, Epist. 324 (copy only).

Frere opposes it] 4 Oct. 1833, Epist. 324.

Lyell urges him on] 27 Dec. 1833, Epist. 324.

91. *Had I been one of the faithful* etc.] *Am. Plat.*, II., cap. 4.

grand tout humanitaire] Aroux to G. R., 21 Nov. 1831, Epist. 278.

92. *Catholic historians*] See Luzio, *op. cit.*, I., p. 236.

William Michael states] See Festing, p. 311. " The innermost arcanum indicated (but not manifestly set forth) in that book [the *Am. Plat.*] is that the writers of whom it treats did not believe in any Supreme Deity at all, but regarded Man as his own sole Deity."

The rest still in MS.] In the Biblioteca del Risorgimento in Rome. For G. R.'s high opinion of it, see *Aut.*, p. 101 ; G. R. to Lyell, 10 March 1842, Epist. 277 ; *Riv. Eur.*, XIV., fasc. 3, p. 530 ; XVI., fasc. 3, p. 583.

thought Beatrice existed] G. R. to Lyell, postmarked 24 Dec. 1828 (Kinnordy).

In the Spirito Antipapale] English version, I., pp. 165–8.

93. *Aroux*] See M. L. Giartosio de Courten, " *La Beatrice di Dante* " *di G. R.*, *Nuova Antologia*, October 1930, Vol. 273. *Je vous avouerai* etc.] Aroux to G. R., 2 June 1852, Epist. 278. *sent Aroux a copy*] G. R. to Aroux, 4 March 1854, Epist. 278. In a letter to a Signor Bolognini in Malta, possibly a publisher's agent, 16 March 1853, G. R. describes the works he has which are available for publication. The best of them he says is the *Beatrice*, the MS. of which he would give " pel modico prezzo di tremila franchi, e voi ne avreste il 10 per 100 ".

worn to pieces] See Frere to G. R., Festing, p. 311.

94. *Westminster Review*] Vol. VII., Jan. 1827, Art. viii. *La Commedia di Dante Alighieri : Illustrata da Ugo Foscolo*. The review, which praises Foscolo highly, ends with this paragraph : " At some future time we propose to ourselves to analyse the commentary on Dante which M. Rossetti has lately published, but which we could hardly dispose of on the present occasion. Its strange fancies are singularly contrasted with that intelligent and informed criticism with which Foscolo has adorned his researches." The article was by Panizzi. See his *Osservazioni sul Comento Analitico*, 1832. *Al Lettore.*

In Italy] See conclusion of *Comento*, II., p. 552.

Reviewer in Quarterly] 1828, January, Art. 3. *History of the Progress and Suppression of the Reformation in Italy.* . . . By Thomas McCrie, D.D. This review was the work of J. J. Blunt (1794–1855), professor of divinity at Cambridge from 1839, and a regular contributor to the *Quarterly*. (His *Essays contributed to the " Quarterly Review "* were published in 1860 —the passage about Rossetti is to be found unmodified at pp. 98–100.) He himself wrote a *Sketch of the Reformation in*

England, London, 1832. Blunt is referred to by Lyell and Rossetti as *Ottuso*. His remarks on Rossetti's *Comento* appear on pp. 57-9, being a digression from the main theme ; he professed to have been indifferent whether the passage was printed or not. (See below, his letter to Rossetti.) It is not altogether uncomplimentary—the *Comento* is " elaborate, learned and ingenious " ; when the Ghibelline theory does not cross his path, Rossetti is an excellent guide, " keeping close to the text, completing the ellipses, and leading his reader by the hand step by step, through the rough places of his difficult author, with an admirable knowledge of the road." Blunt's main objection rather resembles that of Lady Davy—even if the theory were true it would be a misfortune to be versed in it, " it would be the utter ruin of Dante as a poet ".

Let me advise you] Lyell to G. R., 26 Jan. 1828, Epist. 323.
There might be some levity etc.] This letter is of three and a half pages ; in Epist. 323, labelled *Un Critico nel " Quarterly Review "* (? Feb. 1828).

an agitated reply] See draft on notebook pages, in Epist. 323.

95. *Ravina*] See G. R. to Lyell, 27 Sept. 1828, and 9 March 1829 (both Kinnordy).

96. *Thomas Keightley his friend*] Keightley was predisposed to conviction by the course of his own studies. G. R. reports to Lyell, 9 Dec. 1831 (Kinnordy), that K. was about to bring out a new work called *Secret Sects of the Middle Ages*, but had suspended it in order first to see what G. R. had to say in the *Spirito Antipapale*. The book eventually appeared against K.'s wish, consequently anonymously, in the Library of Entertaining Knowledge, as *Secret Societies of the Middle Ages*, London, 1837. It deals with the Assassins, The Templars, and the secret tribunals of Westphalia. Keightley reviewed Panizzi's edition of Boiardo and Ariosto (1830-4) in *The Foreign Quarterly*, Vol. XV., March 1835. He had a grievance of his own against Panizzi—see Fagan, *op. cit.*, I., p. 91. On seeing the review, P. sent a furious letter to the proprietors of the *Foreign Quarterly*, in which, however, he speaks fairly enough about G. R. The letter produced an amusing rhymed address from W. S. Rose.

> My Wife and I are certain you are better
> Than you're reported, reasoning from your letter ;
> In which you've blown your enemy to bits (I
> Think) and deservedly, my dear Panizzi :
> But do not in your honest rage outrun
> The rule the ghostly king enjoined his son ;
> Tho' you " speak daggers—use none "—this I know
> You'd scarcely do—I mean don't use your toe,
> Or break his head, or pull him by the nose.
> Always yours truly, W. S. ROSE. (Fagan, I., p. 93.)

marked advances] G. R. to Lyell, 26 Feb. 1834 (Copy in Taylorian, No. 24) ; G. R. to Mrs. R., 13 Jan. 1834, Epist. 275.

Schlegel] G. R. to Lyell, 12 Sept. 1836, and 16 Nov. 1836 (both Kinnordy).

a year afterwards] G. R. to Lyell, 10 Oct. 1837, Epist. 276. The letter ends with a diatribe against P. in which he is called a mere *nottola ignota*.

P. reviews Amor Platonico etc.] So it appears from G. R. to Lyell, 31 Dec. 1842, Epist. 277. I have not succeeded in finding this review.

goes to the printer etc.] Reported in the same letter.

97. *Adams*] G. R. to Lyell, 4 Dec. 1832 (Kinnordy).

98. *Copy of* Spir. Ant. *given to Schlegel*] Lyell to G. R., 29 May 1834. He sent a copy to Witte at the same time. (See Karl Witte, *Dante-Forschungen*, 1869, Vol. I., pp. 96–133, *Rossettis Dante-Erklärung*. The first part of this, a notice of the *Comento*, appeared in *Blätter fur literarische Unterhaltung*, 1829. The rest was added later, giving a detailed account of Rossetti's reception in France, Germany, Italy, and England, and learnedly dismissing the whole case. The earlier part is the more scornful. See p. 103 : " Es genügt, drei Canzonen, und zwar von denen, auf die Rossetti selber sich beruft, unverstümmelt und unbefangen durchzulesen, um sich zu überzeugen, dass seit Harduin kaum eine lächerlichere, verkehrtere Hypothese ausgeheckt sei.")

Lyell's son etc.] See *Life of Sir C. Lyell*, I., p. 389.

99. *G. R. on Schlegel*] See preface of *Amor Platonico* ; G. R. to Lyell, 12 Sept., 1 Oct., 16 Nov., 1836 (all Kinnordy) Schlegel's review is reprinted in *Œuvres de M. Auguste-Guillaume de Schlegel, écrites en français*, Leipzig, 1846, Vol II., pp. 307–32. He is as scornful as Witte : M. Rossett may think he has accumulated proofs, but " nous n'avons pas trouvé une seule qui pût soutenir l'examen d'une saine critique.' The passage about Goropius, etc., occurs on p. 331.

Heimann] The correspondence is in Epist. 276 : H. to G. R. 3 June 1840 ; G. R. to Lyell, 8 June 1840 ; G. R. to Frere 23 June 1840 ; and G. R. to Frere, 1 Jan. 1841 (Epist. 277) *Frere for instance* etc.] Festing, p. 309.

Veltro] G. R. to Lyell, 7 and 11 Feb. 1828 (Kinnordy).

Who knows etc.] G. R. to Lyell, 1 March 1841, Epist. 277

100. *milleniary hopes*] One of J. H. Frere's brothers, Hatley, had queer views distressing to the rest of the family. He was pacifist ; he invented a reading system for the blind ; and produced a new interpretation of the unfulfilled prophecies He twice fixed the date of the millenium. Whatever hi relatives at home thought, however, J. H. Frere out in Malt

" was disposed to listen to his direful prophecies and look for the end of the world ". See Festing, p. 274. Hatley Frere no doubt was one of " the best and most learned Christians " mentioned p. 107 (*q.v.*). In Festing, pp. 274 ff., there is also information about another strange correspondent of Frere's, Joseph Wolff, traveller and missionary, another millennialist who wrote lengthily about Rabbinical and Talmudic subjects in the intervals of his pursuit of the lost tribes of Israel in Africa and elsewhere.

One of the earliest] ? 1826, Epist. 323. Two of the Kinnordy letters appear to be earlier—7 and 17 Feb. 1826.

101. *confident that . . . must follow*] Lyell to G. R., 11 Feb. 1826, Epist. 323.

cheap edition] Lyell to G. R., 11 Jan. 1828. He suggests 10s. 6d; the text to be " pure and unblemished in each page by note or reference," and thinks that no one who has laid out the 10s. 6d. will be able to resist expending 40s. to possess the larger work.

doubts about the gergo] In same letter.

anagram in Canto I] Ditto.

102. *warning of possible attacks*] Ditto.

No letter upon a literary subject etc.] 1 March 1830, Epist. 323.

in this review] It seems not to have been published however. In *The Edinburgh Review*, Vol. 55, July 1832, there is a review of the *Comento* and the *Spirito Antipapale* together. Its style is not unlike that of Lyell ; its substance however is different from what one would expect from him. The review in the main is complimentary, but the last paragraphs secure a retreat, almost deriding Rossetti's redundancy and assurance, and asking where his system of interpretation is to end. In any case even if Lyell wrote it, it is not the review referred to in the text, which could only have been concerned with the *Comento*. In a review of Wright's translation of the *Inferno*, Vol. 57, July 1833, there is a slighting reference to Rossetti—the reviewer obviously a different person.

103. *Lyell financing a new work*] G. R. to Lyell, 18 and 27 March 1830 (both Kinnordy).

In October etc.] Lyell to G. R., 22 Oct. 1830, Epist. 323.

The whole cost etc.] G. R. to Lyell, 6 Nov. 1830, Epist. 323.

In April next year] G. R. to Lyell, 15 April 1831 (Kinnordy).

Lyell and the dedication] See Lyell to G. R., 22 May 1831, and 24 Jan. 1832 ; both Epist. 324.

four evenings running] G. R. to Mrs. R., 27 May 1831, Epist. 324.

new worlds to conquer] G. R. to Lyell, 21 Oct. 1831 (Kinnordy).

but no nation etc.] G. R. to Lyell, 3 Dec. 1831 (Kinnordy).

extension to 600 pages] G. R. to Lyell, 14 Dec. 1831 (Kinnordy).

Your husband is a great man etc.] G. R. to Mrs. R., 21 May 1832, Epist. 324.

remarks on the Remarks] See Lyell to G. R., 9 and 12 Jan. 1833, both Epist. 324.

104. *That your next volume* etc.] Lyell to G. R., 24 May 1833, Epist. 324.

another supporter etc.] See Lyell to G. R., 22 Sept. 1832, Epist. 324. He had this news from his son, who probably thought his father was wasting money on Rossetti's publications.

whose free-born spirit etc.] Susan Frere to G. R., 29 Oct. 1831, Epist. 324.

Mr. Frere and I etc.] A. Murray to G. R., 20 July 1830, Epist. 323. If we are to believe G. R., Archibald Murray had shown great enthusiasm over the *Comento*. See *Comento*, I., p. 276, where after praising Polidori he goes on to " Signor Arch. Murray, filologo Inglese ornatissimo, il quale fu il primo a giudicare di questo mio scritto. Ei . . . uscendo da un recente esame del poema e degli espositori, rimanea poco persuaso circa al primo, ed assai malcontento de' secondi ; quando all' udire il mio modo d'interpretare fece gran festa ; e in quel suo sentire sentii io stesso la verità del mio trovato." *Enfin Rossetti vint !*

Frere had himself written etc.] See Festing, pp. 305–8.

105. *sent to Frere 5 March* 1832] G. R. to Frere, Epist. 324.

Gone are all his doubts etc.] See Frere to G. R., Festing, pp. 309–11.

If it were lost on the way etc.] G. R. to Frere, 5 Sept. 1832. Festing, p. 311.

too much for Frere] Festing, p. 312. Rossetti indeed felt himself to be a kind of Copernicus. See his letter to Lyell, 15 May 1833, Epist. 324. " Ho letto di Copernico che per 50 anni e più il suo sistema fu deriso e vituperato dalla canaglia de' semidotti. E quanto non dovè mai soffrire quel povero Colombo."

read the book three times] Frere to G. R., 21 March 1833, Epist. 324.

reverted to his Psaltery] Festing, pp. 313–14.

Then comes etc.] Frere to G. R., 29 June 1833, Festing, pp. 315–20.

107. *Pray think well* etc.] Festing, p. 321.

Susan Frere] To G. R., 5 June 1833, Epist. 324.

The dedication etc.] See the very pained letter, G. R. to Frere, 30 July 1833, Epist. 324, where this unkind sentence is quoted.

108. *will take to writing novels*] In the same letter.

I felt as a man does] Frere to G. R., 4 Oct. 1833, Epist. 324. The offending passage is little creditable to Frere and is omitted by Festing.

Rossetti's reply] 31 Dec. 1833, Epist. 324. He declares that he has had great difficulty in getting a copy of *Giovane Italia*, but having read it finds it to be " una vera scimeria Sansimoniana ".

asks Frere to refrain] Festing, p. 324.

answered by an account] G. R. to Lyell, 1 Oct. 1832, Epist. 324.

In the frenzy etc.] G. R. to Lyell, 26 Nov. 1833 (copy in Taylorian, No. 22).

109. *and duly thanked*] No. 23, 4 Dec. 1833.

resume their discussions] See Festing, pp. 324–6.

engages in a translation] See a number of letters Lyell to G. R. 1834 and 1835, in Epist. 275.

Lyell had asked] See Festing, p. 326.

alarm and astonishment] Frere to G. R., 6 April 1836, Festing, pp. 327–9.

110. *Cudworth, father-in-law, Keightley*] Festing, p. 329.

I would not hurry you etc.] Lyell to G. R., 10 Dec. 1835, Epist. 275.

following Sept.] 9 Sept. 1836, Epist. 275.

At the end of 1838] Lyell to G. R., 12 Dec. 1838, Epist. 276.

alterations very numerous] Lyell to G. R., 21 Dec. 1839.

111. *A few days later*] Lyell to G. R., 30 Dec. 1839, both Epist. 276.

To send me your conclusions etc.] Lyell to G. R., 5 June 1840, Epist. 276.

as he tells Frere] G. R. to Frere, 1 Aug. 1839, Epist. 276.

a burning question] G. R. to Frere, 3 March, 1840, Epist. 276.

my own shadow etc.] G. R. to Frere, 1 Jan. 1840, Epist. 276.

with confusion I tell you etc.] G. R. to Frere, 27 Sept. 1840, Epist. 276.

112. *Now I have to confess* etc.] G. R. to Frere, 16 Aug. 1841, Epist. 277.

On 19 Oct. etc.] To Frere, 19 Oct. 1841, Epist. 277.

I renounce the dedication etc.] Lyell to G. R., 31 Dec. 1840, Epist. 276.

four reasons for doing so] See G. R. to Frere, 1 Jan. 1841, Epist. 277.

though my interest etc.] Lyell to G. R., ? Jan. 1841, Epist. 277.

went to post with a letter] See G. R. to Lyell, 8 Sept. 1841, Epist. 277.

He implores Lyell etc.] G. R. to Lyell, 17 Aug. 1841, Epist. 277.

113. *The meditated destruction* etc.] Lyell to G. R., 13 Aug. 1841, Epist. 277.

reported to Frere] 16 Aug. 1841, Epist. 277.

He writes that he is anxious etc.] See Lyell to G. R., 2 Jan. 1842, Epist. 277, and Festing, p. 334. Lyell and Frere had corresponded before this, and the latter had sent a copy of his Aristophanes, his usual token of respect, and a valuable one, since that excellent work was not published until after his death.

20 *to Italy and two to Germany*] Festing, p. 335.

Lyell had 50 *copies*] See Festing, p. 333, and Lyell to G. R., 2 Jan. 1842, Epist. 277.

poem on the cholera morbus] This is *Lisa ed Elvio* in *Versi*, 1847.

clergyman called Nolan] G. R. to Lyell, 31 Dec. 1842, Epist. 277.

Lyell and the Beatrice] See M. L. G. de Courten, *Nuov. Ant.*, Oct. 1930, Vol. 273.

114. *you say that this fancy* etc.] G. R. to Lyell, n.d. (? March 1842), (Kinnordy), quoted Purves, pp. 115–16.

floor me and my theory etc.] Lyell to G. R., 23 May 1843, Epist. 277.

115. *as if of a Messiah*] G. R. to Mrs. R., 6 Sept. 1839, Epist. 276.

discovery of the Dante portrait] See *Aut.*, 144 ff.

sent one for Lyell] G. R. to Lyell, 10 March 1842, Epist. 277.

invited Rossetti] S. K. to G. R., 18 Aug. 1843, Epist. 277. Rossetti was then in Paris.

interested Lord Vernon] See S. K. to G. R. (1843 ?), and 23 Jan. 1844 ; both Epist. 277.

117. *Rossetti's tone*] See G. R. to Lyell, 26 Jan. 1844 (Kinnordy), and 3 Feb. 1845 (in Maria's writing, signed by G. R.), Epist. 277.

Kirkup returns to the attack] S. K. to G. R., 16 April 1844, Epist. 277.

complaints about Lyell] G. R. to Frere, 3 July 1844, 3 Aug. 1844, and 2 Sept. 1844 ; all Epist. 277.

118. *Kirkup in* 1866] See W. M. R., *Rossetti Papers* 1862–1870, pp. 178, 183, 215, 288, 343, 348. In the John Rylands Library, Manchester, there is a copy of Hardouin's *Doutes proposés sur l'âge du Dante*, an ed. with notes by Lyell, 1847, and annotated in pencil by Kirkup. K.'s notes are few but contemptuous. See p. 39, " stolen from Rossetti " ; and p. 43, opposite Lyell's assertion that Dante's invectives against the Holy See are much to be reprobated, " By such as you ".

Dante Alighieri was etc.] *Mem.* DGR. p. 64.

said by Watts-Dunton] See *Old Familiar Faces*, 1916, p. 186.

119. *Christina on Dante*] See *Churchman's Shilling Magazine*, 1867, *Dante an English Classic* (concerned with Cayley's translation). *Century Magazine*, Feb. 1884, *Dante the poet illustrated out of the poem* ; and *CGRFL.*, pp. 184–5.

W. M. R.'s translation of the Inferno] *The Comedy of Dante Allighieri*, Part I., *The Hell*, 1865. This was W. M. R.'s first book ; it was carried no further—wise restraint.

He now says in effect etc.] In various places. But see particularly *Rossetti Papers* 1862–1870, p. 80—a letter from

Keightley, 1 March 1865, referring to the translation of the
Inferno—" It really vexed me to see but one allusion, and that
rather a slighting one, to your father's theory. I infer from
this that you reject it, like Gabriel. It is a curious instance
of the well-known fact of children differing in opinion from
their parents—e.g. the Wilberforces turning papists. I however am unchanged etc." W. M. R. comments that he does
not entirely reject the theory ; he thinks some points correct,
others possibly so, others far-fetched and erroneous. This
letter of Keightley's is entirely in keeping with those quoted,
pp. 249–50.

120. *Perez*] *La Beatrice Svelata*, 1865.
list of the pros and cons] *Ruskin : Rossetti : Pre-Raphaelitism*,
pp. 262 ff.
Luigi Valli] *Il Linguaggio Segreto di Dante e dei " fedeli
d'amore "*, 1928, Vol. II. (*Discussione e note aggiunte*), 1930.

121. *His sight*] *Remin.*, p. 35.
Susan Frere] Letter to G. R., 30 Sept. 1824, Epist. 323.
When you return etc.] *Aut.*, p. 122.
more trouble in 1833] See Susan Frere to G. R., 5 June 1833,
Epist. 324.

122. *I am sorry to hear* etc.] G. R. to Mrs. R., 17 May 1833,
Epist. 324.
Everything is going well here etc.] In Epist. 275.

123. *note*] See G. R. to Lyell, 26 Nov. 1833 (copy in Taylorian,
No. 22).

124. *I have measured* etc.] G. R. to Lyell, 17 Nov. 1834, Epist. 279.
giving up beer] See letter to Mrs. R., 11 Oct. 1836, Epist. 325.

125. *Bacia per me* etc.] Giacopo Ferretti to G. R., Sabato Santo,
1835 (copy), Epist. 275.
has ceased to be rebellious] Lyell to G. R., 19 June 1835,
Epist. 275.
All the children etc.] G. R. to Lyell, 15 Aug. 1835 (copy in
Taylorian, No. 32).
death of Deagostini] Is this possibly the event referred to in
one of G. R.'s letters to F. Leigh (B.M. Add. 36663, f. 290) :
" Essendo morto un degno Italiano, amico mio, sono stato
invitato al suo funerale mercoledì e sventuratamente l'ora che
m'è indicata è la medesima che avea fissato con voi. Vi prego
perciò volermi scusare se, non potendo negarmi ad un luttuoso
dovere, mi veggo constretto a permettermi una piccola man-
canza. . . ." (21 July 1835). Giovanni Amedeo Deagostini
had for many years been a teacher of Italian, and had instructed
Princess Charlotte in that language. He was a subscriber to
Rossetti's *Comento*.
Poor old man etc.] G. R. to Lyell, 1 Oct. 1835 (copy in
Taylorian, No. 33).

The new house etc.] G. R. to Lyell, 13 Jan. 1836, Epist. 275.
No. 50 was a good deal bigger] See *Remin.*, p. 7.

126. *I can answer for* etc.] Lyell to G. R., 24 Nov. 1836, Epist. 275.
as Rossetti has left this space etc.] In Epist. 275.

128. *If you would like* etc.] 27 Jan. 1836, Epist. 275.
Everything here goes well etc.] G. R. to Mrs. R., 16 Jan. 1836
Epist. 275.

129. *the children are absorbed*] See G. R. to Mrs. R., 20 Jan. 1836
4 March 1836.
Marillier] *D.G.R. an Illustrated Memorial*, 1899, p. 211.
an inspiriting muse etc.] *Remin.*, p. 19.
Unlike Gabriel etc.] G. R. to Mrs. R., 20 Jan. 1836, Epist. 275
He does nothing but read etc.] G. R. to Lyell, 11 Feb. 1836
Purves, p. 115 ; and 4 July 1836, *Ibid.*
he is more inclined to arithmetic] G. R. to Frere, 1 Aug. 1836
Epist. 275.
one of R's letters] In Epist. 275.

130. *If only the other two*] G. R. to Mrs. R., 27 Jan. 1836, Epist. 275
Read this alone etc.] G. R. to G. P., 21 Jan. 1836, Epist. 275

131. *A full report was sent*] See G. R. to Mrs. R., 25 Jan. 1836
Epist. 275.

132. *I hear a noise* etc.] G. R. to Mrs. R., 18 Oct. 1836, Epist. 275
At the postman's well-known knock] G. R. to Mrs. R., 30 Aug
1836. Epist. 275 ; and cf. *Mem.* DGR., p. 11.
she hasn't shed a tear] v. supra, 30 Aug. 1836.
Christina has taken Maria's place] Aunt M., Uncle Henry
and G. R. to Mrs. R., 1 Sept., 1836, Epist. 275.
It has to be red etc.] G. R. to Mrs. R., 18 Oct. 1836, Epist. 275

133. *Tell Maria* etc.] G. R. to Mrs. R., 1 Oct. 1836.
six volume Shakespeare] G. R. to Mrs. R., 11 Oct. 1836
Epist. 275.
I was assured etc.] G. R. to Mrs. R., 24 Sept. 1836, Epist. 27
half a shopful of medicine] G. R. to Lyell, 8 Nov. 18?
(Kinnordy).
outbidding etc.] G. R. to Mrs. R., 21 Oct. 1836, *Aut.* 12
quite recovered] G. R. to Lyell, 8 Nov. 1836 (Kinnordy).
He thought whatever a child liked etc.] Note by W. M. R.
G. R. to Mrs. R., 5 Sept. 1839, Epist. 276. Rest of the det
in this paragraph based on descriptions in *Mem.* DGR., *Au*
and *Remin.*

134. *Speaking Likenesses*] See Dedication.
might never have attempted anything etc.] *Remin.*, p. 33.

135. *Outdoor games*] In *Remin.*, p. 25, W. M. R. says, " The id
of playing cricket never occurred to me ; and to this mome
I do not rightly understand what the game consists of."
Regent's Park] See *Times*, 16 Nov. 1834 for announceme
that a part of the Park was to be opened to the public. Co

plaints were made that the part opened was meagre and ill-chosen.

136. *pictures*] See *Remin.*, p. 13.

Princes, ye have etc.] See *Veggente*, Commiato.

They study Latin etc.] G. R. to Lyell, 7 Jan. 1837 (copy in Taylorian, No. 39).

It would be too true to acknowledge etc.] *Mem.* DGR., pp. 69, 75–6.

137. *Take care my dear Friend* etc.] S. K. to G. R., 26 Feb. 1842, Epist. 277.

138. *influenza*] G. R. to Lyell, 12 Jan. 1837 (Kinnordy).

whooping cough] G. R. to Lyell, 25 April, 10, 19, 27 May, 8 and 12 June 1837 (all Kinnordy).

a good year] G. R. to Lyell, 30 Dec. 1837 (Kinnordy).

Mullins] G. R.'s letter in Epist. 276. W. M. R.'s note on this letter says that Mullins was transported for seven years. See also *Remin.*, p. 24, and G. R. to Lyell, 30 Dec. 1837 (Kinnordy), where the sentence is stated to have been for ten years.

139. *By the theft* etc.] Purves, p. 115.

Another school etc.] Festing, p. 330.

If my last hour has come etc.] G. R. to Lyell, 19 Aug. 1838, Epist. 276.

scarlet fever] See G. R. to Lyell, 2 Dec. 1838, Epist. 276.

Illness has entered etc.] 29 May 1839, Epist. 276.

Our children etc.] G. R. to Mrs. R., 25 and 29 Aug. 1839, Epist. 276. The second has a note from D. G. R. at the end : " My dear Mamma, Aunt Margaret says that she will write tomorrow, or on Monday, for there is not time now, as I hear the Bellman. Your loving son, Gabriel. Mr. Sangiovanni begs Grandpapa to send him the receipt which did him so much good in the gravel and which can be purchased at St. Paul's."

140. *Gaetano writes to ask his wife* etc.] The letter accompanies G. R. to Mrs. R., 5 Sept. 1839, Epist. 276.

This will be a novel daily amusement etc.] G. R. to Mrs. R., n.d. (Sept. 1839), Epist. 276.

sonorous Hellenic vocable] Same letter.

Tuscan (or as P. writes it Toscan) *Cottage*] G. R. to Mrs. R., 6 Sept. 1839, Epist. 276.

141 *Polidori's books*] See *Remin.*, p. 30.

Eliza Catchpole and Privitera] *Ibid.*, 32.

W. M. R.'s letter] In Epist. 276.

142. *I have heard from Polidori* etc.] in Epist. 276.

143. *My two boys* etc.] G. R. to Lyell, 16 Dec. 1839, Epist. 276.

Lyell replied] 21 Dec. 1839, Epist. 276.

If it has occurred to you etc.] G. R. to Mrs. R., 16 Sept. 1839, Epist. 276.

144. *doctor and poet*] G. R. to Lyell, 7 April 1841, Epist. 277.
He had written in 1834] 28 April 1834, Epist. 275.
I found your brother etc.] Gabriele Smargiassi to G. R.,
28 Dec. 1836, Epist. 275. This letter announces the com-
pletion of a painting of the Rossetti house in Vasto, which S.
is going to send to R. as soon as he can. See Frontispiece.
Very painful circumstances etc.] G. R. to A. R., 9 Aug. 1838,
Epist. 276.

145. *My kind-hearted* etc.] 13 Aug. 1839, Epist. 276. In the
original Antonio says " il mio genero a settembre di questo
corrente anno cadde malato " ; the dates make it necessary
to translate " last year ".

146. *Another desperate appeal*] In Epist. 276.
Is there anyone in the world etc.] " V'è più di me da deplorarne
alcuno ? " *Veggente*, Commiato.
Ah ! I live in doubt etc.] A. R. to G. R., 26 May 1843, Epist.
277.

147. *in his youth had about him* etc.] D.C., p. 310.

148. *For more than three months* etc.] In Epist. 276.
He complains of having had diabetes] G. R. to Lyell, 15 April
1840, Epist. 276.
Signor Polidori thanks you etc.] G. R. to Lyell, 7 April 1841,
Epist. 277.
if he succeeds etc.] G. R. to Frere, 19 Oct. 1841, Epist. 277.
One would have expected the date 1842 ; it was after the
summer vacation of that year that D. G. R. started upon his
professional training. G. R. must refer to some lessons
received by his son during the school period.
My second son etc.] G. R. to Frere, 16 Aug. 1841, Epist. 277.
audaciously lazy] Remin., p. 27.

149. *invited to Putney Hill* etc.] G. R. to Mrs. R., Easter Monday,
1843, Epist. 277. At the end of this letter he says that the
gentleman who brought the invitation and who spoke with
William on that occasion, " ha fatto del nostro figliuolo il più
grande elogio : dice che ha trovato nel suo discorso una tal
sensatezza ch' è superiore alla sua età : lo chiama il piccolo
filosofo."
I say seems, etc.] G. R. to Lyell, 20 May 1843, Epist. 277.

150. *Florence and Marseilles*] See S. K. to G. R., 14 July 1843,
Epist. 277 ; and Festing, p. 335 (Lyell to Frere, 29 Aug.
1843).
Three doctors have agreed] G. R. to Polidori, 19 July 1843,
Epist. 277 ; G. R. to Miss Polidori, 12 Aug. 1843, Epist. 277.
Having lost the sight etc.] G. R. to Lyell, 18 Oct. 1843
(Kinnordy).
One of my eyes etc.] Festing, p. 337.
The generosity of Frere] Festing, p. 336. It is right to point

out that G. R. did not tell Frere of his distresses until after the latter had heard of them from Lyell.

151. *All my anxiety* etc.] G. R. to Frere, 3 Aug. 1844, Epist. 277.
MS. of Veggente] Since April 1931 in Bib. Ris., Rome.

152. *Autobiography*] This was written between 1846 and 1852; the part here quoted could hardly be earlier than 1848. The poem is in six-lined stanzas, and very informal in style. It was never published in G. R.'s lifetime. W. M. R. published a translation in 1901; the Italian text was printed with elaborate bibliography and notes, by Domenico Ciampoli in 1910.

154. *Heimann*] There is an account of him in L. A. Willoughby, *D.G.R. and German Literature*, 1912, pp. 8–10.

155. *Jelf's acknowledgment*] In Epist. 278.

156. *I expect to receive* etc.] Bedetti, p. 42 (5 Feb. 1848).
I cannot tell you etc.] G. R. to Ricciardi, 24 May 1848, *Riv. Eur.*, XII., fasc. 4, p. 699.
Horrible horrible etc.] G. R. to Mrs. R., 14 Aug. 1848, Epist. 278.
It was providential etc.] G. R. to Lyell, 27 Oct. 1848 (copy in Taylorian, No. 123).

157. *I am so disheartened* etc.] G. R. to Ricciardi, 5 Dec. 1848, *Riv. Eur.*, XII., fasc. 4, p. 700.
between the Rossetti you used to know etc.] G. R. to Lyell, 27 Oct. 1848 (copy in Taylorian, No. 123).
He had in October] Same letter.
I am always alone etc.] G. R. to Ricciardi, 12 April 1848, *Riv. Eur.*, XII., fasc. 4, p. 698.

158. *I entered the small front parlour* etc.] W. B. Scott, *Autobiographical Notes*, 1892, I., pp. 247–8.
As might be expected etc.] F. G. Stephens, *D.G.R.*, 1894, p. 7. The passage is quoted in part in *Mem.* DGR., pp. 19–20.

159. *Ferretti*] Todeas Twattle-Basket [T. de Angelis], *Note di Cronaca*, 1897, p. 23.
Ciocci] "il buon Ciocci," G. R. calls him in a letter to his wife, 8 Aug. 1848, Epist. 278. He was an applicant for the Italian Chair at King's when G. R. resigned. In answer to a query about his religious beliefs, he replied that the Established Church of England was the only one in which he could enjoy peace. His letter ends, " I a Roman exile, and by misfortune formerly a Cistercian monk, and now belonging to the Established Church of England, hope that one day the chains and the double wall which surround my poor Italy will be broken and that I may have the consolation of giving the light of truth to my fellow-countrymen. I remain Sir, Your Umble Servant, R. Ciocci." Quoted from documents in King's College Library, by permission of the College authorities.

Rossetti joined in]   For his religious views as expressed in the
Eco, see Luzzi, *op. cit.*

160. *he complains that the paper is colourless* etc.]   G. R. to Giacopo
Ferretti, 27 April 1850 (copy), Epist. 278.
considerable fame in Italy] See G. R. to Signora [Monti-
Baraldi], n.d., Bedetti, pp. 56–7.
Carducci]   In *Prefazione* of his selection of G. R.'s *Poesie,*
1861 (2nd ed., 1879, p. xiv.).
translated one of them]   *Hymn after G. R.* (two versions),
CGRPW., pp. 183–4.
addresses her father]   In *I do set my bow in the clouds* (Dec. 1847).
letter to Lyell]   End of 1849 (copy in Taylorian, No. 128).
A letter to Ricciardi covering some of the same ground is
dated 11 Sept. 1849, *Riv. Eur.* XII., fasc. 4, pp. 121–3.
In August 1849]   22nd, Epist. 278.

161. *a rich lady of the provinces*]   See the letters to Lyell and
Ricciardi noted above at Sept. 1849.
Gabriel, William, Christina, Maria]   G. R. to Ricciardi, n.d.
(D. G. R. is in Paris, date probably Oct. 1849), *Riv. Eur.,*
XIV., fasc. 3, p. 532.
They will complete their pilgrimage etc.]   G. R. to Lyell, n.d.,
late 1849 (Taylorian, No. 128).

162. *My excellent wife* etc.]   Bedetti, p. 50 (4 Jan. 1851).
a few daughters etc.]   *Remin.,* p. 107.
I am so tired of life etc.]   ? 1850 (copy), Epist. 278.
An habitual melancholy etc.]   9 Jan. 1851 (copy), Epist. 278.
stroke of paralysis]   G. R. to T. P. R., 1 April 1851 (copy),
Epist. 278.
report of his death]   Bedetti, p. 56.
portrait of his father]   See *DGRFL.,* p. 100.   " Mr. Stewart
thought the governor extremely like.   Since you went I have
added the cupboard and a piece of chimney-piece in his background, which improves him much."
I seem still to see him etc.]   T. Pietrocola-Rossetti, *G.R.,* 1861,
pp. 58, 69, 70–4.

163. *The story of our affairs* etc.]   In Epist. 278.

165. *He loitered about a little* etc.]   *Mem.* DGR., p. 79.
And William]   *Remin.,* p. 5.
even a blackbeetle etc.]   *Mem.* DGR., p. 79.
The garden was her familiar haunt etc.]   *T.F.,* Mar. 4.
had never seen a good sunrise etc.]   Bell, p. 70.
love-in-a-mist]   *CGRFL.,* p. 137.
I fled in horror etc.]   *T.F.,* Mar. 4.
Watts-Dunton]   *Old Familiar Faces,* p. 188.

166. *Botany book*]   See *Called to be Saints,* p. xviii.   " Avowing as
I must, a general ignorance of petrology, and even of botany
I ask any who turn to my nature-portraits to accept them as

confessedly no more than loving studies from the outside :
elaborated by one who has written partly indeed from her own
observation of appearances, but mainly from a little reading "
Her person etc.] *Called to be Saints*, p. 468.
Its flowers etc.] *Ibid.*, p. 265.
personal kindness to myself etc.] *CGRFL.*, p. 51.
amuse themselves for hours] At the age of 14 and 15. *Remin.*,
p. 186.

167. *They identified themselves* etc.] *Mem.* DGR., p. 41.
William remarks etc.] *Mem.* DGR., p. 66.
l'amabile Maria etc.] *Ibid.*, p. 58.
Gabriel was the most ingenious contributor etc.] *DGRFL.*, p. 40.

168. *The Blessed Damozel*] Written for the family *Hotch Potch*
DGRFL., p. 293.
Maria . . . could read anything etc.] *Mem.* DGR., p. 37.
Keightley's Fairy Mythology] *The Fairy Mythology, Illus-*
trative of the Romance and Superstition of various Countries,
London, 1828. (Anonymous.) This is a learned book on
very entertaining material, fays, elves, pixies, trolls, dwarfs,
etc., drawn from oriental, Scandinavian, and other European
sources. Full of matter capable of delighting children, but
only very intelligent children. *The Mythology of Ancient*
Greece and Italy, London, 1831, is an even more learned
production. Its usefulness is indicated by the 4th edition
1877, revised by " Leonhard Schmitz, classical examiner to
the University of London ". Keightley gave the Rossettis
copies of his books. The *F.M.* was sent with a letter to Mrs.
R., 8 Jan. 1833, Epist. 324. On 27 Jan. 1836 he brings his
History of Rome, which, says G. R., " will be useful to the
children ". Epist. 275.
Every-Day Book, *Christina and Keats*] Bell, p. 13. (*The*
Every-Day Book and Table Book or Everlasting Calendar of
Popular Amusements, by William Hone, London, 1838, in 3
vols., vols. i. and ii. being *The Every-Day Book* which had
first appeared in 1826–7. Vol. i. has a portion of *The Eve of*
St. Agnes ; Vol. ii. has the *Ode to a Nightingale*.)
morbidly excitable tracts etc.] In one of the *Letters to Alling-*
ham, p. 137, July 4, ? 1855, D. G. R. writes, " I must confess
to a need, in narrative dramatic poetry . . . of something
rather ' exciting ', and I believe something of the ' romantic
element ' to rouse my mind to anything like the moods produced
by personal emotion in my own life." Before " romantic "
the word " schoolgirl " was written and afterwards scored out.

169. *for the sake of his splendid versification* etc.] *DGRFL.*, p. 19.
William had been upset etc.] *DGRFL.*, p. 53.
Keble] *DGRFL.*, p. 11.

170. *writing of a service* etc.] *DGRFL.*, p. 24.

in error on some points] *Remin.*, p. 72.

attempts of their Uncle Henry] " I think he made at times some endeavours (not of a surreptitious kind) to convert my sisters to the Roman Church." *Remin.*, p. 119.

I do not think I shall go to church etc.] *DGRFL.*, p. 6.

Neither he nor his brother] See *Remin.*, pp. 126 ff.

171. *She herself used to say* etc.] Bell, p. 13.

172. *She will indeed be a great loss* etc.] *DGRFL.*, p. 297.

a neatly paved thoroughfare etc.] *DGRFL.*, p. 99.

Her features etc.] *Remin.*, p. 18.

likeness to Savonarola] *CGRFL.*, p. 70.

The execrated Aroux etc.] See his letter, 6 June 1853, Epist. 278, a minute note at the end of which asks Maria to persuade her father that he is mistaken about the writer.

She listens open-eyed etc.] See *Mem.* DGR., p. 54, and Holman Hunt, *Pre-Raphaelitism*, I., p. 154 : " The elder sister was overflowing with attention to all, expressing interest in each individually."

a governess in the Thynne family] The date about 1844 is given by W. M. R., *Remin.*, p. 38. He says she soon left the post, but D. G. R.'s letter quoted on p. 173 complaining of the Thynnes is dated by W. M. R. ' towards August 1847 ' ; (it could not be much earlier since it has a reference to Christina's *Verses*).

I am anticipating etc.] 29 Jan. 1846, Epist. 277.

173. *I hope you told Lady Charles* etc.] *DGRFL.*, p. 33.

Not the least of his gifts etc.] 8 Sept. 1847, Epist. 278.

174. *written for one of the family scrap-books*] *DGRFL.*, p. 18. I am indebted to Mr. T. J. Wise for kindly allowing me to read his copy of *The Rivulets*. I have not succeeded in finding the whereabouts of the other copy—it belonged at one time to W. B. Scott. It was W. M. R. who told Mr. Wise that Maria later disapproved of the story.

Christina chose to think] Bell, p. 57.

175. *Have you heard of Maria's astute plan* etc.] *Rossetti Papers*, 1862–1870, p. 73.

sales of Maria's Exercises] *Ibid.*, p. 329, and *CGRFL.*, p. 188.

Gosse's joke] *Critical Kit-Kats*, p. 160.

176. *If in cultivated society* etc.] *Shadow of Dante* (1894), p. 2.

an Italian writer] De Courten, p. 353.

Swinburne complimented her] December 1871, *CGRFL.*, p. 209.

It is indeed etc.] *Ibid.*, p. 171.

Christina even thought it desirable etc.] *Ibid.*, p. 75.

177. *deep and sincere respect* etc.] *Rossetti Papers* 1862–1870, p. 14.

One of the most genuine Christians] *Time Flies*, April 22 Authority for connection of this with Ruskin is Bell, p. 63.

Charles Allston Collins] See *Remin.*, pp. 151–2.

178. *Poor Maggie is parting with her greyish hair*] W. B. Scott, *Autobiog.*, II., p. 215.
I have really felt very anxious etc.] *DGRFL.*, p. 300.
in this great change] *Ibid.*, p. 320.
It is terrible indeed] *Ibid.*, p. 338.
If Maria's beliefs were correct] *Ashley Catalogue*, IV., 162 ; quoted by permission of Mr. T. J. Wise.

179. *Her Christian faith* etc.] *Remin.*, p. 427.
Mr. T. J. Wise] *Ashley Catalogue*, IV., p. 162.
Sir Edmund Gosse.] *Critical Kit-Kats*, p. 160.

180. *Blake's designs*] See *Time Flies*, April 15, and Bell, p. 61.
mummy room at the B.M.] *Time Flies*, July 4.
enjoying a wedding feast] *CGRFL.*, p. 37.
sad funerals] *Time Flies*, Nov. 7, and Bell, p. 72.
My love whose heart is tender etc.] This appeared first in *Time Flies*, Feb. 15, with the motto " Doeth well . . . doeth better."—1 Cor. vii. 38.

181. *Watts-Dunton*] See his essay in *Old Familiar Faces*.
William Michael declares] *Mem.* DGR., p. 158 ; and *DGRFL.*, p. 71.
Ruskin] *Praeterita*, III., i., 13.

182. *What I ought to do* etc.] *DGRFL.*, p. 93.
a cabman] *PRDL.*, p. 207.
letters to his parents and to William] See *DGRFL.*, pp. 23–31.
Here everything is going well] Epist. 278.
Gabriel continues to carry on] 14 Aug. 1848, Epist. 278.

183. *letters to his brother*] *DGRFL.*, pp. 40–3.
I thank you for writing to Gabriel] 18 Aug. 1848, Epist. 278.

184. *I have the satisfaction* etc.] Epist. 278, and *Aut.*, p. 130 (where the last two sentences are omitted).
diary of Madox Brown] In *PRDL.*
I announce to you with joy] Copy in Taylorian, No. 123.
which you have been pleased to add etc.] 3 Nov. 1848, Epist. 278.

185. *It has been a subject of much regret* etc.] (Kinnordy.) Quoted from Purves.
found occasion to reprehend etc.] *Mem.* DGR., p. 167.
Thinking about what you said etc.] *CGRFL.*, p. 102.

188. *the Bargello Dante*] See the letters about it in *Aut.*, pp. 144–50.
childish compositions] Detail of unpublished items is taken direct from *Mem.* DGR.

189. *His father sent a copy to Frere*] See Festing, p. 341. " That dear first-born son of mine is distressed at the idea that I took it upon me to send you those verses of his . . . for he is now sixteen years old and he himself jeers at his earliest attempts." And see D. G. R.'s own note (about 1881) on " the absurd trash ", *Mem.* DGR., p. 85.

191. *Jan van Hunks*] Published in book form by Mackenzie Bell,

London, 1929. See T. L. S., 10 Sept. 1931, for a letter about earlier printed forms.

192. *I need not say of how much benefit*] Purves, p. 118.
William Michael says etc.] *Mem.* DGR., p. 105.
his son has that day finished etc.] Copy in Taylorian, No. 123.
some five years ago] *Letters to Allingham*, p. 29.
translating canzoni etc.] *PRDL.*, p. 282
a great quantity of translations] *Ibid.*, p. 287.

193. *publishing them in some periodical*] *Letters to Allingham*, pp. 59, 73.
293. *Patmore says* etc.] *PRDL.*, p. 295.
letter to Norton] (July 1858) in *Ruskin : Rossetti : Pre-Raphaelitism*, p. 204.
Benson] *Rossetti*, 1926, p. 152.

196. *Where is my lady* etc.] The original of this stanza is :

> Ov' è madonna e lo suo insegnamento,
> La sua bellezza e la gran conoscianza,
> Lo dolce riso, e lo bel parlamento,
> Gli occhi e la bocca e la bella sembianza,
> L' adornamento e la sua cortesia,
> La nobil gentilia ?
> Madonna, per cui stava tuttavia
> In allegranza,
> Or non la veggio nè notte nè dia,
> E non m'abbella, sì com' far solia,
> In sua sembianza.

Lines 7 and 8 originally (1861) ran

> My lady—she who to my soul so rare
> A gladness brought !

197. *Diego della Ratta* etc.] I am indebted for this correction of Rossetti's mistake to Professor Gardner in the Everyman reprint of his edition of the translations, p. 405.
This Cecco wrote to Dante a sonnet etc.] *Antipapal Spirit* (English version), II., p. 226.

198. *Ford Madox Hueffer*] In *Ancient Lights*.
T. S. Eliot] *Dante*, London, 1929, p. 12 ; and cf. pp 63, 68.
Ever since I have read etc.] Purves, p. 118.

199. *Paget Toynbee's list*] *Chronological List . . . of paintings and drawings from Dante by D.G.R.* (reprinted from *Scritti Varii . . . in onore di Rodolfo Renier*, Turin, 1912).
listed by his brother] In *D.G.R. as designer and writer*. H. C. Marillier's list has 396 items.
The Paolo and Francesca subject] See Marillier, *D.G.R. a Memorial*, 1899, p. 66.
Dantis Amor] Reproduced in Marillier, p. 86.

200. *In these early days*] Holman Hunt, *Pre-Raphaelitism*, I., pp. 153–4.
By 1848 Gabriel was a decided sceptic] *Mem.* DGR., p. 114.

I can make nothing of Christianity etc.] W. B. Scott, *Autobiography*, II., p. 307. Scott may very probably have given a somewhat absurd twist to the remarks he quotes at this point, but there is no reason to doubt their substantial truth.

201. *W. B. Scott's* Rosabell etc.] See *Autobiography*, I., p. 289, and *Mem.* DGR., pp. 164–5.

202. Blessed Damozel] See article by the present writer in *Modern Language Review*, Vol. XXVI., No. 2, Apr. 1931.

203. Ave] The (perhaps faint) parallel with Dante was first suggested by Kurt Horn, *Zur Entstehungsgeschichte von D. G. Rossettis Dichtungen*, 1909.

205. *How earnestly do I hope* etc.] Bell, p. 123.
   beautiful indeed etc.] M. F. Saunders, *Christina Rossetti*, 1930, p. 257.

206. *Dante's sophistries* etc.] See *Vita Nuova*, XXXVIII., and compare *H. of L.*, Sonnet xxxvii. (*The Love-Moon*).
   The passionate and just delights of the body] In his reply to Buchanan ; see *Collected Works*, 1890, I., p. 482.
   It gives only the momentary contact etc.] DGRFL., p. 211.

208. *I wish I were* etc.] DGRFL., p. 294.

209. *brother of brothers*] CGRFL., p. 37.
   You and Gabriel are my resources] *Ibid.*, p. 13.
   Gabriel always suggesting subjects etc.] *Remin.*, p. 33.
   he who wrote so much etc.] *Ibid.*, pp. 33 and 57.

210. *great delight of his father*] ". . . alcune poesie del mio secondo figlio Guglielmo e della mia ultima figlia Cristina, che hanno ritratto grandissimi elogi da quanti l' han lette." G. R. to Lyell, 27 Oct. 1848 (copy in Taylorian, No. 123).
   hoisted him into P.R.B.] William was drawing at the time under his brother's instruction. D. G. R. thought that he would soon be able to give up the Inland Revenue Office and be a painter ; with this prospect in mind he proposed they should make room for William in the Brotherhood (Holman Hunt, *Pre-Raphaelitism*, I., p. 128).
   sonnet which stated the Pre-Raphaelite aims] Printed on the cover.

> When whoso merely hath a little thought
> Will plainly think the thought which is in him,—
> Not imaging another's bright or dim,
> Not mangling with new words what others taught ;
> When whoso speaks, from having either sought
> Or only found,—will speak, not just to skim
> A shallow surface with words made and trim,
> But in that very speech the matter brought :
> Be not too keen to cry—" So this is all !—
> A thing I might myself have thought as well,
> But would not say it, for it was not worth ! "
> Ask : " Is this truth ? " For is it still to tell
> That, be the theme a point or the whole earth,
> Truth is a circle, perfect, great or small ?

" The sonnet ", says its author, " may not be a good one but I do not see why it should be considered unintelligible." (*Germ Reprint*, 1901, p. 15.)

diary of their work] Printed in *PRDL.*

most regretted by its two literary members] *DGRFL.*, p. 137.

211. *Mrs. Holmes Grey*] *The Broadway*, London and New York, Feb. 1868. The style is fairly represented by the following passages. A certain Harling, coming to a seaside town, finds the weather rainy :

> The English " Rainy weather " went from mouth
> To mouth, with " Very " answered, or a shrug
> Of shoulders, and a growl, and " Sure to be !
> Began the very day that we arrived."

He comes across Grey, an old friend, now distracted with grief and jealousy, and is given a newspaper report of the coroner's proceedings to read.

> And this is what he feverishly perused:
> " *Coroner's Inquest—A Distressing Case.*
> An inquest was held yesterday, before
> The County Coroner, into the cause
> Of the decease of Mrs. Mary Grey,
> A married lady. Public interest
> Was widely excited.
>   When the Jury came
> From viewing the corpse, in which are seen remains
> Of no small beauty, witnesses were called . . ."

Their evidence is given in full, ending with a doctor's statement :

> the cause of death
> Congestion and effusion of the ventricle,

whereupon the Coroner sums up, and

> The Jury gave their verdict in at once ;
> Died by the visitation of God.

See D. G. R.'s detailed criticism of the poem in a letter to W. M. R., 8 Oct. 1849, *DGRFL.*, pp. 63–6. D. G. R. calls the poem " very remarkable . . . the best thing you have done . . . more like Crabbe than any other poet I know of."

212. *unless it were politics*] W. M. R. was one of the politically minded Pre-Raphaelites whose discussions could only be carried on in the absence of D. G. R. and Millais. His views constituted a link of sympathy between him and Swinburne ; when Count Ricciardi wished to arrange a convention of free-thinkers at Naples in 1869 to counterbalance the Oecumenical Council at Rome, Swinburne and W. M. R. sent a joint letter of adhesion, theirs being the sole adhesion from England, while there were hundreds from other countries. *Rossetti Papers 1862–1870*, pp. 410, 483.

Snow is a natural phenomenon etc.] *Remin.*, p. 462.

Even were the Scriptural fool etc.] *Letter and Spirit*, p. 42.

213. *W. M. R.'s religious beliefs*] See *Remin.*, pp. 122 ff. For his reading of Shelley, see *Ibid.*, p. 57.

In 1883 he declared] See a letter to Swinburne, *Ashley Catalogue*, IV., p. 151. (Quoted by permission of Mr. T. W. Wise.)

cross over his brother's grave] See the letters on this subject, *CGRFL.*, pp. 128 ff.

refused Christina's dedication etc.] *Ibid.*, p. 193.

less disinclined to believe etc.] *Ashley Catalogue*, IV., p. 151.

Discussing the story of Maude] In the preface to that publication.

She would have been far happier etc.] *CGRFL.*, p. 165.

214. *prayers*] *Ibid.*

unbaptised children] *CGRFL.*, p. 164.

I endeavoured to show her etc.] Quoted from a letter, by Bell, p. 177.

Inscription on gravestone, and comment] Bell, pp. 185–6.

The Past] From *Democratic Sonnets*, 1907.

215. *fell in love*] See *Remin.*, p. 260.

Few things could have been less to my liking etc.] *Remin.*, p. 431.

217. *In a roomful of mediocrities* etc.] *CGRPW.* (1920), p. lvi.

Ask William etc.] *CGRFL.*, p. 138.

218. *mother seems reborn in her*] See p. 151.

grandmother's eyes] See pp. 54 and 56.

She will be the cleverest of them all] See *CGRFL.*, pp. 146–7.

219. *Sing Robin sing*] From *The First Spring Day* (1855).

Lo, in the room the upper] *Young Death* (1865).

I would get quit of earth etc.] *Saints and Angels* (before 1876).

220. *Outer Sister* etc.] See Bell, p. 54; *CGRFL.*, p. 26; and W. B. Scott, II., p. 59. " On Wednesday we drove to the top of Highgate Hill, where is S. Mary Magdelene Home. We spent a pleasant day with the sisters and penitents in the open air, the Bishop of London, etc. etc. . . . Christina is now an Associate, and wore the dress, which is very simple, elegant even ; black with hanging sleeves, a muslin cap with lace edging quite becoming to her with the veil." (Letter from his wife.)

A world of change and loss etc.] *Valentine to her mother*, 1883.

Like an angel watered lily] From a sonnet by D. G. R. on his own *Girlhood of Mary Virgin* ; Christina sat for the Virgin.

221. *The roses bloom too late for me*] *I do set my bow in the clouds*, (December, 1847).

Maude] Published with introduction by W. M. R., 1897.

not dangerously exciting to the nervous system] *DGRFL.*, p. 224.

223. *some paints*] *Remin.*, p. 538.

224. *parted unhappy or deserted love*] See D. M. Stuart, *C.G.R.*, p. 17.

still echoing as late as 1856] See *CGRPW.*, p. 323 (*Look on this picture and on this*), and note, p. 480.

thus securing Dante as his elder brother etc.] *Churchman's Shilling Magazine*, Vol. II. (Oct. 1867), p. 200.

On another occasion etc.] See *CGRFL.*, pp. 184, 5, 8.

Tasso and Ariosto] See *CGRPW.*, p. lxx., and Bell, p. 319.

Keats] Bell, pp. 13, 335 ; and see her sonnet on him (*CGRPW.*, p. 291).

225. *Polidori's enthusiasm*] In his preface to the volume.

228. *Ah woe is me* etc.] *Vanity of Vanities.*

He resteth ; weep not etc.] *Resurrection Eve.*

229. *Love is sweet* etc.] *Love Ephemeral.*

Like breath of summer breezes etc.] *Love Attacked.*

But the face etc.] *Love Defended.*

230. *As to the nonsense about Christina's Verses.*] *DGRFL.*, p. 33.

something above the despicable in them] The letter, which was to Aytoun, is to be found in M. F. Sanders, *C.G.R.*, pp. 85–6.

association with the S.P.C.K. etc.] See *CGRFL.*, p. 92.

Poet Laureate] F. M. Hueffer in *Ancient Lights*, p. 57.

a small thick-necked man] *Mem.* DGR., p. 131. See also the accounts of him in *Remin.*, pp. 65 ff. ; *CGRPW.*, p. lii.

231. *It appears that the Rossettis* etc.] See Holman Hunt, *Pre-Raphaelitism*, I., p. 129 ; and *Letters to Allingham*, p. 134.

did not rise to any distinction etc.] *Mem.* DGR., p. 132.

Meanwhile Gabriel etc.] *PRDL.*, pp. 13–19. Collinson had first explained his feelings to D. G. R., who advocated his cause with Christina. (*Remin.*, p. 72.)

232. *I am glad you like Miss Collinson*] *CGRFL.*, p. 3.

Local converse wearies me] *Ibid.*, p. 5.

Fancy the inflated state etc.] *CGRFL.*, p. 7.

As I lay a-thinking] *Ibid.*, pp. 6, 7, 9.

My correspondence with Miss Collinson etc.] *Ibid.*, p. 10.

233. *I love and reverence God's faith* etc.] *PRDL.*, p. 275. The letter was addressed to D. G. R.

Jesuit seminary] Stonyhurst in Lancashire. On returning to the world he married a sister-in-law of the painter J. R. Herbert ; they had one child, a son. Collinson went on painting, confining himself to humorous or domestic subjects, and exhibited at the Royal Academy and elsewhere. Some of his pictures were engraved—e.g. " To Let ", " For Sale ", " Good for a Cold ". " Collinson ", says Lionel Cust in *D.N.B.*, " lived a very retired life, though he was much respected by those who knew him, and at his death in April 1881 had almost passed out of the memory of his old associates."

Christina noted the event in her diary] Or more accurately, the Diary kept by her on behalf of her mother. *CGRFL.*, p. 222.

I cannot say that she was in love etc.] *Remin.*, p. 73.

Shut Out] See note in *CGRPW.*, p. 480.

234. *saw Collinson in the street*] *Remin.*, p. 73.

continued to ask news of him] *CGRFL.*, p. 13.

recommended a poem of his] Bell, p. 87. She calls it " a blank verse poem of some length on the ' sorrowful mysteries ' of our Lord's life, written by James Collinson, an artist not long deceased ". It is called *The Child Jesus*. Though obviously the work of an unpractised hand, it has a simple sincerity and in places a grace which make it easy to understand why Christina remembered the poem—and its author. *Give me thy heart* etc.] The identity of the writer is stated by Bell, p. 305, but might in any case have been inferred.

unhappy little fragments of verse] *CGRFL.*, p. 15.

235. *Three Stages*] See W. M. R.'s note to these poems in *CGRPW.*, p. 477.

What ?] See Bell, pp. 31–2.

237. *The peace of heaven is placed too high*] *The whole head is sick and the whole heart faint.* (Dec. 1847.)

239. *no special sympathy with them*] Bell, p. 155, quoting W. M. R. : " I do not consider that Christina was particularly fond of children.—In early youth certainly not. As she advanced in years she enjoyed them and their pretty or quaint ways, but still not to any extent comparable to what marks a multitude of women."

Sing-Song] *S.S. a Nursery Rhyme Book*, 1872.

I hope you are glad to know etc.] *CGRFL.*, p. 24.

240. *She considered cheerfulness* etc.] See Bell, p. 163.

241. *I find that you have been perpetrating portraits* etc.] *DGRFL.*, p. 95 (4 Aug. 1852).

with that intense sympathy ·etc.] *DGRFL.*, p. 323.

242. " *successive tergiversations* " and " *ineffective faithful aloofness* "] A reviewer in *T.L.S.*, Centenary article, 4 Dec. 1930.

243. *A certain Rev. Dr. Bennett*] *Remin.*, p. 108.

to leave there these weary bones] Perale, p. 208.

Do you know that I am seventy years old ?] Bedetti, pp. 56 ff., n.d. (1853).

244. *I started this letter* etc.] 11 Sept. 1853, Epist. 278.

some appreciative comments] *DGRFL.*, pp. 114, 123.

grave letter of admonition] Quoted from the translation in *PRDL.*, p. 38, except for a sentence at the end supplied from the original, 4 Oct. 1853, Epist. 278.

245. *In your letter, my dear Father*] *DGRFL.*, p. 123.

246. *Polidori's last letters*] In Epist. 278.

Things with me are but so so] 15 Dec. 1853, Epist. 278.

Christina will have told you etc.] 15 Dec. 1853, Epist. 278. (Original is in Italian.)

247. *Christina saw this letter* etc.] G. R. to Mrs. R., 16 Dec. 1853, Rome, *Autografi*, IV.
Your last letter filled me etc.] 17 Dec. 1853, Rome, *Autografi*, IV.
When are you going to return etc.] 22 Dec. 1853, Rome, *Autografi* IV.

248. *with tears in his half-sightless eyes* etc.] *Mem.* DGR., p. 9.
It is a work of power etc.] Lyell to G. R., 21 Nov. 1848, Epist. 278.
I have great pleasure in informing you etc.] Epist. 278.

249. *John Taylor brought me your last work*] 2 July 1846, Epist. 277.
useless to enquire about your eyes] Keightley himself lost his sight in his later years. Towards the end his services to scholarship (more meritorious than perhaps may appear from these pages) were rewarded by a Civil List pension. He died in 1872.
He has now read all Rossetti's published works] 23 Oct. 1853, Epist. 278.

250. *He was still persuaded* etc.] See note to p. 119 of this book.
Let us take comfort then etc.] 21 Jan. 1846, Epist. 277. The fellow exile was Sperati.
telling Rossetti about the medal] 28 Nov. 1847, Epist. 278. The die for this medal was cut in 1847, but through the death of the leading spirit of the enterprise, nothing more was done until 1871 when 100 medals were struck from the die. (*D.C.*, p. 306.) Christina mentions the receipt of one of them in a letter to William, 28 April 1873, (*CGRFL.*, p. 38). She says she cannot understand the inscription—(A Gabriele Rossetti degli invidiosi veri che da Dante fino al Muratori si gridarono propugnatore magnanimo la Italia riconoscente.) The reference is to the passage in *Paradiso*, x., 138.

> leggendo nel vico degli strami,
> sillogizzò invidiosi veri.

" I taught in my syllogisms truths which made me hated." St. Thomas Acquinas is speaking.
If I can I will certainly come etc.] 1 June 1853, Epist. 278.
You must be very pleased with your children etc.] 12 June 1853, Epist. 278.]

251. *you are alone* etc.] 7 July 1853. Epist. 278.
We shall soon go and find him] 26 Dec. 1853, Epist. 278.
lucky to have his family around him] 21 April 1854, Epist. 278.
Details of G. R.'s end] From *Remin.*, pp. 113 ff.

252. *Maria reported her father's death*] The letter (written in Italian) is given in Bedetti.
note] See note to p. 79 of this book.

253. *We lost my father to-day* etc.] *Letters to Allingham*, p. 7.

Proposed reinterment in Santa Croce] See *Per il cinquantesimo anniversario*, p. 38 ; *Mem.*, DGR., p. 17 ; *DGRFL.*, p. 327 ; Bell Scott, *Autobiography*, II., p. 143.

When my ashes etc.] Bedetti, p. 55.

If ever our dear country is redeemed etc.] *Riv. Eur.* XIV., fasc. 1, p. 126.

BIBLIOGRAPHY

MANUSCRIPTS

IN THE BIBLIOTECA DEL RISORGIMENTO IN ROME

Epistolario. [Epist.] In six files, 323, 324, 275–8. Files 279, 280 contain various MSS. of G. R., copies of others, and matter collected by Domenico Ciampoli for his edition of *La Vita Mia* and for his intended edition of the *Epistolario.*

Autografi di G. R. These may be subdivided :
 (*a*) *Autografi.* Four small files, containing a few letters and various MSS. in prose and verse.
 (*b*) The MSS. detailed by D. C. 199–248.
 (*c*) The following books, presented to the library in 1931 by Signora Rossetti Agresti :
    1. Large MS. volume, p. 534, containing *Il Veggente in Solitudine* (handwriting of Mrs. R., C. G. R., W. M. R.; here and there G. R., D. G. R., Ricciardi).
    2. Three small MS. volumes containing earliest extant form of the *Salterio.* Written by Ponssielgue circa 1824, revisions by G. R. See p. 20.
    3. MS. notebook containing parts of *Salterio*, *Veggente*, and various verses and notes.
    4. Similar book containing scattered passages of *Veggente*, *Lisa ed Elviro*, and other matter.
    5. Small notebook, beginning " ai 30 di Giugno del 1815 "; contains various poems and epigrams.

IN THE MUSEUM OF VASTO

Poems of Antonio Rossetti.
 (There is a copy of these in Bib. del Ris., Rome.) For other Rossetti MSS. at Vasto, not used in this book, see D. C. 249–53.

IN THE TAYLORIAN INSTITUTE, OXFORD

Copies of 127 letters from G. R. to Charles Lyell. The originals are, with a few exceptions, in Epist. The copying was done by V. de Tivoli in 1883.

BIBLIOGRAPHY 299

In the Possession of the Lyell Family at Kinnordy

162 letters from G. R. to Charles Lyell.
(The article by J. Purves [see below] is based on these. I have not had access to the letters, and quote either from the article or from the lengthy abstract very kindly put at my disposal by Mr. Purves.)

In the Library of King's College, London

Letters concerning G. R.'s appointment to the chair of Italian in the College, and concerning his retirement.

In the British Museum

Panizzi MSS. Add. 36714, ff. 84–8. [Three letters from De Marchi to Panizzi, 1827, about the Italian chair at University College.]
Leigh MSS. Add. 36663, ff. 288–95. [Four letters from G. R. to F. Leigh, 1835–7.]

PRINTED BOOKS

The following are the chief works referred to or quoted in the present work.

Ancona, D', A. *Varietà Storiche e Letterarie. Prima Serie.* Milan, 1883.

Adami, Colomba. *Gabriele Rossetti e i lirici pattriottici.* Brescia, 1898.

[Angelis, De, Tommaso] Prof. Todeas Twattle-Basket. *Note di Cronaca, ossia i giornali, gli instituti e gli uomini illustri italiani a Londra durante l'era vittoriana 1837-1897.* Bergamo, 1897.

Angelis, De, Tommaso. *Gabriele Rossetti da Vasto.* S. Maria C. V., 1904.

Baum, P. F. (ed.). *The House of Life. A Sonnet Sequence.* By Dante Gabriel Rossetti. Cambridge, U.S.A., 1928.

Bedetti, Alessandro. *Alcune Lettere e Poesie Inedite di Gabriele Rossetti.* Bologna, 1892.

Bell, Mackenzie. *Christina Rossetti.* London, 1898.

Bellott, H. Hale. *University College, London, 1826-1926.* London, 1929.

Benelli, Zulia. *Gabriele Rossetti. Notizie Biografiche e Bibliografiche.* Florence, 1898.

Beolchi, Carlo. *Reminiscenze dell' Esilio.* Turin, 1852.

Brooks, Constance. *Antonio Panizzi.* Manchester, 1931.

Carducci, G. *Il Veggente in Solitudine di G. R.* In *Collected Works,* Vol. X. Reprinted with some emendations from *La Tribuna,* Rome, 26 Nov. 1884.

COURTEN, M. L. GIARTOSIO DE. *I Rossetti. Storia di una famiglia.* Milan, 1928.

"*La Beatrice di Dante* " *di Gabriele Rossetti. Storia di un manoscritto e di un plagio. Nuova Antologia,* Oct. 1930. (Vol. 273.)

FAGAN, LOUIS. *Life of Sir Anthony Panizzi, K.C.B.* 2 vols. 2nd ed. London, 1880.

FESTING, GABRIELLE. *J. H. Frere and his Friends.* London, 1899.

Germ, The. Facsimile Reprint, with introduction by W. M. Rossetti, London, 1901.

GOSSE, SIR EDMUND. *Critical Kit-Kats.* London, 1896.

[HALLAM, ARTHUR] T. H. E. A. *Remarks on Professor Rossetti's Disquisizioni sullo spirito antipapale.* London, 1832.

HEARNSHAW, F. J. C. *The Centenary History of King's College,* London, 1828–1928, London, 1929.

HORN, KURT. *Zur Entstehungsgeschichte von D. G. Rossettis Dichtungen.* Bernau, 1909.

HUNT, HOLMAN. *Pre-Raphaelitism.* 2 vols. London, 1905.

LUZIO, ALESSANDRO. *La Massoneria e il Risorgimento Italiano.* 2 vols. 1925.

La Madre di Giuseppe Mazzini. Turin, 1923.

LUZZI, GIOVANNI. *Le Idee Religiose di Gabriele Rossetti.* Florence, 1903.

LYELL, CHARLES. *The Canzoniere of Dante Alighieri.* London, 1835. *Ibid.* London, 1840.

The Lyrical Poems of Dante Alighieri. London, 1845.

LYELL, SIR CHARLES. *Life, Letters, and Journals.* 2 vols. London, 1881.

MANZONI, ROMEO. *Gli Esuli Italiani nella Svizzera* (*da Foscolo a Mazzini*). Milan, 1922.

MARILLIER, H. C. *Dante Gabriel Rossetti. An illustrated memorial of his art and life.* London, 1899.

MÉGROZ, R. L. *Dante Gabriel Rossetti, Painter Poet of Heaven in Earth.* London, 1928.

[PANIZZI, ANTONIO.] *Osservazioni sul comento analitico della Divina Commedia pubblicato del Sig. Gabriele Rossetti Tradotte dall'inglese con la risposta del Sig. Rossetti corredata di note in replica.* Florence, 1832.

PERALE, GUIDO. *L' Opera di Gabriele Rossetti.* Città di Castello, 1906.

Per Il Cinquantesimo Anniversario Della Morte di Gabriele Rossetti. A Solenne Ricordanza la Città nativa. Rome, 1904.

PIETROCOLA-ROSSETTI, T. *Gabriele Rossetti.* Turin, 1861.

Pre-Raphaelite Diaries and Letters. Ed. by W. M. Rossetti. London, 1900.

PURVES, JOHN. *Dante Gabriel Rossetti and his Godfather, Charles Lyell of Kinnordy.* In *University of Edinburgh Journal,* Vol. IV., No. 2. (1931.)

ROSSETTI, CHRISTINA. *Dante, an English Classic.* In *Churchman's Shilling Magazine.* Oct. 1867. Vol. II.

Commonplace and other Short Stories. London, 1870.

Sing-Song. A Nursery Rhyme Book. London, 1872.

Called to be Saints. London, N.D. [1881.]

Letter and Spirit. London, N.D. [1883.]

Dante, The Poet illustrated out of the Poem. In *The Century Magazine.* Feb. 1884.

Time Flies. A Reading Diary. London, 1895. (1st ed. 1885.)

Maude. A Story for Girls. With introduction by W. M. Rossetti. London, 1897.

Verses by Christina G. Rossetti reprinted from G. Polidori's edition of 1847. Ed. by J. D. Symon. London, 1906.

Family Letters. Ed. by W. M. Rossetti. London, 1908.

Poetical Works. With *Memoir* and Notes by W. M. Rossetti. London, 1920. (1st ed. 1904.)

ROSSETTI, DANTE GABRIEL. *Sir Hugh the Heron. A legendary tale in four parts.* London, 1843 (privately).

Collected Works. 2 vols. London, 1890.

Family Letters, with a *Memoir* by W. M. Rossetti. 2 vols. London, 1895. Vol. I. is *Memoir,* Vol. II. is *Family Letters.*

Letters to Allingham. Ed. by G. Birkbeck Hill. London, 1897.

Jan van Hunks. With introd. by Mackenzie Bell. London, 1929.

ROSSETTI, GABRIELE. *Odi Cittadine.* Naples, 1820.

La Divina Commedia di Dante Alighieri con comento analitico di Gabriele Rossetti. In sei volumi. Vol. I. London, 1826 ; Vol. II. London, 1827. (No more appeared.)

Discorso Inaugurale per la Cattedra di Lingua e Letteratura Italiana nel Collegio del Re. London, 1831.

Il Corsaro, Scene melodrammatiche con cori, tratte dal Corsaro di Lord Byron. London, N.D. [*circa* 1831–3].

Medora e Corrado. Cantata Melodrammatica con cori. Tratta dal Corsaro di Lord Byron. London, N.D. [*circa* 1831–3].

Iddio e l'Uomo. Salterio. London, 1833.

Disquisitions on the Antipapal Spirit which produced the Reformation. Translated by Miss Caroline Ward. 2 vols. London, 1834.

Il Mistero dell' Amor Platonico del Medio Evo. London, 1840. (Divided into 5 vols., but the page numbering continuous.)

Ditto. J. H. Frere's copy with pencil annotations. In British Museum.

Roma verso la Metà del Secolo decimonono. London, 1840.

La Beatrice di Dante. Ragionamento Prima. London, 1842. (The remainder of this work is among the MSS. in the Bib. del Ris., Rome.)

Il Veggente in Solitudine. Poema Polimetro. Paris, 1846.

Versi. Lausanne, 1847.

L'Arpa Evangelica. Genoa, 1852.

Poesie. Ordinate da G. Carducci. Florence, 1879. (1st ed. 1861.)

Letters to Ricciardi, in *Rivista Europea,* Vols. XII., XIII., XIV., XV., XVI. (April to December 1879.)

A Versified Autobiography. Translated and supplemented by W. M. Rossetti. London, 1901.

La Vita Mia. Ed. by Domenico Ciampoli. Lanciano, 1910.

Opere Inedite e Rare. Vol. I. *La Lira Popolare.* (Two more vols. were promised to subscribers but have not yet appeared.) Vasto, 1929.

ROSSETTI, MARIA FRANCESCA. *In Morte di Guendalina Talbot, Principessa Borghese. Ode del Cavaliere G. P. Campana Romano con traduzione inglese.* London, 1841 (privately).

The Rivulets. A Dream not all a Dream. London, 1846.

Letters to my Bible Class on 39 Sundays. London, N.D. [printed Oxford, 1872].

Exercises in Idiomatic Italian through literal translation from the English. London, 1867.

(Key to the last.) *Aneddoti Italiani. Italian Anecdotes selected from Il Compagno del Passeggio Campestre.* London, 1867.

A Shadow of Dante. London, 1894. (1st ed. 1871.)

Rossetti Papers. 1862-1870. Ed. by W. M. Rossetti. London, 1903.

ROSSETTI, WILLIAM MICHAEL. *The Comedy of Dante Alighieri. Part I. The Hell. Translated into Blank Verse.* London, 1865.

Dante Gabriel Rossetti as Designer and Writer. London, 1889.

Some Reminiscences. 2 vols. London, 1906.

Democratic Sonnets. London, 1907.

Dante and his Convito. A study with translations. London, 1910.

Ruskin ; Rossetti : Pre-Raphaelitism. Papers. 1854-1862. Ed. by W. M. Rossetti. London, 1899.

SANDERS, MARY F. *Christina Rossetti.* London, 1930.

SCOTT, W. B. *Autobiographical Notes.* 2 vols. London, 1892.

STEPHENS, F. G. *Dante Gabriel Rossetti.* London, 1894.

STUART, DOROTHY M. *Christina Rossetti.* London, 1930.

TOYNBEE, PAGET. *Chronological List of paintings and drawings from Dante by D. G. R.* (Reprinted from *Scritti Varii di Erudizione e di Critica in onore di Rodolfo Renier,* Turin, 1912.)

VALLI, LUIGI. *Il Linguaggio Segreto di Dante e dei " fedeli d'amore ".* Rome, 1928.

Ditto. Vol. II. (*Discussione e note aggiunte.*) Rome, 1930.

VANNUCCI, ATTO. *I Martiri della Liberta Italiana del* 1794-1848. 7th ed. Milan, 1887.

WATTS-DUNTON, T. *Old Familiar Faces.* London, 1916.

WILLOUGHBY, L. A. *Dante Gabriel Rossetti and German Literature.* Oxford, 1912.

WISE, T. J. *Catalogue of the Ashley Library.* Vol. IV.

APPENDIX

Page 1.

Antico municipio de' Romani
Ove apersi le luci ai rai del giorno,
Tu che ornando la spiaggia dei Frentani
Hai l' Adria a fronte, e lieti colli intorno,
Ed a mostrarci dei tuoi figli il merto
T' inghirlandasti di palladio serto,

Vaghi lidi, il cui specchio, il cui susurro,
Sol per interna imago or sento e miro,
Ove in me riflettea vivido azzurro
D' un bel ciel, d' un bel mar l' emul zaffiro,
Bei campi ove offre il dì che sorge e cade,
Quasi smeraldi e perle, erbe e rugiade,

Coronato di nubi, alto Appennino,
Ai cui fianchi pascean torme lanose,
Colline apriche, ove scherzai bambino,
Ove adulto cantai, vallette ombrose ;
Addio per sempre : innanzi al guardo mio
Non verrete mai più ; per sempre addio !
(From *Il Veggente in Solitudine, Commiato* I.)

Page 3.

No, diversa tu non sei ;
Ti ravviso ; sei pur tu,
Che presenti agli occhi miei
Le stessissime virtù.
(From *La mia prima Villeggiatura con la mia sposa Fanny nella
Villetta del mio suocero Polidori*, 1826. In *Versi*, 1847.)

Page 6.

Invito per la primavera

Di tremoli fioretti
Già s'orna la pendice :
Deh lascia, o bella Nice,
L' incomoda città.

303

Vieni : a più puri affetti
 S'apre nei campi il core :
 Premio d' un fido amore
 Un fido amor sarà.

Il rio che vien gemendo
 Da questa balza aprica
 Par che passando dica :
 —E quando mai verrà ?
Per lei men vo nudrendo
 I fiori in sulle sponde ;
 Serbo per lei quest' onde,
 Specchio alla sua beltà.

Vieni : di nuove rose
 T' intesse un serto Amore ;
 Regina del mio core
 Ti vuole incoronar.
E l' aure rugiadose,
 D' april pudiche figlie,
 Le guance tue vermiglie
 Desian di ribaciar.

Sul colle un' ara io misi
 Cinta di timo e croco,
 Ed alla dea del loco
 La volli consegrar.
Vieni : de' tuoi sorrisi
 Quest' aure avviva e bea :
 Non manca che la Dea
 Al loco ed all' altar.

(From *Versi*, 1847.)

Page 11.

Di sacro genio arcano
Al soffio animatore,
Divampa il chiuso ardore
Di patria carità :
 E fulge omai nell' arme
 La gioventù raccolta :
 Non sogno questa volta,
 Non sogno libertà !

(Opening of *Ode Estemporanea fatta nella Brigata degli
Amici della Patria, la sera del 9 di luglio, con argomento
e intercalare dati della Società, e desinanze consonanti
somministrate a cerchio.* In *Odi Cittadine* 1820. Also
Veggente in Solitudine, Novena II., Giorno i., 8, where
a note by Ricciardi states that the poem was truly
improvised in the circumstances described by the poet.)

Sei pur bella cogli astri sul crine
Che scintillan quai vivi zaffiri,
È pur dolce quel fiato che spiri,
Porporina foriera del dì.
   Col sorriso del pago desio
Tu ci annunzi dal balzo vicino
Che d'Italia nell'almo giardino
Il servaggio per sempre finì.

   Il rampollo d' Enrico e di Carlo
Ei ch' ad ambo cotanto somiglia,
Oggi estese la propria famiglia
E non servi, ma figli bramò.
   Volontario distese la mano
Sul volume de' patti segnati ;
E il volume de' patti giurati
Della patria sull' ara posò.

   Una selva di lance si scosse
All' invito del bellico squillo,
Ed all' ombra del sacro vessillo
Un sol voto discorde non fu.
   E fratelli si strinser le mani
Dauno, Irpino, Lucano, Sannita ;
Non estinta, ma solo sopita
Era in essi l'antica virtù.

   Ma qual suono di trombe festive !
Chi s'avanza fra cento coorti ?
Ecco il forte che riede tra i forti,
Che la patria congiunse col re !
   Oh qual pompa ! Le armate falangi
Sembran fiumi che inondin le strade !
Ma su tante migliaia di spade
Una macchia di sangue non v'è.

   Lieta scena ! Chi plaude, chi piange,
Chi diffonde vïole e giacinti,
Vincitori confusi coi vinti,
Avvicendano il bacio d'amor.
   Dalla reggia passando al tugurio
Non più finta la gioia festeggia ;
Dal tugurio tornando alla reggia
Quella gioia si rende maggior.

   Genitrici de' forti campioni,
Convocati dal sacro stendardo,
Che cercate col pavido sguardo ?
Non temete, chè tutti son qui.

Non ritornan da terra nemica,
Istrumenti di regio misfatto,
Ma dal campo del vostro riscatto,
Dove il ramo di pace fiorì.

O beata fra tante donzelle,
O beata la ninfa che vede
Fra que' prodi l' amante che riede
Tutto sparso di nobil sudor!
Il segreto dell' alma pudica
Le si affaccia sul volto rosato,
Ed il premio finora negato
La bellezza prepara al valor.

Cittadini, posiamo sicuri
Sotto l'ombra de' lauri mietuti,
Ma coi pugni sui brandi temuti
Stiamo in guardia del patrio terren.
Nella pace prepara la guerra
Chi da saggio previene lo stolto:
Ci sorrida la pace sul volto,
Ma ci frema la guerra nel sen.

Che guardate, gelosi stranieri?
Non uscite dai vostri burroni,
Chè la stirpe dei prischi leoni
Più nel sonno languente non è.
Adorate le vostre catene
Chi v'invidia cotanto tesoro?
Ma lasciate tranquilli coloro
Che disdegnan sentirsele al piè.

Se verrete, le vostre consorti,
Imprecando ai vessilli funesti,
Si preparin le funebri vesti,
Chè speranza per esse non v'ha.
Sazierete la fame de' corvi,
Mercenarie falangi di schiavi,
In chi pugna pe' dritti degli avi
Divien cruda la stessa pietà.

Una spada di libera mano
È saetta di Giove tonante,
Ma nel pugno di servo tremante
Come canna vacilla l'acciar.
Fia trïonfo la morte per noi,
Fia ruggito l'estremo sospiro;
Le migliaia di Persia fuggiro,
I trecento di Sparta restâr!

E restaron coi brandi ne' pugni
Sopra mucchi di corpi svenati,
E que' pugni, quantunque gelati,
Rassembravan disposti a ferir.
    Quello sdegno passava nel figlio
Cui fu culla lo scudo del padre,
Ed al figlio diceva la madre :
" Quest' esempio tu devi seguir."

    O tutrice dei dritti dell'uomo
Che sorridi sul giogo spezzato,
È pur giunto quel giorno beato
Che un monarca t'innalza l'altar !
    Tu sul Tebro fumante di sangue
Passeggiavi qual nembo fremente,
Ma serena qual' alba ridente
Sul Sebeto t'assidi a regnar.

    Una larva col santo tuo nome
Qui sen venne con alta promessa ;
Noi, credendo che fossi tu stessa,
Adorammo la larva di te :
    Ma nel mentre fra gl' inni usurpati
Sfavillava di luce fallace,
Ella sparve qual sogno fugace,
Le catene lasciandoci al piè.

    Alla fine tu stessa venisti
Non ombrata da minimo velo,
Ed un raggio disceso dal cielo
Sulla fronte ti veggio brillar.
    Coronata di gigli perenni,
Alla terra servendo d'esempio,
Tu scegliesti la reggia per tempio,
Ove il trono ti serve d'altar.

  (*Il Dì Nove di Luglio del MDCCCXX.* The text given is that
of the *Veggente in Solitudine*, Novena II., Giorno i., 13.
In *Odi Cittadine*, Naples, 1820, where it first appeared,
it is printed in quatrains, and the stanzas (i.e. eight
lines) are numbered. There are also variants in the
text.)

Page 17.

      Addio, terra sventurata ! . . .
      Ma la terra era celata.
      Ei nel duol che l' aggravò
      Chinò 'l capo e singhiozzò.

Ahi l' amor della sua terra,
Ahi qual guerra—in sen gli fa !
Infelice !—il cor gli dice
Che mai più non tornerà !
(From *Il Veggente in Solitudine.* Novena II., Giorno ii., 1.)

Page 22.

Sire, che attendi più ? Lo Scettro Ispano
Già infranto cadde al suol, funesto esempio
A chi resta a regnar ! Vindice mano
Gli sta sul capo, che ne vuol lo scempio.
Sire, che attendi più ? l'orgoglio insano
Ceda al pubblico voto : il foro, il tempio
Voglion la morte tua—resiste invano
Il debil cortegiano, il vile e l'empio !
(From a sonnet in T. Pietrocola-Rossetti, *Gabriele Rossetti*,
1861, p. 31. See note to p. 22 of this book.)

Page 30.

Care donne, belle siete,
Non vel voglio contrastar,
Ma più belle ci parete
Dopo un lungo navigar.

Non saprei da che deriva
Quest' incanto al vostro sesso ;
So ch' io provo ognor lo stesso,
Nello scendere dal mar.
(From *Il Corsaro. Scene melodrammatiche*, etc.)

Page 33 note.

Del presente sarei giusto
Nel lagnarmi ? certo no ;
Son sanissimo e robusto,
Mangio, dormo, stommi, e vo. ·. . .
Ho consorte che sovente
Fosca e torbida esser suol ;
Ma ci sembra più ridente
Se di rado splende il Sol.
Cinque figli belli e gai
Stanmi intorno a festeggiar :
Per l' Imperio del Catai
D' essi un sol non vorrei dar.
(From *A me Stesso Anacreontica*, in *Versi*, ? 1805-6.)

Page 36.   (Translation by W. M. R.)

Quel giorno che la visita gli resi,
E cinto il vidi da gentil famiglia,
Fissai due volte e tre gli occhi sorpresi
Sulla beltà della seconda figlia.

Decide della vita un punto solo ! . .
Il mio cor fu magnate, ella fu polo.
>   (From *La Vita Mia*, Pt. x.)

Page 37. (Translation by W. M. R.)
Io gridai *Vita Nuova* al par di Dante ;
Ma s' ei la scrisse, io volli portar in uso. . . .
Sorgan, diss' io, nella mia nuova sorte,
Novelli affetti a popolarmi il seno.
>   (From *La Vita Mia*, Pt. x.)

Page 38.

Picciol orto ed umil tetto,
Fanny mia, ci accoglierà,
Felicissimo ricetto
Di campestre libertà. .

Campicello avventurato,
Te doman saluterò. . . .
Redivivo Cincinnato
Di sua man ti coltivò.

>   .   .   .   .   .

Salve, albergo, in cui l' esempio
Offrirem d' un mutuo ardor :
Tu d' Imen sei fatto un tempio,
Dove un' ara ha posto Amor.

Salve, o bosco, a cui sì grate
Ombre ed aure april già diè :
Di colombe innamorate
Nuova coppia accogli in te.
(From *La mia prima villeggiatura*, etc., *Versi*, 1847.)

Page 43.

Germe d' amore, cresci pur felice
Qual vago fiore a dolce zeffiretto.
Al genitore, ed alla genitrice
Tu pungi 'l core di soave affetto.
(In *Autografi* I., Biblioteca del Risorgimento, Rome.
Handwriting of Mrs. Rossetti.)

Page 47.

Brindisi improvvisato
nel dì che Carlo Lyell Esq. tenne al fonte
battesimale il mio figlio Gabriele Carlo Dante.

Fra la gioia convivale
Liberò l' auspice vino :
Pel mio picciolo Dantino
Breve voto io formerò.

Cento voti in un sol voto
Concentrar per lui desio :
Al gentil suo padre in Dio
Rassomigli : e basterà.

8 di Giugno 1828.

(From J. Purves, *Dante Rossetti and his Godfather*. In
University of Edinburgh Journal, IV., 2.)

Page 52.

Vuol giusto vanto, e non orgoglio insano,
Ch' io faccia noto all' avvenir più tardo
Che il primo Professor d' Italiano
Nel Collegio del Re fu l' esul bardo.
Oh quai diversi re, dissi talora,
L' un mi volle impiccar, l' altro m'onora.

(From *La Vita Mia*, Pt. ix.)

Page 70.

A te, Mazzini, io pria rivolgo il ciglio,
Che per la patria tua daresti il sangue ;
Tu sfidasti per lei morte, e periglio,
E in te sì vivo ardor giammai non langue. . .
Ma che ! la patria che tuttor ·s' affanna
Il troppo e non il poco in te condanna.

(From *La Vita Mia*, Pt. xi.)

Page 72.

O d' alme sublimi
Perenne alimento,
Delizia e tormento
D' un nobile cor,
O d' ogni mio male
Sorgente e radice,
Di patria infelice
Santissimo amor !

Tu sola mia colpa
Agli occhi d' altrui,
La colpa per cui
Più patria non ho !
Ma indarno m' incalza
Maligna procella,
Di colpa sì bella
Pentirmi non so.

. . . .

Volgendomi addietro
Nell' ultimo addio,
Bel nido natio,
Mi parve morir ;

E quando mi suona
Sul memore core,
Lo stesso dolore
Ritorno a sentir.
(From the *Salterio*, Part iii., Salmo 3. In the 1843 edition
Sorgente in the first stanza is replaced by *Compenso*.)

Page 73.

Qui dritto e dovere
Si libra e compone,
L' umana ragione
Qui colpa non è.

Tu prima e possente
Dall' Abila al Nilo,
Tu l'ultimo asilo
D'afflitta virtù ;
Chè 'l vasto tuo giro,
Di porti munito,
Al giusto inseguito
Mai chiuso non fu.
(From the *Salterio*, Part iii., Salmo 5.)

Page 74.

Così fondar potrai scuole ed ospizj :
Nutri i poveri tuoi, non i suoi vizj.

Ed onde i figli tuoi n' abbian bei frutti
Sian Cambrigia ed Ossonia aperte a tutti.
(From *L' Inghilterra* in *Poesie Inedite e Rare*.)

Page 76.

Tu soffri, nota e spera. Ordin fatale
Vuol che tu varchi del dolor la valle.
Ben so per prova come sa di sale
Il pane altrui, so come è duro calle
Lo scendere e il salir per l'altrui scale ;
Pur tutto mi gettai dietro alle spalle ;
E se di pari ardir ti ferve il petto,
Tu per la causa soffrirai l' effetto.
   Ambi scacciati dai paterni lari,
Ambi a gran torto : ma qual più di noi ?
Io da' miei cittadini a me sì cari,
Tu da spergiuro re sì crudo ai tuoi.
Mostra in pari destin costanza pari,
Merto e mercè di celebrati eroi.
Vanne : a te come a me nel dubbio corso
Fia compagno il dolor, non il rimorso !

Nobil dolor di grandi idee fecondo,
Ond' uom divien de' vari casi esperto.
Delle cantiche mie l' ordin profondo
Ti svelerò di tua fortezza in merto.
Purgate le caligini del mondo,
Intenderai nel mio parlar coperto
Quell' ineffabil ver che assiduo invochi,
Quel ver che, oscuro ai molti, è chiaro ai pochi.

(From *Il Veggente in Solitudine*, Novena II., Giorno iv., 1.)

Page 80.

In due libri gli occhi miei
Posson leggere qual sei :
La natura è libro immenso
Dov' è scritto il tuo poter,
Libro interno a me che penso
È il medesimo pensier.

(From *Inno a Dio*. In *L'Arpa Evangelica*, Serie Prima, II.)

Nel più puro amor fraterno
Per te l' alma è sublimata :
La ragion santificata,
Santo libro, io trovo in te ;
E in te scerno—il Verbo eterno,
Che favella alla mia fè.

(From *Il Veggente in Solitudine*, Novena II., Giorno iii., 11.)

Page 143 note.

Non grande, non pigmeo, offeso il volto
Dal vaiuolo ; non grosso il naso molto ;
Gli omeri curvo ; nero il crine e folto.
Lumi loquaci, libero di mente,
Gote vermiglie, bocca ognor ridente,
E raro il mento dell' onor crescente.
Sensibil core, in conversar gentile ;
Non mai superbo, nè adulator, nè vile ;
Sordo un po', fido amico, e sempre umile.
Del golfo Adriatico nato all' alme arene,
Dei cigni di Talia e Melpomene
Esperto attore in su le patrie scene ;
Mai sempre acceso del calor Tebeo ;
Non culto vate, ma cantor plebeo
Perchè nemico fummi il fato reo.
Di maschere inventor, di gloria vago ;
Di parrucche son fabbro e ne son pago.
Ecco, o lettore, la mia vera imago.

(From the poems of Antonio Rossetti ; in the copies in the
Bib. del Risorgimento, Rome. Epist. 279.)

Page 145.

Alla virtuosissima Signora N.N.
Sonetto.

Sensibil mia degnissima cognata,
 Mi scrive il mio german tuo caro sposo
 Che tu a mio pro ver lui sei l' avvocato.
 Io rendo grazie al cor tuo virtuoso.
Del ben che a me tu fai guiderdonata
 Verrai dal Cielo giusto e generoso ;
 Tu un' alma chiudi in sen predestinata
 Al pari al tuo consorte il cor pietoso.
Senza il soccorso ch' ei mi ha favorito
 Mercè la tua pietà, mia protettrice,
 Di fame ah sì, sarei di già perito !
Ne' vostri casti amplessi coniugali
 Ricordi a Lui, ch' io son vecchio infelice,
 Qual Giobbe carco ognor di molti mali.
   (In a letter to G. R., 13 Aug. 1839, Epist. 276.)

Page 146.

Miei vaghi Nipotini amabilissimi
Deh ! dite al vostro degno Genitore
Spesso così : caro Papà, d' inedia
Il misero zio nostro Antonio muore
Se non gli manderai la carità.
Deh ! stendergli la man, caro Papà.
Tu chiudi in sen un cor pietoso, e umano ;
Caro Papà, deh ! stendegli la mano.
Egli è zio nostro, ed è pur tuo germano.
Se ad esso voi così spesso direte
A me la carità pur voi farete ;
Perchè, spint' ei da voi, di me pietà
Avrà tuttora, e mi soccorrerà.
Vi bacio infin, nipoti miei diletti,
E siate, sì, dal cielo benedetti.
   (In a letter to G. R., 23 Oct. 1839, Epist. 276.)

Page 151.

Colei che pria di padre il dolce nome
Mi die' con l' infantil labbro rosato,
Bruna il volto, brunissime le chiome,
D' un trïennio i tre lustri ha già varcato,
E in lui l'alma paterna arde e sfavilla
Nel raggio della fervida pupilla.

Maria l' ordine aprì, Cristina il chiuse,
In cui la madre duplicò se stessa,
Chè non sol le sue forme in lei trasfuse,
Talchè mi sembra ingiovanita in essa,

Ma l' alma armonizzata dalle Muse
In ambe le figliuole ella ha trasmessa ;
E forse anche la mia che vi si mesce,
Geninando la face, il lume accresce.

. . . . . .

Quando al fioco chiaror d' un dì che spira
Seggo accerchiato dalla mia famiglia,
E pingo Italia che di duol sospira,
Mentre il mostro bicipite l' artiglia,
Io veggo in ambi or di pietade or d' ira
Inumidirsi e sfavillar le ciglia,
E assai più forte per commosso affetto
Battere il cor nell' agitato petto.

. . . .

Oh quante volte al tramontar del giorno
Supplici entrambi ci prostriam dolenti,
E inginocchiati ci fan cerchio intorno
I cari al nostro amor quattro innocenti !
Quel più bel tempio che un rural soggiorno
Dove s' ergono al ciel preghi ferventi ?
Sei voti da sei cuori alzati a volo
Nel concorde desir non fan che un solo.

(From *Il Veggente in Solitudine*, Novena II., Giorno v.
3 and 5.)

Page 153. (Translation by W. M. R.)

Figlie amorose, in cui quest' alma trova
In virgineo pudor mente celeste,
D' ingegno e di moral fulgida prova
In prosa e poesia voi già ne deste :
Da doppio specchio par che in voi si scerna
Riflessa sovra altrui l' alma materna.

Come da fonte gemine zampillano
Sgorghi di vivo umor che un prato inondano,
Come da doppia fiaccola sfavillano
Vividi rai che misti si diffondano,
Così talor l' anima stessa abbellano
Pittura e Poesia che s'assorellano.

Ed ambe in te, mio Gabriel, s'uniscono
E ti fecondan l' alma e te l'accendono :
Come due fonti ambe da te fluiscono,
Ambe come due faci in te risplendono ;
E mentre chiare in te si manifestano
Entrambe ad opre eccelse in te s'apprestano.

Corri ed attingi pur la doppia meta
Benchè sii della vita al primo albore :
Già salutar ti ascolto abil poeta,
Ammirar già ti veggio abil pittore :
Va pur, la doppia via trascorri omai ;
Quel ch'io far non potei tu lo farai.

Se vanità non è, quasi rinato
Mi sento di persona e più di viso
In te, dolce Guglielmo, imberbe Plato,
Ch' hai negli occhi il pensier, sui labbri il riso ;
In te rinacqui, amato figlio, e spesso
Te vagheggiando io contemplai me stesso.

Ma di tua mente le potenze attive
Ricercano la Stoa, non l'Elicona :
Già con due lingue morte e quattro vive
La verità nel tuo pensier ragiona ;
E già più d' un quando di te favella,
Giovinetto filosofo t' appella.

(From *La Vita Mia.* Pt. x.)

Page 163.

Cade nel mar la gocciola
Ed eccola—è sparita.
È gocciola la vita,
È mar l'eternità.

(From T. Pietrocola-Rossetti, *Gabriele Rossetti*, 1861, p. 74.)

INDEX

Abatemacco. 262.
Achilli, Giacinto. 159.
Acquinas, St. Thomas. 114, 296.
Albert, Prince. 59.
Albigenses. 88, 90.
Alfieri, Vittorio. 32, 261,2.
All Saints Home. 117.
Allingham. 178, 253.
Angeloni, Luigi. 64,6 ; 269–70.
Angiolieri, Cecco. 196,7.
Anichini, B. 62,3 ; 268.
Apocalypse, The. 187, 202,3 ; 225.
Arabian Nights, The. 186, 226.
Arditi, Cavaliere. 7, 258.
Ariosto. 187, 224.
Arlington St., No. 38. 161,2 ; 238.
Aroux. 82, 93, 172, 288.
Arrivabene, Count Giovanni. 22.
Athenæum, The. 96,7 ; 210.
Aulisio, Signor. 262.

Baldacconi, Dr. 37, 263.
Barclay, Mr. 51.
Bath, Marchioness of. 161.
Bell, Mackenzie. 235.
Belluomini, Dr. 69.
Benelli, Signor. 30.
Bennett, Rev. Dr. 243.
Benson, A. C. 193,4.
Beolchi, Carlo. 52,6 ; 266.
Betsy. 128, 130–2,8.
Betti, Benedetto. 4.
Bianchi. 10.
Bible, The. 65, 80, 187, 225,7 ;
  269–70.
Biscione, Canon. 271.
Blake, William. 180,7 ; 239.
Blunt, J. J. 94, 274–5.
Boccaccio. 103, 119.
Bolognini. 274.
Borghese, Princess. 173.
Boyley, Mr. 123.
Brigand Tales. 187.
Broadway, The. 211.

Brontë, Emily. 179.
Brontës, The. 240.
Brougham, Lord. 43,4,5 ; 264.
Brown, Ford Madox. 64, 184.
— Lucy Madox. 240.
Browning, Robert. 187,8 ;   201,
  224.
— Mrs. 187, 240,2.
Buchanan, Robert. 45.
Bulwer, Edward. 187.
Burnett. 272.
Bunyan. 90, 109.
Buonaparte, Joseph. 9.
Bürger. 154, 190,1.
Byron, Lord. 30,2 ;   92,   169,
  181,6,7.

Caine, Hall. 58.
Calderai, The. 10.
Campana. 173.
Campbell, Thomas. 27,9.
Carbonari, The. 9, 10,9 ; 77,8 ;
  83, 106, 253.
Carducci, Giuseppe. 61, 160, 267.
Carleliani, The Sisters. 163.
Carlyle, Thomas. 70, 99, 266.
— Mrs. 68.
Cary, H. F. 44, 83,4 ; 273.
Castlereagh, Lord. 21.
Catchpole, Eliza. 141.
Cathari, The. 90.
Cavalcanti. 101, 196.
Cayley, C. B. 157, 213, 242,2 ;
  280.
Chamisso. 187.
Charles Albert. 155,6 ; 266.
Charlotte St., No. 38. 42, 57,8,9 ;
  63,8 ;   75,   101,   118,9 ;
  121,5,6,8 ; 133,6 ; 141, 161,7.
Chaucer. 89, 90,9 ; 103,5.
Chiappini. 257.
Cianis, The. 64.
Cimitile, Principe di. 51.
Ciocci, Raffaele. 159, 285.

317